William Taylor

Christians adventures in South Africa

William Taylor

Christians adventures in South Africa

ISBN/EAN: 9783743301337

Manufactured in Europe, USA, Canada, Australia, Japa

Cover: Foto ©ninafisch / pixelio.de

Manufactured and distributed by brebook publishing software (www.brebook.com)

William Taylor

Christians adventures in South Africa

CHRISTIAN ADVENTURES

IN

SOUTH AFRICA.

BY

REV. WILLIAM TAYLOR,

OF THE INDIAN MISSION CONFERENCE,

AUTHOR OF

"CALIFORNIA LIFE ILLUSTRATED," "ADDRESS TO YOUNG AMERICA
"SEVEN YEARS' STREET-PREACHING IN SAN FRANCISCO,"
"RECONCILIATION: OR, HOW TO BE SAVED,"
"THE MODEL PREACHER," ETC.

"St. Paul declared particularly what things God had wrought among the Gentiles by his ministry. And when they heard it they glorified the Lord."—*St. Luke.*

ELEVENTH THOUSAND.

New York:
NELSON & PHILLIPS, 805, BROADWAY.
1877.

PREFACE.

THE numerous facts and incidents contained in this volume are illustrative, first, of the history, extent, resources, population, and varied life of South Africa; and second, of Christian adventures in South Africa, in great variety, through a period of fifty years, but especially of the recent great work of God in Cape Colony, Kaffraria, and Natal. I had no "guide books" from which to copy, but derived my facts from their original sources. I am indebted for some historical matter to *Wilmot's Essay* on the "Rise, Progress, and Present Condition of Cape Colony," and to Rev. Wm. Shaw's very interesting work, *The Story of my Mission*, and for statistical matter to the Colonial *Blue Books*, but the mass of my facts and incidents are fresh from their original life sources, accompanied by the names of their living actors and observers.

THE AUTHOR.

London, November 30th, **1867.**

INTRODUCTION.

1. As this interesting and remarkable narrative will probably be read by many who are but partially informed respecting Christian Missions in South Africa, it appears desirable to state, that, within and beyond Cape Colony and Natal, four of the principal English Missionary Societies, one American, two Scotch, and five Foreign Societies, occupy among them about two hundred and twenty-four principal Stations, and employ above two hundred and seventy European Missionaries, besides Native

Assistants. This appears to be a large supply of Ministerial Agency to meet the spiritual wants of a population not exceeding by the highest calculation much more than a million of souls; and contrasts strangely with the disproportionate number of Missionaries labouring in India and China; but, on the other hand, it must be kept in mind that this population is widely scattered over an area of more than a million of square miles: rendering a larger amount of agency necessary than where the population is more dense; and, further, that many of the Missionaries, acting as Pastors of European and native congregations in the Cape and Natal Colonies, as well as in the two Dutch Republics, are, to a great extent, supported by local resources. The leading Societies have, of late years, been paying special attention to the training of a native ministry, and with some measure of success. Meanwhile, the languages of South Africa have been mastered: grammars and dictionaries compiled: and translations of the Word of God and of other books have been executed with considerable ability. A small reading population has been called into existence, and the civilizing influences of Christianity have been widely spread. The Wesleyan

Mission, with which Mr. Taylor came most in contact, occupies fifty-three Stations, employs sixty-one Missionaries, and reports ten thousand one hundred and eight church members. It is calculated that nearly sixty thousand persons, including members and scholars, are regular attendants on the public ministry of the Missionaries of this Society. Other Societies have equal reason, in the retrospect of their labours, to thank God for the measure of success vouchsafed to them, and to take courage for the future.

2. Compared with the accounts of the success of Romish Missionaries in pagan lands, the results of Protestant Missions appear to disadvantage. But Popery is satisfied with conformity to forms and ceremonies. The administration of baptism and a professed assent to the creeds of the Church, are its main conditions of membership; while Protestant Missionaries are not satisfied without a reasonable proof of genuine sincerity, and of the beginnings at least of a spiritual work. It is possible that they err on the side of scrupulousness, by requiring a higher degree of knowledge and of moral progress before baptism than is absolutely necessary; but this is an

error on the right side. The increase of the churches in heathendom must, under such circumstances, be very slow in the beginning; but we must not judge of the success of such Missions by the paucity of genuine converts. This habit of "numbering the people," which was David's sin of vanity and self-confidence, when applied to modern Missions, is a temptation to certain minds to despair. We forget the "upper room" and that "the number of names together were about one hundred and twenty." (Acts i. 13-15.) Spiritual influence cannot be represented in figures. It baffles our arithmetic. Half a century or more of preparation and labour may present few converts in response to our eager inquiry for results; and then we are in danger of crying in unbelief, "Can these dry bones live?" At such a crisis it frequently occurs, that some man of God is raised up "to prophesy upon the bones, and to cry unto them, 'O, ye dry bones, hear the word of the Lord;'" and thus "a noise" and "a shaking," followed by the breath of the Spirit infusing spiritual life into those who had been spiritually dead. (Ezek. xxxvii.) In this mode of procedure, God vindicates His sovereignty, teaching us that "neither is he that planteth anything, nor he that watereth: but God that giveth the increase." (1 Cor. i. 37.)

3. It is no disparagement of Mr. Taylor's services, to apply to him the words addressed by our blessed Saviour to the disciples " And herein is that saying true, One soweth and another reapeth. I sent you to reap that whereon ye bestowed no labour: other men laboured; and ye are entered into their labours." (John iv. 37, 38.) The toilsome and perhaps thankless labours of more than one race of Missionaries had prepared the people to understand and receive good from the ministry of this honoured servant of God, and to God alone be ascribed all the glory. It is pleasing to observe the cordial reception given by the Missionaries to this stranger from afar, and their no less hearty rejoicing over the results of his ministry. All human littlenesses disappeared in the presence of these spiritual manifestations, which solemnly testified that Jehovah-Christ was passing by; "forgiving iniquity, transgression, and sin." (Exodus xxxiv. 7.) Mr. Taylor's unassuming manners, together with his scrupulous delicacy in abstaining from interfering in matters properly the exclusive business of the pastors and

church officers, contributed, no doubt, materially to the ready acceptance and grateful acknowledgment of his services. Ministers in general, honoured the gift of God in him, manifesting, on this occasion, the enlarged sympathy of the great Jewish legislator, when he said:—" Would God that all the Lord's people were prophets, and that the Lord would put His Spirit upon them." (Exodus xi. 29).

4. No one can read the Notices of the Wesleyan Methodist Missionary Society from October 1866, to November 1867, and the Annual Report for 1866, without being convinced, that, a great and glorious revival of religion has taken place in South Africa, among Europeans and natives, and not only among the Methodist Societies, but also among other religious bodies. The native work has partaken largely of this blessed outpouring of the Spirit. Whilst believers have been strengthened and confirmed, the careless have been quickened, sinners have been convinced of sin, and have found peace with God. The extraordinary nature of the work, the power which attended the preaching, and its immediate results, seem to have affected even the heathen mind. It appeared as if God were speaking to them in the

words of the prophet: "Behold ye among the heathen, and regard and wonder marvellously: for I will work a work in your days, which ye will not believe, though it be told you." (Habakkuk i. 5.) Revivals of religion were not unknown in South Africa, but hitherto they had been of a local character; this was more general, and, is we trust but the beginning of a great spiritual work which shall go on until the most distant tribes and nations partake of the blessing. South Africa is one of the most accessible gates of entrance into a large portion of the continent. The prospect of extensive usefulness in regions far beyond our present field, we regard as the justication of our large outlay on the comparatively small population of the Colony and its adjacent territory. Such were the views and the hopes of the two great and good men who were the pioneers of Wesleyan Missions in South Africa. They knew that in their very nature they must be aggressive, and that the Colonial and Frontier Stations were to be regarded but as stepping-stones to the regions beyond. BARNABAS SHAW has gone to his reward. WILLIAM SHAW happily yet lives to rejoice in the "showers of blessing" which have been poured out

CONTENTS.

CHAPTER I.

PROVIDENTIAL MISSION TO SOUTH AFRICA.

                                                                                                            Page

The author leaves California. Labours as an evangelist in most of the United States and Canadas. Visits England, Ireland, Asia Minor, Palestine, Egypt. Labours nearly three years in the Australias, New Zealand, and Tasmania. Dr. James Brown. Dr. A. Moffatt. Author's trip to Wallaroo. Rev Mr. Flockhart. Startling telegram. Glad tidings. Rev. Mr. Caldwell. His undying energy. His death. His widow. Rev. C. T. Newman. Evil tidings. Church opening at the "Moonta." Hasty retreat. Voyage to Sydney. Author meets his family. Touching scenes. Watches a sick son at the gates of death for many weary weeks. Returns to South Australia. Sails for the Cape of Good Hope. Rev. James Calvert. Safe arrival. Parkes' Hotel. Rev. John Thomas. Rev. Samuel Hardey - - - - - - 1-11

CHAPTER II.

CAPE COLONY.

Synoptical History of the Colony. Population. The Dutch. The English. The Malays. The Hottentots and Basards. The Kaffirs. The Fingoes. Government of the Colony - - - - - - - 12-25

CONTENTS.

CHAPTER III.

CAPE TOWN.

Its topography, surrounding scenery. Population. Institutions. Churches. Sir George Grey. Rev. A. Murray, Junior. Historic reminiscences. Henry Reed, Esq. His Malay boatman. His detention in Cape Town. His adventures in Small-pox Hospital. Mrs. Gunn's boarding-house. Reed's interview with Rev. Mr. Hodgson. The native Christian hero and the lion. Author's first Sabbath in Cape Town. Sunday-school Anniversary. Mr. Filmer's speech. Special services in Cape Town, and results. Rev. Wm. Impey. Voyage to Port Elizabeth - 26-37

CHAPTER IV.

PORT ELIZABETH.

Rev. John Richards. Roman Catholic Church opening. Independent minister installed. Too late for posters. The chapel. Visit among the shops. Incredulous laugh of the Local Preacher. Mr. Sidney Hill. Series of services, with facts and incidents. Preaching in Courthouse Square. Wayside illustrations. The old Californian and his story. Joseph Tale, the tall Kaffir. Preaching to the natives. Calls from the interior - 38-47

CHAPTER V.

UITENHAGE.

Jones's carriage and pair. Travelling companions. The beard question. Captain George Appleby. Rev. Purdon Smailes. Wool-washing on the Zwart Kops River. Dutch Reformed Church. Rev. Mr. Steytler. A chapel ready for the "moles and bats." Services in the Dutch Church. Plan of conducting a prayer-meeting. The dash of the Dutchman. "Satan is getting more polite each day of our meeting." Preaching to the Kaffirs in a wood-shed. Post-cart travelling - 48-61

CHAPTER VI.

GRAHAM'S TOWN.

History, topography, churches, population, &c. "Commemoration Chapel." Mr. W. A. Richards. Hon. R. Godlonton. Rev. W. J. Davis. Rev. G. H. Green. "Horse sickness." Opening of the campaign. Disappointment of the friends. Removing hindrances. Ventilating the chapel. "Brother Atwill." "The Apollos of South Africa." "Caed mela faltha." Christian statesmen. The widow Ayliff and her tall sons. "Old Brother Sparks" - - - - - - - 62-74

CHAPTER VII.

GRAHAM'S TOWN (CONTINUED).

Review of the series of three weeks. Fellowship-meeting. Rev. Mr. Holford. Illustrative facts and incidents. Celebration of the Queen's birthday. "Mr. Taylor, I have come to ask your pardon for what I have been thinking about you." "The right impulse at the right moment." Getting off the old Jewish track of "going about to establish their own righteousness" into the only way of salvation. The Sergeant's long struggle. Sudden conversions. Sir D—— and the barber. Preaching through an interpreter. Mr. D. Penn. Seventy miles journey - - - - - - - 75-87

CHAPTER VIII.

KING WILLIAM'S TOWN.

The old pioneer, Rev. John Brownlie. Wesleyan Chapel. Rev. J. Fish. A Colonial audience. "Bar of reserve and prejudice broken down." The missionary's account of the work. "A Kaffir came running with the message that four missionaries were in 'the path.'" Rev. John Scott. Rev. Robert Lamplough, and his Kaffir preachers. Rev. Brother Sawtell and his Fingoes. Charles Pamla.

Letter to Mr. Impey. Rev. J. W. Appleyard and his Kaffir Bible. George Impey, Esq., and his dying triumphs. Rev. Mr. Hillier, his success, his sudden death. Mr. Joseph Walker. Kaffirs mounted on young bullocks. Journeying incidents - - - - - 88-107

CHAPTER IX.

ANNSHAW.

Chief Kama and his Kaffirs. Mr. Shaw's mission among them. Rev. Wm. Sargent. Kama's refusal to take a second wife. His piety and courage. Kaffir huts. "Brother Lamplough gave me Charles to interpret for me." Private lecture on "naturalness." Lights and scenes of the first service. Grandeur of the night service. Hymn and tune put into Kaffir on the first hearing. "Don't send them off to the river to battle with Satan alone, and take a bad cold as well." Stirring scenes. Glorious results. Mr. Harper. Trip to Lovedale. Rev. J. Wilson. Fort Beaufort. Good tidings from Annshaw. Lamplough's reports. Illustrative incidents. The heathen lame man. The old heathen convert and his two wives. "Our last stroke is being levelled against Kaffir beer." Witnesses for Jesus. How the deaf and dumb testified. How the heathen try to explain it. Persecutions - - - - - - - 108-135

CHAPTER X.

FORT BEAUFORT.

Population and surroundings. Rev. John Wilson. Strong force from Graham's Town. Specimens of the work of the Spirit. "A sacrifice, indeed? Why, it's a glorious riddance!" Mrs. D—— changed her mind. Mr. James Roberts, a man of Providence for Kaffrarian adventures. "Wars in the path." Missionary's report of the work as "great and glorious." Work among the natives. "That shawl! that shawl!" - - - - 136-148

CHAPTER XI.

HEALD TOWN.

"Industrial School." Governor Grey. Rev. Wm. Sargent. Rev. John Ayliff. Theological Institution. Rev. Wm. Impey. Rev. R. Lamplough. Mission press. The monkeys by the way. Mr. T. Templer. Barnabas. Siko Radas. The marriage. The sermon. The missionary in his report of that day says, "What a day! I know not how to record it!" Second day greater than the first. "I realized by faith, on that occasion, what I never can explain." "If you know all this time that black fellow going to hell, why you no tell black fellow till now?" Caring for the lambs. "Satan is conquered," &c. "My Father has set me free," &c. Marvellous results. Continued progress. T. Templer's poem. Permanency of the work - - - - - - - 149-177

CHAPTER XII.

SOMERSET EAST.

Journey. Adelaide. Rev. P. Davidson. The Dutch "Nagmal." Benjamin Trollip and his son. Bedford. Mr. Francis King. Rev. Mr. Solomon. King's adventures among the "Bushmen." "Dig away, you'll find plenty of honey in there!" "I was awakened by something cold touching my toe." Rev. John Edwards. Rev. Wm. Shaw. R. Hart, Esq. "Government Farm." Large circuit. Mr. Nash. Mr. Burch. Work among the whites and natives. Remarkable narrative of missionary adventures, from Rev. J. Edwards. Daniel, the Fingo Prophet - - - - - - - 178-191

CHAPTER XIII.

CRADOCK.

Mr. Sargent, senior. "Dagga Boer." The Trollip family. The rebel Hottentots. Prejudices against the native races.

Kaffir fidelity. Dr. Adam Clarke's prayer. Rev. W. Chapman. Cradock. Dutch farmers. Rev. John Taylor. Hon. Henry Tucker, M.L.C. Hon. Samuel Cawood, M.L.C. John and William Webb. Mr. H. Park. Jack, the Kaffir. The Gospel preached in three languages at once. Glorious results - - - - - 192-205

CHAPTER XIV.

QUEEN'S TOWN.

Journeying with Brother Tucker. Mr. Hines. "Tarkisstaat." Queen's Town. Rev. H. H. Dugmore. Governor Cathcart's generosity. Messrs. Shaw, Barnes, Elliott, and Jakins. "Joyful tidings to write to my sister in Tasmania." The blind widow and her sons. Dugmore's preaching on "The American Preacher." Lesseyton. Rev. J. Bertram. Wm. Bambana, "the head man." "Dear me, this is horrible! Here are hundreds of thirsty souls, and I can't tell them how to come to the river!" James Roberts. M. Stuart Taylor. Charles Pamla. Tidings from Annshaw. Fellowship-meeting. John Weekly. Wm. Trollip, twenty years a seeker, and thirty years a Christian. A soldier's courage tried - 206-223

CHAPTER XV

KAMASTONE.

Rev. Wm. Shepstone. Moonlight stroll with Stuart. Kaffir pony for Stuart. Description of the audience. Remarkable scenes. "I never knew that I was such a sinner till the Holy Ghost shined into me." "O, I felt nasty." "Walked forty-six miles to get to this meeting." "She seems to be a near relation to the antediluvians." Perfect loyalty, faith, and love preached to Kaffirs. The "ivy" and "milkwood" illustration. Effect of Pamla's address on Mr. Shepstone. Report of the numbers saved. Great baptismal service for saved heathen. Missionary's report of progress. "O mother, my dear mother, I have found Jesus!" - - - - 224-241

CHAPTER XVI.

LESSEYTON.

Interpreter lost in the scrub. First night's service, and lodgings with a native. Wonderful scenes of the next day. A heathen woman shouting the praises of God. The forgiven Kaffir who could not forgive himself. Bambana's two sons. "I went away and left the oxen, wagon, and precious cargo standing in the road." "We have heard of washing the disciples' feet, and of kissing the Pope's toe; but to kiss the sole of a Kaffir's boot is a new idea." "The milk is good, and you have given us a great feast." Starting for Kaffraria. Dugmore's letters reporting the advance of the armies of the Lord in Queen's Town, Lesseyton, &c. - - - - - 242-250

CHAPTER XVII.

WARNERS.

J. C. Warner, Esq. "British Resident for Kaffraria." Warner and Shepstone on the true principle on which to establish Mission Stations. ("Likaka laba Fasi.") Both sides of the question fairly stated. Long day's journey. Travelling in the dark. "A sudden jolt sent us both over the 'larboard,' head foremost down the hill." Rev. E. J. Barrett. Campaign of one day in the open air, and its results. Chief Matanzima among the seekers. Fellowship meeting in a stable. The man who saw a great light, could not pass. "The devil ordered his Hottentot servant to make off with the goat to Krielie's country." Colonel Barker at the Tsomo. Captain Cobb. "The road rough and dangerous." - - - - - 251-268

CHAPTER XVIII.

BUTTERWORTH (IGEUWA).

Rev. W. Shaw. Rev. Mr. Shrewsbury. The great chief Hintza. "A cake of bread from the house of Kauta."

Conspiracy against Rev. John Ayliff. Revs. Davis and Palmer come to his rescue. The "great wife" Nomsa. "Sing again." "If he remains he might tramp on a snake in the grass." Destruction and re-establishment of the mission-station. Chief Krielie. Great drought. Protracted meeting of the rain-makers. "No rain while the missionaries were allowed to remain in the country." Davis took the bull by the horns. "Stop all this nonsense,—come to chapel next Sabbath and we'll pray to God to give us rain, and we will see who is the true God, and who are His true servants." Station "destroyed the third time. Chief Krielie's "daring desperate plan for forcing his people into an exterminating war against the Colonists." Sir George Grey's great bread victory. Mission established the fourth time. Rev. John Longden. Description of the congregation by the river-side. "What has that old red blanket to say for himself?" "Loaves and fishes" needed for the hungry multitude. "Brother Longden told the father that if he meant to sell his daughter to the heathen, he must at once leave the station." The great snake-killer. He "chose rather to retain his skull for his own personal use." Umaduna. "A martyr-spirit under a sheepskin." • • 269-290

CHAPTER XIX.

CLARKEBURY (UMGWALI).

W. Shaw's visit to the great chief Vossanie. Rev. Mr. Haddy. Mr. Rawlins killed. Massacre of Rev. J. S. Thomas. Chief Vadana's expedition to seize Mr. Davis dinner-pot. "Well, this is a strange thing. Here's a man who is not afraid to die!" Rev. Peter Hargraves and his wife. Rev. Edwin Gedye in exile. Mr. Joseph Walker. Mr. Crouch. H. B. Warner. Great chief Ngangelizwe. "They are determined to have a heathen chief to rule over them, and I'll let them feel the power of a heathen chief." "He threw an assegai through the arm of one of them." "Go home, and sit down in peace, and take all your cattle, I don't want them." "The cavalry of the train consisting of about forty councillors, fell into line, single file, the chief being about the middle." Prince Usiqukati. Preaching to the great chief and his councillors. H. B. Warner's appeal to them. Kaffir proposition to unite Church and State. King Thackenbau of Fiji, and King George of the Friendly Islands,—illustrative examples. Rev. Peter Turner, the apostle. Pamla's grand talk to the chiefs. Ngangelizwe's child dying. "The chief must return to the Great Place at once." Striking testimonies in the fellowship-meeting. "Isikunisivutayo." "My heart was as tough as the hide of a rhinoceros." Mr. Wm. Davis. Rev. Wm. Hunter, D.D. "The Eden above." "Icula Elitota Ngelizwe eli Pezulu." - 291-321

CHAPTER XX.

MORLEY (INCANASEUE).

Rev. Wm. Shepstone. The invasion of the bloody chief Qeta, a deserter from his more bloody master Chaka, the great Zulu. Shepstone's narrow escape. The Amapondo chief, Faku. Rev. Mr. Palmer. Mission re-established under Rev. Wm. B. Rayner. "Smelling out." J. C. Warner, Esq. on "Kaffir laws and customs." Witchcraft and the witch-doctors. Different methods of torturing witches and wizards. Man roasted for thirty-six hours. The ant-eaten woman. "We can't kill such a witch! She won't die!" Out-door preaching scene. Chief Ndunyela, with his warriors and wives at preaching. How they devoured the bullock. Missionaries' report of the work. Horrible case of "smelling out" and torture after the revival. - - - - - - 322-341

CHAPTER XXI.

BUNTINGVILLE—ICUME.

Rev. Wm. B. Boyce. "We eat the dogs to make us more fierce and powerful in battle." Boyce's Kaffir Grammar. "Euphonic concord." Theophilus Shepstone. Chief

Faku's plan for getting rain. Mr. Fainton. Rev. Mr. Satchell. Rev. James Cameron. Rev. Thomas Jenkins. New Buntingville. Rev. Wm. Hunter. Dahveed's "new road." Umtata Drift. "Pezulu! pezulu! pezulu!" Chief Damasi and his division of the Pondos. Chief Vava and his marriage feast. The chief and his warriors at preaching. Visit to Damasi's "Great Place." The chief, his hut, his wives, his royal robes and tiger's tails, his cattle kraal, his bloody "cliff." How a neighbouring chief took down our "umfundisi." Damasi's war with Chief Umhlonhlo allowed "to sit still a little while," during Umhlonhlo's marriage. Damasi's hospitality. Lodgings in a Kaffir hut. Preaching at the "Great Place." Penitent meeting in the hut. Traders and Kaffirs saved. - 342-360

CHAPTER XXII.

SHAWBURY—ELUNCUTA.

Beauty of scenery. Rev. Wm. H. Garner. Dreadful war complications involving the mission. Escape of the missionary and his family. Rev. Mr. Solomon. Demoralization of the mission people. Kaffir beer-feasts. How we got through the lines of Umhlonhlo's warriors, and across the Tsitsa Drift in the dark. Rev. C. White. First great audience, and the preaching. Small audiences and hard work. Visit to the Tsitsa Falls. Kaffir-corn "holes." Serious case to be settled. Kaffir lawyers, Elijah and Job. The cause debated, bringing out startling developments, and important issues. " Ah, if we had had that counsel on the first day of our series here, instead of the last, we would have had a glorious work of God!" The great work of God which followed. - - 361-383

CHAPTER XXIII

OSBORN—TSHUMGWANA.

Rev. Mr. Hulley. Rev. Charles White. Amabaca tribe. Pondo invasion under chief Umgikela. Chiefs Tiba, and

Makaula. Dreadful slaughter of the Pondos near the mission. "These men have placed their lives in my hands, and if you want them you will have to pass over my dead body." "You are both liars; neither of you killed me!" "Do please let me lie still and die." Stuart's description of the route from Shawbury to Tshumgwana. "Bring out all your men, women, and children, and we will sing you a song about the country above." St. Paul's method of preaching to heathen. Bringing heathen Kaffirs to an acceptance of Christ under a single discourse. Specimen of the preaching God thus owned in saving raw heathens. A sermon. Its immediate results. Specimen extracts of another sermon, showing the analogical points between Kaffirism and Judaism. Text the last day, "Choose ye this day whom ye will serve." Points of analogy between Kaffir superstitions and sacrifices, and the service of the true God. Testimony of 113 witnesses. "I asked God for a great gift, and He showed me my sins." "I had an old shield full of holes." Great harvest of souls. - - - - - 384-430

CHAPTER XXIV.

EMFUNDISWENI.

Stuart's description of the route from Tshumgwana. Rev. Thomas Jenkins and his wife. Rev. Daniel Eva. Adventures of Mr. Jenkins in Pondo-land for thirty years. At a district meeting, 150 miles from home, he learns that the Zulu warriors have swept the country, and that his family was slain. Perilous adventures. "The Umfundisi is killed!" "I will not fly! I am in the Lord's hands; if He delivers me to the Pondos, they shall kill me in my own house!" WITCHCRAFT as seen by Jenkins. "The exterminating decree was so terrible, that not even a dog was allowed to escape." A woman roasted. INFLUENCE OF THE GOSPEL ON WITCHCRAFT. Sanctuary for the victims of the witch-doctors. Faku's mother. Faku's great wife. "The witch-doctors make it out that he died through the Word of God." "My Umfundisi, you have saved

Cingo! He shall not be killed!" DEBASING EFFECTS OF HEATHENISM ON THE MIND. "If there is a God why can't we see Him?" Favourable change within thirty years. POLYGAMY. "She bit the other woman's nose right off!" "I wish I had no wife at all!" Contrast between the state of the Pondo nation twenty-five years ago and its present state. "I am going to the King above!" "The assegai dropped from his hand, for the Holy Spirit's two-edged sword was piercing him." "When God gave me a new heart I vowed to Him that I never would kill another man." Special services. Mr. Alfred White. Visit to Palmerton or "Izala." Rev. John Allsop. Return to Emfundisweni. "I now saw that God would answer my prayer indirectly, by giving my mantle to my Elisha." "In spite of the devil and his heathen host a grand victory for God was achieved." Dismal journey to "Kok's Camp." "Roberts, we have got into Nomansland sure." "While we were trying to dry one side the other was getting wet with the fast falling rain." Preaching at "Kok's Camp." Trip across the "Zuurberg." "Alfredia." "Ulbricht's." "Blom's." Preaching in Hulley's "Hut Chapel." Mr. Hancock and family. Adventures in crossing the Umkomas river in the night. "Our man of Providence." "Your horses have fallen into the ditch!" "Indaleni." Rev. W. H. Milward. Pietermaritzburg, Natal. Pamla's arrival. Report of his labours at Indaleni. Review of the situation at Emfundisweni. "My children, you have done right! Go and sit down in peace! We want to remove to that part and be converted also as you have been!" "When Jenkins gets to heaven he won't stay there without me!" "If my blessed Jesus is coming, I can't wait for anybody!" "Some of the heathen chiefs have expressed a strong desire for Charles to come and visit them" 431-464

CHAPTER XXV.

NATAL.

Geographical position. Climate. Productions. Various

industrial pursuits. Population. Revenue and appropriations of Government. Missions. Schools. Pietermaritzburg the capital. Edendale and its beautiful surroundings. D'Urban and the "Berean Hill." Verulam. Ministerial helpers in Natal. "I commended my sable brother to the missionaries, and bespoke for him an open-field and a fair fight." Bishop Colenso. Grand rally of the hosts on both sides. The Lord's glorious victory. PPOMISCUOUS EXAMPLES OF NATAL ADVENTURES. Colenso's attempt to popularize the Gospel to the Kaffirs. Trying to astonish the natives. "Wondering all the time why the man did not put his shirt inside of his trousers!" Charming a lion with music. Colenso's ark taken down by a Kaffir. Tom Palfreyman and the tiger. The Dutchman and his Holland Bible. Rev. Mr. Butler and the alligator. The lawyer and his advocate. Theory of the wiseacres. George C. Cato, Esq. Colenso's call at Mr. Grant's. Francis Harvey, Sen. "Open there, right and left, and let his Majesty's brave tars come near me." Bishop Colenso and the "Local Preacher in the Wesleyan Establishment." "SAW YE HIM WHOM MY SOUL LOVETH?" Harvey's contrasts between the effects of Colenso's preaching and the saving power of the Spirit at the special services. Incidents of the work in Verulam. Charles and the heathen man at Inanda. "Jim, believe sharp!" Roman Catholic saved. F. B. Fynney's conversion. J. W. Stranack's account of his scepticism, conversion, and call to the ministry -   -   465-504

CHAPTER XXVI.

THE MISSION-WORK IN SOUTH AFRICA.

Voyage from Natal to Cape Town. Mr. James Roberts. Letter written on the voyage. Rev. Barnabas Shaw. Rev. William Shaw. Wesleyan Missions in South Africa. Base line and depôt of supplies. Old plan of establishing Mission Stations. The new development. Kaffir population. Providential indications in favour of the new plan proposed. Evangelical platform, Gospel facts, and our demonstration of them in South Africa. Apostolic plan. Ineffectiveness of modern methods. How to carry out Apostolic methods. Kaffir standard of ministerial education. Where is the money to come from? "I've a share in the concern." "Hard work, hard fare, and a martyr's crown if they can win it." Mr. George Cato's question. Heroic type of Christianity. "They would die for Jesus as cheerfully as the martyrs of the Apostolic age." Ultimate effects - - - - 505-519

CHAPTER XXVII.

REVIEW OF THE WORK AND ITS PROGRESS TO THE PRESENT TIME.

Rev. Thomas Guard's letter. Graham's Town, Queen's Town, Somerset, Cradock, Fort Beaufort. "Annshaw heads the list." Missionary's report of the number saved in Kama's tribe. Success of the Annshaw workers. Triumphal procession. Red heathen's conversion and testimony. Report from Chairman of Queen's Town District. "It was I who stole the thatch." "Take them off! take them off!" "He would have no praying in his family." "The old grey-headed polygamist." Report of Rev. J. Cameron, Chairman of Natal District. Young evangelists. Rev. Ralph Stott's letter. Rev. R. Hayes's letter. Rev. H. S. Barton's report. Tabular view of Graham's Town and Queen's Town districts. Statistical grand total. Indications of progress in Kaffraria, given by Rev. P. Hargraves. H. B. Warner's success. New Mission at the Tsomo. Emfundisweni. Progress of the work in Natal. Thomas Garland. J. W Stranack. F. B. Fynney and his fellows among the Zulus. "I came and found, ah, alligators!" Snake transmigration. Fynney at the American Mission Station. Work at Umhlali. The old toper reformed. Rev. F. Kirkby. The dying Zulu maid. "The wagon is coming to fetch me." Reports from Graham's Town District. W. A. Richards. Rev. W. J. Davis. Anniversary revival services. "'Tis worth living for, this." Rev. R. Lamplough on his new circuit. "Disappointing business to my dear Brother Lamplough." Charles Pamla. Chief Maxwayana and his two converted wives. Pamla's visit to Heald Town. His great success in Newtondale. Heathen objections against him. How he battled for the truth at the "Great Place" of Chief Fundakube. The Chief's decision. Pamla's triumph. "In the habitation of dragons were each lay," there is "grass with reeds and rushes." The End - - - - - - 520-557

CHRISTIAN ADVENTURES

IN

SOUTH AFRICA.

CHAPTER I.

PROVIDENTIAL MISSION TO SOUTH AFRICA.

My mission to South Africa was purely the result of a providential arrangement quite outside of my own previous plans.

In the autumn of the year 1856, under a leave of absence from the California Conference, to which from its organization I belonged, and of which I am still a member, I commenced a tour of evangelistic labours in the Eastern, and then in the Western States of America, and then into the Canadas, which I continued for five years. In the winter of 1861, while labouring in Peterborough, Canada West, I met with Dr. James Brown, who had spent several years in Australia. Through Dr. Brown's persuasive agency, and subsequent indications, to my mind unmistakably Divine, I felt it my duty to visit the Australian Colonies, and assist the churches in those antipodal regions in the prosecution of their great work. When I sailed for Australia, my family, from their own preference, returned to their home in California. I spent seven months in England and Ireland, made a tour round the coasts of Asia Minor and Syria, explored Palestine, and passing on through Egypt took steam by the Peninsular and Oriental Company's line at Suez for Ceylon and Melbourne, so that nearly a whole year was spent en route from New York to Melbourne. The first year of my labours in Australia was devoted to the Colonies of Victoria and Tasmania; the second year to New South Wales, Queensland, and New Zealand; and six months of the third, to South Australia.

During the term of my labours in New South Wales, my friend, Dr. A. Moffitt, of Sidney, often tried to persuade me to visit South Africa. He had spent six years on the east and west coast as surgeon in her Majesty's ship of war, *Penguin*. He had become well acquainted with missionary operations in those parts, and felt a great interest in their success, and believing that I could render them essential service, he was importunate in his entreaties. I could only reply, that "however great my interest in African missionary movements, I cannot go; there is no steam communication direct from Australia to Cape Town, and but few opportunities by sailing vessels; moreover, I have to consider the claims of my Conference, and my family in California, and my limited time for foreign evangelical work. These things together utterly preclude my going to Africa."

The Doctor, however, maintained that it was his firm belief that God would, in His providence, send me to Africa.

"Very well," I replied, "whenever I get an order from Him to go to Africa, I will be off by the first ship His providence may provide."

I had not seen my dear wife and children for more than three years—the time required for a cruise by the men who "go down into the deep" to catch whales—such a separation from my family was a heavy uphill business all the time; but since so many men endure similar privations in whale fishing, merchant marine, army, and naval service, I should have been ashamed to complain, even if I had felt a complaining spirit; but having the conviction that God had appointed me a messenger to the churches in the "Southern world," confirmed by the conversion of about six thousand souls to God during those two and a half years, I patiently waited the issues of Providence in regard to my family. At their request I had consented for them to come from California to Australia, and I would accompany them back, via India, Egypt, and England. But they afterwards hesitated and seemed rather to decline so serious an undertaking, and I was quite in doubt whether they would come or not. I therefore made plans for returning home by that route, and staying a few months in India, whether my family joined me or not.

In November, 1865, while labouring in a series of services near Adelaide, South Australia, I received a letter from Mrs. Taylor, stating that, having been disappointed in getting passage on the ship that brought the letter, she doubted whether it was the will of God that they should come. That was a bitter disappointment to me, for notwithstanding the uncertainty as to whether they would come or not, which occasioned me an uncomfortable measure of suspense for many months, I had acquired a hope that they certainly would come; so that now I fully realised the truth that "hope deferred maketh the heart sick."

The day after I received this sickening letter I travelled 120 miles, ninety by mail-coach, amidst clouds of dust, under a broiling sun 110° Fahrenheit, in the shade, to the mining town of Wallaroo, on York's Peninsula. The Rev. Mr. Caldwell, the superintendent of the Wallaroo circuit, had died but a few days before. It was at his pressing invitation some months previously that I arranged to assist him for a fortnight in his great work: but now, when the time arrived, he was gone. He left a wife and one child, and a large circle of friends, to mourn his loss, for he was a young man of extraordinary talents and usefulness, and assisted by his energetic colleague, the Rev. C. T. Newman, he was rapidly developing an important circuit, embracing three mining towns with a population of from four to six thousand each. The annual yield of copper, in solid bars, from the principal mine (the Moonta) amounts to forty-five hundred tons.

Brother Caldwell's work was very heavy, and his health had been failing for some months; but his undying energy had kept him up to the last, and then, instead of remaining quietly at home to die, he went to Adelaide, 100 miles distant, to attend the district meeting. He put in one appearance at the district meeting, represented his work, returned to his lodgings, and died that night. The ministers of the district, thus assembled, buried their brother, and appointed, as a temporary supply to Wallaroo, Rev. Mr. Flockhart from the North Adelaide Circuit, who accompanied me to Wallaroo. We arrived at the mission house a little after dark, and were kindly entertained by our bereaved sister, the widow Caldwell.

A telegram from Sydney arrived that night, sent by my friend Mr. Macafee, of the firm of Messrs. McArthur and Co., saying, "Mrs. Taylor and her children have just arrived. All well."

I had just given up all hope of seeing them for many months to come, but now my dear wife, and Morgan Stuart, Ross, and Edward, aged nineteen nine, and six years—four, between the ages of nineteen and nine, having left us, and gone up to the "land of the living"—had, indeed, arrived in Australia. I had travelled east, and they west, and having compassed the globe, we were now, by the mercy of

God, on the eve of a meeting in those ends of the earth. That was one of the few nights of my life that sleep departed from my eyes. Surprise, and joy, and gratitude to God, combined, so filled my heart, that sleep was sought in vain. It being Saturday night, I could not respond till Monday morning. Several telegrams were exchanged with my wife up to Wednesday, when I received one saying that my son Morgan Stuart was thought to be dying, and I must haste to see him alive; I was over one thousand miles away, and no steamer till the next week. My feelings I will not try to describe, but my heart was stayed on God, and I continued the services that week, and on the following Sabbath opened a new church at the "Moonta." It contained about 1,000 persons; I preached three sermons, made good collections for the "trust fund," and had a good work of salvation that night.

By four a.m. Monday morning I was in the coach, bound for Adelaide, hoping it might be the will of God that I should return from Sydney, and resume my contemplated services among those miners. When I reached Adelaide I received another telegram saying that my son had a malignant fever. The Australian summer had fully set in, and I thought if it should please God to spare my son, the sooner I could get him away to sea the better; and hence, at once "packed up" for a final departure from South Australia, where I had hoped to do two months' more work for God. I could not get a passage till Thursday p.m., which gave me time to speak to my family along the wires. Just as I was stepping aboard the steamer I received a despatch "in haste." I feared it might contain a thunderbolt that might go right through my heart. I anchored my soul down firmly "to the rock that is higher than I," and said, "God loves my dear son more than I possibly can, and His decisions, in regard to him, are exactly right." I quoted for myself, "He shall not be afraid of evil tidings; his heart is fixed, trusting in the Lord." I then tremblingly opened the despatch, and read, "Morgan is somewhat better, but we greatly need you here. Signed, A. Moffitt." Then I thanked God, and breathed more freely. I reached Melbourne Saturday p.m., and had to wait till Tuesday for a steamer to Sydney. Preached in three different churches in Melbourne that Sabbath. Received a telegram while there, stating that Morgan was "convalescing." Here I made conditional arrangements for taking a Melbourne ship direct for London, if I should find Morgan able to travel within a fortnight, and thus get him as soon as possible out of the intense heat. I reached Sydney at three a.m. on Friday. Dr. Moffitt, at whose house my family were staying, had been waiting at the wharf till a few minutes before, and had left his brother-in-law, Mr. James Greer, to watch for my coming. He ordered a cab, and drove me at once to Dr. Moffitt's. My poor wife had not retired to rest, and indeed had not been able to sleep a night for nearly a fortnight, and was nearly worn out with care and weary watching. I found my son was much worse than I feared. It was thought best for me not to go into his room, to excite him, till morning, for though the nervous derangement and delirium occasioned by high fever almost precluded sleep, still every measure of undue excitement was to be avoided.

At day dawn my little Ross was brought to me. He had grown out of my knowledge. I took him into my arms, and wept over him some minutes before I could speak to him. I then asked him if he knew me.

"Yes, papa."

"How do you know that I am your papa?"

"My mother told me so?"

He thus accepted me as his father on the faith of his mother's testimony.

I then received my dear little Eddie—who thought he remembered me very distinctly, though he was but two years old when I parted with him. His memory no doubt got its impression, which he found identical with the person of his pa, from a recent "carte de visite."

I then went into the room which I had occupied as my bedroom while labouring in Sydney, and embraced the bony wreck of my firstborn, and heard him faintly say, "O my father!" Then we sat down just outside the gates of death, and wept, and prayed, and watched our sick son for three months. My dear Dr. Moffitt, at whose residence we were entertained, and his consulting physicians, gave it as their judgment that at least a year would probably be required for his recovery. Our contemplated trip to India was out of the question. To remain through an Australian summer was hazardous in the extreme. To go to the northern hemisphere, just in time to encounter the summer heat there, was not the thing for an invalid of that description.

Our physicians unanimously decided that our best possible plan was to take ship for the Cape of Good Hope. We would have a temperate climate at sea in going, and arrive about the first of April—the commencement of the salubrious winter season of Cape Colony.

Every other way was closed against us as certainly as was "Asia and Bithynia" against St. Paul and Co., and our call to Africa as distinct as was theirs to "Macedonia." I need not speak of the terribly severe and varied, but graciously sanctified discipline of those intervening months, in Sydney, in Melbourne, in Adelaide, and at sea. However God was with us, and not a Sabbath passed that I did not preach from two to three sermons. On the 17th of February, 1866, we bade our dear friends in Adelaide farewell, and went aboard the fine clipper ship, "St. Vincent," Captain Loutett, and after a prosperous voyage of forty-one days, we cast anchor in Table Bay, Cape of Good Hope.

Rev. James Calvert and wife, who had been successfully labouring in the Wesleyan Missions in Figii for twenty-five years, sailed from Adelaide three days after our departure in the ship "Yatala," a rival London ship of the "St. Vincent." Our captain and ship's company were rejoiced to find, as we cast anchor in Table Bay, about sunset on Friday evening, March 30th, that the "Yatala" had not yet arrived. But the first thing we heard in the morning was "The 'Yatala's' in. She cast anchor at four o'clock this morning." Early Saturday morning, I went ashore with Captain Loutett, and selected quarters at Parke's Hotel for self and family, at forty-eight shillings per day. Our passage from Adelaide had cost us altogether over £200, but our son's health was greatly improved, and we thanked God, and felt sure that we were in the providential path, and that having committed "our way unto the Lord, and trusting also in Him, He certainly would bring it to pass"—bring that to pass which was best for us, and the good of His cause. I left a note at the hotel for Rev. Samuel Hardey, Superintendent of the Wesleyan Circuit of Cape Town and Chairman of the Cape Town District, to whom I had letters from our mutual friend, Dr. Moffit. I then returned to our ship for my family.

When we landed, Rev. John Thomas, Wesleyan Missionary to the Dutch-speaking Coloured Wesleyan Circuit of Cape Town, met us, and gave us a welcome greeting, and accompanied us to our quarters. Brother Hardey had called at the hotel during my absence, but was then occupied with Rev. Brother Calvert, whom he took to his own house. He kindly offered to provide for me and mine among the friends, which I respectfully declined. Brother Thomas has been in the mission work in Southern Africa for twenty-six years. He is an earnest good man. Rev. Brother Hardey was for twenty-five years a Wesleyan Missionary in India, his excellent wife is a native of India, born of Missionary parents there, in connection with the Wesleyan Missionary Society. Brother Hardey's health failing in India, he spent some time in Mauritius, and founded a Mission among the Indian coolies there, of whom there are about 200,000 on that island. This promising young mission, not having been founded under any regular missionary plan, and the Secretaries of the Wesleyan Missionary Society not seeing their way clear to adopt it, and enter it on their very extensive list of Foreign Missions, it was turned over to the Protestant Episcopal Church, and is being carried on with success.

Brother Hardey then spent seven years as a missionary in West Australia, and fully recovered his health. He has been but a few years in Cape Town, but has done, and is doing, a good work there. He is one of the most affable, kind-spirited men, I believe, that this world can produce, and is, I am told, a good administrator of discipline, a good preacher as well. He gave me a cordial welcome to Cape Colony, and was ready at once heartily to co-operate with me in special efforts to promote the work of God.

CHAPTER II.

CAPE COLONY.

THE Cape of Good Hope was discovered by the Portuguese in 1486, and called the "Cape of Storms.' The King of Portugal subsequently changed the name to "Cape of Good Hope." In view of the terrible gales which occasionally occur, and the exposure of Table Bay to their fury, it would seem that the first would still be a very appropriate name. Only eleven months before our arrival, a north-west gale swept the Bay with such violence that of twenty-seven vessels in the harbour only nine of them rode out the gale. The remaining eighteen were driven ashore, with great loss of property and life. As the Colonial Government and people are making docks, by an immense excavation in solid rock, and forming a breakwater with the [stone thus obtained, I think there is "good hope" that it will soon afford safe anchorage for the shipping. The breakwater has been carried out 1,701 feet. The rock, with a slight mixture of the soil taken from the site of the inner basin, amounts to 822,055 cubic yards. The whole cost of the work, so far as they have gone up to

December, 1866, amounted, according to their official report, to the round sum of £391,135 14s.

The first European settlement at the Cape was in 1652, consisting of one hundred men, under the authority of the Dutch East India Company, not so much with a view "to establish a colony, as the establishment of a place for supplies, and for recruiting the sick of the Company." It continued under the control of this East India company, by consent of the Home Government in Holland, with a short intermission that the English held it, for 150 years, slowly increasing its population, and extending its territorial lines.

In 1806, the British troops took possession of the colony, and it is to be said to the honour of Lord Caledon, the first English governor, that he struck the first death-blow against slavery, which everywhere prevailed among the Dutch settlers. In 1807 he proclaimed it to be "unlawful to retain Hottentot children as apprentices."

It was in 1834 that slavery was abolished throughout the colony under Sir B. D'Urban. This occasioned great dissatisfaction among many of the Dutch settlers, and large numbers of them left the colony, and went to seek a country in the interior wilds of Africa. A large number of them went to Natal, more than one thousand miles east of Cape Town. But in consequence of their bad treatment of the natives in that country, they got into collision with the English colonial government. Mr.

George Cato, of Natal, then an English trader there, now a wealthy landowner, sugar planter, counsellor-general of the governor and government of Natal, Consul of Sweden, Norway, and Denmark, and Consular Agent for the United States of America, and altogether the most important individual in that colony, wrote a letter to a friend, who showed it to the governor, and British troops were sent to D'Urban, the principal port of entry, called after the governor, to protect the natives and British residents in that quarter. After a great deal of skirmishing, and some hard fighting, the defeated Dutch *trekked* beyond the "Drakensberg," and formed settlements on the Orange River, which have developed into the "Free State," and "Transvaal Republics."

Meantime, the tide of English immigration continued to increase. "In the year 1820, the British Government spent £50,000 sterling in sending British settlers to the Eastern province of Cape Colony, so that, by the gradual diminution of the Dutch element, and the increase of the English, as early as 1822, it was ordered, by proclamation, that the English language should be used in all judicial proceedings." The Dutch population, however, in most places, especially in the Western province, is much greater than the English; and, as it regards their wealth, and superiority of church edifices, the Dutch Reformed Church is, practically, the "State Church" of the country. Though it does not monopolise all the "State aid" of the colony, yet of the £16,000 annually granted by the Colonial Government for the support of religion, the Dutch Reformed Church gets £9,000. The Parliament, during its recent session (1866), came within two votes of abolishing "State Aid" altogether. They will probably come to that before many years, for the most of this money goes, not to support weak churches in poor and sparsely settled portions, but mainly to the wealthy churches in Cape Town.

The population of Cape Colony, according to the "Census of 1865," amounted to an aggregate of 482,240, or, in round numbers, nearly half a million, of which 71,078 are whites, principally Dutch and English, including, of course, the usual proportion of Scotch and Irish.

The native population is subdivided as follows:—

The ancient occupants of this country were "bushmen," a nation of beings of very low stature, low in intellect, and have the character of being a marauding, murderous people. They are now almost extinct. They were superseded by the Hottentots, a race peculiarly marked, with deep set eyes, and very high cheek bones; their faces on a line across the nose and cheek bones are very broad, the forehead not so broad, and the lower part of the face and chin very narrow.

It was this class of natives that the Dutch reduced to slavery, and hence such an amalgamation with the Dutch that the name Hottentot, in many sections of the country, is synonymous with "Bastard."

The Hottentots, throughout the colony, pure and mixed, number 79,996. The "Bastards" hold themselves quite superior to the purely black races, and usually have separate sitting in chapel. Many of them are rising in the scale of education, civilisation, and religion. They are principally under the care of the missionaries of the "London Missionary Society."

Many thousands of these "Bastards," not embraced however in the census of Cape Colony, under the chieftainship of Captain Adam Kok, by the advice and encouragement of the Colonial Government, removed, some four years ago, from "Griqualand," near the Orange River, in the "Free State," to a large district of country in Eastern Kaffraria, bordering on the colony of Natal, called "No-man's-land." Their missionary declined to accompany them to their mountain home; but in building up a town of over 1,000 population, they have built in the midst of their barracks a chapel, which will seat about 600; and there, and in several smaller communities, they have regular services every Sabbath. I preached for them on my journey through Kaffraria, and though it was raining, and sleeting, and bitterly cold, their church was crowded with well-dressed and well-behaved worshippers. Their language is the Dutch, though many of them are learning the English. But a large class of the Hottentots have learned so many of the vices of the white man, especially a love for brandy, that they are dying out very fast.

Before the European occupancy of Cape Colony, the Kaffirs had pressed down from the east into the country of the Hottentots, and had taken a great deal of their land, which they had previously taken from the bushmen.

The Kaffirs in Cape Colony number 95,577. They are naturally a powerful race of people. Those in the colony, and on the eastern border of it, are considered finer specimens of men, than the nations further eastward. Rev. Wm. Shaw says, "The Kaffirs are physically a fine race of people. The Amaxosa are, as a general rule, of greater stature than Englishmen, and in general well made and finely proportioned. Many have well-formed heads and pleasing features, such as would be deemed handsome in a European. They walk erect, and with a firm step, and when occasion presents, they show great agility and fleetness of foot." Mr. Godlonton, the originator and senior proprietor of the *Graham's Town Journal,* which claims the most extensive circulation of any paper in the colony, told me that before they had regular mail facilities in the colony, he had a Kaffir who, twice each week, carried a load of papers fresh from the press, after dark, forty-six miles to Fort Beaufort, and delivered them there at day dawn next morning. The overland mail from the Eastern Province of Cape Colony to Natal, is carried a distance of over 400 miles, by

Kaffirs on foot. The traders and missionaries often send books and other articles in the mail bags, amounting sometimes to a load, as I have seen and handled them, more suitable for a horse than a man, and yet those uncomplaining fellows carry them through with great despatch.

"Kaffir women," says Rev. Mr. Shaw, "when young, generally appear to be quite equal to their countrymen in physical development, only differing in size as in all other nations." "The prevailing colour of the Kaffirs on the border is nearly that of dark mahogany. There are, however, great varieties, from a tawny brown to a jet black. As a general rule, the Zulu Kaffirs are much darker than the Frontier tribes." I have seen a great many myself who are purely a red, glossy, copper colour. Many of them have nearly as good a Jewish physiognomy as any of the sons of Abraham.

The chiefs all hold their rank by hereditary right, and Rev. Mr. Shepstone, and others, have been able to trace the regular succession of the principal ruling chiefs of the country back for fifteen hundred years. The people are divided into nations, tribes, clans, and families.

The Kaffirs speak a most euphonious language, constructed with such precision, that old Kaffir scholars have told me that they never heard a Kaffir make a grammatical blunder in speaking his own language, and almost every Kaffir is a natural orator. The principal nations, beginning in the colony, and

SPECIMENS OF THE KAFFIR FAIR SEX.

going eastwardly, are the Amaxosa, Abutembu (Tembookies), Ambaca, Amapondo, Amapondumsi, and Amazulu.

Besides the 96,000 Kaffirs, in round numbers, in Cape Colony, there are supposed to be at least 300,000 between Cape Colony and Natal, in a strip of country 150 miles wide and 400 miles coast-wise, known as Kaffraria. They have a fine country for live-stock, well watered; and a good supply of cattle, sheep, and goats. Their principal grain is Kaffir corn, which has the general appearance, but with a grain double the size of broom-corn, and maize, or Indian corn. This is pounded in a mortar, and prepared very much like American hominy, and also ground into meal between two stones prepared for the purpose, and worked by hand. As in olden time the women do the grinding.

The name "KAFFIR," by which all these nations of natives, from Cape Colony to Delagoa Bay, three or four hundred miles east of Natal, and their language, are designated by Europeans, "is not a name used by the natives to designate either themselves or any other tribes in the country. "The word," says Rev. Mr. Shaw, "is derived from the Arabic, and signifies an infidel or unbeliever. It is, in fact, the epithet which most Mohamedan people in the East would apply to any European or Christian." It was therefore a term of reproach given by the followers of the false prophet, but has come into universal use as applied to this people, their language, and the literature which has been given them, and indeed is so convenient for the mass of Europeans, who could not understand, or even pronounce the hard names by which many tribes are known among themselves, as to be indispensable.

The remaining 131,992 mentioned in the census, filling up the aggregate of nearly half a million in the colony, are "Fingoes," except some 15 or 20,000 Malays, principally in Cape Town and Port Elizabeth, who were brought originally from the Dutch East Indian possessions. The most of these Malays are Mohamedans, and have their mosques, and peculiar forms of worship in the cities just named.

The FINGOES, which constitute so large a proportion of the native population of the colony, are refugees from the East. They were driven from their homes by Chaka, an Amazulu chief, who waged a most desolating war for eighteen years, from 1817 to 1835, against all his neighbouring tribes. Mr. Shaw says:—"The terror of Chaka's name, and the destructive mode of conducting war by the Amazulu, combined to deprive the surrounding tribes of all hope that they could offer any effectual resistance; and, in numerous cases, they fled from their country on the approach of the smallest detachment of Chaka's fighting men. The victories of his warriors extended east, west, north, and south, over an area of more than one hundred thousand square miles. Some of the more powerful tribes, when driven out of their own districts, invaded the territory of their neighbours, until the whole region from Delagoa Bay to the Griqua country, near the Orange River, and from the Basuto country, in the north to that of the Amapondo in the south, was one scene of war and desolation. Men, women, and children were unsparingly slain by their conquerors. It is believed that fully one half the population of that immense district, just described, during those dreadful eighteen years of slaughter, perished." Many thousands of these refugees were received by the Amatembu, Amaxosa, and other Kaffir tribes, along the eastern border of Cape Colony, as " Amamfengu," or Fingoes, having a meaning corresponding with that of "serfs." They were not slaves to be bought and sold, and separated from their families, but were distributed by families, and clans, among the head men of different kraals; seed and cattle were furnished them, and the free use of the public domain; but their corn or cattle were at any time subject to seizure at the will of the Kaffir chiefs. Thousands of them subsequently took refuge at the Wesleyan Mission stations in Kaffraria. The Kaffir chiefs meantime became very jealous of the Fingoes, and greatly oppressed them. When the Kaffir war against the Colonists in 1835 broke out, many Fingoes rallied around our missionaries at "Butterworth, Clarkebury, and Morley Wesleyan Mission stations, and on the arrival of the British troops many more fled from their masters, and took refuge in the British camp. Governor D'Urban, finding that the

Fingoes reposed great confidence in the missionaries, requested Rev. Mr. Ayliff to take the whole body of the Fingoes under their special care and lead them to the land of the free in the colony. The Governor in his official report says, " When it became necessary to make war upon Hintsa and his people, finding the people called Fingoes living among them in a state of most grievous bondage, and seeing them anxious to be delivered, I at once declared them to be a free people and subjects of the King of England; and it is now my intention to place them in the country on the east bank of the Great Fish River, in order to protect the bush country from the entrance of the Kaffirs; and also that by bringing a large population into the colony, the colonists may supply themselves with free labourers."

In company with the British troops, on their return into the colony, Rev. John Ayliff, during one week, from the 9th to the 15th of May, 1835, led out of bondage into the colony 16,000 of these people, with all their cattle. The policy indicated in the Governor's proclamation has ever since been carried out, and the Fingoes, who now number over 100,000 in the colony, have ever remained loyal to the Government, and they are still specially under the care of the Wesleyan Missionaries. The Government has done much for them in various ways. Governor Grey established "Industrial Schools for them at Fort Peddie, Heald Town, and

Lesseyton, under the Wesleyans; and at 'Lovedale,' under the missionaries of the Free Church of Scotland."

The Kaffirs, never having been in bondage, are open, independent, and manly in their bearing, and seem never to feel that spirit of servility, common among the Fingoes, and for a long time the Kaffirs continued to despise the Fingoes; but the superior political relations of the Fingoes as British subjects, and the fact that many hundreds of them, by their industry, have become the owners of good farms, oxen, wagons, and herds; and that thousands of the younger ones can read and write, and speak the English language, they now command the respect of even of their former masters. The following extract from the *Graham's Town Journal* may serve as a further illustration of this subject:—

"The circumstances of the colonial natives generally may seem, to persons fresh from Europe, supremely miserable; but this is very far, indeed, from being the case. Hardy, with few wants, and having those wants easily supplied, the poorest of them are better off than the lower class of Europeans, while thrifty and industrious men often accumulate a great deal of property.

We could point out at least half-a-dozen natives in a single district, whose properties, if realized, would produce from £3,000 to £5,000 each; and there are hundreds of Fingoes, whose position among natives is one of opulence. The fact is, that with ordinary prudence, any native, not unduly encumbered with wives, may, after a few years of service, save enough in the shape of live-stock to give him a very creditable position among his compatriots. We may mention, for instance, that within the last five months, the following stock—all the property of native immigrants—passed through Queen's Town:— Of sheep and goats, 7,548; of cattle, 627 head; and of horses, 159." In the settlement of the last colonial war complications with the Kaffirs, the Government got from the celebrated warrior chief "Krilie," a large tract of country beyond the "Kai river," which has recently been given to the Fingoes. They have hence become the owners of the soil in which they dwelt as serfs. The immigrants above mentioned were journeying to this land of promise. About 40,000 Fingoes have already settled in their new home, which may appropriately be called "Fingoland."

"This colony, like Australia and Canada, is ruled by a Governor (appointed by the Home Government), assisted by an executive Council, as well as by Upper and Lower Houses of Parliament, respectively named the Legislative Council and the House of Assembly. The Council contains fifteen members, eight of whom are elected by the votes in the western districts, and seven by those in the eastern province, while the Assembly comprises forty-six members, elected by the various constituencies throughout the colony." "The judicial establishment comprises the

THE COLONIAL GOVERNMENT.

Supreme Court, of four judges, who hold sessions in Cape Town, and Circuit Courts in the country districts; also an Eastern Province High Court of judicature." "The numerous Courts of resident magistrates, in all the larger villages, exercise limited jurisdiction in all civil and criminal cases."

CHAPTER III.

CAPE TOWN.

CAPE TOWN, the capital of the colony, is located at the base of Table Mountain, which rises very precipitously to an elevation of about four thousand feet, and is nearly as flat as a table on the top and often covered with a light fleecy mist, gently dropping over the edge like a tablecloth. The mountain constitutes a grand background for the city, and contrasts beautifully with the splendid flower-gardens and groves of oak, and Scotch firs, which abound at its base, in, and around, the city. Cape Town has a population of 28,547, of which 15,118 are whites, about 12,500 Malays, and about 1,000 Hottentots and Kaffirs.

It is well supplied with banks and newspapers, and all the variety of educational and benevolent institutions, common in large towns. In the midst of the city are beautiful Botanic Gardens, Museum, and Library. The *Museum* "comprises a fine series of mammals, birds, reptiles, fish, shells, insects, fossils, and minerals. It has also collections of coins, weapons of various races, and some specimens of metal-work and plastic art." The principal room containing these, "is eighty feet long, forty-two broad, and thirty-nine high."

The Public Library, occupying part of the same building, is said to be superior to that of a y other colony. It "contains books in every b anch of science and literature, and has nearly 40,000 volumes on its shelves. It is open to the public daily from 9 A.M. to 4.30 P.M. free of expense."

In an adjoining room is what is known as "The Grey Library," containing 5,000 volumes, many of them very ancient and rare. It was presented to the colony by her late Governor, Sir George Grey, now Governor of New Zealand.

There are three large Dutch Reformed Church edifices in Cape Town, containing an aggregate of 3,000 members. Rev. Andrew Murray, jun., a pastor of one of them, a liberal, and thoroughly evangelical, man, was "Moderator of the Synod." His father, Rev. A. Murray, sen., an old pioneer minister in the Dutch Reformed Church in Southern Africa, has given three highly-accomplished, and pious sons to her ministry. The father, full of years, and ripe for heaven, died a few months ago in "Graafreinet."

There are three Protestant Episcopal churches in the city, one Presbyterian, one Independent, one Evangelical Lutheran, and two Wesleyan,—one for the English, and one for the coloured Dutch.

As I propose to illustrate a great variety of Christian adventures in South Africa, besides what I saw and did myself, I will insert a few specimens here, and one commendable act, worthy of a Christian, by one of those Malays—a very different fellow, certainly, from the one who stole one of my boots while I was one morning swimming in Table Bay. He might just as easily have taken both boots as one, and I wondered why he did not, till a friend of mine traced it, and bought the boot from him. Having one boot, he counted his chances for a customer for it in the person of the owner.

My friend, Henry Reed, Esq., of Dunorlan, Tunbridge Wells, in one of his voyages to Australia, stopped, in the year 1840, in company with his family at Cape Town. When the ship came to anchor, a Malay boatman tipped his hat to Mr. Reed,—

"A boat, sir?"

"What will you charge to take me and my family ashore?"

"Thirteen dollars, sir."

"Thirteen dollars! Why, that is too much."

"No, sir, it is the regular price, and I can't do it for less!"

"Very well," said Mr. Reed, "we will go with you."

When safely landed he paid the Malay thirteen dollars, about £2 14s. The next morning a messenger called on Mr. Reed at his lodgings, and said,—

"The Malay boatman, who brought you ashore yesterday, is at the door, and wants to see you."

"Dear me," thought Reed, as he was going to the door, "that fellow is not satisfied with his extortionary gains of yesterday, and wants to make another draw on me to-day, the mean fellow."

"What do you want, sir?" demanded Reed.

"You made a mistake yesterday in the money you paid me," replied the boatman.

"Not at all, sir; no mistake about it. You asked me thirteen dollars for your work, and I paid you, and you'll not get any more," and added to the sentence, in his own mind, "these villanous boatmen are alike the world over."

"No," said the Malay, "you are quite mistaken; I charged thirteen dollars—"

"Yes," rejoined Mr. Reed, "and I paid it, and you ought to be satisfied."

"But," continued the son of Mohamed, "I meant Dutch rix-dollars, and you paid me three times as much as I asked, and I have brought your money back," handing him the money.

Thirteen rix-dollars are 19s. 6d., instead of £2 14s.

Mr. Reed was satisfied to receive back his money, but especially delighted to find such an example of honesty, where he least expected it.

Owing to the illness of Mr. Reed's little daughter Mary, whom he finally buried in Cape Town, he was detained there many weeks. It was a time of great distress to the Cape Town people, and Mr. Reed was providentially detained to minister the Word of Life to perishing hundreds who were dying with the small-pox. The disease, which was of the most virulent type, had been communicated to the town from a slaver, which had been captured, and brought into Table Bay, with its living freight of wretched captives. It spread rapidly over the town, causing a panic which nearly suspended all kinds of business, except that of doctors, nurses, undertakers and grave-diggers. Money in payment of debts was refused, until it had been dipped into vinegar, and laid out to dry. The hospitals were crowded, and then the municipal Government had a large building, two miles out of town, fitted up, and filled with decaying, dying sufferers. Mr. Reid and his family were boarding with Mrs. Gunn, who kept a first-class boarding-house, which was well-filled with Government officers and distinguished travellers.

All who are acquainted with Mr. Reid's labours among all sorts of adventurers in Tasmania and Australia, know that he would not stop a day in any place without preaching Christ to the people, publicly or privately; so in Cape Town he at once went to work for his Master, but for a time, for prudential reasons, he avoided contact with the small-pox patients. Soon, however, he was waited on by two pious soldiers, Sergeant Runciman, and a fellow sergeant, who informed him that there were hundreds of men and women dying in the new extemporized hospital beyond the town, and not a soul to speak a word of comfort to them, or tell them how to receive Jesus Christ as their Saviour. The soldiers begged Mr. Reed to become the volunteer chaplain to that hospital, who, upon a little reflection responded, "I will." When Mrs. Gunn's boarders heard of it, they had a meeting, and after discussing the subject, decided that Mr. Reed should not go, lest he might bring the contagion into the house, and hazard the lives of the whole of them, and that if he should persist in carrying out his purpose he must remove from Mrs. Gunn's house.

To all this Mr. Reed replied, "It will be a very great inconvenience for my family, with a sick child, to leave, and go we know not whither, but I believe it is my duty to go, and do what I can for the sick and dying. I will commit the whole matter to God, do my duty, and leave all consequences with Him."

So he went daily till the plague abated. He took them by tiers or sections, as they lay, and spoke to them personally and collectively, and told them how, by the power of the Holy Spirit, they should surrender their poor diseased bodies and souls to God, and receive the sympathizing Jesus, who was saying to them, "Come unto me all ye that labour, and are heavy laden, and I will give you rest." A speechless dying girl, with smiling face, drew a Bible from under her pillow and showed it to Mr. Reed, indicating by signs that her title was clear to a mansion in heaven. On one occasion, two persons, with whom he conversed as he passed in, were dead before he got back. He had hope in the death of some, and the Judgment alone will reveal the number "who were snatched as brands from the burning" through his agency during those trying weeks. God took care of His servant, and he heard nothing more about his having to change his quarters, but remained quietly at Mrs. Gunn's house, which was one of but very few houses in the city that entirely escaped the dreadful visitation.

Rev. Mr. Hodgson, who had been labouring for some years as a Wesleyan missionary among the natives in the Orange River Country, was then superintendent of the Cape Town circuit, and greatly interested Mr. Reed with a narrative of his adventures in the interior, and introduced to him a Christian native man who had just come with a wagon from Orange river to Cape Town.

This native man was a Christian hero, as the following facts related by Mr. Hodgson to Mr. Reed will show. The lions in the Orange River country, when they get old and too stiff, or too lazy to follow their trade of catching bucks and other active animals, sometimes crouch about the kraals, and pounce upon a man; and when they begin that kind of work they soon acquire such cannibal proclivities, as to become very troublesome customers.

An old lion had been making some such unwelcome visits to the kraal to which this Christian native belonged, and one day he and two others took each a

THE LION AND THE CHRISTIAN NATIVE.

gun, and went out in search of him, hoping to make a final settlement with him. A few miles distant from the kraal, passing over the brow of a ridge into a little vale, they suddenly surprised a large lion, feeding on the remains of an animal carcass. The lion preferring fresh meat seemed glad to see them, and without ceremony advanced to give them a greeting. The men, in their sudden fright, declined the interview, and ran for life. The Christian man quite outran his two heathen compatriots; but as he was making away with himself as fast as he could, the thought struck him, "One of those men will be killed; neither is prepared to die! I am prepared, thank God! I had better die, and give them time for repentance!" He instantly stopped, and faced about; the two men passed him, and before he could transfer his thoughts from his heroic consent to die for his heathen neighbour, to a purpose of self-defence with his gun, the lion was upon him. With the force of a mighty bound, the lion struck him on the breast with his paw, and tore off the skin and flesh to the bone. Then with his fore-feet upon the body of his victim, he took one of his arms in his mouth, and craunched and mangled it. Then he got the stock of the gun between his teeth, and ground it to splinters. Meantime the other two men looked back, and seeing their friend down, braced themselves up for the rescue. They returned near enough for a sure shot, and both together took good aim, and the lion dropped dead beside his bleeding victim.

D

Brother Reed examined the deep scars left by the paw of the lion, which the noble fellow would carry to his grave. "Scarcely for a righteous man will one die, yet peradventure for a good man some would even dare to die; but God commendeth his love toward us, in that while we were yet sinners Christ died for us." And here was one of Africa's sable sons so imbued with the self-sacrificing spirit of Jesus, that even for a bad man he was willing to die.

On my first Sabbath in Cape Town—April 1st —I preached at half-past 10 A.M., in Burg Street Wesleyan Church, which will accommodate about 500 persons. On this occasion it was not filled by onethird; but the Holy Spirit was manifested in mercy to many hearts. Rev. Brother Calvert, and wife, were present, and in the afternoon and evening Brother Calvert preached there, while I, at the same hours, preached at Rondebosch Wesleyan Chapel, four miles out. The limited capacity of the chapels, and the smallness of the congregations, contrasted unfavourably with the fine churches, and packed audiences, of Australia. During that week, after several days of inquiry, we secured, what we considered, under the circumstances, good boarding accommodation, at a more reasonable rate than we were paying at the hotel, and sought information in regard to the field I might successfully cultivate during my sojourn of six months. I learned that the English work in the Western

Province was very limited, the mass of the people composing our societies being coloured, speaking Dutch, to whom I could not preach. I learned that we had a much better English cause in the Eastern Province, 500 miles distant, and in Natal 1,000 miles distant, but that there were only two places in the Eastern Province, and two in Natal, where I could get a congregation of any size speaking English, so I began to conclude that my working-time in Africa would be reduced to three instead of six months. On the 7th of April I attended the anniversary meeting of the Wesleyan Sunday-schools, and delivered an address on the Gospel doctrine of having all the children converted, and trained for God. Rev. Andrew Murray followed with words of earnestness on the same subject.

Brother Filmer, one of the superintendents, in his speech, said, "Seventeen years ago we had a revival in this town; about fifty souls were soundly converted to God; some of them have become missionaries, and others remain useful members of the Church. Then, five years ago, we had another revival, principally among the Sunday-school children. About forty professed to find peace with God. Some of them have fallen away, but the most of them have remained steadfast; and I find some of them among our Sunday-school teachers now, and others are useful members of the Church. I am now feeling, hoping, and believing, that we are on the eve of another outpouring of the Holy Spirit." I thought, "Well, such revivals during a period of seventeen years are much better than nothing, but fall very far short of God's purpose, and provisions in Christ, and the spiritual demands of nearly 30,000 sinners."

On Sabbath, the 8th of April, I commenced a series of special services in Burg Street Wesleyan Chapel, which was kept up for nine days, during which I preached thirteen sermons. A few seekers came forward the first night, ten, and upwards, each night of the series, till the last, when the altar was crowded with about thirty seekers; but our congregations were not large, and the whole machinery of Church agency seemed very weak. The members of the church seemed very willing to do what they could, and I believe they were much strengthened; 'and twenty-one souls were reported by Brother Hardey as giving satisfactory testimony to the fact of their conversion to God.

On the Wednesday night, of our week of special services, we had with us Rev. Wm. Impey, Chairman of the Graham's Town district. He had been twenty-seven years a missionary in Africa, a good preacher, and a man of fine administrative ability. He is a son-in-law of Rev. Wm. Shaw, so well known as the apostle of Methodist Christianity in the Eastern Province and Kaffraria, and the President of the English Wesleyan Conference for the year 1866. Rev. Mr. Impey was on his way to England as a representative to the Conference, and Mrs. Impey to see her father and friends. He had with him a most complimentary testimonial, for Mr. Shaw, signed by 1,400 persons in the Eastern Province, to remind their old pioneer friend that they had not forgotten him.

Brother Impey, on his own behalf, and on behalf of the ministers in his district, gave me a cordial welcome to South Africa, and a pressing invitation to visit Graham's Town. "I'll give you the keys," said he, "and you may go into my circuit and do as you please."

"O, I thank you, Brother Impey," I replied, "for your expression of confidence, but I do not wish the keys of any man's circuit. When I accept the invitation of a minister to work in his circuit or church, it is simply that, under the leading of the Holy Spirit, I may assist him and his people in their great work. It is my rule not to work in a church in the absence of the pastor; but as you have left such a noble brother as Rev. Thomas Guard—two of whose brothers, ministers in the Irish Conference, I know —as your representative, I accept your kind invitation."

We had so many seekers the last night in Cape Town, that I felt rather sorry to leave; but I had to go then, or wait probably a month for the next regular steamer. So, on Wednesday the 18th of April, I took passage in the steamer "Natal," a clean, comfortable little boat of 400 tons, for PORT ELIZABETH. We expected to reach Algoa Bay on Friday; but in consequence of head winds and rough weather, we did not arrive till Saturday afternoon.

CHAPTER IV.

PORT ELIZABETH.

Rev. John Richards, the superintendent of Port Elizabeth Circuit, met me at the wharf, and kindly conducted me to his house. Brother Hardey had written to him that I was coming, but he did not know definitely when, so there was no announcement of our contemplated meetings. Brother Richards was very glad to have me hold a series of services, but thought it a most unfavourable time to commence, because of a number of counter attractions :—

"1. The new Roman Catholic Church, in Port Elizabeth, is to be opened to-morrow, with imposing ceremonies, to be continued through most of the week, and a great deal of public interest and curiosity have been excited, and large expectations are entertained."

"2. The newly-arrived Independent minister is to be installed to-morrow, and to preach his first sermons, and receive his friends at a public tea-meeting on Wednesday evening."

These great coming events had been duly announced, and were the talk of the town; but it was not known that I was even expected, for Brother R. himself had only notice of it a day or two before.

I replied, "I have come, I believe, in the order of Providence, knowing nothing of these things. We are not responsible for any of these adverse influences, nor under any obligation to turn aside for them; I have nothing to do, but go forward and do what God may open before me, as my duty."

As it was important that the public should have notice of our contemplated series of meetings, I modestly said to Brother R.

"In Ireland, they would in such a case get a lot of little handbills printed for private circulation, and send them to all the families they might desire specially to invite to our meetings. In Melbourne they would have large posters put up all over the city straightway, and let everybody know what we proposed to do."

He thought it rather late for anything of that sort. "But," said he, "I will go down town and tell some of our friends, and request them to inform others."

I proposed to accompany him. We went about a quarter of a mile down the principal business street, and I was conducted into a substantial stone chapel, with end gallery, deep pews, and doors to guard the way into them; an organ in the gallery, and at the opposite end, well up toward the ceiling, a small old-fashioned pulpit. That was the Wesleyan

Chapel, large enough to seat about 400 persons. It had stood there twenty-five years, our principal place of worship in a town containing a population of 11,633, of whom 7,120 are whites, and, for the most part, English. Port Elizabeth too, which was founded as early as 1820, is the principal "Port of entry," for the Eastern Province of Cape Colony, the "Free State," and "Transvaal Republics," in the interior, and boasts a much larger export than Cape Town. The Episcopalians, Roman Catholics, Independents, Presbyterians, and even the Mohammedans, have each a good church edifice. Brother Richards said :—

"We were the first in this field, and have lost a good congregation for want of suitable church accommodation. I tried hard, three years ago, to persuade the trustees to build a good church, and the Wesleyans here were then well able to do it; but divided councils prevailed, and the thing was postponed. Since then great financial reverses have fallen on the town, and now we are obliged to wait for better times."

In came the chapel-keeper and Brother R. said to him, "Tell the people that a stranger will preach for us to-morrow."

Then we went to several shops, and I waited outside, while Brother R. went in to tell them about the arrival of a stranger. But I thought my good brother was not "raising the breeze" fast enough, and that if we had to "blow our own trumpet," we had better do it effectively. So I then went in too. He introduced me as "Rev. Mr. Taylor, who has been preaching recently at the Cape."

Thought I, "Dear me, if I have no greater prestige than what I gained at the Cape, it will not fill our little chapel to-morrow." So when he told the shopkeepers to tell their customers that "a stranger would preach at the Wesleyan Chapel to-morrow," I threw in a few qualifying terms, such "as California,"—"Australia,"—"A work of God,"—"Bring your friends, and have them saved by the mighty Jesus; God hath sent Him for that purpose, and they ought to receive Him gladly." In passing along I was introduced to a Local Preacher, and to help him gird on his armour, I gave him our plan of procedure, with a few illustrative facts. When I told him that we had very orderly meetings, and closed them as early as 10 P.M., he broke out in one of those incredulous laughs for which the Lord reproved Sarah. "I would be glad," said he, "to see such things in Port Elizabeth, but cannot see how they can be brought about; why, our people here," he added, "can hardly wait till 8 o'clock, much less 10."

"O, well," I replied, "we will dismiss them each night as early as eight o'clock, at the close of the sermon, and give all an opportunity to leave who wish to do so."

He replied, "You don't know the Port Elizabeth people as I do, or you would not entertain such hopes." After we had made our round among the shops, we spent the evening with Mr. Sydney Hill, of the mercantile firm of "Savage and Hill, 41, Bow Lane, Cheapside, London, and Port Elizabeth." Brother Hill is a very intelligent thorough business man, a zealous Wesleyan Christian, Superintendent of the Sunday-school, Class-Leader, and altogether one of those noble men whom the Lord distributes through the world where they are most needed. His lady too is a person of rare excellence. Brother Hill was full of hope, "and believed that the work of God in the awakening and conversion of sinners had already commenced, and we would see better days in Port Elizabeth." After spending a couple of days very pleasantly with Brother and Sister Richards, I then, according to previous arrangement, made my home at Brother Hill's.

On Sabbath morning we had the chapel more than half full. Brother R. read Mr. Wesley's abridgment of the "Morning Service," I preached, and the Holy Spirit wrought as in days of old.

At 3 p.m. I preached to the children. The chapel was well filled, but not crowded; but we had still more out in the evening. About 8 p.m., after the sermon, I dismissed the congregation; but most of them kept their seats, preferring to remain for the prayer-meeting.

After explaining our method of conducting a prayer-meeting, I said, "If there are any sinners here who feel the awakening power of the Holy Spirit, and, like the awakened souls on the day of Pentecost, wish to know what to do, they may come forward to this altar of prayer, and we will tell you what we did when we were in your sad state, and how we obtained salvation through Jesus Christ." Thirteen adults came forward as seekers, and about half of them professed to find peace with God. I found we had some good workers, who came up promptly, and wrought effectively.

At a quarter past nine Brother R. said, " With Brother Taylor's consent we will close the meeting for this evening." I felt sorry to close so early, for a number were near the strait gate, and striving with many tears to enter in, whom I had not had time to speak to personally, but I deferred to my superintendent, as the best thing probably under the circumstances, and the meeting was promptly closed.

When we got back to the Mission House, Brother R. said, "I feel rebuked, for I did not think that one person would come forward to the altar at this early stage of the meeting, and especially the persons who did come." Sister R. also upbraided herself for having her faith outdone. They were both, however, greatly delighted and encouraged.

Brother Richards was one of Dr. Hannah's first graduates from "Didsbury." He is a thorough student now, and I believe a man of scholarly attainments. I am told that he is a good preacher, a most industrious pastor, and an ardent friend. His wife, though delicate in health, is a true missionary helper. He came first to the Colony in 1837.

I spent two weeks in Port Elizabeth, preached sixteen sermons, and lectured one night on "Reminiscences of Palestine." We had from ten to twenty seekers forward every night, and conversions to God on each occasion, but how many were saved I know not, as the minister said he knew them, and did not, so far as I know, keep a record of their names. I had preaching service on Saturday night for the natives—Kaffirs and Fingoes. The chapel, which will seat 350 persons, was filled. William Barnabas, "a good man," Local Preacher and native teacher, was my interpreter. I felt so awkward in preaching through an interpreter, and being very weary from excessive labours through the week, I did not enjoy the service, and saw but little indication of good from the effort. On the second Sabbath, besides the regular morning and evening preaching for the whites, I preached in the afternoon from the Court-house steps. A little shower of rain at the time of assembling kept many away, but we had out about 600 persons, and it was a profitable service; I thus preached the Gospel to two or three hundred who would not otherwise have heard it from me. During preaching a funeral procession passed close by. The subject suiting the occasion, I illustrated it by the dead returning to dust.

Then, a little later, the police came along with a bloody-faced prisoner, followed by a rabble, and I said, "Look at him, 'The way of transgressors is hard,'" and got an illustration of my subject out of him.

At the close, a man came and shook my hand, saying, "I have heard you preach to the gamblers in San Francisco, and to the sailors on Long Wharf, and I heard you give a singular reproof to some sailors that I'll never forget. They were loading a barge with coal, and one, with a profane oath, wished the coals in H——. 'That is quite unnecessary, my friend,' said you, 'for if you are so unhappy as to go down to that place, you will find it hot enough, and plenty of fuel.'"

When I went to the Eastern Province it was with the purpose of spending one month there, dividing the time between Port Elizabeth and Graham's Town, and another month in Natal. I had my return-ticket, for which I had paid £17, extending to three months, but I soon found that the English population of the Eastern Province was much greater than my limited information had led me to suppose, and that my time should be extended to at least two months for the Eastern Province alone.

On the evening of my arrival in Port Elizabeth, Brother Richards introduced me to the first Kaffir I had ever seen. He stood before me six feet four inches, with finely developed form, good head, very pleasant countenance, and a superior display of ivory. "This man," said Brother R., "is one of our Local Preachers, Joseph Tale, from the Annshaw

Circuit, about one hundred and fifty miles in the interior." Through Wm. Barnabas I asked him many questions about the work of God among his people. He gave a very encouraging account of the number and steadfastness of their people on the Annshaw Mission. I told him that when my boxes were opened I would give him some books. He said his children could read English, and they would read them to him. I felt great sympathy with the native work, and deep regret that I could not preach to them. I had no faith in successful preaching through an interpreter. I asked my new tall brother to attend our meetings next day, but he said his teams had gone out of town that day, that they had to go out some distance homeward to get grass for their oxen, but that he and a party of wagoners would keep the Sabbath on the road, and that he had an appointment to preach to them there. A good example for their white brethren.

Brother Richards made me a plan for a two months' tour, embracing Graham's Town, King William's Town, Queen's Town, Cradock, and Somerset, each appointment about eighty miles apart, in travelling from one to the other. I would have two weeks for Graham's Town, and a week for each of the other places, and a week at Port Elizabeth, on my return, in waiting for a steamer to take me on to Natal. He accordingly informed the ministers of my arrival, and they all wrote me a cordial invitation to visit them, and with them came pressing invitations from Salem, Bathurst, Fort Beaufort, and Uitenhage Circuits. The last two I added to my plan. I made no provision for preaching to the natives, for not knowing their language I did not hope to be able to work successfully among them, but prayed and hoped that indirectly they would derive much good from a revival of God's work among the English.

My next move was to Uitenhage, which is an old Dutch town, twenty miles distant from Port Elizabeth.

CHAPTER V.

UITENHAGE.

On the 5th of May, I came from Port Elizabeth, to this beautiful town. At Port Elizabeth, I had been sojourning a few days at the house of Mr. W. Jones, a somewhat eccentric but very clever genial Welshman, and a superior Local Preacher in the Wesleyan Church. His wife, a very good woman, is a class-leader; his daughter Jessie, a fine young lady, and several sons were unconverted.

Brother Jones gave me the use of his carriage and two horses, and his son Philip to drive me to Uitenhage. We took with us, Mrs. John Richards, and Miss Jessie Jones. Sister Richards was in such a poor state of health when I arrived, that she feared she would not be able to attend many of my meetings, but, as she entered into the work, her health improved, and after two weeks' special services at home, was now going to help me a week among her friends in Uitenhage, among whom she was blessed in doing a work for God. During our journey that day, she took occasion to say, that she had been greatly edified by my Gospel ministrations, and was much pleased with me in everything she had seen, except my beard, in regard to which she put me on my defence. I said, "Sister Richards, when I was in Belfast a few years ago, a Primitive minister waited on me to say, 'There are some very good people in this city who are greatly prejudiced against a beard, and I think you can be more useful among them if you will go to a barber and get shaved. In reply to that brother I said, 'I certainly would not do anything which would be damaging to any person following my example; for instance, I don't use tobacco in any form, I don't use wine or spirits, except sacramentally or medicinally. I have been a total abstainer from my youth, for the good of others, as well as for myself. As to the beard, while in the genial climate of California, with youthful vigour on my side, I did not feel the need of it, and wasted much precious time in cutting it off, but having returned from California to the Eastern States of America, my thin jaws were exposed to the north-west blasts of New York, Wisconsin, and Iowa, which gave me neuralgia, and I suffered what appeared to be almost the pains of death. So I found that I was obliged to seek protection for my face, and instead of bundling up in a sheep-skin, and an artificial respirator, the constant re-adjustment of which would consume time and give trouble, I just threw aside that barbarous instrument, the razor, to see what the God of Providence would do for me, and this flowing beard was the result, and it answered the purpose exactly. I soon got well of neuralgia, and have never had it since. I have found it a good 'comforter,' a good respirator, a good shield against the reflecting rays of the summer sun, which used always to blister my face, and crack my lips till I could neither laugh nor sing without the shedding of blood. Moreover, it was a protection against gnats and flies. By a deep inspiration in preaching, which is essential, I used sometimes to take down one of those pestiferous little fellows into my throat, and then followed a sudden change in the exercises. I have suffered from none of these things since I submitted to the Lord's arrangement, planting the beard where it was needed. I have found it of great service to my vocal organs, and hence necessary to my work of preaching the Gospel, and to cut it off is to impair my working effectiveness, and so far a sin against God. With that, the Irish brother said, 'I suppose it is not worth while to say anything more about it.' 'No, my dear brother, I cannot do a wrong thing on any account, and I also like to help break down an unreasonable prejudice in this matter, under the influence of which many a poor Irishman is daily shedding tears, under the operations of an old dull razor.' The good people of Belfast soon got over their prejudice against my beard, and we had a blessed work of God during my stay among them." I repeated this Irish discussion to Sister Richards as we drove along, and she could not help joining Miss Jessie in a laugh at some parts of it, but still it did not convince her of the propriety of a beard on a minister's face. I then said, "Surely Sister Richards, it cannot be a moral impropriety for a minister to wear a beard, since the Master Himself had a beard?"

"But you have no proof," she replied, "that He did wear a beard."

"Well, Sister Richards," said I, " if I prove to you from the Bible, that the Great Teacher did have a beard, will you allow that to end the discussion in favour of the beard?"

"Yes, I'll rest the case on the Scripture proof, if you can produce it."

"Lest there should be some ground of mistake in identifying the person of Christ, when He should come into the world, God, through His holy prophets, advertised to the world, hundreds of years in advance, all His leading characteristics, by the exact fulfilment and counterpart of which, in the person of Christ, He should certainly be recognized as the Messiah ; Sister Richards, believest thou the prophets?"

"Certainly, I do."

"Very well, in describing the prophetic scene of the humiliating, and excruciating abuses, to be endured by Christ, Isaiah, employing the language of the Divine Messenger of the Covenant, says —'I gave my back to the smiters, and my cheeks to them that plucked off the hair.' To pluck the hair off the head, or back part of the jaw, is nothing in comparison with the pain of plucking it off the cheeks." The good sister then subsided. We were now nearing our journey's end, and after a little talk on personal holiness of heart, we drove into the village, and I was welcomed to the very pleasant home of Captain George Appleby, who had formerly been a shipmaster, but now for many years a resident in South Africa. He has a large wool-washing establishment, nearly a mile above the town, on the Zwart Kops river, employing a powerful steam-engine, and from seventy to one hundred working men and women, principally native Africans.

Rev. Purdon Smailes, the superintendent of the circuit, called in soon after my arrival, and expressed his pleasure in having me to help him in his important work. He was formerly a school-teacher, but for many years a learned, zealous, and useful Wesleyan minister, in South Africa. Sister Appleby is one of the largest women I ever saw, but says she has not increased in weight since she was fourteen years old, so that having learned to carry such dimensions in her youth, it seems no burden at all, for she seems as active as a lass of twenty years. She is very energetic, but very kind-hearted and hospitable.

UITENHAGE is an old Dutch town, located on the slope of a beautiful valley, near the banks of Zwart Kops river, with fine vales and table lands in the background, bounded by a range of mountains' east and north. Across the river, at the rise of the hills, we see a heathen village; along the river we see some large buildings, and the smoke and steam of the engines. These are large wool-washing establishments. Now we learn why we saw hundreds of teams loaded with wool passing out of Port Elizabeth, where it had been taken, and sold, the day before, and often the same day. It is brought out here twenty miles to be washed, because of the abundant supply, and superior quality of the water of this river for the purpose. The town is supplied with water from a large spring rising out of the base of the mountain, which flows in, and is so distributed as to furnish several streets, with each a bold stream, almost sufficient to propel the works of an overshot-mill.

The streets are lined on each side with rows, and, in some cases, double rows, of large oaks, and Tasmanian blue gums. The buildings are nearly all large one-story cottages, painted white, with long verandahs in front. Altogether the town, and surrounding scenery, are very beautiful. The population of Uitenhage district is 7,202, of whom 2,859 only are whites, mostly Dutch, the rest are natives.

The Dutch Reformed Church have a large commodious place of worship in Uitenhage, with a good evangelical minister, Rev. Mr. Steytler, and a large congregation. As the English population is small, and divided between the Presbyterians and Wesleyans, we cannot muster a very strong force there. We have, however, some very respectable and influential Wesleyan families in the town, but the Wesleyan chapel is a very poor concern indeed. For many years it was the residence of some old denizen, but, in course of time, it fell into the hands of a little pioneer club of Wesleyans, who had learned not to "despise the day of small things," and they did it up, and dubbed it a Wesleyan chapel, but the ceiling is very low, and it is every way unsuitable. One would think, on seeing it, that it should have been delivered over to the "moles and bats," long ago; at any rate, the "bats" have so far asserted their claim as to take possession of all the upper part of it, from the ceiling to the roof. Whoever may dispute their right of possession, none are able to dislodge them, for 'tis said there are thousands of them, and they have lined their floor with an excremental nuisance which will fairly drive the white folks away before long. It will seat about two hundred persons, but they cannot stay in it more than another summer. Sister Appleby was working hard to raise funds to build a decent chapel, and, I believe, she will succeed.

On Sabbath morning, the 6th of May, we assembled in the said Chapel to commence our series of special services. The place was filled with a very genteel-looking audience, and I felt encouraged to believe that we had some good stuff to work upon.

Brother Smailes read the service, and commented sensibly on the lessons. The audience did not seem to take much interest in the prayers, as only one man responded with audible distinctness, and he did not seem to be well up in the business, for he put in a response at the wrong place, producing a ludicrous surprise that somewhat excited the risibilities of some of the youngsters. The Holy Spirit graciously helped in the preaching of the Gospel that morning, and we had a solemn and profitable occasion.

By the kindness of Mr. Steytler, the Dutch Reformed Church minister, whom I had met in Port Elizabeth, and his trustees, we had the use of their church at 3 p.m., and in the evening. Our congregations there were large, and though most of them were Dutch, they knew the English well enough to understand my preaching, and listened with serious attention. We did not attempt to follow the preaching in the evening with a prayer-meeting there, lest some of our kind friends would think we were making too free with the privileges they had granted us. I was glad to have the opportunity of preaching to them, and hoped they would carry the good seed into their closets at home, and have it watered with the dews of grace which descend there.

On Monday, at 11 a.m., I preached again in the Wesleyan Chapel to a better audience than I supposed we could get in a week-day.

After preaching on Monday night, I explained the order of our prayer-meetings, somewhat as follows:—
"A prayer-meeting should have more of the social element in it than a preaching service. We have two varieties of worship in a prayer-meeting:—

public singing by the congregation, alternately with prayer, in which one person leads audibly, for general worship. Then, in an undertone, which need not interfere with the solemnity and order of the general worship, we give the largest liberty for individual efforts to bring souls to Christ. Any brother who knows the Saviour, and has a friend here who knows Him not, pray for that friend, and if you feel that by the help of the good Spirit, you can, by telling him what Jesus hath done for you, or by any persuasive appeals to his conscience, induce him to turn to God, you are entirely at liberty, any, or all of you as the Spirit may lead you, thus to work for God during the prayer meeting. I make this explanation at this early stage of our series of services, lest some, seeing this variety of exercise, might think it a disorderly proceeding, when indeed it is in accordance with the order and design of the meeting; the low-toned conversation to seekers who may be inquiring 'What must I do to be saved?' and the earnest ejaculatory prayer of sympathizing hearts for such, do not indeed produce the least discord in the harmony of the general worship.

"We have nothing new to introduce, but rather the old simple methods of the Gospel. In the great Pentecostal awakening the poor sin-stricken souls cried out, 'Men and brethren, what shall we do?' Peter did not tell them to go home and meditate in the quiet solitude of their closets, and call at his house next day, and he would have a talk with them on the subject. Nay, when the Spirit awakens a poor sinner, He is then waiting to lead that soul directly to Jesus. But the poor stricken sinner does not know the Holy Spirit who hath smitten him in love, and does not know Jesus, nor where to find Him. How appropriate, then, that such should avowedly ask, 'Men and brethren, what shall we do?' Should not the 'Men and brethren' then, and there, tell such poor sinners what to do, and go to work every one of them and lead the poor seekers to Jesus? That is just what they did in Jerusalem, and three thousand of them, not only heard from the lips of the 'Men and brethren,' who were 'working together with God,' to save them, what to do, but at once, openly and honestly, yea, 'gladly received the Word, and were baptized,' that day. Now this is the kind of thing we want to have here in Uitenhage; no new thing but the blessed old thing, which worked so well long before our new-formed methods of nice propriety were invented. We are now ready to converse with any who feel the awakening of the Holy Spirit, help you to grapple with your difficulties, tell you how we went through the same ordeal f hardness, darkness, grief, guilt, despair, hope, esire, fear, and the terrible swaying between two mighty forces, the one attracting towards Christ, the other repelling by the force of a thousand bad associations, and a mighty power of satanic influence. Poor sinners, we know well from sad experience what you feel. We sympathize with you profoundly, and we are anxious to help you. **We** cannot save you, but God may use us as agents to lead you to Jesus, according to his Gospel method. But unless you indicate your desire to turn to God, as did the awakened souls in Jerusalem, in some way or other, we know not to whom to speak, nor for whom personally to pray. We are willing to meet you in any part of the house, but we recommend as the most prompt and orderly means to the great end proposed, that all those who have counted 'the cost,' and who have intelligently, deliberately, determinately, resolved to seek the Lord now, 'while He may be found,' to come forward to this altar of prayer.

> Come sinners to the Gospel feast,
> Let every soul be Jesu's guest;
> Ye need not one be left behind,
> For God hath bidden all mankind.
> Come all ye souls by sin opprest,
> Ye restless wanderers after rest;
> Ye poor, and maimed, and halt, and blind,
> In Christ a hearty welcome find.
> This is the time, no more delay,
> This is the acceptable day.
> Come in this moment, at His call,
> And live for Him who died for all."

While singing this invitation hymn, about a dozen adult seekers came forward. Just at the close of the prayer that followed, as we rose to sing again, when everything was going on in an orderly way according to the method I had just defined, a tall young Dutchman rushed up the crowded aisle to where I was conversing with the seekers, and addressed me in an angry shouting tone,—" How dare you introduce such blasphemous proceedings in this town ? I demand your authority for such outrageous proceedings under a pretence of worshipping God," repeating similar expressions several times. I took him by the arm, and kindly explained to him what from its novelty to him seemed so strange, and begged him to be seated near the front, and see and hear all that was done there, and satisfy his own mind that this was, indeed, the work of God; but he turned and hastened away, like the young man who seemed suddenly to be waked out of sleep, and ran into the garden of Gethsemane, and laid hold on Jesus on the night of his betrayal. The young fellow was very respectably connected in family relations; but as I learned, got no sympathy, unless from one man, but a great deal of contempt for his rash interference with the peaceable worship of his neighbours. The meeting then went on quietly, and several persons obtained peace with God. But our working force was very small. The Class-Leader, a fine old man, was sick, so that we were deprived of his help.

On Thursday morning we were reinforced by the arrival of Rev. Brother Richards, and Sister Hill, my kind hostess from Port Elizabeth. At eleven A.M., I preached again to an audience of increased dimensions and interest. At the day services we get the wheat without the chaff, less bulk, but greater weight. Tuesday evening we had our little chapel packed, and at the prayer-meeting the altar was crowded with seekers. During the progress of the prayer-meeting, which was solemn, but very quiet, a Mr. B. sent me, by a boy, the following note:—"The Rev. Mr. Taylor will oblige by not interfering with the devotions of this meeting by his audible conversation." I was simply conversing with a seeker in a low tone, according to our announced plan, but Mr. B., who, I was informed, is not friendly to the cause of God in any form, was not satisfied to allow us to proceed in our worship according to the dictates of our own conscience. I, of course, made no reply to his note, but said to some of my friends after the meeting, "Satan is getting more polite each day of our meeting. Last night he rushed in like a roaring lion to devour the prey; but to-night he addressed me in a note as the Rev. Mr. Taylor; by to-morrow night he will not dare even to mutter in the dark, unless it is round the corners out of sight, or in the canteen." Wednesday, at eleven A.M., I preached, and at the prayer-meeting following we had some very interesting conversions. On Wednesday night, after preaching, we had thirty persons forward as seekers, a number of whom found peace; and, as I anticipated, Satan could not command an agent that could "face the music." The silent solemnity of the occasion seemed to subdue opposing forces. I preached again on Thursday at eleven A.M., and several persons were saved. At three P.M. of that day, I preached in Brother Appleby's woolshed to the Kaffirs in his employ. We had an audience of about seventy, most of whom had often heard the Gospel, but a portion of them were raw heathens. I got an unconverted, bare-footed, ragged Kaffir to interpret for me, and got on much better than I had done before with a professional interpreter, for he talked in a simple, natural way. On Thursday night I delivered a lecture in a public school on "Reminiscences of Palestine," and "St. Paul and his Times."

The number of converts, during our brief series in Uitenhage, was not reported to me; but there was manifestly a deep and general awakening in the town, and among the converts were some influential persons, who will make valuable members of the Church, I doubt not.

On Friday we returned to Port Elizabeth, where I delivered a leture on *St. Paul and his Times;* and at five A.M., Saturday, my kind host, Brother Sydney Hill, saw me safely into the "Post cart," a rough conveyance on two wheels, drawn by four horses, and that day, while I was resting, I was jolted over a rough road, ninety miles, to Graham's Town.

CHAPTER VI.

GRAHAM'S TOWN.

Graham's Town was founded as a military post in 1812, but received its life and proportions from the famous immigration of 1820. The Colonial Settlement of that year in Albany, a few miles distant, having, by the appointment of the Home Government, the Rev. William Shaw for their minister, contained much sterling stuff for the foundations of empire in a new country. Those of them better adapted to mechanical, commercial, and literary pursuits than to farming, soon left their "wattle and daub" huts in the country, and have gradually built up this flourishing town.

It is situated in a valley, bounded by high hills, near the sources of the "Kowie River." Its houses are principally of brick and stone, covered with slate and zinc. They are not generally over two stories high. It contains many fine gardens; and the streets are ornamented, and shaded with rows of trees, principally English oak, eucalyptus (or Tasmania blue gum) and Kaffir boom. The last is indigenous, and grows a large beautiful scarlet-coloured flower. There is an extensive barracks for troops, both at the east and west ends of the city. And the continual presence of a regiment or two of English soldiers, with their daily drill, and martial-music, reminds the stranger that, though every thing he sees there, is so thoroughly English, and home-like, he is nevertheless in a country where Europeans have to watch, as well as pray, and while they trust in a gracious Providence, to take Cromwell's advice, and "keep their powder dry."

Graham's Town has, according to the census of 1865, a white population of 5,263, all English, and a few thousand Hottentots, Kaffirs, and Fingoes. It has good churches; three Episcopalian, three Wesleyan, two Baptists, two Independent, and one Roman Catholic. It has a public library, museum, and botanical gardens: two banks, one high school—Wesleyan, called, in honour of the old Methodist pioneer of that Province, "Shaw College," besides the full compliment of educational and charitable institutions common in such a city.

The first Wesleyan Chapel there was dedicated in 1822. It would seat 400 persons. It was followed by another in 1832, twice its size, which cost £3,000. The former house was given to the natives. The present principal Wesleyan Church of Graham's Town—"Commemoration Chapel," is thus described by Mr. Shaw:—"The building is in the pointed style (Gothic), well-sustained in all its parts. The front, from the level of the floor, is seventy feet high to the top of the centre pinnacle, and it is about sixty-three feet wide, including the buttresses. The interior dimensions are ninety feet long by fifty broad, and from the floor to the ceiling it is thirty-four feet in height. There are two side, and one end, galleries; and the building is capable of accommodating, in great comfort, a congregation of about fourteen hundred persons." It cost over £9,000 sterling, and is quite superior to any other church of any denomination in the city.

The subscription for it was commenced on the anniversary day, celebrating the arrival of the " Albany Settlers" in Algoa Bay, on the 10th of April, 1820; and in memory of that event, it was called "Commemoration Chapel."

Rev. Mr. Shaw remarks further, that owing to the embarrassments occasioned by the Kaffir War of 1846, the debt on " Commemoration Chapel," at the time of its dedication, was upwards of £5,000, and adds, " I had already appealed to the Legislative Council of the colony for assistance, seeing that we had never received a shilling from the Colonial Treasury in aid of our religious institutions in Graham's Town, while nearly the entire cost of St. George's Church had been defrayed from that source, and the Episcopalians and Roman Catholics of the town were receiving about £1,000 per annum towards the support of their respective clergy." After some disappointments and long delay, they succeeded in obtaining the grant of £1,000 in aid of the building fund. Mr. Shaw says further by anticipation, "I trust that the few settlers, who may survive the fiftieth year, or jubilee of their arrival in the country, will take care that, if any debt unhappily still remains on Commemoration Chapel, it shall, on that occasion, be entirely extinguished by their grateful and liberal thank-offerings." Well, when I reached Graham's Town, there was still a debt of £3,000 on it. But through a letter, recently received from Rev. T. Guard, I shall be happy to inform Brother Shaw that the friends there, recently had a meeting to take the subject under consideration, and paid the whole amount that day.

After a rough ride in the post-cart, ninety miles from Port Elizabeth, I arrived in Graham's Town at six P.M. My home was with Mr. W. A. Richards, one of the proprietors of the "Journal," a large Tri-weekly, having the largest circulation of any paper in the colony. He is stepson of the founder, and senior member of the firm—the Hon. R. Godlonton, who is a "Colonist of forty-six years' standing, and an old Wesleyan as well, and though for many years a member of the "Legislative Council," or Upper House of the Colonial Parliament, yet he is really a spiritually-minded useful member, and active worker in the Church. I had a delightful home in the spacious house, and more spacious hearts of my dear friends, Brother and Sister Richards. During my first evening, Brother Atwell and several other leading laymen called in to bid me welcome, and also

Revs. Davis, Green, and Holford. Brother Guard, acting superintendent during the absence of Brother Impey, had been away on a visitation of the churches for a short time, and had not returned. Brother Holford, an earnest young minister, was a junior colleague in the circuit. He has been but five or six years in the colony. Brother John Scott was the single young preacher in the circuit. He is the son of my friend, Rev. George Scott, the old Swedish missionary of the British Conference. John was brought out into the work in Africa, and I believe will become a useful minister.

Rev. W. J. Davis was sent out by the British Conference, in 1831. He is a brave man; has been most of his time in the purely mission work among the Kaffirs; has encountered wars, and a very great variety of perils among them. He now has charge of a large native station in Graham's Town. He is, I believe, a thorough Kaffir scholar, and is the author of a grammar of the Kaffir language. I afterwards proved him a valuable helper in our prayer-meetings in leading souls to God.

He has a large, interesting family, and, I believe, all converted to God. Two of his daughters, who know the Kaffir language as well as the English, the wives of Rev. Brothers Hargraves and Sawtell, are in the missionary work, and his son William has recently commenced to preach in Kaffir.

Rev. George H. Green, superintendent of Bathurst

circuit, had come to Graham's Town on duty, and was detained by the sudden death of one of his horses, and was unable to leave till after the Sabbath. Many hundreds of horses had recently died in the province, from the "horse sickness," with which the country is sometimes visited. A hotel-keeper on the road, from Port Elizabeth, who keeps a relay of coach-horses, told me that day, that within a month he had lost eighty horses by this disease.

Brother Green was sent out in 1837, and has, during the most of the time since, been devoted to the English and Dutch work. He is an open, laughing brother, but thoroughly devoted to God, and His work, and has the reputation of being a superior preacher. I was highly entertained with the missionary narratives of these brethren till the hour for retiring. I will note some of them at a suitable time.

On Sabbath, May 13th, we had "Commemoration Chapel" crowded three times with a superior-looking class of people, with a sprinkling of red-coats (English soldiers) among them. In the morning Brother Green read the service, and I preached from "the last words of Jesus," "But ye shall receive power, after that the Holy Ghost is come upon you: and ye shall be witnesses unto me, both in Jerusalem, and in all Judæa, and in Samaria, and unto the uttermost part of the earth." In commencing a series of special services, I always preach first to believers on a subject embracing the personality, immediate presence, and special mission of the Holy Ghost, and the adjustment of human agents to His gracious arrangements, essential to success.

At three P.M. I preached to the children, with as many adults as could crowd into the church. At night I preached specially to sinners. At the opening of the prayer-meeting which followed, I invited seekers of pardon to present themselves at the altar of prayer, but not one came. I knew that the awakening Spirit had thrust His "piercing" sword into the hearts of many sinners, but did not press them to come forward. Many believers were greatly disappointed in not seeing some go forward, but thought it was the pleasure of the Holy Spirit, thus to set the church more fully back to their homework of self-examination, and more thorough preparation for the coming struggle for the rescue of perishing souls.

On Monday many leading brethren called to bid me welcome; but all expressed their disappointment at the results of the labours of the previous day, and their great sorrow that the Church was in such a low spiritual state. They spoke gratefully of a work of God in 1822, at Salem, twenty miles distant; a second revival in 1830, in Graham's Town, which extended to some of the country circuits. Their third, and "great revival," was in 1837, when about 300 souls were saved. A fourth revival, less extensive, but really a very good work, especially among the young people, in 1857; but now they felt a painful sense of coldness and ineffectiveness. I assured them that as soon as they were ready for an advance movement, the Holy Spirit would certainly lead them on to victory. I reminded them of the carnal obstructions to the work of God in the Church, which must be sought out and removed by individual repentance and reformation, through faith; and that there was at least one serious physical difficulty in the way. "Your beautiful church is not sufficiently ventilated for a large audience, by one half. The immense amount of carbonic acid gas thrown out from the lungs of fourteen hundred persons, and the porous discharge of fœtid matter from their bodies, must on each occasion poison the atmosphere in the church in a very short time. This poison being inhaled, corrupts the blood, blunts the nervous sensibilities of the people, and hence precludes vigorous mental action, produces headache, and drowsiness, and sadly injures their health; and when it comes to that, the best thing is to quit, and go home as quickly as possible. We can't afford to spend our precious evenings there in poisoning each other, for that is the very kind of stuff that killed the British soldiers in the 'blackhole of Calcutta.' It is out of the question to have a great work of salvation without a good supply of oxygen."

They could not readily realize that their really splendid church could be so defective in anything; but expressed a willingness to make such changes as might be found to be necessary.

They were decidedly of opinion that we would get on better to have the prayer-meetings, after preaching, in the basement lecture-room, as the brethren felt more at home, and could work more freely there.

I replied, "Before this week is out, we will require all the room the body of the church can afford to accommodate the people who will remain for prayer-meeting; and as your people will have to get used to working above, they may just as well break in first as last, and then we will lose no time in needless changes."

We had to go thoroughly into the subject of ventilating the chapel. I begged them to employ a competent mechanic to put ventilating apertures in the windows, above and below. They had two such on each side of the chapel in the windows below, but none above. But to make any permanent change, a meeting of the trustees must be called, and perhaps much time consumed in the preliminaries before the work could be effected. So to close the debate, and secure the end by a short method, Brother Atwill, one of the trustees, who is allowed to do daring things, without being called to account, because all who know him feel sure, that under all circumstances, he will do what he conscientiously believes to be the right thing, went into the gallery, hammer in hand, and knocked a pane of glass out of each window on both sides, which afforded a good supply of fresh air, for our crowded audiences, and thus removed a physical barrier to our success, and gave us a wide awake people to preach to.

On Monday night we had the church well filled above and below. Nearly enough remained for the prayer-meeting to fill the main audience-room of the church. Over thirty seekers came promptly forward to the altar of prayer, and about a dozen of them were "justified by faith," and obtained "peace with God, through our Lord Jesus Christ."

On Tuesday morning Brother Green, who had meantime provided himself with another horse, was about to return home, taking with him his daughter "Libbie," who was not converted to God. The young lady was in sad bereavement, and was disposed to complain of God's dealings with her. She was within a few days of being married, a year before, to the son of Rev. John Edwards, one of our old South African Missionaries, but the young man, in crossing Fish River, on his way to the home of his bride, was drowned. I said to Brother Green, "Don't take your daughter away from our meetings. Just leave her here to be converted, and go ye and bring Sister Green and your daughter Hannah, and let them all share the blessings of God at our meetings. There are crowns to be distributed, and the gift of eternal life to be granted to all who will come to God, and I don't see why your family may not as well have their full share of blessing."

Brother Richards seconded my motion by a cordial invitation for Brother and Sister Green to sojourn with me in his house. Brother Green consented at once. The result was, we got two valuable helpers in the persons of Brother and Sister Green; and during the series of meetings, their daughters were both converted to God; and, subsequently, their son Arthur, at our Somerset meetings, and their son John, at our Cradock series, were saved. They are very interesting girls, and their brothers give good promise of becoming useful men.

On Tuesday, the 15th of May, Rev. Thomas Guard returned. As he had before given me a cordial invitation, so now he gave me an Irish "Caed mela faltha" —"100,000 welcomes"—to Graham's Town. He is the Apollos of Southern Africa. I believe it is conceded by all parties who have heard him preach and lecture, that no man in Africa can approach to his standard of logical fascinating sublime eloquence. It was said, however, that he succeeded better in stirring the romantic and poetic elements of man's nature, and in feasting the intellect, than in arousing the conscience, and leading sinners to repentance. But he threw all his energies into the work at our meetings, publicly, and in social circles, and was greatly owned of God as an agent in the work that was done, and himself received, as he testified to the praise of God, an extraordinary baptism of the Holy Spirit, under which he "had grown more than during a period of fifteen years before." His talents now, more than ever, are employed by the Spirit in the direct work of winning souls for Christ.

He has been but a few years in Africa, but his name is a tower of strength in both colonies.

He was induced to leave the Irish Conference, and take an appointment to Africa, because of the failing health of his highly-talented wife. Her health is greatly improved; but it would be a calamity to the work in Southern Africa if they should return to their "Emerald Isle."

We have many wealthy influential Wesleyans in Graham's Town, who, I believe, shared largely in the rich blessings of grace poured out from their Infinite Source during our series. Seven members of Parliament from Graham's Town are Wesleyans. Hon. George Wood, senior; Hon. Robert Godlonton, Hon. Samuel Cawood, Hon. J. C. Hoole, belong to the Upper House, or "Legislative Council," four out of the seven members to which the Eastern Province is entitled. Hon. John Wood, George Wood, junior, sons of George, senior, Jonathan and Reuben Ayliff, and J. C. Clough, are members of the Legislative Assembly; William Ayliff also, from Fort Beaufort. These are all class-going Wesleyans, except Messrs. Hoole and Clough, who are, in other respects, identified with us.

These are, for the most part I learn, wealthy men, and very influential for good. The Ayliffs are sons of Rev. John, recently deceased, one of our most laborious and successful pioneer missionaries, who led the Fingoes out of their bondage, as before stated. His widow, daughter, and two of his sons live in Graham's Town. The widow still has the genuine missionary spirit, and is driven round daily in her carriage to all parts of the town, visiting the sick, and doing good to the souls and bodies of the needy. At her request I visited some of her patients; among them was "old Brother Sparks," who had been bound, lo! these thirty-six years, with rheumatism. Many of his joints have been drawn quite out of place; but he said, "God has been very kind to me. He has, all through my long period of suffering, so filled my heart with His precious love, that I never felt a spirit of impatience." He seemed greatly to enjoy my singing. I thought his poor wife, who has daily attended him during his long illness, must have developed patience almost equal to that of Job. I have made the acquaintance of all four of Father Ayliff's sons. They are all over six feet in height, born in the mission-field among the Kaffirs, fluent in the Kaffir language, pious, "well-to-do" men, and leading men in the Government.

Volumes might be filled with the details of what was said and done in connection with our series of meetings in Graham's Town; but I will simply give an outline and a few specimen illustrative facts of a work which, in extent, numerically, was limited compared with the numbers saved during my series of the same length in any of the Australian cities. But the work in Graham's Town is of vast importance, not only in its local effect, but in its far-reaching influence on the extensive mission-field among the surrounding African tribes.

CHAPTER VII.

GRAHAM'S TOWN (CONTINUED).

DURING my first week in Graham's Town I preached eight sermons, each followed by a prayer-meeting, of about two hours in time. The second week the same as the first, with the addition of four mid-day prayer-meetings.

During the third week preached four sermons; delivered three lectures on "Reminiscences of Palestine," and "St. Paul and his Times." We had fine mid-day prayer-meetings that week, and occupied one evening by a fellowship meeting, at which I gave a lecture on Christian Fellowship, and over one hundred and twenty persons, nearly all adults, came forward and gave their names as candidates for membership in the Wesleyan Church, and eighty-four persons stood up in their places promptly, one after another, and clearly gave their testimony to the saving work of the Holy Spirit in their hearts.

The number of persons professing to have found pardon and peace with God, meantime, whose names and address had, on a personal examination, been taken down by Brother Holford, one of the ministers of the circuit, amounted to over a hundred and seventy, which number swelled to over two hundred soon after I left. The daily prayer-meetings have been kept up ever since, and will, I trust, to the end of time.

I found the people of Graham's Town a very attentive, social, affectionate people. I formed among them many personal acquaintances, and strong bonds of Christian friendship, which will abide for ever.

On Thursday, the 24th of May, out on the hills overlooking Graham's Town, in the Mimosa Scrub, we had a Wesleyan celebration of the "Queen's birthday." It was a delightful social entertainment, where I had an opportunity of speaking to many friends, and among them many of the young converts. Mr. H., a tall man, with heavy beard, came to me as soon as I alighted from Brother Richards' carriage in the grove, and said, "Mr. Taylor, I have come to ask your pardon for what I have been thinking about you. I felt so badly under your preaching, that I went forward to the altar last Thursday night, but I felt worse and worse. Just beside me was a woman who was in such an agony of distress that I soon began to neglect my own case in my sympathy for her. I wondered that you did not come at once, and do something for her; and while I was looking and hoping that you would come, I saw you walk past her. Now I am telling you this, that I may ask your pardon for what I had been thinking about you. When I saw that woman's flowing tears, and saw you pass without seeming to notice her, I got angry, and wanted to pull your beard. Knowing that such a procedure would not be suitable to the occasion, I got up and went away. But on last Sabbath, when you preached in Market Square, I stood so near to you, that I could see into your eyes, and saw there such a flood of sympathy for sinners, that I was fully convinced that I had done you great injustice in my mind, and felt ashamed that I had allowed such feelings so to influence my conduct. Then I began again in earnest to seek the Lord. Last night, during the prayer-meeting, I surrendered my soul to God, and accepted Jesus Christ as my Saviour, and immediately I was filled with 'unspeakable joy.' Now I see that you were right all the time, and that you understood the woman's case, and that I did not; that she had to feel her own utter helplessness and surrender herself to God." (The fact is, as I then told him, I had explained the way of salvation to the woman before she got his attention.) "This is the man," continued he, pointing to a small man by his side, "who spoke to me last night, when I was just poising in an even balance. I required but the weight of a feather, and he gave the right impulse at the right moment, and I yielded, believed, and was saved."

Several very respectable persons, who had been a long time acceptable members of the Church, found out that they were on the old Jewish track of "going about to establish their own righteousness," but had never submitted themselves to the righteousness of God," and were hence really destitute of salvation. Brother R. came to see me, and told how he had been trying for years to serve God, but could not tell whether or not he had even the witness of pardon. I tried to help him ascertain his facts, and define his spiritual whereabouts, but in vain. Then I told him to drop the discussion, and come directly to God in a present unreserved surrender, and claim in Christ what was the privilege of every poor sinner in the world, who had any desire to come to God, a present salvation from sin. I then fully explained to him the simple way of salvation by faith, the only way to be saved. He at once ceased to debate the question of doubt, and very soon obtained salvation by faith, and the clear witness of the spirit that he was then indeed a child of God. He afterwards became a successful worker in leading souls to Jesus.

On the second Sabbath night of our series, I saw an interesting-looking man at the altar of prayer, in an agony of soul on account of sin. Several good brethren stood near him, and said to me, as I was about to speak to the penitent, "This is one of our best members," pointing to the man at the altar. "He is not simply a nominal member, but an active worker, reproving sin, and trying to do good daily, and also the superintendent of one of our Sabbath schools. He is subject to seasons of great darkness, and is now under a cloud; but it is all the result of severe temptations." At the close of the following week the said seeker came to see me, and related his experience, in substance, as follows :—He was first awakened when twelve years old; but having no one to instruct him, gradually lost his convictions of sin. Then, twenty years ago, he was greatly awakened, and resolved to be a servant of God, and joined the Wesleyan Church. "For several years I strove hard to live right, and attended all the means of grace within my reach. Then I became acquainted with a very bad man, who was the means of leading me astray, and for a short time I was out of the Church, but I was very wretched, and made a sincere and humble confession, and was again admitted to the Wesleyan Church. I then doubled my diligence in trying to work out my salvation with fear and trembling. I often fasted from Wednesday till Friday.

"Once during my fast I received an order to perform a hazardous duty, as a sergeant in the army. Some of my fellow-soldiers begged me to break my fast, or I could not accomplish my work; but I kept to my fast, and though in a very weak state, fulfilled my duty. I have spent many days in prayer, in the kloofs and caves of the mountains, and often wished that by laying down my life, I could get relief for my soul. I once resolved to die on my knees, or get relief. I got some relief, but did not get salvation. I have for some time been teaching school, and have been trying to do good in the Sunday-school, but got no 'rest for my soul.' During the first week of your preaching, I was thoroughly waked up, but I felt very bitter against you. By last Sabbath I felt so badly, so guilty before God, that I could not show my face; but spent the day alone in the hills, trying to pray. But on Sabbath night, I went again to hear you preach, and when you appealed to murmurers against God, and asked them if they would be willing to have their miserable existence terminated by annihilation? I responded in my heart, 'Yes, I would hail such an opportunity with gladness.' I then went forward to the altar of prayer, and cried for help, but found it not.

"But the next night, in your sermon on believing, you unraveled every knot of unbelief, by which I have been held down all these years. Your account of that man in Mudgee, New South Wales, who said, 'I can't believe, O, I can't believe,' suited my case exactly, and I said, 'I'll never use that fatal expression again.' I do submit myself to God, living or dying, to do with me just as He likes. I do believe His record concerning His Son. I do have confidence in Jesus, as an all-sufficient Saviour of the very chief of sinners. I do accept Him as my Saviour now.' I began then at once to get hold on Christ by faith; and while they were singing, 'O, the bleeding Lamb! He was found worthy,' I clearly realised, what I had always admitted in theory, that though I should 'give all my goods to feed the poor, and my body to be burned, it would profit me nothing;' but the Lamb of God slain for sinners, was indeed a sufficient sacrifice for my sins, and I do accept Him now as my Saviour.' I returned home, quietly resting on Christ as my Saviour. About one o'clock that night, while steadily clinging to Jesus, the Holy Spirit so manifested the pardoning love of God to my heart, that I could not restrain my joyous emotions, but went and waked up Mr. G., and told him that I was saved, and we praised God together. If a legion of angels had told me that all my sins were forgiven, I could not have had a clearer evidence than I had within my heart, through God's witnessing Spirit. Before that I did not love you; but ever since, I have loved you so, that I could cheerfully lay down my life for you. I ask your pardon for the hard feelings I entertained against you, during your first week's services. I see now that I was under the influence of the carnal mind and Satan. The devil has often come since with his old suggestions of unbelief; but, thank God, the snare is broken, and I am a free man in Jesus." I had a season of prayer with Him alone, and God manifested himself in great mercy to our hearts.

In contrast with this, another class of converts, after the style of the Philippian jailor, may be illustrated by the experience of Mr. J. W., of Graham's Town, who was saved through the preaching of Rev. Brother Guard, a few weeks after I left. Brother W. brought his brother, burdened with sin,

107 miles, to my meeting in Cradock, who returned full of joy unspeakable. During our Cradock series, at a fellowship-meeting, Brother W. said, "Under the preaching of the Rev. Mr. Guard, I was awakened by the Spirit of God, to a sense of my sad condition as a sinner. I had not bowed my knee in prayer for fifteen years, but utterly without hope of improving my condition, by anything I could ever do, I knelt before God, and in the simplicity of a little child, told Him all about my sad state, and reminded Him of his abundant provision of mercy in Christ for just such poor sinners as I was, and that I then and there thankfully accepted Jesus on His own terms, as my Saviour, and before I arose from my knees I obtained the forgiveness of all my sins, through Jesus Christ, and now for twenty-three days I have walked in the light. I had every facility a man could ask for enjoying this world, and sought pleasure at every source that leisure and money could command; but I have enjoyed more real happiness during the last twenty-three days, than in all the thirty-nine years of my life before."

It must not be supposed that such a work can be wrought in any place, without strongly exciting the antagonistic forces of carnal nature and Satanic power in the hearts of many worldly men and women, and not unfrequently we find some misguided good people who will forbid any person "to cast out devils" who will not follow them.

Many false things, and many hard things were

said in Graham's Town during the progress of our work, by the wicked; and much opposition was manifested in certain quarters, where we had a right to expect better things; but as I seldom ever read, or listen to such things, I will not burden my pages with them. It is said that Sir P. D., commandant of the British forces there, inquired of Mr. Green, the barber, "Who is this man Taylor, who is causing such a stir in the town?"

The barber replied, "Have you not read, Sir P., of certain men of whom it was said, 'These men who have turned the world upside down have come hither also?'"

"Yes," replied Sir P., "I have read something of that in the Acts of the Apostles."

"Well sir," replied the barber, "Mr. Taylor, I believe, is a relation of those men."

My three lectures, in Commemoration Chapel, were well attended, and for defining and defending the Gospel methods of evangelization, I think they were better adapted to general instruction and edification than the same number of sermons.

An extract from a letter, written by "mine host," Mr. A. Richards, a month after my departure, may serve to illustrate the continued progress of the work of God in Graham's Town.

"Everything is going on very satisfactorily here. The work of God is widening, extending, deepening. Many are seeking the higher spiritual blessing of holiness of heart. Our house has reason to be thankful, and to praise God. We have a prayer-meeting in our dining-room every Monday evening. Last night seventy were present. At the midday prayer-meeting there were 100 to-day, and a gracious influence was at work." Then, after speaking of a number by name, who had recently been saved, he adds, "The number of seekers are daily increasing. I should think the devil must feel rather bad at seeing so many of his soldiers returning to God. He can't say they are rebels, for they all belong to God." "The work is going on here too among the natives. About 100 are converted; twenty in each of the last three nights."

That was the beginning of a work among the natives there, after I left; I did not work among them, except to preach one sermon through an interpreter, and found it a very slow business. However, I believe I did better than a good brother I heard of there, who undertook to give an address to an audience of Kaffirs. He was a brother accustomed to use long, hard words, which would sound well to English ears; but rather too abstract and lengthy for a Kaffir interpreter.

When he delivered his first sentence, the interpreter said, in effect, "Friends, I don't understand what he says."

Then came another sentence,—

"Friends, I have no doubt that it is very good, but I don't understand it."

Then came another deliverance, long and loud.

"Friends, that is extraordinary, no doubt, but it is all dark to me."

By that time the eyes of the whole audience glistened, and they began freely to show their ivory, and the speaker seemed to think he was doing it, for he could not understand a word that the interpreter said, and he waxed eloquent in the flow of his great words; and the interpreter went on to the close replying to each sentence, closing with, "Friends, if you have understood any of that, you have done more than I have. It is a grand discourse, no doubt." The Kaffirs there are blessed with the ministry of my friend, Rev. W. J. Davis, who needs no interpreter, and now reports several hundreds of them saved since I was there.

After my lecture, on Friday night the 1st of June, I gave my last words of counsel and exhortation to my dear brethren and sisters in Graham's Town. It was a solemn occasion, for though I never preach "farewell sermons," or encourage any ado on the occasion of my final departure from any place, still, I am always reminded that Christian love and sympathy, so beautifully illustrated at Miletus, is the same in all ages, and among all people.

God's messenger of mercy to their hearts "kneeled down, and prayed with them all. And they all wept sore, and fell on Paul's neck, and kissed him, sorrowing most of all for the words which he spake, that they should see his face no more." Brother Davis, and two of his daughters, Brother and Sister Guard,

Brother Holford, and a few others, accompanied us to the house of my host; and after a good supper, and good social cheer, we together sang,

> "And let our bodies part
> To different climes repair,
> Inseparably joined in heart
> The friends of Jesus are," etc.

And upon our knees again commended each other, and our young converts, to the special care of our covenant-keeping God, and said farewell. It was then midnight, and I had a rough journey of seventy miles between me, and my work in King William's Town the following Sabbath. After a little sleep, at four A.M., of Saturday, June 2nd, Mr. D. Penn called with his cart and-two, and we commenced our long day's journey. Brother Penn had a pair of fine travellers, which took us thirty miles to breakfast. Then we got a pair of fresh horses, which he had sent on two days before, and they made the rest of the journey just as the sun sank from view in the western horizon. Much of our route lay through a broken, rocky country, all the way hilly, with the usual variety of deep gorges, little creeks, precipices and cliffs, rich grassy ranges, and patches of African jungle, with their peculiar intermixture of aloes, and the euphorbia-tree. We saw one deer on the route; met many scores of wagons, drawn by the finest oxen I have ever seen; we saw in the distance too, many Kaffir huts, and passed a very few houses of colonial settlers. Brother Penn is an old colonist; has been in the Kaffir wars; has had a great variety of experience, and entertained me all the way with marvellous narratives, illustrating colonial life; while I enjoyed them very much, I was too weary to note them.

Brother Penn had been a servant of God for some years, but had lost ground in the Christian race; at our recent meetings he had received a rich baptism of the Holy Spirit, and was now very happy, and very active in the work of winning souls.

Arriving at King William's Town, he found lodgings with an old friend, and I was kindly entertained by the superintendent of the circuit, Rev. J. Fish, and his excellent young wife.

CHAPTER VIII.

KING WILLIAM'S TOWN.

KING WILLIAM's TOWN, located on the banks of the Buffalo River, in the midst of a fertile grassy country, was commenced by the establishment of a military post there in 1835. It was subsequently abandoned by the authority of the Home Government, but re-established in 1848, and became the capital of British Kaffraria—a large tract of country extending from the old eastern boundary of Cape Colony to the "Great Kie River." It was settled by an enterprising class of people, and became a flourishing province. The people prayed earnestly for a Colonial Government of their own; that being denied them, British Kaffraria was in April, 1866, annexed to Cape Colony. As this annexation was subsequent to the taking of the Colonial census in 1865, the population of British Kaffraria is not included in that census, and must therefore, whatever it may be, which I know not, proportionately swell the real aggregate colonial population above the figures I have given from the census; since the census was taken, however, about forty thousand

Fingoes, included in the census of Cape Colony, have removed to Fingo-land, so that the Colony has upon the whole no numerical gain in these changes, but a real gain of a fine tract of country, and a most enterprising Colonial population.

King William's Town has a population of about 6,000, probably one half of whom are Europeans, principally English. It is a strong military post, and a large force of soldiers are quartered there. There are in the town two weekly papers published, and the Episcopalians, Roman Catholics, Presbyterians, and Wesleyans, have each one church edifice. Besides which, the Wesleyan, London Missionary Society, and the Berlin Missionary Society, have each a chapel for the Kaffirs. Rev. John Brownlie, one of the oldest pioneer missionaries of Southern Africa, established a mission there among the Kaffirs, under the direction of the London Missionary Society, long before the town was laid out.

The first Wesleyan Chapel was built at a cost of £400, with sittings for 150 persons, in 1849. It is now used as a schoolhouse; next to it stands a substantial stone dwelling, which is the "Mission House," and next to that, separated by a few rods of ground for garden and shrubbery, in one of the best sites in the town, is the new Wesleyan stone chapel, built at a cost of £2,000, with sittings for 500 persons.

Rev. J. Fish, the Superintendent, is from the "Richmond Institution," an energetic, talented young minister, and though but a few years in Africa, honourably maintains the responsible position of Superintendent of this very important circuit. On Sabbath morning, June 3rd, we had the chapel crowded with a well-dressed, very intelligent-looking congregation, for whatever may be said of the rustic lives and manners of pioneers, they have a bearing of self-possession, wide-awake spirit of discrimination and thoughtfulness, which are very manifest, even in the quiet of an assembled audience in the house of God. Having had much experience in pioneer life in California, I think I understand pretty well how to reach the hearts of such people; yet though we had three very interesting preaching services that day, and a gracious quickening in the Church, there were no conversions so far as we could learn. I preached each evening during the week except Saturday evening, but having a heavy attack of influenza I was not in good working condition, still the interest increased in the Church, and on Wednesday evening, as Mr. Fish states in his letter to the Missionary Society, "the bar of reserve and prejudice was broken down, and some twenty-eight young people gathered round the communion-rail; many of whom, as the "first-fruits" of a gracious work, were enabled by faith in Jesus Christ to realize the forgiveness of their sins. "It was a moment of delicious joy," continues Brother Fish, "when I saw them come forth one by one as penitents, but the joy was more blessed as, one by one, a score of them stood up, and in a few broken sentences told how Jesus had pardoned their sins." We often, near the beginning of a series of services, invite those who have just "believed unto righteousness," to make "confession unto" the "salvation" they have received, that the Church, and the unbelievers also, may get an appreciative idea of the character of the work from the testimony of a variety of witnesses just saved, and have hence learned nothing to say but the simple, glorious, conscious facts of the "demonstration of the Spirit" in their hearts. Why not have them confess publicly all through the services? Because we get so many seekers requiring attention, that we cannot spare time to listen to the interesting words of the new-born souls, but arrange to have them tell their experience to their minister, who writes down the fact of their conversion, with their names and addresses, so as to put them at once under pastoral care, as lambs in the fold of Christ. Most of the persons professing to obtain pardon that week were young persons. Our special series of preaching services closed on Monday night of the week ensuing. Mr. Fish goes on to state in his letter, "On Sunday, the 10th of June, the Holy Ghost fell upon the people, and twenty-six adults came forward to declare themselves seekers of God's pardoning mercy; eight or ten of whom were enabled to rise up and declare that God had, for Christ's sake, forgiven all their sins. On the following evening twenty-eight adults came forward. No sooner was the invitation given, than, as if resolved to press into the kingdom, they walked from their pews to the communion-rail. It would be in vain to describe our feelings, as now and then the low sobbing cry for mercy was blended with words of praise, uttered by those who had found Christ. With the exception of eight seekers, all entered into the liberty wherewith Christ maketh His people free.

"This was the last sermon of Mr. Taylor's series; and thus God set His seal upon His servant's faith. A day or two afterwards he left us. His name is a 'household word' among us. We are thankful to him for his self-denying efforts, but more thankful to the Master who sent him."

Lectures on Tuesday and Wednesday nights closed my labours in King William's Town. The visible result is thus stated in Brother Fish's letter: —"The work thus graciously commenced has gone on slowly and gradually. In order to conserve and extend it, we held daily prayer-meetings at one o'clock, and continued special services every evening; as the result of which, about twenty more souls have been converted. The number of Europeans converted in this revival is, children included, about eighty. Some of these were members of society, who had not before enjoyed the evidence of their acceptance 'in the Beloved.' The rest have been received on trial, either in this or other circuits."

On Wednesday the 6th of June, in the midst of our series of services in King William's Town, a Kaffir came running with the message that four missionaries were "in the path," and would arrive—pointing where the sun would be—a little after noon. In due time we saw in the distance four Englishmen on foot coming into the town, accompanied by a few Kaffirs. Their appearance suggested the sacred historic scene of the Master and His rustic-looking fishermen, whom he was teaching to be "fishers of men," walking into the city of Capernaum. These brethren had walked from Annshaw Mission station, twenty-five miles distant. We watched them with peculiar interest as they approached. One of them I recognized at once as Rev. John Scott, from Graham's Town, and I was introduced to Revs. Lamplough, Hillier, and Sawtell.

Rev. Robert Lamplough had for nearly six years been, and then was, the Wesleyan missionary to Chief Kama's tribe of Kaffirs, the residence of the chief, and head of the mission circuit, bearing the name of Rev. Wm. Shaw's missionary wife—"Annshaw." I had heard much of Brother Lamplough's faithful ministrations in Graham's Town, where he had laboured before his appointment to the Kaffir work. I had learned also that though he was not much acquainted with the Kaffir language, he was preaching successfully through an interpreter, and was the best disciplinarian in South Africa. It was gratefully stated by his Graham's Town friends, that there were many noble ministers, and administrators among them; yet, in the Kaffir work, where Lamplough's administrative talents had specially been called into requisition, he was, confessedly, in wise, firm, persistent and effective discipline, superior to any man in South Africa. I was, therefore, very glad to meet with Brother Lamplough; but could not anticipate the glorious results of our acquaintance with each other. He expressed his deep regret that I had arranged to spend but one night on his station. Having no hope of working successfully through an interpreter, my plan of appointments, extending then more than a month in advance, was confined to the English work, except this one night for Annshaw, which I had given more in deference to Brother Lamplough, of whom I had heard so much, than from any hope of doing much good to his people.

Brother Sawtell was, by appointment, junior minister on Annshaw circuit, engaged specially in establishing a new mission among a tribe of about 15,000 Fingoes in Amatola Basin, in the mountains, about fifteen miles distant from Annshaw. He is son-in-law of Rev. W. J. Davis, an industrious young minister, who will, I think, become very useful. I heard him preach a very good sermon, through a Kaffir interpreter, in King William's Town, the only English sermon I had heard for nine months, being all the time so occupied myself. I followed with an exhortation, and was encouraged to hope that I might do some good after all, by preaching through an interpreter.

Brother Hillier was junior minister on Fort Peddie circuit. We'll hear from him again.

Brother Lamplough introduced to me his two native candidates for the ministry, whom he had been training for several years. One was Wm. Shaw, son of Chief Kama, the other was Charles Pamla, who belongs to a family of Amazulu chiefs. These, with two others, are the first South African natives proposed for the ministry among the Wesleyans. The Free Church of Scotland have one educated Kaffir minister, Rev. Tio Soga. Wm. Shaw Kama had given up the prospect of becoming the successor of his father in the chieftainship of his tribe, that he might be a missionary to the heathen, and desired "to be sent far hence," among those who had not the Gospel.

Charles Pamla had sold his farm, and good house, that he might devote his undivided time and energies to the one work of saving sinners, by leading them to the only Saviour. He is about six feet high, muscular, well-proportioned, but lean; quite black, with a fine display of ivory; good craniological development, regular features, very pleasant expression, logical cast of mind, sonorous powerful voice. He is the man whom God appointed, through the instrumentality of Brother Lamplough, to open for me an effectual door of utterance to the heathen.

Charles Pamla's providential training for our great work was going on quite independent of me, yet simultaneously with the progress of my work in another part of the colony. This is forcibly illustrated by a letter written by Charles, to Rev. Wm. Shaw, dated June 1st, which was the day I closed my campaign in Graham's Town. The letter was published in the *Wesleyan Missionary Notices*, for September, 1866. Any one reading it will require of me no apology for inserting the whole epistle.

My dear Sir,—Since I came to Annshaw, by reading Wesley's Sermons, I was convinced to seek after entire sanctification, and since last District-Meeting I have been praying for it, and trusting to obtain it. I had a sure trust, that through the blood of Christ I would obtain the blessing promised to those who come to Christ by faith. About a month ago, one morning very early, I went to pray for the same thing, entire sanctification; and while I was praying and trusting in the blood of Christ, I felt a small voice speaking through my soul, saying, "It is done, receive the blessing." The first thing I felt was ease from the different kinds of thoughts, ease from the world, and from all the cares of the flesh. I felt the Spirit filling my soul, and immediately I was forced to say in my soul, "For me to live is Christ." And I gave up my body, soul, thoughts, words, time, property, children, and everything that belongs to me, to the Lord, to do as He pleases. One evening, while I was thinking about the promises, a young man came to me, and told me that he felt his sins. I told him to come in, and so he did; and we began to pray to God. I took my book, and read one of Wesley's Sermons on Justification by Faith; also showing that it is not through the works of a man that God justifies a sinner; the sinner has only to repent and give up his sins, believe and trust to the atoning blood of Christ. At the same time there were two others who had never found peace with God : one of them was a member; but the other two were unbelievers. I kept on praying and showing the way to their great Creator God, and they all three began to cry aloud with a broken and contrite heart. I went on praying. First one found peace, and then another, until they all found peace. And they almost showed in their appearance that they were new creatures in Christ Jesus. The following evening we had another meeting, and three found peace.

I went to Keiskamma Hoek the next Sunday, and took the same subject,—Justification by Faith; and I put a few strong words in to make it plainer to the hearers. It seemed as if God was there; the congregation were shaking; it seemed as if every one of them were condemned by the power of the Holy Ghost, and Christ seemed to be there. They began to cry aloud through these words, beginning from the Leaders to the members, and also the heathen who were there. After that we had a Prayer-meeting, and again preaching about "the way to the kingdom—repent, and believe the Gospel." (Matt. i. 15.) It was the same thing, several found peace during these two services, and many cried out for mercy ; and I proposed another service at the Tshoxa in the evening. Several came from different places, and we began our services, and God visited us that night with a great baptism of the Holy Ghost. Some were crying for mercy, some were rejoicing, those that had just found peace, saying, "We were in darkness, but now we are in light; our eyes are open to-day; we were dead, but to-day we are alive." I was praying, and talking, and addressing them, quoting different passages for their benefit, and my heart rejoiced more and more in that great work of God. The next morning we had another meeting : it was. the same thing,—some were crying, and some found peace. I examined them carefully through one of Wesley's Ser-

H

mons on the "Witness of the Spirit." They answered satisfactorily. There were twenty-six members found peace that day and night; also one backslider, one little girl about ten years of age, and nine people who were heathens. These thirty-seven all found peace with God, and are now willing to join class and serve God with all their heart, and mind, and soul, and strength, and give up Kaffir beer, and all other heathen customs, and every sin, and be fully on the Lord's side all the days of their life, by God's help. This is the salvation which is through faith, even in the present world. My dear Sir, we rejoice in this great work, seeing that God has not altogether given up His people the natives.

Brothers Lamplough, Hillier and Sawtell gave us valuable assistance in our prayer-meetings in King William's Town, their Kaffir candidates for the ministry, and companions in the local ranks, looked on, listened, and learned what they afterwards turned to good account. I spent much time with these missionaries and our kind host, in conversation on the best methods of missionary enterprise. While in King William's Town I became acquainted with Rev. J. W. Appleyard, a mild, sweet-spirited brother, superintendent of our Mount Coke Mission Station, ten miles distant, and manager of the Wesleyan Kaffir printing-establishment at Mount Coke. Brother Appleyard was appointed, by the Wesleyan Conference, to South Africa in 1839, and has become a thorough master of the Kaffir language, and is the author of a grammar of that language of high repute among the missionaries. With the assistance of some fragmentary translations of the Bible, by Brothers Davis, Dugmore, and others, Brother Appleyard has translated the whole book of the Old and New Testament Scriptures into the Kaffir language, which, under his immediate supervision, was published in one neat volume in London, by the *British and Foreign Bible Society*. Some parties, not believed to be friendly to Wesleyan successes in South Africa, made a representation to the managers of the Bible Society, stating that Appleyard's translation was a miserable failure. This led to a critical examination of it by competent Kaffirs, well-read in the English, as well as their own language, who have pronounced it an excellent translation.

Brother Appleyard believes that the Kaffir language is spoken by one million souls in South Africa, and probably by some millions in Central Africa, whence these South African Kaffirs appear to have emigrated. In King William's Town I also met with Rev. John Longdon, Wesleyan missionary at Butterworth, in Fingo-land, who gave me a pressing Macedonian call to help him; not recognising it then as a call from the Lord, I did not promise to go, but afterwards went, nevertheless, by the will of God.

I visited Mr. George Impey in his last illness, the father of Rev. William Impey. The dear old man had been confined to his room for four years, suffering from paralysis. He had been a resident of the colony for twenty-two years, and of King William's

Town for seven. He was for some years manager of the British Kaffrarian Bank, and was, as I learned from them, who knew him long and well, a consistent, cheerful Christian, and a Wesleyan Local Preacher of superior abilities. He was not able to converse much when I saw him, but was steadfast in faith, and his victory over sin and Satan complete.

I sang to him the dying sentiments of Bishop McKendree :—

What's this that steals, that steals upon my frame?
   Is it death? Is it death?
That soon shall quench, shall quench this vital flame,
   Is it death? Is it death?
  If this be death, I soon shall be
  From every pain and sorrow free,
  I shall the King of Glory see!
   All is well, all is well.

Weep not my friends, my friends weep not for me;
   All is well, all is well.
My sins are pardoned, pardoned, I am free:
   All is well, all is well.
  There's not a cloud that doth arise,
  To hide my Saviour from my eyes,
  I soon shall mount the upper skies:
   All is well, all is well.

Tune, tune your harps, your harps, ye saints, in glory,
   All is well, all is well.
I will rehearse, rehearse the pleasing story,
   All is well, all is well.
  Bright angels are from glory come,
  They're round my bed, they're in my room,
  They wait to waft my Spirit home,
   All is well, all is well.

Hark! hark, my Lord, my Lord and Master calls me,
  All is well, all is well.
I soon shall see, shall see His face in glory,
  All is well, all is well.
  Adieu, adieu, my friends, adieu,
  I can no longer stay with you,
  My glittering crown appears in view,
  All is well, all is well.

All through the singing of this hymn, which has given expression to the triumphant joy of multitudes of dying Christians to whom I have sung it, the face of this dying patriarch was covered with smiles, and streams of tears; and his hands were waving, as though, in the rapture of his soul, his dying body could not wait its appointed time, "to wit, the redemption of our bodies," but would fain mount up and fly, and at once accompany its immortal tenant to its "house not made with hands, eternal in the heavens." For a time he seemed hardly to know whether he was "in the body or out of the body;" but his acute bodily sufferings soon reminded him that the mortal struggle was still pending. He then grasped my hand, and with tears, exclaimed;—" Oh, my brother, my dear brother, it will not be long! All is well." He lingered a few weeks, and sank to peaceful rest.

Rev. Brother Hillier begged me to visit Fort Peddie, one of the largest mission stations in the country; but I had passed that *en route* from Graham's Town, and my appointments had been announced in advance, for every day for weeks, taking me quite into another part of the country, so I had to say nay. He was a young man of great promise, recently united in marriage to a daughter of one of our old missionaries, Rev. J. Smith. A few months after, in a letter from Brother Lamplough, I received the following sad intelligence:—" You will remember our Brother Hillier, who accompanied Brother Sawtell and myself to King William's Town. He died about a fortnight ago, after an illness of three days. The last sermon he heard of yours was that on going 'on to perfection.' Under that sermon he received a wonderful blessing; indeed, he was not like the same man afterwards, either in his spirit, or in his preaching. After he returned to his circuit, he sought, and found a fresh baptism from on high, which led him to preach and pray for a revival of God's work, and it was not long before it came, and some hundreds of souls entered into liberty through Brother Hillier's instrumentality. I need not say that he died trusting in Christ, and in sure and certain hope of everlasting life." As I am usually but a week on a circuit, in its largest and most central place of worship, it is quite as much my business, under the leading of the Holy Spirit, to labour for the "perfecting of the saints," as in the "work of the ministry" of reconciliation to sinners, so as to assist the Church in the development, and increasingly effective employment of her home resources and agencies, that she may go on, in humble reliance on God, without foreign special agency, conquering and to conquer.

A number of the leading business men, of King William's Town, are the sons of our old missionaries and members, such as R. Giddy, Esq., the son of Rev. Richard Giddy, chairman of the Bechuana District, Messrs. Joseph and Richard Walker, sons of Rev. Father Walker, of Graham's Town, one of our old pioneer missionary Catechists, and others which my space will not allow me to introduce. These men are an honour to their parents, and to the Church. Mr. Joseph Walker presented me with a fine walking-stick, turned out of the horn of a huge African rhinoceros. It came just at the time I needed it, to support me in my subsequent out-door preaching to the Kaffirs, in the absence of pulpit, or even chairs, for we generally sat on the grass.

After spending a few days at our series of services in King William's Town, on Saturday, the 9th of June, Charles Pamla, and Boyce Mama, a very eloquent and successful native Kaffir preacher, went to Mount Coke and preached, and conducted prayer-meetings through the Sabbath, and Brother Appleyard told me that upwards of seventy souls professed to find peace under their labours that day.

On Monday they returned and held a short, but very successful, series of services for the natives in King William's Town. Rev. Brother Fish, in his letter before-mentioned, says, " While Mr. Taylor was preaching to our English congregation, Charles Pamla devoted two or three days to preaching at the native location of this town.

"His 'word came not in word only, but in demonstration of the Spirit and with power.' It pierced the consciences of the people. The Holy Ghost fell upon them; and during three services, nearly eighty persons, chiefly young men and women, were converted. Since that time, to a great extent by the instrumentality of my native preachers and leaders, nearly forty more have been saved at the same place. The work is still going on. Every week, at my native Leaders' Meeting, I receive the names of new converts."

On Thursday morning, the 14th of June, Mr. Joseph Walker sent his carriage and pair to take me to Annshaw, and after the usual shaking of hands, and solemn pledges of fidelity to God, and a joyful meeting, but never a parting, beyond the river, we were soon on our way across the Buffalo, a beautiful stream, and up a long range of hills to their summits. Then we have a beautiful view of the town we have left, and in every direction a measureless extent of grassy hills and valleys, interspersed with occasional groves of the Mimosa, and wild aloes, and patches of jungle, of a great variety of shrubbery and intertwining vines. The most striking feature of the African jungle is the euphorbia-tree, standing thickly and high above the rest. Its trunk resembles somewhat the New South Wales "cabbage-tree," which is a very tall, beautiful variety of the palm. The euphorbia, however, does not usually grow to a height exceeding thirty feet; its limbs and leaves are rather lobes, more like the cactus than anything I can think of, and is sometimes called the "cactus-tree." A few miles out we overtook an Englishwoman, well dressed, on foot. It looked strange to see such a respectable-looking person travelling alone, so we asked her to accept a seat in our carriage, which she did, without a second asking. She said her teams had gone on before, en route to the neighbourhood of Kaskama Hoek, where she lived, twenty-five miles distant, and having stayed in town longer than she expected, she would have trouble to overtake them. We put her about five miles on her way, for which she was glad and grateful. We found her earnestly desiring to find her way to heaven, but knew not the way; so I gave her definite instructions which, if followed, will surely lead her to Him who is "the Truth, the Life, and the Way." I was glad also to have the opportunity of indirectly preaching the Gospel to my Roman Catholic driver, who went to my native service that night to hear me preach, and saw the marvellous effects of the Holy Spirit's work, such as but few persons ever see. I hope I may overtake both of my wayside hearers some day on the hills of glory, and hear the result.

As we drove along I saw, for the first time, the Kaffirs in their nude state.

Having travelled about fifteen miles we "outspanned" at a public-house, and got our dinner, and food for our horses. I walked down into a field a few hundred yards from our hotel, where some men were thrashing barley with a machine propelled by four oxen. They said they used horses till they all died with the prevailing "horse sickness," and then "inspanned" the horned cattle. While I was there one of their oxen seeming to get suddenly sick, fell down, and they could not get him up.

Looking to the hills east of the valley in which we were stopping, lo, a novel sight, four naked Kaffir young men, each mounted on a young bullock, and dashing along like Jehu. They used a kind of bridle, by which they guided them at will. Sweeping across the valley at a great rate, they rode up to the public-house. Their animals were fat, and apparently almost as fleet as deer; they came up panting like racers, as they were, and seemed quite impatient to stand. Two of the men dismounted, and beckoned to a couple of naked boys to hold their animals, while they, in imitation of their white brethren, went into the bar-room. Whether they got anything to drink, I know not, as I do not patronize the bar; but like prompt men of business, they were soon off, and we saw them cantering across the valley again to their native hills. About two P.M., we saw the silvery serpentine flow of the Keiskamma, and the mission-village of Annshaw on its banks.

The natives were assembling from all directions, and standing round in groups, waiting the arrival of the strange "umfundisi," and as we descended the hills, they came running to meet us, and bid us welcome.

CHAPTER IX.

ANNSHAW.

THE first Wesleyan Mission, established among the Kaffirs, was in the Amagonakwabi tribe, Amaxosa nation, under Chief Pato, and his brothers Kobi and Kama, in the year 1823, by Rev. W. Shaw, assisted by Rev. William Shepstone.

Mr. Shepstone came out from "Bristol" in the great immigration of 1820. Though not a minister, he was an earnest young Wesleyan, and came to Africa specially to try to do good. In addition to his usefulness as a successful Local Preacher, he had other talents specially adapting him to missionary work in Kaffraria—where ordinary mechanics were afraid to go, lest the Kaffirs should kill them—in that his craft was not only to build tents, but to build houses. In due course of time he was received by the British Conference, and ordained a minister of the Gospel, and has been actively engaged in the South African missionary work ever since. He is now superintendent of Kamastone Mission

FIRST KAFFIR CONVERTS. 109

Station, and chairman of the Queen's Town District.

Nearly two years after this first mission station was commenced, Mr. Shaw makes the following record :—

"On the 22nd of March, 1825, I held the first Methodist Class-meeting in Kaffraria, at which six of the natives were present. We were exceedingly gratified with the truly earnest manner in which they expressed their desire to save their souls." Of their next meeting the following week, he says, "It was a pleasing and profitable occasion. We had good reason to hope well of all who were present; but they are very weak in the faith, and very ignorant, and must be treated with much tenderness and forbearance. We shall consider them on trial for an indefinite period, and when it is deemed expedient they will be baptized." "In August, 1825, three natives were baptized, in the presence of a large assembly of people." The first-fruits of a glorious harvest. This first mission station grew into a native village, which Mr. Shaw named "Wesleyville."

"Amongst the natives whom I baptized at Wesleyville," says Mr. Shaw, "were the Chief Kama and his wife. The latter is a daughter of the great Chief Gaika, and sister of Makomo, the noted leader in the late Kaffir wars.

"Kama and his wife, amidst many temptations,

and serious difficulties, designedly put in their way by the heathen chiefs, to seduce them from their steadfastness, are still members of the Church, and are very regular in their attendance on its ordinances."

Wesleyville was destroyed in the Kaffir war of 1835; but afterwards rebuilt, and destroyed again in the war of 1848. The great chiefs Pato and Kobi, came to grief in those wars. One has spent years as a prisoner on "Robin Island," in Table Bay; but their tribe, with Kama at their head, remained true to the British Government, and hence have found a peaceful home on the banks of the Keiskamma, in British Kaffraria. The fragments of Wesleyville Mission were formed into a mission in this new home of the tribe, with a change of the name to Annshaw.

Chief Kama, who is now an old man, is about six feet in height, well-proportioned, and corpulent. He has a large head, a broad face, very benevolent expression, with the usual, not black, but dark copper-colour of the "royal line" of Kaffir Chiefs. He is altogether a noble-looking old man. The Colonial Government allows him a small pension. About 12,000 of his tribe are settled about him, and are under his rule, subordinate to the English Government in the colony. It is a sad fact, but may be said to illustrate the uphill work of the missionaries among such people, that Kama is the only "paramount chief" in Southern Africa who is connected with any Christian Church. Rev. William Sargent, who established the Annshaw Mission Station, and hence knows Kama well, told me he heard him, in a missionary address, tell his experience, in which he said, "When I became a Christian, my fellow-chiefs and many of my people laughed at me, said I was a fool, and that I never would become a ruling chief, that my people would throw me away—that I would become a scabby goat, and a vagabond in the earth, without home or friends; but just the reverse of all that has come to pass. I was then young, and had no people, my older brothers had a great people, but they rejected Christ, and lost their people, and everything they had, and I remain the only ruling chief of my tribe." Kama has ever remained true to the Wesleyan Church. It was said, with great regret, by some of the missionaries, that he had become cold in religion, and was too fond of strong drink; but during the recent revival among his people, he has been fully reclaimed, and is happy in God. His only wife still lives, and is, I am told, a superior woman.

The paramount chief of the Amatembu tribe, from which nearly all the ruling chiefs get their "great wives" (the mothers of the ruling line of paramount chiefs), sent, by a deputation of his counsellors, with all the ceremony due to such an occasion, a young woman to Kama, to become his "great wife." In the olden time a refusal, on Kama's part, would have furnished an occasion for war. When this party arrived near Kama's "great place," they "sat down," according to the ceremony to be observed in approaching a chief, to wait his pleasure. Kama refused to see them, but sent them a bullock that they might slay, and eat, and then go about their business. They tarried but a night, and left unceremoniously in the morning.

Kama has but three sons; the first was a Wesleyan at one time, but was ensnared by the trap laid for his father, and took a second wife, became a heathen, and is such a wreck that it is not likely that the tribe or the Colonial Government will ever promote him to ruling power. His second son, William Shaw, is a man of great amiability, sound intelligence, and sterling Christian integrity. He would, no doubt, succeed his father in the chieftainship, but has devoted himself to the ministry, and was with Charles Pamla and two others, "received on trial," at the recent session of the British Conference (1866). His third son is a good young man, but is thought to be dying with consumption.

Since writing the above, I have received, by a letter, the following corroborative and additional facts concerning the Chief Kama from Rev. Robert Lamplough, who has been his missionary for the last six years:—"The Chief Kama is a fine, tall, very dignified-looking man, nearly seventy years of age. He first became known to Rev. W. Shaw, when he and his tribe lived near the sea in the Peddie District. He was then a young man, and a red heathen; and he and his tribe had no friendship with the white man. When Mr. Shaw went among them about forty-three years ago, they showed him where to build his place remote from their kraals, for they said, "This word of God will bring sickness among us." Mr. Shaw, however, refused to go so far away from them, and they at last consented for him to live near their kraals. Mr. Shaw soon taught them about the Sabbath-day, and that on the Sabbath they were expected to attend the services, and hear the Word of God preached. On one occasion Mr. Shaw asked Kama to accompany him to Graham's Town, but his people were very much opposed to this, saying, that Kama would "be killed by the English."

Mr. Shaw said, "I shall leave my wife with you, and if Kama is killed, you will kill her." At this they knew not what to say, and, finally, they consented to Kama's going to Graham's Town. It was on this, and subsequent journeys, that Kama and Mr. Shaw became great friends. The people of Kama's tribe observed this, and were evidently afraid of the consequences; they tried to prevent Kama from going so often to visit Mr. Shaw, and they told him that if he was so much with the minister he would be converted. Kama at this time was poor, and Mr. Shaw advised him to buy a wagon, telling him that it would help him very much. When

Kama told his people that he was going to buy a wagon, they were still more afraid, and they tried to hinder him in every possible way. But Kama would not listen to them, and so he gave Mr. Shaw ten fat oxen that he might buy a wagon for him in Graham's Town. That wagon made Kama rich, so that in time he had three kraals full of cattle.

One morning Kama went to visit Mr. Shaw; he found him writing. Mr. Shaw said to Kama, "Do you know my face and name?" Kama replied, "Yes." Mr. Shaw said, "And I know your face and name," and then went on to talk to him, telling him that in the next world they would know each other as they did in that room. This word came home to the Chief's heart, and led eventually to his conversion; there soon followed others, a brother of Kama's amongst the number.

Some years after this, when Kama was living at Newtondale, about ten miles from Peddie, and being now a member of the Wesleyan Church, another Kaffir chief sent his daughter to Kama that he might marry her for his second wife (his first being still alive), Kama sent word to the Chief that he could not take a second wife, for he was a Christian and feared God. This word of Kama's might have caused war between his people and the other chief and his tribe, and his brothers and people did their best to make him take this woman, saying that they were afraid they would be killed by the other chief and his people. Kama nobly replied, "I am ready to die, rather than take two wives," and forthwith he sent away the Chief's daughter without seeing her, with a present of four cattle.

After this the small-pox broke out amongst the people, and many died of this fearful disease. The other chiefs were for killing all the people living at infected places. Kama said that he would not allow such a thing; but notwithstanding all his efforts to prevent it, some were killed secretly. When Kama heard of it, he spoke much to his people about it, and told them that God would not approve of such things. The other chiefs said that they would prepare to make war upon Kama, and kill him, for preventing the killing of all who lived at the places where the small-pox was. To this Kama replied, that he would not consent, though they should fight with him.

In consequence of this and other things, Kama determined to leave that part of the country; but first he informed the English Government about it, who gave him full permission to go where he chose. Some of his people did not accompany him, but others would not forsake him, and they set forth, intending to go as far as Moshesh's country; but finally they settled in what was then the Tambookie country. Whilst living here Kama preached to the people, for they had no minister; but Kama got them together on Sundays,—his eldest son Samuel used to read for him out of God's Word, and Kama preached to the people regularly. None of his sons were converted at that time; but after some time his two sons, Samuel and William Shaw (who was at the last session of the English Conference admitted to the ministry), together with several others, were brought to God, and the Rev. Wm. Shepstone afterwards came and baptized the young converts, and took charge of the people; and thus were laid the foundations of the Mission Station, so wonderfully visited by the Holy Spirit of late, called after the Chief—" Kamastone."

Chief Kama lives in a good substantial house of English style, about three hundred yards from the chapel. The mission-house is a large, one-story cottage, with verandah, extending all along the front. The chapel is a wood building, plain, but neat, and will seat about six hundred persons. These, with a few square native houses, stand out as the prominent buildings of the place; next to these, what is more interesting to a stranger, the humble dwellings of the natives. These are, for the most part, round huts, one class of which, shaped exactly like a haycock, consists simply of a framework of small poles and twigs, covered all over and down to the ground with long grass, beautifully thatched. A hole about two feet wide, and three feet high, is left on one side as the door. The fire is built in the centre, and the smoke slowly works its way up through the thatch, making it black inside and out. Europeans would not enjoy a residence in such an establishment I'm sure. Others are built up of "wattle and daub," in a perpendicular wall, from four to five feet high, and covered with thatch, just like the former. A third class of huts are built just like the second, except that the round wall, rising from five to seven feet high, is made sometimes of sod, but more frequently of solid blocks of clay, somewhat like the Mexican "adobes," plastered over with mortar. These are very comfortable dwellings for the higher classes.

At the time of my arrival at Annshaw, there were in the circuit a Wesleyan membership of six hundred, most of whom were Kama's Kaffirs, the rest were Fingoes. Charles Pamla, an Amazulu Fingoe, had been labouring, principally among Kama's Tribe, as an unpaid evangelist, for several years. He is one of the evangelists mentioned in last year's (1865) official reports of the Annshaw circuit, an extract from which may serve to illustrate the breaking up of fallow ground in that important field. "This circuit has prospered spiritually during the year. Discipline has been beneficially exercised. Conversions have resulted in several instances. The officers of the church have been much quickened. Three evangelists have been diligently employed in preaching at the heathen Kraals, during the greater part of the year. There is reason to believe that, partly through their efforts, one or two conversions have taken place among the heathen, and in other respects their labours have been attended with good."

Brother Lamplough gave me Charles Pamla to interpret for me.

Before the service, I took him alone, and preached my sermon to him, filling his head and heart full of it. After he had heard me preach in King William's Town, I asked him if he could put my sermon into Kaffir.

"No, Mr. Taylor, I think I could not. I understood the most of it, but I can only interpret low English, and you speak high English."

I at once determined to study "low English." And now when I was preaching to him alone, I told him to stop me at every word he could not fully understand. I was fully committed to make one more effort at the second-hand mode of preaching, through a spokesman. Having gone through with the discourse, I gave my man a talk on naturalness.

"But," said he, "I must speak loudly sometimes."

I then saw that by naturalness he thought I meant simply the conversational style.

"O, yes," I replied, "as loudly as you like at the right time. The scream of a mother, on seeing her child fall into a well, is as natural as her lullaby in the nursery. God hath given us every variety of vocal power and intonation adapted to express every variety of the soul's emotions, from the softest whispers, like the mellow murmurs of the rippling rill, up to the thundering, crashing voices of the cataract. I however, put it into "low English," so that he understood me perfectly.

FIRST REVIVAL SERVICE. 119

At four P.M. of Thursday, June 14th, we commenced our first service. Brother Lamplough opened with singing and prayer. I stood in the small pulpit, and Charles on the top step by my side. In front we see the crowded audience of natives, packed in to every square foot of space, including the aisles. The mission-station people—men and women—are all clothed in European dress, the head-dress of the women consisting of a handkerchief, usually red, turbaned round with some display of taste. The heathens are painted red with ochre, the men wrapped in a blanket, the women wearing a skirt of dressed leather, with head-dress, similar to the fashion of the station women. To our left, in the corner, are my Romanist driver, and Mr. Harper, who had come to drive me next day to Lovedale, also Sister Sawtell, Sister Lamplough, and her children; in the altar below us were the two circuit ministers; on our right, next the wall, were Chief Kama and the Fingoe Chief, Hlambisa, from Amatola Basin, fifteen miles distant, who rules a tribe of fifteen thousand Fingoes in the Amatola mountains. He is Brother Pamla's uncle, but a hardened old heathen, with about a dozen wives. We announced as the text the last words of Jesus, " Ye shall receive power, after that the Holy Ghost is come upon you, and ye shall be witnesses unto me both in Jerusalem, and in all Judea, and in Samaria, and unto the uttermost parts of the earth." The sermon was entirely to believers. I believe Charles gave every idea and shade of thought as naturally and as definitely as if they had originated in his own brain. Indeed, black as he was, he seemed a transparent medium through which my Gospel thoughts, rendered luminous and mighty by the Holy Spirit's unction, shone brightly through the soul windows—the eyes and ears of my sable hearers—down into the depths of their hearts. All through the discourse of one hour and a quarter there was a profound silence throughout the assembly, rendered awful in solemnity by the deep consciousness that every one seemed to feel of the presence of a power which, like a slumbering earthquake, would soon break forth in manifest grandeur. After a season of silent prayer, at the close of the discourse, silent for a time, but slightly interrupted by the uncontrollable emotions of the people, we dismissed the assembly to give a little time for refreshment and reflection before the evening service.

After a hasty tea I went alone with Charles, and gave him in detail the sermon for the evening, and we again stood before the people at 8 P.M., and preached to sinners from the text, " As I live, saith the Lord God, I have no pleasure in the death of the wicked; but that the wicked turn from his way and live. Turn ye, turn ye from your evil ways, for why will ye die?" We had about the same congregation, in the same order, as in the afternoon. During the preaching of over an hour, the beaming faces of believers, the distorted features of sinners, the tearful eyes of both, all in solemn silence before the Lord, and the voices of His prophets, presented altogether a scene which neither painter nor poet can describe; and yet, to be felt and witnessed, was to receive an impression never to be effaced while memory endures.

At the close of the discourse I said, "Charles, I will sing a hymn suitable to the subject, but I only know it by memory to the time of the tune, and can't line it for you, but I will sing a line at a time, and you will put it into Kaffir." I then sang as follows, line by line, leaving time for the translation into another language, the hymn called—

WHY WILL YE DIE?

"SINNERS, hastening down to ruin,
    Why will ye die?
Jesus is your souls pursuing,
    Why will ye die?
Though from Him you still are flying,
All His power and love defying,
Hark, how loudly He is crying!
    Why will ye die?

Sinai asks in loudest thunder,
    Why will ye die?
Heaven and earth cry out with wonder,
    Why will ye die?
Sinners, sunk in degradation,
While rejecting God's salvation,
This is Heaven's expostulation,
    Why will ye die?

Jesu's groans, on Calvary's mountain—
    Why will ye die?—
Speak with blood that fills the fountain,
    Why will ye die?

> Blood that ransomed every nation,
> Fits for heaven's exalted station.
> Sinners, now accept salvation.
> > Why will ye die?
>
> Death and hell cry out, while hasting,
> > Why will ye die?
> And your feeble strength while wasting,
> > Why will ye die?
> When you cross cold Jordan's river,
> And your doom is fixed for ever,
> God will ask no more—no, never,
> > Why will ye die?
>
> But through everlasting ages,
> > Then you must die!
> While hell's howling tempest rages,
> > Then you must *die*!
> Stripp'd of every earthly pleasure;
> Lost for ever, heavenly treasure;
> Burning vengeance without measure;
> > But cannot die!

Charles not only put every line into Kaffir, but after the first verse, he gave them the tune as well, though he had never heard it before. When spoken to about it the next day, he said that he was not aware of the fact that he had sung it, as he only meant to give the words.

The ministers present seemed to think it the result of an extraordinary inspiration of the Holy Spirit, which was true in a very glorious sense, but I believe the Spirit's work on the whole occasion was perfectly adjusted to the human conditions employed, and did not miraculously rise above, or suspend any physical law. The fact was, I had a very apt scholar for my interpreter. He had so thoroughly digested my lecture on *Naturalness*, that, though he has a voice for variety, pathos and volume, so grandly superior that he could not be an ape, yet in his own natural voice he gave every intonation of mine, running through at least two octaves, during the discourse, so when he commenced to render the lines which I was singing, he seemed at first a little confused, for he had lost the key-note of my intonations, but soon his voice mounted up into the regions of song, and echoed, perfectly as a keyed instrument, my singing tones, just as he had before echoed my speaking tones. Charles, however, was not simply a medium through which my thoughts were conveyed to the people. He had been under Brother Lamplough's training for several years, and was well read in Bible doctrines, and, better still, had a holy heart, and the prophetic unction of the Holy Spirit; and, having the subject fully impressed on his retentive memory by my personal preaching to him alone, he uttered every sentence from his heart, just as I did myself, so that by the union of two heads and two hearts, under the Holy Spirit's power, we worked a double heart battery, which seemed to give the preaching through an interpreter much greater power than singly and directly, without an interpreter.

Through all the preaching service addressed mainly to the intellect, conscience, and will, there was the keen piercing of the Spirit's sword, and deep awakening, but profound silence. Before the prayer-meeting commenced, I explained the simple plan of salvation by faith to the seekers collectively, just as I would to each one personally. Then we invited all who had intelligently and determinately decided to surrender themselves to God, and accept Christ as their Saviour, to come forward to the front forms. They at once came as fast as they could press their way. Beginning at the front forms, they filled form after form with seekers, till at least two hundred penitents were down on their knees. There was no loud screaming of any one above the rest, but their pent up emotions now found vent in audible prayers, sighs, groans, and floods of tears. When the prayer-meeting had thus progressed for about fifteen minutes, Brother L. said, "Had we not better dismiss them, and let them go off alone, and seek by the river? The old missionaries have told me that it will not do to let them give way to their feelings, lest they run into wild extravagance. They will go off to the river and pray all night."

"Why, my dear brother," I replied, "this is not a rush of blind emotional excitement. The most of these people have been under your teaching for years, and we have just explained the way of salvation to them, so that under the enlightening power of the Spirit, every child here of ten years can understand it. They are now intelligently coming to Jesus. The Holy Spirit is leading them. Why interrupt them at this most important juncture, and send them off to the river to battle with Satan alone, and take a bad cold as well? They are emotional beings, to be sure, and have not the same control of their feelings as the mass of Europeans; but all the noise of this occasion is in beautiful harmony with all the facts in their case. This is unquestionably the work of God. We will just keep our hands ' off the Ark of God,' and let the Holy Ghost attend to His own business, in His own way."

Upon reflection, Brother Lamplough heartily concurred with my views of the subject, and entered most earnestly into the work. It was not long till they began to enter into the liberty of the children of God. I soon saw that Charles Pamla, Wm. Kama, and others, were quite at home in the work. As fast as they found peace, the new converts were separated from the seekers, and seated apart on the other side of the chapel. They were then quiet as the Gadarene, "sitting at the feet of Jesus clothed, and in his right mind." All were personally examined as to their experience, and the names of those who gave a satisfactory testimony to their having obtained peace with God, through an acceptance of Jesus Christ, were written down, that the pastor might the more readily find them, and get them at once into the visible fold of the Church. At the close of the prayer-meeting, it was found that seventy souls had professed to find remission of their sins that night. To me it was the harmony of heaven. I felt an indescribable joy, not simply on account of the great work of God in the salvation of the Kaffirs, which was an occasion of great joy to "the angels of God," but especially because the spell that bound me within the lines of my native language was broken. I could now preach effectively through an interpreter, and the heathen world seemed suddenly opened to my personal enterprise, as an ambassador for Christ. The service was continued that night till midnight. No one then seemed willing to leave; but knowing the danger of violating physical laws by excessive labour, and loss of sleep, and hence involving damaging penalties, we prevailed on them to retire and seek a little rest. The natives, however, were back to a sunrise prayer-meeting, and seemed fresh and earnest as before.

That day, Friday, the 15th of June, at 10 A.M. we preached again to about the same crowd we had the preceding day, and continued the prayer-meeting service till two P.M. During the three services one hundred and fifteen persons, professing to obtain the pardon of their sins, were examined, and their names and addresses recorded.

After a hasty dinner, Mr. Harper took me and Sister Sawtell into his cart and drove us over the hills, thirteen miles to his house in "Alice,"—also called "Lovedale." One of the industrial schools, established under the patronage of Governor Grey is located in that lovely dale. It is under the direction of the Scotch Presbyterian Missions, and is being carried on, I was informed, with a good degree of success. Getting in late, and leaving next morning, I could not do myself the pleasure of visiting the institution. The Wesleyans have a comfortable chapel there, small, but large enough for the demands of the village. It belongs to the Fort Beaufort Circuit, but the little society had dwindled down, I was informed, to such a dwarfish, sickly state, that they could not keep up a class or prayer-meeting. I preached there that night to a full chapel. Most of them were very serious and attentive, but one man, well-dressed and apparently influential, kept up a sort of incredulous scoffing, grinning all the time. In extraordinary contrast with the results of the preceding night, not one seeker responded to the call so far as to say, "What must I do to be saved?" Many, I believe, however, were awaked, who followed us to Fort Beaufort, thirteen miles distant, and afterwards there, and at Heald Town, embraced Christ, and a good work in "Alice" followed, and a healthy young society was organized there. The widow of one of our old missionaries, Rev. Mr. Garner, lives in that village; but my weariness from excessive labours, and limited time, prevented me from calling to see her. Several of her family, however, were saved at my services in different places. On Saturday morning the 16th of June, Rev. John Wilson, Superintendent of Fort Beaufort Circuit, drove me, in a cart and pair, to his house at the Fort, where I spent six days.

While at Fort Beaufort, twenty-five miles distant

from Annshaw, I received a letter from Brother Lamplough, dated June 19th, an extract from which will illustrate the progress of the work in Kama's tribe.

"My dear brother,

"You will rejoice to hear that 165 profess to have found peace since you left, making altogether 280 since your arrival at Annshaw on Thursday last. Besides these, from what I can learn, there are at least twenty more at the out-stations, who are not yet reported. More than two-thirds of this number were not members, some were heathens, others were notoriously hard and wicked characters, whilst a few had been professedly seeking salvation for ten or fifteen years, and could not find it, but have now entered into liberty. Never was such a work seen among the natives of Kama's tribe before, and I question whether there has ever been such a work for power and rapidity in this country before. To have about 300 souls brought to God in less than five days, is indeed a glorious thing, especially when we consider that not more than a thousand people have been brought within the sphere of the influence. I suppose the congregation at Annshaw was about 600 souls, and I can scarcely find one who heard you preach who is not now converted. Indeed, so thorough has been the work, that to keep the supply of seekers, we have had to send out every day for fresh batches of heathens and formalists from the out-stations, who very soon enter into liberty.

On Annshaw station I cannot call to mind a man or woman, and hardly a boy or girl, who is without a professed sense of pardon. The Church is wonderfully revived, and the Leaders and Local Preachers are stirred up to look for yet greater things. Charles Pamla and Wm. Shaw Kama are especially useful. They returned on Sunday from their appointments, bringing a list of the spoils taken from the enemy, amounting to thirty-four. They are going out again to-day, and intend to remain all night. I doubt not the Lord will bless their labours abundantly. I hope soon to be able to go out to some of the heathen kraals, and try the plan suggested and adopted by yourself (that is St. Paul's plan of 'disputing with them daily,' till all Asia shall hear the word of the Lord). I wish I could get out at once, but so many things have to be attended to. These new converts have to be formed into classes, under the care of suitable leaders, and this is a work that cannot be neglected."

A few additional facts and incidents, illustrative of the work of God at Annshaw, I extract from Brother Lamplough's report, published in the *Wesleyan Missionary Notices*, for October, 1866.

"One very pleasing feature in this good work," says Brother L., "is the clearness with which nearly all are enabled to testify, respecting their conversion to God. Almost all who have professed to find peace, have been carefully examined, and closely questioned, by Mr. Sawtell, or myself, Charles

Pamla, or William Shaw Kama, and the result has been most satisfactory; especially as regards the children, and those who, until recently, were living in heathenism.

"The effect of Mr. Taylor's visit upon the Local Preachers is wonderful, and they are six times as efficient as they were before. Charles Palma, Boyce Mama, and a few other natives have been used as the principal instruments in this work."

ILLUSTRATIVE INCIDENTS.—Brother Lamplough continues:—"Generally speaking, penitents were enabled very speedily to lay hold of the Saviour, and rejoice in a sense of forgiveness; and very wonderful was it to see the effect when some of these entered into liberty. For a few moments the face appeared transfigured with light; and the smile of joy which shone forth from their eyes was such as I shall never forget. I cannot attempt to describe such cases; but I have several present to my mind whilst I write. One man, I noticed, came forward every morning and evening for some days. He was a heathen, and I noticed him because he was lame, and as he came forward he hopped on one leg. At the close of the meeting he generally had to be carried out by three men, being too much exhausted to move. The morning he found peace, he was led to the seat reserved for the new converts, where he sat for a little time, apparently in deep thought; he then burst out into such a laugh of joy and surprise as I shall never forget; and he kept on in this way for some ten minutes, as though perfectly unconscious of all outward things,—feasting his soul with the wonderful love of Christ, which filled him with surprise and joy."

Charles Pamla gave me the following incident. An old heathen who lived eight miles from the station, was waked up by songs in the night, sung by some of his converted grandchildren, returning from the meeting where they had found Jesus. The old man, hearing the wonderful story these young witnesses had to tell, took up his sticks, and hobbled off straightway to Annshaw, arriving about the break of day. Hearing the voice of praise in the chapel at the morning prayer-meeting, he went in and heard the prayers and prophesyings of God's people. "The secrets of his heart were made manifest, and, falling down on his face, he worshipped God," and was enabled that morning "to report that God was in them of a truth," from a blessed experience of salvation in his own heart. When he reported himself among the young converts of that meeting, he asked the minister what he should do about his two wives.

"You will have to give one of them up."

"Well," replied the old man, "one is a young woman, and I love her; the other is an old woman, the first wife of my youth. She is old, and can't work much, but she is my true wife, and she has always been kind to me, and I will keep her, and give up my young wife. But I am not angry with her, and I don't know how to tell her to go away. I will bring them both here to-morrow, and let you explain it to them."

"Very well," replied the missionary, "that will do."

So the next day, the old man was seen in the distance, hobbling along on his two sticks, close after him his old woman, and next, in single file, his young woman and her three children. It was a painfully interesting, and yet pleasing sight.

The old man brought his two wives into the chapel, and marched straight to the missionary. Brother Lamplough went into an explanation of the whole matter to the astonished women, who, it appears, did not know what was to be done. When the minister's decision was announced, the old woman cried out:

"I am glad of that. I always loved my dear old man, and did not want him to give half of his heart away to another woman. Oh, I am so glad to get him back to me, and now he is all my own!"

The younger woman stood weeping, and all naturally thought, that to be "thrown away," as the Kaffirs would term it, in that style, was an occasion of great grief, which would lead to an unpleasant scene; but when her turn came to speak, she said, "I thank God for this. I am not angry with the old man, but I have been living in sin, and now I want to find Jesus Christ, too," and, as she wept and commenced tearing off and throwing away her heathen charms and trinkets, she said—"What is to be done with my children? May I take them with me? I will go home to my people, and serve Jesus Christ, but I want to take my children with me."

The old man, under Kaffir law, could have held the children, but he promptly said, "Yes, take the children, and teach them to love Jesus Christ."

TOTAL ABSTINENCE.—"Our last stroke is being levelled against Kaffir beer," says Brother Lamplough. "I do not know a single Leader or Local Preacher, who touches beer now in this circuit. This is a grand thing, and the result of five years' hard fighting."

WITNESSES FOR JESUS.—"About twelve days after Mr. Taylor's visit," continues Lamplough's report, "we had a fellowship-meeting, in order to give the new converts an opportunity of testifying of the grace of God. The chapel was crowded; more than half the congregation being composed of those who had just found peace. About fifty spoke, several of them were very old people, not a few were children; many had just left heathenism, and two were deaf and dumb men, who could not speak, but pointed to the heavens and the earth, and laid their hands upon their breasts, to signify that the great God who made the heavens and the earth had come into their hearts, and then they smiled in a peculiar way, to intimate that their souls rejoiced. Who will say that these men were not taught of the Spirit, in a way which we cannot understand? Only less wonderful than this was the testimony of children not more than ten or twelve years of age, many whom had heathen parents. The way in which these little ones (with only a sheep-skin on) testified to what they had experienced of the saving grace of God, was truly amazing."

How the heathen try to explain it.—" The visit of Mr. Taylor," says Brother Lamplough, " was so short, and the effects so wonderful, that some of the heathen say he came down from heaven. Others say that he came to destroy the country, and that he brought a medicine with him, which he has left at my house, and which I give to the Local Preachers, and it makes them mad, so that they are able to work wonders among the people. They say that when the people come to Annshaw Chapel, they are invited to come forward, and that as soon as they touch the 'wood' (communion-rail) they must be converted; for I have some blood with which I sprinkle them, and some flour which I scatter upon their heads, and then we blow in their ears, and they are believers!" We will see in due time how some of the white people in Natal try to explain away the work of God.

Persecutions.—"At many of the heathen villages," reports Brother Lamplough, " the people will not go near the services, for fear they should be converted. When a woman wants to repent, the husband takes a stick and beats her; and some of the children of the heathen are beaten, and not allowed to come to class. Indeed, there is much persecution going on in many parts of the circuit, and several are by compulsion

CHAPTER X.

FORT BEAUFORT.

FORT BEAUFORT, "situated on the lower part of the Kat river, was first established as a military post soon after the Kaffir war of 1835," and has gradually developed into a good average African town. It is in the midst of a good sheep-farming country, and some of the valleys produce good crops of maize and tolerably fair crops of wheat. The district, including the town, contains a population of 13,048, of whom 2,648 are whites. The Wesleyan Church was organized there in 1837, and a chapel was built the same year, which was a few years later superseded by the present chapel, which has sittings for about 400 persons.

My home was at the house of the Superintendent of the Circuit, Rev. John Wilson, a man of an excellent spirit, and an earnest minister, who, with his truly missionary wife, has been in the South African work for many years. Two of their daughters who had long been seeking, were saved during our series of services. I was agreeably surprised to meet a large force of my Graham's Town workers and friends who had come forty-seven miles to Fort Beaufort to attend our services. The principal ones were my Graham's Town host, Mr. Wm. A. Richards, his good wife, and four children; Mr. J. B. Janion, an earnest worker for God, and, I was informed, a superior Local Preacher; Mr. B. B. Atwell, "a chief man" in Commemoration Chapel, who extemporised the ventilators there by knocking out a pane of glass from each gallery-window, no one presuming to ask "What doest thou?" Also Ben Atwell, son of the good brother last named. Brother Ben is the organist in Commemoration Chapel, and got his soul into harmony with God during our series there. Mr. D. Penn, who drove me seventy miles in one day with two pair of his own horses, to King William's Town; Dr. Exton, who joined the Wesleyan Church at our "fellowship-meeting" in Graham's Town, and will, I think, make a very influential and useful member; Mrs. Rev. Thomas Guard too was among them; she, with Sister Richards and their children, had come in an ox-wagon, making a journey of three days, and enjoyed the romance of the trip greatly. Besides those were Messrs. Wm. Roberts, C. H. Webb, R. Frumble, J. Green, the barber, W. Oates, C. Gowie, D. Gowie, W. Barnes, his wife, and Miss Cheney, all earnest seekers after wandering souls. Last of all was, to me, a stranger of the Graham's Town party, a prodigal son of a truly Christian widowed mother, who afterwards became my friend and travelling companion,

Mr. James Roberts. I was told that when this little army arrived, the Fort Beaufort people were greatly astonished, not knowing of anything like the "Derby races" to attract such a multitude, and some would hardly believe that they had left their business, and travelled so far, to be on expense at the hotels for days, purely for spiritual purposes, getting and doing good at our services. At one of the hotels our friends had prayers, morning and evening, in one of their private sitting-rooms, and were a little surprised when the hotel-keeper and his wife asked to be allowed to be with them in their worship, and still more surprised and delighted afterwards, to find them among the seekers of salvation. They did not get into liberty that week, but the landlord with a few brethren who were converted that week, attended my meetings a few weeks afterwards in Queen's Town, distant about eighty miles, and there the hotel-keeper received Jesus. He gave up his "Canteen," took down his sign, and opened a temperance hotel, to furnish good accommodation, without the bad associations and bad effects of a "bar." On Sabbath morning, the 17th of June, we commenced our services at Fort Beaufort. The place was too much crowded to be comfortable, but there was a gracious manifestation of the Spirit to the hearts of believers. As we were returning from chapel Dr. Exton said, "I went into chapel this morning a moderate drinker, but came out a teetotaller." His decision on that subject was occasioned by some illustrative narrative bearing on another subject, and but incidentally reflected on drinking customs. At three P.M. we had a good time in preaching to the children. In the evening after preaching, we invited persons awakened by the Holy Spirit, who wanted to know "What they must do to be saved," to come forward that we might tell them. The altar-rails were soon crowded, and a good number were saved that night. I found there were a few good workers belonging to the Fort Beaufort society. We had a very good brother too from Eland's Post, a remote point on the circuit, and the Graham's Town friends were fully equipped for the war.

On Monday, at eleven A.M., I preached to believers, and we had a gracious season. On Monday night the work went on gloriously. A number of leading citizens, under the smitings of the Spirit, were down among the seekers. On Tuesday, at eleven A.M., I preached at Heald Town, seven miles distant. On Tuesday night I preached again at Fort Beaufort. Nearly all our early seekers were now rejoicing in the pardoning love of God; but the altar was as greatly crowded as ever with new seekers. On Wednesday, at eleven A.M., preached to the Church on *Christian Perfection*, with blessed spiritual results in the experience of believers, and on Wednesday night closed our special series of preaching services at Fort Beaufort. After preaching we had a great breaking-down among the sinners, and some very striking cases of conversion to God. During our brief service, sixty-five whites professed to find peace with God. Some of them give promise of great usefulness to the Church.

Many interesting examples might be given; but one or two illustrative cases may suffice.

Mr. E——, a very large man, who had been forward several times as a seeker, exclaimed, with tearful eyes, as he entered into liberty, "Talk about sacrificing all for Christ! What had I to sacrifice but my sins, and all my wicked abominations. A sacrifice, indeed? Why, it's a glorious riddance! And in return I have received in Christ the priceless gift of eternal life. Glory to God!"

Mrs. D—— had heard a great deal said against that "Foreign preacher," and she never would disgrace herself by going to hear such a man.

A friend said in reply, "Well, now, Mrs. D., you see that the most respectable people do go to hear him, and would not miss a subsequent opportunity, on any account; and for you to form such an unfavourable, and unjust judgment of a servant of God, without even hearing him for yourself, is alike discreditable to your intelligence and your honesty. Now, Mrs. D., go and hear him to-night, and then we will talk about the preacher to-morrow." She consented, and that night the "Spirit's two-edged sword" pierced her heart, and she wept aloud, and begged us to pray for her. She soon afterwards found her Saviour, and became a happy intelligent witness for Christ.

Mr. James Roberts was absent from Graham's Town during my series of meetings there; but on his return, found so many of his friends and kindred converted to God, that he at once felt a desire to learn something more definitely about "this way," and hence came with the Graham's Town company to attend my meeting at Fort Beaufort. After a day or two of deep awakening, without much emotion, on his return from the Tuesday meeting in Heald Town, he turned aside in the woods alone to meditate and pray. He had been secretly very sceptical, and though blest with one of the best mothers to be found in any land, he was a great prodigal; but he had read Mr. Hamilton's "Metaphyics," and by the study of the constitution of his own mind; he was profoundly impressed with a kind of realizing belief in the existence, and power, and all pervading presence of his Maker. From that step, he logically worked out the fact, as a matter of faith in his mind, that such a Creator would certainly reveal His will to His creatures, and he accepted the Holy Scriptures as the revelation, meeting the demands of the case. Its delineations of human guilt, pollution, bondage, and condemnation, he felt to be true in his own experience. The Almighty Saviour revealed, according to God's descriptions of Him, and God's promises through Him, was exactly suited to the demands of his soul. When he fully realized these facts, as he was walking alone in the wild wood, he stopped, took off his hat, and said, "O, thou God, who made me, and redeemed me with the blood of Christ, I surrender my wicked soul to Thee, and I now accept Jesus Christ as my Saviour. If there is any mistake about this thing, it must be in Thy revelation concerning Him; but Thy statements are very clear, they are Thine own words, and I can't doubt them, and I do accept Christ as my Saviour, and entrust my whole soul to Him. I don't believe there can be any mistake or failure in the matter."

Soon after Brother Janion met him, and said,—

"Well, Brother Roberts, have you accepted Christ?"

"Yes, Mr. Janion, I have."

"Have you found peace in Him?"

"No, I have experienced no change in my feelings; but I have taken Christ as my Saviour, and shall trust Him till I die to save me from all my sins."

He maintained his position unwaveringly for three days, clinging to Jesus by simple faith, without much emotion, and without any relief, beyond the power to hold on, till the third night; then, while I was delivering a lecture on *St. Paul and his Times*, the witnessing and renewing power of the Spirit came upon him like a flood of light and glory, and his heart was filled with "unspeakable joy."

He became a man of Providence in connection with my mission among the Kaffirs. While I was working at Graham's Town, Mr. Alfred White, one of the oldest pioneers in the country, who lives on the "Umzimvubu River," in Kaffraria, nearly four hundred miles east of Graham's Town, persuaded me to go overland, through Kaffraria to Natal, instead of by sea, as I had contemplated. I did not then hope to be able to do much good, but I wanted to see the practical working of the Mission Stations among the heathen in their own country, and learn what I could.

I knew not how I should go, but Mr. White said he would meet me thirty miles west of the "Umzimvubu," and convey me hence across the river, and give me any assistance I might need, in getting on thence to Natal. He also made me a plan of travel, embracing the whole of the Wesleyan Missions in Kaffraria. A few days later we learned that Dumasi, Chief of the western tribe of the Amapondo, and Umhlonhlo, Chief of the Amapondumsi, were at war, and the Shawbury Station was just in the midst of it, and that the missionary and his family were in great jeopardy; we learned further that the eastern half of the Amapondo nation, under Chief Faku, were at war with the Amabacas, and that "Osborn" Mission Station, under the superintendence of Rev. C. White, brother to my friend Alfred, was the scene of great slaughter. So Mr. White said I could not travel through that district, and planned for me a more southerly route, leaving out the two troubled stations. I wrote to Cape Town to have my son, Stuart, who was recovering from his Australian illness, to join me, and bear me company, I then expected to have to buy horses, and go on the independent line.

My friend, Rev. John Richards, of Port Elizabeth, was not very well pleased with the change in my plan, and would fain have persuaded me to give it up. He exhibited an array of all the difficulties as follows:—" We shall be intensely disappointed in your not returning here to preach our missionary sermons, and hold another series of services, which we believe God would own and bless; but apart from this, I think you have not been wisely advised. Much precious time and labour will be comparatively wasted by a journey through Kaffirland to Natal. To me it appears that your calling is especially to the English-speaking portion of the population of this country; the natives will be benefited indirectly. How are you going to travel through Kaffirland to Natal? How long will it take you? You cannot remain on each station for a series of services; if so, poor Mrs. Taylor may hope to see you sometime, if the Lord will. Then how are you going to ford the rivers? How is your baggage to be conveyed? You will have difficulties before you, which will be new to you; possibly, you may surmount them if time enough be allowed you. Think, my brother, think. I believe you would act most wisely in coming back here, after the tour I have marked out for you; then, after helping us, go by sea to Natal." I felt a great desire to accommodate Brother Richards, for he had been very kind to me; but I had not promised to return, and now firmly believed it would be more for the glory of God to go through Kaffraria, and the difficulties were nothing to me, since others had so often overcome them, on errands of much less importance.

When I was at Annshaw, I made arrangements with Brother Lamplough, to have Charles Pamla go with me through Kaffirland as my interpreter. At Fort Beaufort, a week later, the Lord provided me a "dragoman," in the person of my friend Mr. James Roberts, who hearing of my contemplated trip, came the next day after his conversion to God, and asked me to allow him the pleasure of furnishing conveyance and horses, and of driving me to Natal. Under the circumstances I could not deny him "the pleasure," but thankfully accepted his kind offer.

The Lord not only selected me a man from the fruits of the Fort Beaufort revival for my Kaffrarian tour, but raised up others to remain in the "Fort" for home defence, and the aggressive work of the Church. One of the converts has become a useful Class-leader and Exhorter; another, who is a Member of Parliament, has become a Local Preacher; and the work has gone on, I learn from Brother Wilson, and from other sources, very prosperously in Fort Beaufort, Alice, and other parts of the circuit. But while many were saved, some, by resistance of the Spirit's call, we fear have perished. I remember well one man who became so interested in our meetings at Fort Beaufort, that he accompanied us to Heald Town, and witnessed one of the most extraordinary displays of the saving power of the Spirit I ever saw, and was greatly awakened, and almost persuaded to be a Christian, but, so far as we could learn, refused to accept Christ. A short time afterwards he was found dead in his room. Of course no one knew the poor fellow's heart; but had he accepted Christ, as many of his neighbours did, and "witnessed a good confession," it would have been a sure thing for himself, and a great comfort to surviving friends.

An extract from a letter written me by Rev. Brother Wilson, dated Nov. 14th, 1866, may serve to illustrate the further progress of the work of God in Fort Beaufort: "The work in this circuit has been great and glorious. At our last Quarterly Meeting we had a net increase of thirty-eight members and sixty on trial. Besides there has been a very delightful work among the natives here, and many of them have been enabled to rejoice in Christ their Sviour. The testimony of some is exceedingly pleasing. A case or two was rather striking: Two native girls, who were servants in the same family, were convinced of sin; one of them came to my house to receive instruction; I talked to her and prayed with her, but she got no rest for her soul. I left her, and Mrs. Wilson went to her, and while she was praying with her the poor girl found Jesus. Her joy was unspeakably great. She fell on her knees and kissed Mrs. Wilson's feet, and then crawled to the young woman who came with her and kissed her feet, and when I came she fell down and kissed mine, and so overwhelmed with rapturous joy and so humble, that she knew not how to express it. Her fellow native servant was in great distress, but did not get relief so quickly, I found her in an agony at the penitent-rail, and in her bitter confession of sin, she said, 'That shawl I bought at Mullett's—that shawl! that shawl!'

"'What about it?' I inquired.

"'O, Sir, part of the money for that shawl was stolen; I stole one and threepence of it from my mistress. I'll pay my mistress, I'll pay her all, I'll pay her double!' Her mistress was an unconverted woman, would receive no money, but forgave her freely. Then the poor girl took the shawl, tore it to shreds and burnt it. She had a hard struggle, but at last the dark cloud of guilt and sin rolled away, and she was made happy in Jesus her Saviour.

"We have formed two extra classes here among the English, and two for the natives. I have made Brother Shaw" (a merchant who was saved at our series) "an Exhorter and Leader, and he is a very active, zealous man, quite disposed for liberal things. His wife and mother are now members of our Church. Mr. Ayliff, who was saved just after you left, is now on the Local Preacher's plan. Mr. Elliott is going on well, and prays in the prayer-meetings. His place is now a Temperance Hotel. We have a fresh class in Alice, and it is a very interesting one. Mr. Harper is the Leader. Truly we have great cause of thankfulness to God for the rich blessings He hath bestowed upon us here. A glorious visitation has come to this land."

INSTITUTION AND CHAPEL AT HEALD TOWN.

CHAPTER XI.

HEALD TOWN.

HEALD TOWN, called in honour of James Heald, Esq., Treasurer of the Wesleyan Missionary Society, is a large Fingoe settlement and Mission Station, six miles distant from Fort Beaufort. This is the site of the largest Industrial School established under the patronage of Sir George Grey. The accompanying cut, from a photograph taken on the spot, will represent, on a small scale, the School buildings and Mission Chapel. "The principal building is two hundred and twenty feet in length, and fifty in width; there are also two wings extending to the rear, each ninety feet in length. It is built of brick, on a stone foundation, the roof is of slate from Wales. The floor of the verandah, which extends along the whole front of the building, is several feet above the ground. The internal arrangements afford spacious apartments for the governor, chaplain, and their families, with large and airy dormitories, school, and work-rooms, refectory, kitchens, &c., for the accommodation of a large number of boys and girls who were boarded, clothed, educated, and trained to various industrial pursuits." The exact statistics of the cost of these buildings, the annual appropriations, and the number of pupils trained in this establishment, I have not been able to get; but the following figures, furnished me by Rev. William Sargent, Wesleyan Missionary, in charge of it when I was there, will furnish the facts with sufficient approximate correctness for our purpose. The cost of the buildings, paid by the Government, through Sir George Grey, was about £7,000. The Government appropriation, which was subsidized by the Wesleyan Society, was about £1,000 per annum for about nine years. While this appropriation was continued, the school, under the administration of the memorable missionary, Rev. John Ayliff, contained about eighty boarded scholars, and an addition of nearly two hundred day-scholars, making an aggregate of nearly three hundred, and was going on prosperously, but when Sir George Grey was removed to New Zealand, about three years ago, the Government appropriation was partially withdrawn from that and kindred institutions, and between the removal of their liberal patron by the Government, and of their devoted missionary by death, the Heald Town institution came to grief. The boarding and industrial departments, from a want of funds were abandoned.

A day-school has been kept up with success. It contained, at the time of my visit, two hundred day-scholars, conducted by Mr. T. Templer, head teacher, a fine spirited brother, and I believe a successful educator, assisted by Siko Radas, a young native teacher. They have also three schools taught by native teachers at three different "out-stations" connected with this mission establishment. The whole cost of these schools at the present time is £322 per annum, of which the Government pays £252; and the Society £70. Some thousands of natives have here, from first to last, been taught, not only to read their own language, but the elements of an English education.

Rev. Wm. Impey, during his recent visit to England, appealed strongly to the Missionary Committee, and not in vain, to authorize the establishment of a High School, and Theological Institution at Heald Town. James Heald, Esq., gave five hundred pounds towards the enterprise, and Mr. Impey's success was such that the District Meeting in Graham's Town, last January, resolved to carry it into effect. The following is a statement of their action, furnished to me by Rev. Wm. Sargent, in a recent letter. as follows:—"Our District Meeting decided to form a training institution at Heald Town to include two or three classes of agents.

"1. Men for the full work of the ministry, and pastorate.

"2. Native evangelists, who shall have no fixed pastorate, but be employed in going from place to place preaching the Gospel.

"3. Young men as schoolmasters for the native schools.

"It was also agreed to move the press from Mount Coke to Heald Town. Mr. Appleyard goes to Heald Town in charge of the press. Mr. Lamplough was appointed to superintend the institution, and take charge of the native agents; a better supply could not been have got in the district. Bro. Lamplough possesses peculiar abilities for such a work, his whole soul is in it."

I firmly believe myself that Bro. Lamplough is the man for that responsible post, for he will teach them how to win souls to Christ, and administer good discipline in the Church of God.

The Lord, in mercy, help him, and make of him an Elijah, and make his "school of the prophets" an hundred-fold more effective than that of Bethel or Mount Carmel!

The Wesleyan chapel at Heald Town, which will seat about eight hundred natives, is a cruciform in shape, the transverse portion of which, with a front vestibule, is seen in the accompanying engraving.

Rev. Wm. Sargent, the missionary at the time of my visit, was brought up in the colony, and having been in the mission-work for many years, is quite at home in the native language, manners, and customs; he is a true friend to the natives, and an earnest missionary. He removed his whole family to Fort Beaufort, so that they all might enjoy the benefit of our week of special services there. He had written me requesting a visit to his natives in Heald Town, but not having the natives in my plan of appointments, and having engaged to labour with the whites for weeks a-head, I could not promise, but at our first interview I arranged to give them a week-day service. So on Tuesday the 19th of June, Brother Sargent took me up with his cart and pair, and set off for Heald Town. As we pass the lines of Fort Beaufort we at once see the white mission buildings before described, six miles distant. It is a beautiful sight through a narrow valley, bounded by high hills on each side, rising to the altitude of respectable mountains, but the town itself, which, besides the school buildings and chapel, is composed almost entirely of native huts, is perched above the head of this beautiful vale on the plateau of a transverse range of little mountains. The scattering huts, seen in the cut, represent but a small part of the native town, the body of which is hid from view by an intervening hill. In our little journey, we pass over a broad undulating valley, rich and grassy. To our left are several native "kraals," surrounded by fields of maize, pumpkins, and Kaffir-corn. Ascending the narrow vale, we cross many times a bold mill-stream, the banks of which are lined with wild olives, willows, and a great variety of shrubbery and vines, forming in some places a dense jungle, which furnish a grand retreat for the monkeys. Half-a-dozen of them made a stand in the road before us long enough to inquire "who are you, and where are you going ?" and then scampered off into their native wilds.

The mountains to our left are partly cultivated by the Fingoes, and we see some fine herds of their cattle. The mountains to our right are rugged, but beautified by a thick undergrowth of the wild African aloes just coming into bloom, with stately sentinels of the euphorbia-tree. We have a long, rocky steep ascent from this valley to the high land of the town; the surrounding scenery, with the high cliffs at the head of the valley, just below the town, is not only beautiful, but grand. When we arrived, a little before the hour appointed, the chapel, with sittings for about 800, was packed with about 1,000 natives and twenty whites.

The head teacher, Mr. T. Templer met us, and said, "We have Barnabas here, from Graham's Town, he is a splendid interpreter, and we'll get him to interpret. He says he would rather not, as he's here on business, in his working clothes; but I'm sure he'll consent if we press it."

"Give me anybody else," I replied. "I tried him in Graham's Town, and he got his voice up an octave too high at the start, and sang out the whole sermon in two or three monotonous tones that did not suit me at all. He is a good fellow, and we must not hurt his feelings, but if you are not committed to him, and can give me any other Kaffir who can talk English, don't engage Barnabas."

"We are not committed to him, but consider him the best we can get. We have a Kaffir boy, my assistant teacher, who understands English, but he is not a professional interpreter."

"He's my boy; send him to me quickly, as our time is nearly up, and the people are waiting."

Brother Sargent immediately sent for him, and brought him into a private room in the "Institution," a real black boy, about twenty years old, five feet six inches in height, prominent forehead, good eye, pleasant countenance, a quiet, unobtrusive youth, a good singer, can write music, and play on the harmonium, but rather a feeble voice for addressing a large assembly—Siko Radas.

Brother Sargent said he had to celebrate a marriage, either before or after preaching. We at once arranged that Brother Sargent should open the service in the usual way, and attend to the marriage, and allow me that time for drilling my young interpreter.

I preached my sermon to Siko, and gave him a lecture on naturalness. We entered the church before the marriage ceremony was over. The bridal party were all black, but well dressed, and presented a very genteel appearance, and signed their names to the marriage records with self-possession and neatness of execution. The bride was covered from head to foot with a fine white veil.

The bridal party sat in the front form, just before us. I did not occupy the little pulpit, but stood beside my interpreter in the altar. Siko put my sentences into Kaffir very rapidly, but distinctly; and, as I learned, correctly. There was evidently an extraordinary power of the Holy Spirit resting on the audience during the preaching, but silence reigned, except the slight murmur of suppressed sobbing and tears. At the close of the preaching we dismissed the assembly, giving all who wished an opportunity to retire. The bridal party and a few others left.

Before we proceeded further with the prayer-meeting, I explained in Gospel simplicity, the way of salvation by faith, so that the seekers might intelligently come to Christ without further personal instruction. We then invited the seekers to come forward and occupy the forms from the front, as far back as might be necessary. They rushed forward with that violence which the kingdom of heaven suffereth, and many of "the violent took it by force" that day. At least three hundred seekers were down on their knees within a few minutes. They were all praying audibly, the floor was wet with tears, yet none seemed to be screaming louder than his neighbours. Brother Sargent seemed, for a few moments, fearful, thinking it might lead to confusion, but I reminded him of the undeniable evidences, that God the Holy Spirit was moving in the matter, and however much of human dross and infirmity might be mixed into such a mass of superstition and sin, the people had been well instructed, and the Holy Spirit was fully competent directly, and through the agencies available, to manage the business, and we will work with Him, but let us not interfere with His work. Brother Sargent at once heartily acquiesced in my views, which were supported so thoroughly by Scripture teaching and precedent, and by the logic of facts before our eyes, that we could do but little else than "stand still and see the salvation of God." We had Brothers Janion, Attwell, Webb, Roberts, and other Graham's Town brethren present. They seemed a little confused at the first shock, for my meetings at Graham's Town, as in every other place among the whites, were conducted in quietness; but in a few minutes they were re-assured by their faith in God, and the power of His Gospel, and entered into the work with their characteristic earnestness. In the recess there were fourteen whites down on their knees, as seekers, so that the brethren who could not speak the Kaffir, found ample employment among them.

As fast as the seekers entered into liberty, they were conducted to seats, first in the right wing of the chapel, and then in the left, and then in front, where they gave their testimony to their minister, Rev. Brother Sargent, who wrote down their names in his pastoral book. The services closed at 4 P.M., having extended through five hours. Some of us, however, went into Brother Templer's house about 2 P.M., and took in haste an excellent lunch which good Sister Templer had prepared for us, and immediately returned to "the front." Seven whites reported themselves among the converts, having, during the service, embraced Christ, and found salvation in Him. Six of them were one whole family, a grandmother, her daughter, son-in-law, and three children. It was a touching scene to see the poor old woman in the centre, and her children and grandchildren embracing her, and with flowing tears praising God, and telling her how happy they were in the love of Jesus.

Of the natives, Brother Sargent recorded the names of one hundred and thirty-nine, who professed to find peace with God during our service of five hours. We then hastened back to Fort Beaufort, where I preached, and had a glorious work among the whites that night.

On Thursday morning, the 21st of June, Brother Sargent, in company with Mrs. Rev. T. Guard, drove me again to Heald Town, according to the announcement made the preceding Tuesday. When we arrived, Brother Barnabas came to me and said he was sorry he had declined to interpret on Tuesday, but if I would consent he do so on that occasion. He is a good man, and remembering that I had not learned to preach through an interpreter, when I tried to preach through him in Graham's Town, and that the fault might therefore be more in myself than in him, I replied, "I am well satisfied with Siko, and would not propose a change, but if Siko chooses

to have you take his place, I have no objection."
Siko readily deferred to his elder brother, and Barnabas became my spokesman. While Brother Sargent was opening the service, I was privately preaching to Barnabas. He is a tall lean brother, not very black, well-acquainted with the English language, a professional interpreter for years, and famous for his exact literal rendering of a discourse into Kaffir. He is now well-advanced in years. Notwithstanding his long experience as an interpreter, I took the liberty of giving him a good talk on naturalness, and in return learned from him what I could in so short a time about some of the customs and peculiar sins of the Kaffirs.

We went before our crowded audience fully equipped, trusting to the immediate presence and saving power of the Holy Spirit. Barnabas was ready, natural, and effective. The prayer-meeting was conducted as on the first day. Among the seekers were many aged persons. The awful presence and melting power of the Holy Spirit on this occasion surpassed anything I had ever witnessed before. I tried to find an illustration of what I saw and felt, by the historic fact, that in creation's morn, "The spirit moved upon the face of the waters," and brought order out of chaos: I thought of what Ezekiel saw, and thus described, after giving an account of his vision of the valley of dry bones, "Thus saith the Lord God unto these bones; Behold, I will cause breath to enter into you, and ye shall live: and I will lay sinews upon you, and will bring up flesh upon you, and cover you with skin, and put breath in you, and ye shall live; and ye shall know that I am the Lord. So I prophesied as I was commanded: and as I prophesied, there was a noise, and behold a shaking, and the bones came together, bone to his bone. And when I beheld, lo, the sinews and the flesh came up upon them, and the skin covered them above: but there was no breath in them. Then said he unto me, Prophesy unto the wind, prophesy, son of man, and say to the wind, Thus saith the Lord God; Come from the four winds, O breath, and breathe upon these slain, that they may live. So I prophesied as he commanded me, and the breath came into them, and they lived, and stood up upon their feet, an exceeding great army." I thought of the waiting disciples in that upper room on Mount Zion, when "suddenly there came a sound from heaven as of a rushing mighty wind, and it filled all the house where they were sitting," and the glory that immediately followed. "The wind bloweth where it listeth, and thou hearest the sound thereof, but canst not tell whence it cometh nor whither it goeth."

The atmosphere, the symbol of the Holy Ghost whom God hath sent to administer the bounteous provision of salvation to a perishing world. The air, everywhere present, enveloping the world, mysterious, invisible, yet always abiding with us, now at rest, then moving in the gentle zephyr, then in the breeze, then in the gale, then in the hurricane. This mighty Spirit of God abiding with us, and to "abide with us for ever," and yet adjusting His mighty power to the laws of the human mind, and moral nature.

I realized by faith on that occasion what I never can explain, even with the help of this Scripture teaching. If the dispensation of the Spirit is to extend to "that great and notable day of the Lord, when He shall judge the quick and the dead," and if the ever-abiding Spirit is as available now, and as willing to fulfil His mighty mission now, as He was on the day of Pentecost, why is the world not saved? I wept over the defective faith, and ineffective methods, of the Church, and thought how the Holy Spirit is grieved in not having suitable agencies for the successful prosecution, and consummation of His work, according to God's purpose, and most adequate provisions in Christ. As I saw dead souls by the score stand up by the power of the Spirit, till they became like an army around us, and heard them witnessing to the saving mercy of Jesus in their hearts, I felt the keen retort of the South Australian black fellow, "at Lake Alexandrina, on the Murray." A man whom this native had known for twenty years was warning him for the first time against the danger of losing his soul, and the sable son of nature said with great vehemence, "If you know all this time that black fellow going to hell, why you no tell black fellow till now?" A majority of those before me, to be sure, had been born and brought up under Gospel teaching; their old friend and minister, who led them out of Kaffir bondage, had lived and died among them at that very spot; in the chapel before us, was a slab to his memory, on which it was stated that the last prayer he ever offered, just as he was stepping into Death's dark river, was that God would bless and save his "dear Fingoes;" his prayer was now being answered among the ones to whom he last preached, but I thought of the millions beyond, who have not to this day heard of Jesus. Oh, I felt that, dearly as I loved my country, my conference, my home, and, above all, my dear family, if it were the Lord's will to adjust my relations satisfactorily in regard to those sacred interests, and call me to this work, I would hail it as a privilege, to lead a band of Black native evangelists through the African Continent, till "Ethiopia" would not only "stretch out her hands," but embrace Christ, through the power of the Holy Ghost, from the Cape of Good Hope to the Mediterranean.

At the close of this second service at Heald Town, Rev. Brother Sargent reported the names of 167 native, and three European, converts, during the service of five hours, making an aggregate for the two services of 306 natives, and ten whites saved, "by the washing of regeneration, and renewing of the Holy Ghost, shed forth abundantly upon us, through Christ Jesus our Lord." These, added to the sixty-five Europeans at Fort Beaufort, will make a total of 381 souls brought to God, and "justified freely by His grace" during the space of five days. The name of each one was written down by the ministers in charge, after a personal examination, and the testimony of almost every one was clear and satisfactory. My instructions to the pastors were, that if they should find any with whose experience they were not satisfied, they should kindly send them back to the altar of prayer, and have them continue to seek the Lord till they should obtain pardon, and the satisfactory "witness of the Spirit.".

Of course we cannot see the hearts of any, but in connection with clear Gospel teaching, and all the outward signs of awakening, repentance, and faith in Christ, followed by the distinct testimony of each convert, we take their names that they may be gotten immediately into the classes, and receive the pastor's care.

A shepherd, on the purchase of a large addition to his flock, would not be satisfied to allow them to wander off, without even identifying, and so marking them, as at least to know them himself. His care would extend to every little lamb, and the weak ones he would often bear in his bosom. At the close of our service at Heald Town, I gave the Local Preachers, Leaders, and members generally, an address on the care necessary to the healthy growth of the young converts.

If the stirring incidents and scenes of those two services could be recorded, they would fill a volume;

but they were really indescribable; I will, however, for further illustration of that great work of God, insert the following letter, written by the Rev. Brother Sargent to the secretaries in London, which appears in the *Missionary Notices*, for October, 1866.

"Tuesday, June 19th.—What a day! I know not how to record it. I never witnessed anything which so reminded me of what is recorded of the Day of Pentecost in the 2nd of Acts. At 9.30 A.M., I started with Mr. Taylor for Heald Town. The people had already collected in the chapel, and were engaged in an earnest prayer-meeting. Mr. Taylor addressed them, through an interpreter, from the words, "But ye shall receive power after that the Holy Ghost is come upon you." The effect was manifest. The truth told with wondrous power on the congregation. At the close, those who were desirous of seeking the Lord were exhorted to stand up, and then kneel round the communion-rails. About three hundred fell simultaneously upon their knees, among whom there was a considerable number of Europeans, many of whom had come from Beaufort. There was now a great weeping. At first all seemed chaos and confusion. Even the native Local Preachers and Class Leaders were confounded; and it was some time before I could get them into working order. The first paroxysm of excitement having subsided, the native agents distributed themselves all over the chapel, speaking to, and praying with, the penitents. The distress of some souls was extremely great, but after awhile one after another entered into the liberty of the children of God, passing from the excess of grief to the excess of joy. The scene was indescribable, as first one and then another rose to praise God, with eyes sparkling, and countenance beaming with joy, and tears flowing in copious streams from their eyes. One exclaimed, 'Satan is conquered! Satan is conquered! Satan is conquered!" Another, a very old woman, lifted her eyes and hands towards heaven, and exclaimed, for five or ten minutes, at the top of her voice, " He is holy! He is holy! He is holy!' A very old man, who had been in an agony of distress, when set at liberty, exclaimed, ' My Father has set me free! My Father has set me free! My Father has set me free!' These are merely specimens. We were five hours hard at work; and, at the close, 140 persons professed to have a obtained a sense of the pardoning love of God.

"Thursday, 21st.—Returned to Heald Town in company with Mr. Taylor; a great number of Europeans following us from Fort Beaufort. The chapel was crowded to excess. Mr. Taylor preached a very searching and powerful sermon on the 'Ten Commandments:' After the sermon those seeking salvation were invited to the communion-rail. I suppose more than 200 fell upon their knees, crying aloud for mercy; sobs, and sighs, and groans filled the chapel. After the first burst of powerful emotion, I got the Local Preachers and Class Leaders to distribute themselves among the penitents. After a while, the shouts of the pardoned strangely mingled with the cries of the penitents. We continued the meeting for five hours; and at the close 160 professed to have 'found peace and joy through believing,' making, in the two days, 300 who had professedly 'obtained peace.' (This report does not include the white converts.)

"I am happy to say that the work is still progressing; and we seldom hold a meeting for inquirers without a number coming forward, and several of them getting into liberty. These have not numerically increased our Church members, as much as some might suppose, as the majority of those who have 'found peace' were already members of society, but had never obtained a clear sense of pardon, or, having obtained it in years gone by, had lost it through unfaithfulness. Yet I may add, that a considerable number consists of young people who have been brought up in our Sabbath- and day-schools. These I am now forming into juvenile classes. There are still many seekers in the congregation, especially among the young; and at the close of every evening service the bushes and rocks about the station are for hours vocal with the prayers of those who are earnestly pleading for mercy. Since this work began the desire for learning among the young people of the station is something wonderful. Children now came to the day-school who never came before; and the numbers have been almost doubled. The difficulty now is to find books and teachers for them.

"The work has not been confined to the natives; but the few European families living on the station have likewise 'been made partakers of the benefit.' Nearly all who were not members before have now joined the Society, and are rejoicing in a sense of the Divine favour. Several European children have been formed into an interesting class; and not satisfied with this, they have, at their own instance, formed themselves into a juvenile prayer-meeting, which I allow them to conduct in their own way, without the presence or interference of any adult."

An extract from a letter I received from Brother Sargent, dated July 17th, nearly a month after I left, may serve to illustrate the continued progress of this work in Heald Town:—"I am thankful to say that the good work of the Lord is still progressing favourably at Heald Town. About sixty more have found peace since you left, and I have no doubt but that there would have been a much larger number, but for the fact, that I have had to be away so often, that the penitent meetings have not been held so frequently as I could wish. There is much earnestness manifested among the people, both old and young. You would be amazed and delighted to hear their cries of a night till after nine or ten o'clock; and, in some cases, till daylight in the morning, pleading for the pardon of their sins. The valleys and rocks below the mission-house are literally vocal with the cries of penitents, morning, noon, and night. You will be glad to be informed that last Saturday, in our Local Preacher's meeting, the local brethren, in receiving several new candidates on the Local Preacher's plan, passed a resolution, that no one using Kaffir beer, or any other strong drink, shall be allowed to exercise the office of Local Preacher among them. Next Saturday the Class-leaders intend passing the resolution respecting themselves; not allowing any to exercise the office of Class Leader in Heald Town, who will not give up the drinking of Kaffir beer, and all other intoxicating drinks."

The Kaffir beer is made of maize or Indian corn. It was considered by many good people a wholesome nourishing drink, and as the Kaffirs do not usually have tea or coffee, the Kaffir beer was tolerated on the mission-stations; but its use wrought all manner of mischief, especially at the Kaffir beer-feasts, which are very common among the Heathen Kaffirs. resulting in drunkenness and all its consequent evils. The total abstinence reform movement commenced among the Kaffirs at Annshaw about five years ago. Charles Pamla was one of the leaders in the movement, and endured a great deal of persecution from the old school beer-drinking members; but he never struck his colours, and now all the leading men at Annshaw, Heald Town, and other stations are fully with him. I was very sorry that Brother Sargent's engagements called him away, so that the work in Heald Town was not pushed with the same vigour as at Annshaw. The next Sabbath, after I was there, he was, according to a previous engagement, preaching at Adelaide, twenty miles distant, and soon after that he was called away to King William's Town, fifty miles distant, to take Mrs. Sargent to see her dying father, Mr. George Impey. Those poor penitents crying day and night in the woods, should have been brought at once to Jesus, the only Saviour of sinners.

Recurring to that memorable Thursday once more, I may add that Mr. Templer, the native teacher, though not a poet, perpetrated a poetic effusion, which was published and pronounced good; so much of it relates to myself, that it is hardly safe for me to insert it, yet, as its descriptive power may arrest the attention of some poetic reader and do good, I may be excused for copying thirteen of the twenty-three verses of the poem. Beholding the scene, with his eye alternately on the preacher and the audience, he says:—

Equipp'd, with "the whole armour of his God;"
Prepared to fight the battles of his Lord;
His willing "feet, with Gospel peace well shod,"
And holding in his hand, the "Spirit's sword."

"The righteous breastplate, and faith's mighty shield,"
Adorn'd his front, and turn'd hell's dart aside;
The law of "truth," which God to man reveal'd,
"Begirt his loins," and was his strength and guide.

"Salvation's helmet," did his head secure;
   His Captain's name, his "forehead" render'd bold;
Eternal truth, his mind did richly store,
   And thence he drew his weapons "new and old."

With simple, earnest, "supplicating prayer,"
   And labour hard, he made his armour shine:
Did all thy servants, Lord, such 'quipment wear,
   The fallen race of man, would soon be Thine.

He saw a motley throng before him rise,
   Whose blood 'neath skins of various hues did run;
Yet souls alike redeem'd with highest price—
   The precious blood of God's beloved Son.

His voice, "like trumpet loud," God's law, declar'd,
   On Sina given, was "holy, just, and good:"
With this, the lives of old and young compar'd,
   And then their guilt in crimson colours stood.

"Now think awhile," said he, "let conscience live;
   Yourselves your judges be; then thus inquire—
Can God be just, and yet my sins forgive,
   Or must I dwell with the devouring fire?"

With speed more swift than lightning's swiftest dart,
   His soul flew up in silent, earnest prayer,
To God the Holy Ghost, to break the heart—
   Convince, and start the penitential tear.

He did his work—conviction seiz'd the soul,
   With godly grief; then prostrate on the ground
They fell, and tears of penitence did roll—
   One Pentecostal scene was spread around.

"The powers of darkness" raged; "it was their hour.
   Souls, long in bondage held, and captive led,
Were struggling to be freed, from Satan's power,
   Which held them bound, though Christ had bruis'd his head.

With tongue of seraphic fire, the herald cried,
  " Believe in Christ—this is the record true—
To save a guilty world, the Saviour died—
  He tasted death for *all*—he died for YOU."

A ray of light appear'd; then Satan, thron'd,
  His greatest efforts made, to " keep in peace
His house and goods " which he so long had own'd :
  But Jesus came and gave the soul release.

Then shouts of joy, and songs of highest praise,
  To God the Father, Son, and Spirit rose;
And others heard the vivifying lays,
  Were pierc'd and felt the guilty sinner's throes.

As we returned from Heald Town to Fort Beaufort, accompanied by a large number of Europeans on horseback, and many natives on foot, though we drove rapidly to be in time for the evening appointment, some of the black fellows, happy in the Lord, and light on foot as Elijah before the chariot of Ahab, ran so fast, as to keep up with us most of the distance of six miles.

Passing a jungle, we saw a mob of monkeys perched on the thickly-matted tops of the trees, clearly defined above the branches. They seemed surprised to see so many persons in their unfrequented woods, and stood erect looking at us till we passed out of sight.

Mrs. Thomas Guard witnessed all the scenes of that day, and possessing a very refined taste, a nice sense of propriety, and not favourable to noisy religious exercises, I was a little surprised to find her enthusiastic in her expressions of admiration of all she had seen and heard. I had observed that she looked on and wept, and smiled alternately, during most of the service, and as we drove along she said, "I have seen most of the crowned heads of Europe, was at the opening of the Great Exhibition in 1851, have witnessed, and felt the thrilling effects of the most imposing pageants of royalty, but I never saw anything for sublimity and soul-stirring effect to compare with the scenes of this day. I would not have missed the meeting of to-day for anything that could be offered."

"But dear me," says one, "such sudden work as that must be very transient—over three hundred persons professing conversion at two day's services, and working weekdays too, why it must have been a straw fire that will soon die out."

Indeed, after so long a preparation, why should not "the Lord whom ye seek come suddenly in His temple?" Was not that the way the Holy Spirit did it when He first entered on His great work in Jerusalem? If He hath changed His methods of working, it is a wonder He hath not informed us, so that we may adjust ourselves to them. That was a quick work by which three thousand souls were saved in one day, under the first Gospel sermon they ever heard in their lives, and yet thirty-three years afterwards St. Luke testified to their steadfastness, saying, "They continued steadfastly in the apostle's doctrine, and fellowship, and in breaking of bread and in prayers."

To illustrate the genuine character and permanency of this work, of the same pentecostal Spirit, at Heald

Town, so far as we can in the time which has since elapsed, I may be allowed to copy part of a letter written me by Rev. Wm. Sargent, who has recently been sent to Graham's Town circuit, but who is best prepared to testify of this work, nearly ten months after my visit. His letter is dated Graham's Town, April the 4th, 1867, in which he says:—

I am thankful to be able to say, that up to the time of my leaving Heald Town, and since my departure, the work has been widening and deepening. At the time of our District Meeting in January, besides about two hundred old members, who had either obtained for the first time a sense of their acceptance with God, or had recovered what they had lost, and many who had been raised to a higher platform of Christian experience, there were three hundred and fifty-eight, principally young persons, who had been received on trial, most of whom had been made happy in God's pardoning love. With the experience of some of these young people I was truly astonished at the Quarterly Visitation, describing their conversion to God in a way that would have been impossible, had they not been taught of God. Out of about *four hundred* professing conversion to God, not above *two or three persons* had, up to the time of my leaving Heald Town, discontinued meeting in class. This, I may remark, has been a striking peculiarity in the recent revival during your visit in these parts. Immediately after every previous revival, there was always a considerable falling away; but the cases of defalcation, in this instance, have been exceedingly few compared with the numbers brought in.

In reference to the effects of the recent work of God at Heald Town, I may remark,—

1st. The members of the church have all been greatly quickened, and raised to a higher standard in the Divine life than they previously enjoyed.

2nd. The Local Preachers and Class Leaders have been aroused to a sense of their duties and responsibilities, and have devoted themselves, with renewed energy, to the work of the Lord. Some of them, in addition to their ordinary work, have associated a number of the new converts with themselves, and have gone from hamlet to hamlet preaching the Gospel, and conducting prayer-meetings. These meetings have often resulted in the conversion of individuals who seemed to be otherwise inaccessible.

3rd. New Leaders and Local Preachers have come forward in a way we never anticipated, and have helped to carry on the work of the Lord with efficiency and success.

4th. Our native agents have shown a determination to battle with the remains of heathen customs, towards which they were formerly disposed to be lenient, such as polygamy, circumcision, the drinking of Kaffir beer, etc. They seem determined to purge out of themselves, and out of the society the very last elements of "the old leaven, that they may be a new lump." In respect to the very injurious custom of Kaffir beer-drinking, the Local Preachers first, and then the Class Leaders afterwards, bound themselves by a solemn pledge that, for the influence of their example, they would not henceforth use this pernicious drink, and that they would do all they could to put it down, both in and out of the church. Had it been in their power, many of them would have gone so far as to make it a condition of membership, allowing no one to be a member of the church who would not consent to give it up, in every form and degree. But others felt that this could not be done without an enactment of Conference, which should render "total abstinance" a *sine qua non* of membership throughout all our societies. (Mr. Wesley's enactment in the " general rules of our societies," has been sufficient to make "total abstainers" of all the Methodists of America, numbering in the aggregate two millions of members, and fourteen thousand travelling ministers. The poor Kaffir Christians feel something of the same apprehension of danger in tampering with drinking customs—which have killed their tens of thousands, to the tens of hundreds slaughtered by the sword—that Mr. Ashbury's preachers felt in America nearly a hundred years ago, when they made Mr. Wesley's rule practical and effective, prohibiting the " buying or selling spirituous liquors; or drinking them, unless in cases of extreme necessity "—by " spirituous liquors " Americans understand all intoxicating drinks, wine, Kaffir beer, and all the rest; by the terms " extreme necessity," they understand the medical necessity of sick persons.

5th. The Sabbath schools and day schools, in a short time, almost doubled their members, and the thirst for learning among the young people became most manifest in an unprecedented application for school-books, and that from children upon the adjacent hamlets, who previously cared for none of these things.

Many of these young people formed themselves into prayer-meetings, which they hold in the fields alone. One Sabbath afternoon, not long before leaving Heald Town, I was walking a little below the institution towards the 'kloof,' (a deep gorge or ravine) when I saw some twenty or thirty native children making their way down into the 'bush.' I was suspicious that they were meeting for purposes of play, and therefore watched them. I soon found, to my agreeable surprise, that they were a company of Sabbath-school children, met for a prayer-meeting, spending an hour after school in alternate prayer and singing. The six or eight European children at Heald Town, besides attending class, formed themselves into a select prayer-meeting.

My little girl of nine years, after having cried to be permitted to meet in class herself, went from house to house among the Europeans upon the station, and invited all their children about her own age to a little room, the use of which she had obtained for that purpose, and formed them into a prayer-meeting.

One day she came to me saying, " Pa, what can I do for that poor sick man ? "

She had heard me speak of a sick native man, whom I had been visiting. I said,

" What do you mean, my dear ? "

" Oh," she replied, " I would like to do something for him ? "

I told her that she might go and buy a few groceries at the shop, and take them to him. She did so; but took her New Testament under her arm, and having given him the groceries, she read several portions of God's Word to him, and then asked him if he was happy. I knew nothing of it till the man told me himself, what a comfort it had been to him. This same man had been a vile backslider, but had been recovered during your visit to Heald Town. He now thought himself upon his deathbed, but was filled with the light of God's countenance, and anticipating a speedy admission into His presence, where "there is fulness of joy." He, however, subsequently recovered, and is " adorning the doctrine of Christ his Saviour." * * *

Our last District Meeting was one of the most harmonious and profitable we have yet had. The reports of the different circuits were such as to warm and encourage every heart, and all the brethren seemed as if they were baptized afresh for their great work. A record was entered upon the Minutes of your visit among us, and it was resolved to hold special meetings in all the circuits in May or June next, to seek for another revival and still greater extension of God's work among us. We are looking for great things. I know not why we should not have constantly repeated baptisms of the Spirit. Why not?

CHAPTER XII.

SOMERSET EAST.

On Friday morning, the 22nd of June, Brother Sargent, in company with his son and daughter, drove me twenty miles with his cart and pair, to the village of Adelaide, on my way to Somerset, which is about eighty miles distant from Fort Beaufort. At half-past two P.M., I preached at Adelaide in the Presbyterian Church, Rev. Peter Davidson, pastor, with whom I dined. I had dined with his brother, the Rev. William Davidson, at his own house, in the town of "Clare," South Australia, and had become acquainted with another brother, Rev. James Davidson, King William's Town, British Kaffraria, so instead of strangers, we seemed to meet as friends. The Wesleyans have no society at Adelaide, but we have a few good men there, who, in the absence of their own Church, have united with Mr. Davidson. Mr. Francis King sent his cart and pair, to convey me that afternoon to Bedford, twenty miles further on my way, Brothers Sargent and Davidson accompanying. I was weary and allowed them to do all the talking.

brother Davidson gave us an interesting history of himself, and brother ministers, and their widowed mother, and how they struggled up the hill of difficulty, in acquiring an education, and preparing for the ministry. It was altogether a very interesting narrative. Brother Davidson is a very genial Scotchman, and I am told an earnest evangelical minister of the Gospel. The Dutch Reformed Church in Adelaide are building a church edifice there which will cost £25,000, and a minister's house to cost £3,000, altogether the sum of £28,000. The village is very small, but it is the centre of a large Dutch farming community. The Dutch, being the first European settlers in South Africa, own the majority of the best farms, and build very large churches in accessible centres, and put up small houses contiguous, for temporary home comfort during their sojourn at their "nag mals." The "nag mal," or "night meal," is the sacrament of the Lord's Supper, which is administered at their churches quarterly. The farmers, within a radius of twenty or thirty miles, attend on those occasions, with their families, and spend several days in religious duties, embracing the sacraments of baptism, and the Lord's Supper, preaching the Gospel, and confirmation; and a social reunion with their friends. For a sparsely settled pastoral country, like Southern Africa, I think it a very good arrangement indeed, and might be made very useful among the the Wesleyans, as a kind of "camp-meeting," to promote the spiritual life of the scattered country societies. The appointment for my preaching in Adelaide was circulated after our arrival, and a company of about sixty persons assembled, to whom, for the first and last time, I presented the offer of Christ as their only Saviour. Five months afterwards, Rev. Brother Sargent, in a letter to me, makes the following allusion to that occasion. "You will remember our visit to Adelaide, I feared it was rather discouraging to your own mind, having but a small attendance at the chapel, but I have heard of at least one young man by the name of Trollip, whose friends you met in Queen's Town, who was that day savingly impressed, and has since died happy in the Lord." In a letter dated April, 1857, Brother Sargent makes another allusion to that occasion, as follows: "Mr. Benjamin Trollip, whose soul was greatly blessed under your ministry at Queen's Town is lying upon his death-bed in Graham's Town, unspeakably happy in God. He is the father of the young man who was converted under your sermon at Adelaide, and died happy in the Lord shortly after."

BEDFORD is a small village with one little church, which is under the pastoral care of Rev. Mr. Solomon. Mr. Solomon was for many years a missionary to the Griquas, Adam Kok's Hottentots, and Dutch bastards, then near the Orange River, now in "Nomansland," Kaffraria. They are at present, and ever since their removal to their new home, without a missionary. Yet under the effect of former missionary teaching they have their chapels, and regular services among themselves. The Wesleyan Missionaries occasionally visit them, and administer the sacraments to them.

Mr. Solomon, after a separation of several years, had just returned from a visit to them, of several weeks. He is greatly interested in their welfare, and says, that but for his family relations he would go and live with them. Rev. Mr. Solomon is a brother of the celebrated Saul Solomon of Cape Town—celebrated for his littleness of stature, about three and a-half feet high, and for his greatness as a politician, and member of the Colonial Parliament, for literary and commercial enterprise, conducting a large paper in Cape Town, and a variety of business pursuits—the greatest man of his size, I suppose in the world. I preached for Rev. Mr. Solomon that night. His church, being the only one in the place is made up of all denominations," among whom are some excellent Wesleyans, especially Francis King, his brother, and their families.

The Kings are of the Graham's Town stock of Wesleyans, where their good old father still lives.

They are sheep and cattle farmers. Being native-born "Africandas," as the native Europeans are called, they have had many adventures, both in times of war and peace. Francis King said he and another young man were once travelling together to Namaqualand, to explore the copper mines (350 miles west of Cape Town). They were on horseback, but were unarmed. Away in the wilds, two hundred miles west of Cape Town, they were suddenly surrounded by a dozen "Bushmen," who seized the bridles of their horses and stopped them. "I knew," said King, "from their general character and their movements, that they designed to rob us, and perhaps kill us too, but fearing that we had concealed weapons they offered no violence except to hold us fast. My companion was greatly alarmed, and said, 'We're sure to be killed;' but I said, 'Jim, don't show the least fear, keep perfectly cool, and we may providentially find a way of escape.' After we had waited some time, a square, burly-looking fellow came up, having six toes on each foot, and joined the rest in holding on to our bridles and stirrup-leathers. I soon found that this six-toed fellow could speak a little Dutch, so I said to him, 'Take us to the water, we want to drink.' They immediately set off with us, holding our bridles on each side, and took us a mile or two to a spring. We dismounted, and holding our horses with one hand, managed to get a little water, for we were nearly famished. I talked to them familiarly all the time, as though I of course thought they were our friends. I told them I wanted to buy ostrich feathers, and I wanted them to go and get me some. Two of them ran away, and after an absence of nearly an hour came back with a few feathers. I paid for them, and said, 'This is not half enough; I want you all to go and bring me all the feathers you can get, and I'll pay you a good price for them,' so they all started off under the impulse of the moment to get feathers. As soon as they got out of sight, we mounted, and rode off for life. That was in the after part of the day. We travelled all that night, and till late in the P.M. of the next day before we stopped long enough to make a cup of tea. That afternoon as we passed along. I discovered a bees' nest in the rocks. Near sunset, over forty miles from where we left the Bushmen, we encamped for the night. We had just taken a cup of tea, and were talking of our narrow escape, when lo, the six-toed fellow and his party were upon us. They came and seated themselves in a circle around us, without saying a word. I talked Dutch to Six-toes, but he made no reply. I laughed and talked as though nothing had happened, or was likely to happen, while I was trying to invent a method of escape. I knew if we showed fear, or if they should find out that we were unarmed, it would be all up with us. All at once I thought of the bees' nest, and said I to Six-toes, 'Wouldn't you like for me to show you a bees' nest? You all must be hungry after your journey, and I'm sure a little honey will do you good.' Then he began to talk a little, but in a very surly spirit. I said, 'Come with me, and I'll show you a bees' nest, and you can get a good feed of honey.' I got up and started, and they followed Jim said, 'Frank, you are not going to trust yourself alone with those savages, I hope.'

"I replied, 'Get the horses ready, and take them to the other side of the ridge beyond the bees' nest, and wait there till I come.' I took the Bushmen to the nest, and they all at once began in great haste to work their way into the rocks, to get the honey; finally, one of them drew out a fine piece of comb, full of honey, and I ran up and snatched it, and began to eat. They looked at me, and began to mutter, but said I, 'Dig away, you'll find plenty of honey in there,' so they went to work with greater eagerness than ever, while I began to walk backwards and forwards, eating a little honey, and humming a tune, watching my opportunity. While their attention was taken in their scramble, each trying to get his full share of the honey, I got out of sight, and ran for life. The horses were ready, and we put them up to their best speed for about thirty miles. In almost utter exhaustion, we then off-saddled and knee-haltered our horses, and half-buried ourselves in the sand and soon fell asleep.

"We had not been long asleep, as I afterwards found, when I was awakened by something cold touching my toe. It was a bright moonlight night, and I instantly recognized the dog of those Bushmen smelling my feet, but was glad to see him trot away without barking at us. 'I shook Jim, and whispered to him to keep a sharp look out, but not to move a muscle unless attacked. In a few minutes I heard our pursuers run past, but a few rods distant from us. They lost their scent, we took another direction, and saw them no more." This is one of many tales I heard by the way, which I relate to illustrate the adventures of pioneer life in South Africa.

Rev. John Edwards, Superintendent of Somerset Circuit, met me at Bedford, and drove me hence, nearly forty miles, in his "cart-and-four," to his own house in Somerset. Brother Edwards was sent as a missionary to Africa in 1831, and has had a great variety of missionary life in the English, Dutch, and Kaffir work on the frontier, and the Bechuana work in the interior.

SOMERSET was visited by Rev. Wm. Shaw as early as 1822, on the invitation of R. Hart, Esq., who had been an officer of the Cape regiment, a good man, and though aged, still lives near Somerset, and takes a great interest in the work of God. At that early day Somerset was simply a Government farm, under the superintendency of Mr. Hart, to raise supplies for the frontier troops, but when the general farming interests of the colony were sufficiently developed to supply this demand, the farm was converted into a township. The district of Somerset now has a population of 10,022, of which 3,784 are Europeans. The village has probably one-third of the whole population of the district. The Wesleyan chapel, for the whites, had recently been enlarged to double its former size, by the addition of a transept as large as the old chapel; altogether it will now seat over three hundred and fifty. The native chapel is about the same size. Our cause among the whites there was considered very feeble. The circuit is geographically very extensive. Brother Edwards keeps four good horses to enable him to do the travelling work necessary, and our cause was said to be much stronger in the country than in the town. Indeed Brother Edwards told me at the start that he had but two white members in town, besides his wife, who could pray in public, so our prospect for a work was not very bright. On Sabbath I preached three sermons, and collected £23 towards the late enlargement of the chapel. We had two services for the whites on Monday. One day service for natives on Tuesday, preaching to whites at night. Preached twice to the whites on Wednesday. Preached for the natives on Thursday, lectured on Thursday night, and left early on Friday morning.

A number of persons had come fifty, and others seventy, miles to attend the meetings. Among them was a Mr. Nash, from "Ebenezer," fifty miles distant. He was a good farmer, a kind-hearted man, with an interesting family, but I was told that he was given to drink, so that his life and all that he had were in jeopardy. He called to see me on Saturday evening soon after my arrival. Said he, " I never would have thought of coming to this meeting but for Hon. Mr. Burch, of Uitenhage. He used to be my neighbour before his removal to Uitenhage, and recently he was in our neighbourhood, and was telling myself and others about your preaching in Uitenhage, and what surprised us most was that he said that he had found the pardon of all his sins at your meeting. We thought it was a wonderful thing. We knew that Burch was not a man to be deceived in such a matter, and that he would not lie; indeed, we could all see that there was a wonderful change in him. He begged us to attend your meeting here, and we have come. I am a dreadful sinner, and I can see no hope for me, but still, when such a man as Burch finds peace with God, I don't see why anybody need despair." I was pleased with his honest simplicity and earnestness.

He attended all the services, but did not yield till Wednesday, when he surrendered to God, accepted Christ, and was saved. Nearly all those who came so far, through the testimony of Mr. Burch, went home happy in God.

At each native service the chapel was crowded I was greatly favoured in having Siko Radas, from Heald Town, to interpret for me. He was having holiday during his vacation, and spent it in riding nearly eighty miles on his own hired horse to help me at Somerset, and thence eighty miles to Cradock to help me there. We had not such a mass of people to preach to in those towns as at Heald Town, but, in proportion to the population, we had a blessed harvest of souls. At the two native services in Somerset, over fifty natives were examined by their minister, Brother Edwards, and reported converted to God. Over twenty-five whites were saved at our series for them. In a letter from Brother Edwards, written the following week, he says, "On Sunday July 31st, both at the preaching and at the prayer-meeting in the evening, the power of God the Spirit was graciously manifested in a way I never felt before. A great concern is found among the English families; many have yielded, others are deeply awakened. Many natives belonging to other churches have found peace. They will be lost to us, but not to God. The young converts are happy, and are working well; among others, none more so than my son Walter. To God be the praise. Fully one hundred have found peace." In another letter from Brother Edwards, four months later, he says, "Most glad to hear from you, and of the prosperity of God's work. God hath blessed us much here. Those brought in remain steadfast. Mr. Nash is a miracle of grace, he holds on his way, and is very happy."

Among many missionary stories related to me by Brother Edwards, I will record one, as it will illustrate several facts in connection with missionary life and adventure in Africa. Many years ago the natives of three mission stations, with their missionaries, Mr. Edwards being one of them, went in search of a new home. They travelled about a thousand miles before they found a suitable place, and hence the establishment of our missions in the *Free State* in the "Bechuana District," which was first established by Messrs. Jenkins, Edwards, and others. The following narrative is from Brother Edwards's own pen, written at my request. "Previously to the year 1830, there was a great slaughter among the native tribes living in the north. Owing to their making war with one another, whole native towns were depopulated. Those who escaped fled for their lives, and wandered they knew not whither. Among them was a lad who found his way into Basuto country" (the Basutos are the people under Moshesh, whom the Dutch of the Free State have been fighting for several years). "After many days of lonely wandering, living on pumpkin-peelings, found in the deserted huts of the depopulated country through which he passed, he fell in with Sikonyele's tribe, called the Mantatees. They looked upon him as a poor little thing, and treated him roughly, as a refugee. After being there for some time, he told the chief men of the tribe that he had a vision to make known to them, which was, that a large army would come down upon them from the north, destroy many of them, and take their cattle. Most of them paid no attention to his revelation, but said, 'Who can conquer us?' It was a tribe at that time strong, warlike, rich in cattle, and proud. Not long after, however, there came down from the north some hostile tribes, which robbed them of the most of their cattle, and destroyed many of their people.

"Then many of them began to believe in their little refugee prophet. Some time after that, the boy said he had another vision to make known to them Some were opposed to hearing him; however, he told them that another attack would be made upon them by another sort of people. A copper-coloured people, on horses, having guns to fight with, would come upon them, and would take away their goats and sheep, and many of their children, and would kill many people. Not long after a lot of "Corannas" (Hottentot bastards, who, being so long among the Dutch, had learned the use fire-arms, and were well-supplied with guns), "came and did just as the boy had described. These two attacks reduced the Mantatees much, and brought them into a state of great humiliation and fear. Again the prophet boy gave notice that he had received another vision, and had something to tell them. They were now all anxious to hear what he had to say. Then he told them that 'a large lot of people will come into the country to reside. They will not come to fight or destroy. They are men of peace, and will bring good tidings. There will be among them men dressed in black clothes, but men of peace.' They all listened attentively, and asked him what more he had to tell them? 'No more,' said he, ' but only to listen to what the men of peace will tell you.' Shortly after that," continues Mr. Edwards, "we arrived in that country with the people of three stations, in all about twelve thousand souls, under the care of three missionaries. We were afterwards told that if we had gone into that country, while the Mantatees were in their pride and prosperity, not one of us would have escaped death. Here we saw the hand of God. That prophet lad was one of our first converts to Christ, and I baptized him, *Daniel*, not knowing then that he had been such a prophet aforetime. The boy remained steadfast in the faith.

"The Mantatees had no correct idea of God; but believed that a great Being lived above, to them unseen, whom they called 'Morimo'—'Mo'—him—'rimo' above—Him above."

CHAPTER XIII.

CRADOCK.

On Friday, the 29th of June, Mr. Sargent, brother to Rev. W. Sargent, one of the principal Wesleyans in Somerset, drove me, in company with his wife, from Somerset, forty miles on my way towards Cradock to "Dagga Boer." We spent the night, and preached at the house of Mr. John Trollip. The Trollip family is a very old and numerous family, very well-to-do, respectable, and everywhere known as Wesleyans, though not all saved as yet. We were hospitably entertained at Mr. John Trollip's for the night, and took breakfast with his aged parents in a separate house on the same premises. They have had their share of the sweet and the bitter of old pioneers in a new country. In their family burying-ground, surrounded by a stone wall, I read on a tombstone the following :—" Sacred to the memory of Henry Trollip, aged twenty-eight years two months and ten days ; and his brother Edward, aged nineteen years and five days, sons of William Trollip, who, on returning home were waylaid and shot by a band of rebel Hottentots, on the 31st of

December, 1851. 'They were lovely and pleasant in their lives, and in their death they were not divided.' 2 Samuel i. 23."

These were John's brothers, and sons of the honourable aged pair, at whose board we were entertained. Their bereavement but illustrates the bereavement of many in the colony, and explains, in part, the deep, but not very discriminating, prejudice of the white colonists against the natives. The murderers of those young men belonged to a colony of highly favoured Hottentots, settled on lands ceded to them by the Government, near the "Kat Mountains." Unlike the Fingoes, who have always been true to the Government, in the Kaffir War of 1851, these Hottentots rebelled, and did great damage to the colonial cause, and greater damage still to their own. The repeated Kaffir wars have done much to deepen prejudice against the blacks, still it should be remembered that they claimed to be the original owners of the soil, and that they were heathens, and knew nothing of what Europeans consider the honourable modes of conducting wars, and killing people; but whatever the conduct of those heathen warriors, it does not justify an indiscriminate bitter hatred of the race, which has operated seriously against the success of the Gospel among them, and the raising up of native missionaries. This prejudice, to be sure, is not universal, but very general, and very outspoken.

It usually breaks out in declamation about the inefficiency and dishonesty of native servants and then goes off into general charges, such as "they are a nation of thieves," "they won't work;" "you'll never make anything out of them," and so on. I have often replied to such charges against the servants, by saying, 1st. "The better class of Fingoes and Kaffirs have their own cattle, and comfortable homes, and don't go into service. Those who know them well, say they are industrious, honest, and many of them as consistent Christians as can be found among the whites. 2nd. Good servants get a good situation and keep it. I have met many such in South Africa, whose masters say, 'they never have much trouble with them, and they can trust them with anything they have. It is a notorious fact, that if you entrust, even a Kaffir thief, with your property to the amount of even thousands of pounds, and let him see that you have faith in him, you may go away where you like, and take your pleasure or your rest, and be sure that your Kaffir servant will faithfully attend to your interests. 3rd. The coloured servants so often in the market, and changing continually, from whom you get your grounds of complaint against native servants in general, and against the mission-stations, because, as wandering refugees, they may have found quarters there for a time, are just like a thriftless class of servants to be found in all countries, and of all nationalities. 'Tis said that a gentleman once inquired of Dr. Adam Clarke if he could tell him where he could get a good English servant?

"Why," replied the Doctor, "I have been praying to the Lord for three weeks to send me one, and I do believe if He had one out of a situation, He would have answered my prayers before this time."

While proper vigilance should be maintained to prevent the organization of seditious bodies of natives, everything possible should be done to Christianize all classes of them, develop their manhood, and fully ally the best interests of both the Europeans and natives. The missionaries alone cannot do all that work, they need the intelligent, discriminating moral power of all good colonists to aid them.

Rev. W. Chapman, Superintendent of Cradock Circuit, met me at Mr. John Trollip's, and drove me in his cart and pair, through a gale of wind and blinding clouds of dust, a distance of about forty miles to Cradock. Brother Chapman spent a number of years in the mission-work, in that charnel-field of martyr missionaries—the West Coast of Africa. When his health failed there, he was transferred to South Africa, where he recovered his health, and has for some years wrought succesfully as a missionary.

CRADOCK is located near the Great Fish River, 550 miles east of Cape Town, and 107 north-west of Graham's Town, in a fine sheep-growing country of extensive valleys and mountains. The mountains do not rise in regular ranges, but stand out in every direction, clearly defined in the peculiarly transparent atmosphere of that region, in isolated grandeur. Huge granite mountains with many perpendicular lines, especially near their summits, shaped like the roof and gable-ends of a house, yet rising to an altitude of six or seven thousand feet. Cradock was originally established as the seat of a magistracy, and centre of a large district of wealthy Dutch farmers. Rev. John Taylor, the Dutch Reformed Minister there, has the reputation of being a very liberal and useful man. The town has grown up to a place of considerable commercial importance. The population of the district amounts to an aggregate of 12,136, of whom 5,845 are whites; a good sprinkling of these are English. "Rev. Thornly Smith was the first resident Wesleyan minister appointed to Cradock, which was in 1842. He was soon succeeded by Rev. John Edwards, who could preach in both Dutch and English. The first Wesleyan chapel there was built in 1842. That was subsequently given to the Kaffirs, and the present commodious chapel, with sittings for about 500, was built under the superintendency of Rev. G. H. Green."

Our party, consisting of Brother Chapman and son, Brother and Sister Sargent, Siko Radas and myself, arrived a little before sunset. Our first business was to dispose of our surplus "real estate," in the form of a very uncomfortable accumulation of dust, completely covering our persons and baggage. I then paid my respects to a good ham of venison, well-prepared by good Sister Chapman, and was after dinner conducted to my Cradock home, in the family of Hon. Henry Tucker, M.L.C. I found there most comfortable quarters, through the kindness of Brother and Sister Tucker. Though a merchant and a politician, I found Brother Tucker to be a thorough and active teetotaller, the superintendent of our Sabbath-school, and an earnest Christian. The cause of total abstinence had a stronger hold in Cradock, than in any South African town I visited, and, as a consequence, we had no disorder in the streets, nor about the doors of our chapel, and a larger proportion of the people were prepared *soberly* to wait on God under our Gospel ministrations, and hence a proportionately large number of them were converted to God during our series. Being "drunk with wine," instead of being "filled with the Spirit," is one of the greatest hindrances to the success of the Gospel. Many of our ministers in South Africa have waked up to this fact, and for the sake of their influence upon society in this matter, have become total abstainers. Hon. Mr. Tucker gave me the following melancholy instance of the damaging effect of a tippling minister's example. "A hotel-keeper in Graham's Town, was greatly addicted to the use of spirits. I laboured with him, and had him on the eve of becoming a teetotaller. He had given up the use of it for weeks, and I finally believed that I would succeed in saving him. He was a genial good-hearted fellow, I was boarding with him during the session of Parliament—its only session in Graham's Town—and I felt a great interest in him, on his own account, and on account of his family. But just at the time, when I thought my efforts were about to be permanently successful, a minister came in and dined with us, and at the dinner-table he held up a glass of spirits, and, in quite a little speech, expatiated on it, as one of the good gifts of God to be enjoyed by His creatures, and then drank it. The next morning I made some remark to my landlord about the danger of drink, and he replied abruptly: 'Mr. Tucker, I don't wish you to speak to me again on this subject, after the eloquent remarks of Rev. Mr. ——, yesterday. I see now clearly that it is all right to use it, as a good gift of God to be enjoyed.' In two weeks from that day he died in delirium tremens."

I believe Brother Tucker has been the means of saving a number of men from a similar end, and in his position of life, his example and active labours tend greatly to promote the temperance movement in South Africa. I was pleased to meet some of my Graham's Town friends in Cradock, who had come to attend the meetings—Hon. Samuel Cawood, M.L.C., who rendered us good service in our prayer-meetings, and Messrs. John and Wm. Webb, and others.

I commenced my work in Cradock on Sabbath morning the 31st of June. My first service was to preach to the Kaffirs, through Siko Radas, at seven, A.M. There was a gracious moving of the Holy Spirit, but we had no time for a prayer-meeting.

I preached to the whites at eleven A.M., three P.M., and half-past six in the evening. We had the altar crowded with seekers, and twelve persons professed to find peace with God at our first prayer-meeting. Had two successful services for the whites, Monday, at eleven A.M., and seven P.M. On Tuesday, at eleven, A.M., I preached to the Dutch-speaking natives. About one-half the natives of Cradock speak Kaffir, and the other half Dutch, making it necessary to have two native chapels, and separate services in each language.

Mr. H. Park, a discharged old soldier, and Dutch interpreter in the magistrates' court there, was my interpreter. The language is not nearly so euphonious as the Kaffir, but I was interested in marking its near relationship to the English. Our principal difficulty on that occasion was the want of room to accommodate the multitude who wished to hear. During our prayer-meeting, after the preaching, over thirty persons gave their names as new converts to Jesus. On Tuesday night, and Wednesday, at eleven A.M., and seven P.M., preached to the whites, followed in each case by a prayer-meeting, and the salvation of souls. On Wednesday night, during the prayer-meeting, Mr. Wm. Webb, who had come from Graham's Town to attend our meeting, and who had been forward a number of times as a seeker, was suddenly delivered from the power of darkness, and translated into the kingdom of Jesus. He arose and addressed the audience, testifying very intelligently and clearly that, after forty-six years of rebellion against God, he had now obtained reconciliation and unspeakable joy.

When we had sufficient time at command, we often gave the young converts an opportunity to testify publicly, and rising one after another, they witnessed distinctly to the facts in their experience, demonstrating the truth of the Gospel, and the saving power of Jesus in their own hearts. Many doubting ones have thus been convinced, and led to decision for God.

It was arranged that I should preach again to the natives on Thursday, but their new chapel, which will seat between four and five hundred, was not ready, and it was finally announced that I should preach to the natives and whites together in the court, back of the mission-house.

At eleven A.M. the heterogeneous mass nearly filled the court. We take our stand on the back verandah of the mission-house. The court is bounded on our left by a wall, in front, by a carriage-house, and the garden fence, on the right, by the stables and a wall, altogether affording almost as good protection from outside intrusion, if the danger of such had existed, as the sacred precincts of a church. The central group of our audience is composed of Kaffirs and Hottentots of every colour, and of every variety of native costume. They have brought their sleeping-mats, each about three feet wide and six in length, and have spread them out to sit and kneel

GOSPEL PREACHED IN THREE LANGUAGES AT ONCE. 201

on. Many of them are seated on benches provided for them, but many more are down on their mats. Next, in a massed circle and in scattered groups, we see all classes of the whites. Brother Park stands ready to put my sermon into the Dutch language, but we see so many Kaffirs in the audience, who know neither English or Dutch, that we say "Poor souls, can't we have another interpreter? I wish we had Siko Radas here, but he has gone back to his school." "There's a Kaffir here just up from Port Elizabeth, called Jack, who can speak English," said Brother Chapman, "but I don't know whether he can interpret." "Jack, come here, my man," said I, and up came a black Kaffir, about five feet eight, very plainly dressed, wearing an old straw-hat. "Brother Jack," said I, "can you put my words into Kaffir?" "Yes, sir," replied Jack. "Brother Park will put them into Dutch, and you will follow him, and put each sentence into Kaffir just as you would talk to them about shearing sheep." I had no time, under this extemporized arrangement, to give Jack my sermon privately, as I was in the habit of doing for my interpreters, but proceeded at once to business. The three of us stood side by side, Park close to my right, and Jack next. I gave every sentence in a clear but condensed form, and for over an hour the piercing light and melting power of the Gospel flowed out through the medium of three languages at once, without the break of a single blunder or a moment's hesitation. Men, women, and children weep, and I doubt not angels gaze and rejoice. At the close of the preaching we invited all who wish to surrender to God and accept Christ to "kneel before the Lord" at once. Scores of the Kaffirs kneel down on their mats, with cries and streaming tears. The whites, with no such provision, go down on their knees in the dust, bench after bench is crowded with them, and, ah! what a scene ensued.

While I was without, pointing these struggling souls to Jesus, Brother Chapman came to me, saying, "Brother Taylor, will you please come into the house and speak to a woman in despair? She is a very clever, influential woman, and will make a noble Christian if she is saved; but she says her day of grace is gone, and that nothing remains for her but the blackness of darkness for ever." I go and find her in a sad state of mind, to be sure, but after some time we get her composed, so as to converse and reason on the subject, and convince her that this dreadful discovery of extreme heart wickedness is the result of the Holy Spirit's awakening mercy. "Though you can see no way of escape, my dear sister, God sees the way of salvation open for you, and the proof of that is the fact that He has sent His Spirit to show you your bondage, and lead you to Jesus. Now if you consent to surrender yourself to God, consent that He take your case in hand, and do with you as He wishes, take from you all your sins, impose on you whatever is right, you may at once accept Christ as your Saviour. God hath sent Him into the world to save sinners—even the chief of sinners. That was His business when manifest in the flesh; that is His business through His invisible Spirit now, as really as then. God offers Him to you in His Gospel as your Saviour, the Holy Spirit presents Him at the door of your heart as your Saviour. He is knocking at the door. Now you will accept Him, and be saved by Him, or reject Him and perish. Accept Him now by faith. It is not presumption, but confidence in God's most reliable record concerning His Son. If what God says about Him is true, then Christ is worthy of your confidence, and if so, why not receive Him now? You cannot improve your case by anything you ever can do, and you cannot add anything to God's ransom, and remedy; then, on the faith of God's testimony, receive Jesus now as your Saviour from sin. You must say, 'I accept Him. I accept Him on His own terms, I accept Him on God's recommendation, I accept Him now, I accept Him'—say it till your heart says it, and in that moment God will justify you freely by His grace, and His Holy Spirit will bear witness with your spirit to the fact, and fill your heart with His pardoning love." Finally she began to say, "I accept Christ, I accept Him," and in a few moments she received the witness of forgiveness, and was filled with "joy unspeakable," and oh, how she wept and talked of the amazing love of God. My Dutch interpreter's wife and daughter were saved that day, and a large number of whites, Dutch, and Kaffirs.

I have given but an inadequate glance at the scenes of that day.

To try to describe any of those occasions of the out-pourings of the Spirit at different places, of which I have been speaking, is like trying to describe the lightnings of Heaven. When we say we witnessed a grand thunderstorm, those who are familiar with such scenes know what we mean, but it cannot be put into words, nor spread upon the canvas, so when we speak of hundreds of souls bowed before God in penitential grief, and of their accepting Christ, and then in rapturous joy telling of their deliverance, those who are familiar with such scenes know what is meant, "but the natural man receiveth not the things of the Spirit of God, neither can he know them, because they are spiritually discerned." A lecture on Thursday-night closed my labours in Cradock. Rev. Mr. Chapman, reported over seventy whites, and over fifty natives converted to God, during our series of five days. By a letter from Brother Chapman, dated November 9th, over four months after I left, I learn that the work of God in Cradock has gone steadily on, with increasing power. "After you left," he writes, "some of our oldest members came up as seekers. One man, near eighty years old, long a member, and others who had been fifteen or twenty years in the Church, and had never obtained peace before. I believe we have now but very few members without this blessing." He goes on to give me the names of many whole families who had been saved, and were walking happily in the light, and states that up to the time of writing, the number of converts among the whites had gone up to about " 150, and about 160 coloured," making an aggregate of over 300 souls justified, besides a number wholly sanctified to the Lord.

My next field was Queen's Town.

CHAPTER XIV.

QUEEN'S TOWN.

AT early dawn on Friday morning, the 5th of July, I was seated beside Brother Tucker, my host, in his splendid carriage, behind his two fine grey Arab steeds, *en route* for Queen's Town, over eighty miles distant. Brother Tucker accompanied me thirty miles on my way, where we dined at the house of his brother, and I bade my dear friend adieu. Mr. Hines was in waiting, and drove me that afternoon twenty miles in his cart and four, to his own house in the village of "Tarkisstaat." The Wesleyans had a small chapel there, but no society. The Dutch Reformed Church being a little more central, and having been kindly offered for our use, I preached that night in the Dutch Reformed Church. We did not hold a prayer-meeting, but a respectable citizen of the town, Mr. J. F., called next morning to inform me that, after preaching the night before, he went home and wrestled in importunate prayer, till he was enabled to submit to God, and accept Christ, and was made happy in the assurance of pardon.

On Saturday, Mr. Hines, accompanied by his

daughter and son, drove me thirty-five miles to Queen's Town, where I put up at the house of the resident Wesleyan minister, Rev. H. H. Dugmore. Brother Dugmore is one of the old pioneer missionaries of Southern Africa, yet of colonial production. He is a minister of superior abilities in the pulpit, as a preacher, in his sanctum as a student and writer, in the social circle as a companion, and musician, playing a variety of musical intruments. He preaches in English, Dutch, and Kaffir. He is considered one of the best Kaffir scholars in the country; has translated large portions of the Scriptures into Kaffir, and is the author of the most and best hymns contained in our Kaffir Hymn Book, and sung by the Kaffirs. There is but one of our Wesleyan hymns in the Kaffir language, so says the Rev. W. Shepstone, and that is the 143rd, "Jesu, lover of my soul." Excellent as they are in English, they cannot be readily made to fit Kaffir ideas and idioms.

QUEEN'S TOWN is situated in the midst of a beautiful and fertile district of country, composed of beautiful vales, extensive plains, and sublime mountains. It was formerly occupied by bushmen and Tembookie Kaffirs, but after the war of 1850-2, it fell into the hands of the Government, and was added to the colony. The Wesleyans for many years before had two mission-stations among the Tembookies in that district, and the natives of those stations proving true to the Government, as usual, the Governor, Sir

George Cathcart, allowed them to remain in the undisturbed possession of their lands, on which we now have the flourishing mission-station of Lesseyton, eight miles distant from Queen's Town, and Kamastone, twenty miles distant. The Government gave a good lot in Queen's Town to the Wesleyans for church purposes. A church and "mission-house," were soon after built, and a Wesleyan Society organized by the present incumbent, Rev. H. H. Dugmore. The first chapel, near the mission-house, has been given to the natives, and a spacious and beautiful chapel, more centrally located in the town, has been erected for the whites. The population of the district amounts to an aggregate of 44,542, but 3,632 of whom are Europeans. The white residents of Queen's Town, as in Graham's Town, are nearly all English.

We had a number of visitors at our services from different parts of the colony; Messrs. Shaw, Barnes, Elliott, and others recently converted to God at Fort Beaufort, were there, and rendered us good service. Mr. Shaw is a Fort Beaufort merchant, who has since become an Exhorter and Class-leader. Mr. Elliott was the said hotel-keeper who gave up his "canteen." We had a few from Graham's Town, and Mr. Jakins, from Salem Circuit, one hundred and twenty miles distant.

Brother Jakins is an old pioneer Wesleyan, who has been very useful, I am told, as a Local Preacher for many years. He called on me soon after my arrival in Graham's Town, and said, "About a year ago I received a letter from my sister in Launceston, Tasmania, stating that she and her two sons and two daughters had found peace with God, and had united with the Wesleyan Society, at a series of meetings recently held in their town, by the Rev. William Taylor, from America, and gave me a glowing account of a wonderful work of God which had spread throughout the colony of Tasmania. When I saw your name announced in the Cape Town papers, it struck me that you must be the same minister mentioned by my sister, and I have taken the liberty to call on you to ascertain whether indeed that is so." When he learned that he had thus strangely enough met with the man whom God had used in saving his dear kindred in a remote colony in the Indian Ocean, he wept in gratitude before God.

At our Graham's Town series, two of Brother Jakins' daughters and a son-in-law were saved, and now he had come one hundred and twenty miles to attend my Queen's Town meeting, with the hope of seeing his two sons, who are farmers in that district, brought to God. He did us good service at our meetings, and had the happiness of seeing his sons happy in Jesus before he returned. "Now," said he, with tearful eyes, "I will have joyful tidings to write to my sister in Tasmania, that all my own family, too, have been converted to God at your meetings."

Some whole families were saved at our Queen's

Town series, and many sweet surprises and affecting scenes were witnessed. A dear mother in Israel, named Turvey, had two grown-up sons, both unconverted, but one was so wild in his career of sin that she almost despaired of ever having him brought back to God. The mother had brought up a large family of children, in affliction and darkness, for she was blind and had not seen the light of the sun for many years. She was a real daughter of sorrow, but a patient Christian. The great grief of her heart was her prodigal son.

One night during our series, a brother went to her, and said, "Mrs. Turvey, your son is at the altar of prayer among the seekers, and wants you to come and talk to him." Her gushing tears were the index to the unutterable emotions of joy and grief which thrilled her heart as she exclaimed,

"Oh, I thank God that my dear George is coming to Jesus, but my poor prodigal! I'm afraid he'll never be saved!" She was then conducted to the place, and feeling her way down to her penitent son, she cried, "O George, my dear son, I'm glad to find you here; but poor Edward! Would to God, he was here too!"

"Mother," exclaimed the young man, "you are quite mistaken, it is not George; I am indeed your prodigal son, and I want you to forgive me, and to pray that God will forgive me." The prodigal returned that night, and was admitted into the royal "household of faith." George, who had always been a comfort to his mother, was not saved till the following week, at Kamastone, when the mother got the joyful news, she rode twenty miles to Kamastone to greet her dear son, and rejoice with him in thanksgiving to the God of the orphan and the widow.

Our services at Queen's Town extended through five days, from the 8th to the 12th of July. Three sermons on the Sabbath, and two each week-day, except Tuesday, when I preached at Lesseyton. During this series of services, about one hundred Europeans were reported by the minister as new witnesses for Christ.

My next field of labour was Kamastone. On the Sabbath I spent at Kamastone, Rev. H. H. Dugmore preached a sermon in his own pulpit, from the text, "Stand still, that I may reason with you before the Lord." The subject of his discourse, singularly enough, was the—

I. The American preacher.
II. His preaching.
III. Its effects.

He was, no doubt, prompted to deliver such a discourse, by the active efforts of a clergyman of the town, in trying to prejudice the public mind against our meetings, and more especially to vindicate and extend the work of God. The sermon was published by Mr. David S. Barrable, of Queen's Town, and as I was leaving the colony, a few months afterwards, a few copies were sent me. In glancing over it, I think a few extracts from the "third division" will serve to illustrate some important phases of the work of God in connection with our series of services there, and generally in other places.

1. ITS EFFECTS.

It was *Awakening*. Some thirty or forty persons came forward on the first evening, to request the prayers of the ministers in their behalf. The numbers increased on succeeding evenings. Now, among these were persons of every age, from ten years to sixty. There were the married, as well as the unmarried, fathers and mothers of families; persons constitutionally calm and impassive, as well as those of excitable temperament. There were persons who had a strong instinctive horror of making "fools of themselves," persons who had resisted most strenuously their own penitential impulses—persons who, in the first instance, had swelled the ranks of the revilers, persons who knew that the penalty of their procedure would be the ridicule and scorn of their former associates, persons of nearly every social grade that Queen's Town affords. They came not under the impulse of terror, for nothing had been said to excite it. They avowed themselves suddenly made sensible— vividly and sorrowfully sensible—of the sinfulness of their hearts, and the "evil of their ways." I ask, could the grief of such persons be unreal? "But so much of the feeling was unnecessary." (It has been said). The feeling was awakened by a consciousness of having violated the most sacred of obligations—those of duty to God. Will any one dare to say that such sorrow ought to be less poignant than that awakened by any human ills? Is deep-impassioned grief allowable when earthly sources of sorrow are opened, and yet not to be warranted when the "exceeding sinfulness of sin" is felt? "But its manifestation was violently unnatural." Let us look at the facts. I stood in the midst of forty or fifty persons, who were sorrowing unto repentance. I did so from evening to evening; and this is my testimony concerning them. The grief of two-thirds of the number was silent grief, or expressed in whispered earnestness; of the rest, one half wept audibly, and a few, chiefly youths from the country, were in a state of mental distress still more loudly manifested. Now was there anything unnatural in this? Various temperaments were variously affected. Had all been demonstrative alike, it would have supplied a plausible objection.

2. THE COMFORTING EFFECTS.

Most of the persons who had been brought into mental distress, obtained, after a shorter or longer period of penitential earnestness, not merely a sense of relief, but a gladdening consciousness of pardon, accompanied by a peace " which, to their own minds, passed understanding." They felt their souls brought out of a state of deep distressing " darkness " into one of " marvellous light " and joy. They experienced an inward assurance of personal adoption into the Divine favour which they believed to be the inward voice of " the Spirit itself, bearing witness with their spirit that they were now the children of God." This assurance produced at once a feeling of grateful love to God for His mercy. The manner in which this change of feeling was manifested, varied with the various temperaments of the persons who experienced it. Some sank into silent adoration, some looked around in wonder, as though they were then for the first time conscious of real existence; some smiled with an expression of indescribable rapture; some practically adopted the language of the Psalmist, " Then was our mouth filled with laughter, and our tongue with singing." Many began at once to speak to those who were kneeling in the distress from which they had themselves just escaped, to urge them to exercise the appropriating faith which they had found so efficacious in their own case. But amidst these diversities of outward expression, the language of all was virtually this:—" Being justified by faith, we have peace with God through our Lord Jesus Christ, by whom also we have access by faith into this grace wherein we stand, and rejoice in hope of the glory of God."

3. THE PRACTICAL EFFECTS.

This religious excitement does not evaporate in mere feeling, but manifests its Divine life in the fruits of the Spirit in their Scriptural order. The "joy" that springs from the "love," is succeeded by the "peace," which becomes the settled habit of the soul, and, though less ecstatic than the first gush of rapture, *rules* in the heart and mind. And from the "love, joy, and peace," which thus lie at the root of the Christian life, spring the other graces, of the Christian character in due order—" long-suffering, gentleness, goodness, fidelity, meekness, temperance." Now, in strict accordance with this newness of life, which thus affords a test of the reality of conversion, the change in feeling, in manners and in action, displayed by those whom God hath brought to himself by this man's instrumentality, has astonished and confounded their former associates. Leaders in vice have become champions in defence of the religion they had reviled. Men of profligate lives have, with bitter shame, made confession, and are endeavouring to repair the evil of their former courses, by zealous and courageous activity in a new one. Drunkards, who were the terror of their families, and the pest of their neighbourhood, have renounced the use of intoxicating liquors, and the very alteration in their outward appearance proclaims the change within. Profane swearers are shuddering at the recollection of their favourite oaths and blasphemies. Frauds and wrongs have been acknowledged, and restitution made.

Men who had taken advantage of the detected villany of others to escape from their own responsibilities, have come forward and paid the demands which they had asserted were forgeries. Long-standing family discords have been healed, and quarrels that had lasted for years, ended in the overture for reconciliation by the parties most aggrieved. These are specimens of the *practical* effects of this man's preaching. They tell their own tale.

On Tuesday, the 10th of July, pending my series in Queen's Town, I went, in company with Rev. Brother Dugmore, Rev. Brother Wakeford, and others, to preach at Lesseyton. Rev. J. Bertram, a successful missionary, who was converted to God during the "Graham's Town revival of 1837,' was the superintendent. He was, in 1847, the founder, and is the present superintendent of Lesseyton Station, which is the seat of one of the three industrial schools, established under the Wesleyans, by Governor Grey. The school-buildings here are not so large as those in Heald Town, but very substantial, and large enough for all demands at present. The mission-house and chapel are good, and many of the natives live in substantial brick cottages. Altogether, the Lesseyton Station is said to be in advance of all others in the colony in education, and civilization, among the natives. Brother Bertram was absent on a necessary engagement that called him away for some weeks. He was at my services at Fort Beaufort and begged me to visit his people at Lesseyton, and also wrote to Brother Dugmore, asking him to arrange for me, and accompany me to his station. It is a rule with me not to work in any charge in the absence of the pastor, but under all the circumstances in this case, I could not refuse. During the minister's absence, there was not a white man on the station, but all the services were kept up, and good order maintained in every department of society, under the able administration of their "head man," William Bambana. He is an Amatembu Kaffir, as are the mass of his people on the station. He is a tall, large, fine-looking old man, of commanding influence among all classes in Queen's Town district.

When we arrived, at eleven o'clock A.M., the chapel, which is a commodious stone building, to seat about 600, was crowded. My interpreter was the son of Rev. Brother Wakeford, a fine young man, who had just been converted to God at my meetings in Queen's Town. The young man was born and brought up among the Kaffirs, and was said to be a fine Kaffir scholar, so I anticipated a glorious harvest of souls that day. The people had heard of the great work of God at Annshaw and Heald Town, and their eyes glistened with a spirit of expectation.

Brother Dugmore, who conducted the preliminary part of the service, remained seated in the pulpit. As the small, old style of pulpits, which are found in all the chapels in South Africa, did not afford space for me and my interpreter, and as I wished always to stand beside my spokesman, and not behind and above him, as many do, I took my stand in the altar, which has an elevation in this chapel of more than a foot above the level of the floor. Now we proceed :—Brother Dugmore, in his perch in our rear, Brother Wakeford seated by the wall to our left, the anxious native crowd on all sides and front, back to the door, my young interpreter standing just to my left.

Text :—" The Spirit and the Bride say come," &c. I proceed to say, " The provision of salvation for all sinners is compared to a river." A pause— " What do you mean by provision ? " says my interpreter. I explain, and he renders.

Then follows a baulky baffling tug. Every few minutes when I discharge a Gospel shot, which I expect will bring down some Goliath in penitential humiliation, the whole charge comes rebounding with most humiliating effect upon the shooter. Now Brother Dugmore gives my man a helping-hand, which conveys the thought to the anxious crowd, but only increases the confusion of the young man. Now his father gives him a word, worse still for him. Now I leave him standing alone in not a very pleasant position, while I step back and give a whole illustration to Brother Dugmore to give to the people, and we both stand and wait till the old missionary is through, and then try again. The longer the worse, confusion becomes double confounded.

Say I to myself, "Dear me, this is horrible! Here are hundreds of thirsty souls, and I can't tell them how to come to the river, and I shall never have another opportunity of speaking to them this side the Judgment. Oh, if I only had my Charles here! I wipe off the perspiration and try again, hoping for a favourable turn in the tide, but all in vain. Not willing to endure the apparent defeat of stopping short in the middle of the discourse, abridging it as much as possible, we struggle through with it, and sit down in confusion and disappointment. My "fine Kaffir-scholar," alas, did not know English sufficiently, and was so confused, that what he did know was not available in our time of need. We did not attempt a prayer-meeting for seekers. Brother Dugmore covered our retreat by a few remarks, followed by singing and prayer, which closed the scene. I had found so many good interpreters on my round, after leaving Annshaw, that I thought if anything should prevent Charles Pamla from accompanying me through Kaffraria, as my interpreter, I could probably get on well nevertheless, but now I began to realize how helpless I should be if he failed to come. I had not received any communication from Rev. Brother Lamplough, nor from Brother Pamla on the subject since our agreement at Annshaw, and began now to feel very uneasy, lest something might interfere to prevent his coming. I, however, took comfort in the fact that I was going on the Lord's business, and that He would afford all necessary facilities and helpers.

The next day, Wednesday, 11th July, Mr. James

JAMES ROBERTS.

Roberts and my son, Morgan Stuart, arrived from Graham's Town, preparatory to our Kaffrarian journey. Brother Roberts had a light, strong buggy, built for the purpose, at a cost of £54. He had purchased four horses, at a cost of £75. His outfit altogether cost him about £150. Being so amply provided for myself, I set the expenses of my son and my interpreter, on horseback, to my own account. We were now nearly ready, except that Charles Pamla had not arrived, and we had no tidings from him. But the next day Charles arrived all right, bringing good news concerning the progress of the work of God in the Graham's Town district, and a letter from Brother Lamplough, dated July the 9th, an extract from which will illustrate the progress of the work at Annshaw, and the man God had sent me in my need.

My dear Brother,—I just drop you a line by our Brother Charles Pamla, who leaves here to-day for Queen's Town. I have not time to enter into many particulars about the work since I last wrote to you at Beaufort; but I may just say, that altogether since your coming to Annshaw, about six hundred profess to have found peace with God, and after careful examination into every case, I cannot doubt the reality of the work in any of those who profess to be justified. We have now about twelve hundred in this circuit, formed into about eighty classes. This is by far the largest number of any circuit in South Africa, and I rejoice to say the work is still going on. Last week was a glorious one, more than one hundred and ninety entered into liberty. God is greatly honouring our Brother Charles Pamla. He has been the means of the conversion of about three hundred souls during the last six weeks. Others of our native brethren are also very useful in this good work, and it seems to me that God is plainly showing the Church that this is the instrumentality that He intends to employ in converting this continent.

I rejoice in this with all my heart. As yet I have not been able to go out among the Heathens, but as the tickets will be finished to-day, I hope soon to try a week at a Heathen village, though, in this work, I have lost my best man so long as Charles is away; but I am willing to sacrifice a little for the benefit of the work beyond the Kei.

During our week of special services in Queen's Town, I had no opportunity of preaching to the Kaffirs there, but arranged to give them a service on Wednesday afternoon of the following week, on our return from Kamastone. The Kaffir chapel in Queen's Town is a good building, next door to the mission-house, fronting the principal street, and will seat about three hundred, but by the Kaffir art of packing, will hold about five hundred. Our service commenced at four P.M. The venerable Dugmore, with a smooth and beautiful flow of the euphonious language of the Kaffirs, opened the service by singing (all the congregation joining) as with one voice, thrilling the sympathetic chords of many souls. In a note appended to the said printed sermon, Mr. Dugmore makes the following allusion to the sermon which followed:—"Mr. Taylor preached to the natives in their own chapel here. He took for his text the ten commandments, explaining and applying them, and dwelling specially on the evils to which the natives are specially addicted—theft, falsehood, and licentiousness. Persons who listened to the discourse remarked, that had the preacher been twenty years among these people, he could not have preached a more suitable sermon. The usual effects followed." Over one hundred came forward as seekers, and a fair proportion of them received Christ, and were saved. I remained with them till dark, and left Brother Pamla to go on with the prayer-meeting till nine P.M., while I, meantime, should conduct a fellowship-meeting for the European friends in the other Chapel. It was a pleasing scene to witness a crowd of happy worshippers filling the chapel, kneeling before the Lord, and uniting with their venerable pastor in prayer, and thanksgiving to God for His showers of blessing.

I gave them an address on Christian-fellowship, adducing the Scriptural authority for it, and illustrating the best methods of promoting it. Then, in the space of one hour, fifty-three persons stood up in their places, and testified distinctly to the fact of a conscious knowledge of "peace with God, through our Lord Jesus Christ." Among these were a number of old Christians, but the greater part were persons who were converted to God the preceding week. They gave brief details of their awakening, penitential struggle, and the time when they obtained salvation—some on Sabbath night, others on Monday night, and others on other different days and nights all through the series of services. Most of them had found peace at the altar of prayer; but some had found it at their homes. I will simply record a few illustrative specimen testimonies:—

Mr. John Weekly, a merchant in Queen's Town, said, "When I was a young man I thought that all I needed to make me happy was a good wife. God gave me a good wife; but gave me to see that I I needed something more to make me happy. I was deeply convinced of sin by His awakening Spirit, sought and found peace with God, then I was happy, and have been preserved in the fear and love of God for twenty-four years."

Mr. William Trollip said, "I found peace with God here three days ago. These have been the happiest days of my life."

A venerable-looking old man arose and said, "I wonder to see so many here at this fellowship-meeting, and to hear so many tell of the saving power of God in their souls; but my greatest wonder is to find myself here. I commenced to try to serve God fifty years ago. I was not instructed in the simple Gospel way of salvation by faith, and was, for twenty years, a seeker. I then obtained salvation by faith, and for thirty years have walked in the light. My race is nearly run; my crown is in view. By the grace of God in Christ I shall soon join in the fellowship-meeting of the Church triumphant in Heaven."

A soldier said, "When I commenced to seek God

my heart was so full of shame and pride, that to face a line of bayonets in battle, would not be half so hard as to face the eyes of the people upon me as a seeking sinner; but last Monday night I bowed at that altar of prayer, humbled my proud heart before God, surrendered my poor soul to Him, and by faith in Jesus, obtained the pardon of all my sins. Glory be to God!"

CHAPTER XV.

KAMASTONE.

HAVING closed our week of services in Queen's Town, on Saturday the 14th of July, Mr. Wm. Trollip, cousin to John Trollip, who with his wife found peace with God, a couple of days before, took me and my son Stuart up into his carriage and pair, with his good wife, and drove us twenty miles to Kamastone Mission Station. We were cordially received and kindly entertained by the missionary, Rev. Wm. Shepstone, who, as we have before seen, assisted Rev. Wm. Shaw in the establishment of the first Wesleyan Mission Station among the Kaffirs, in Pato's (now Kama's) tribe. He has been actively engaged in the missionary work ever since, extending through a period of more than forty years. He is now, not only the missionary of this large station, but also the chairman of the Queen's Town District, which embraces all our Kaffrarian missions, west of the Umzimvubu river. The stations of Palmerton, and Emfundisweni, lying east of that river, belong to the Natal district. Brother Shepstone is a very kind, cheerful, earnest brother,

thoroughly imbued with the missionary spirit of his Master. After a good tea, and a social hour with Brother and Sister Shepstone, I strolled through the mission-grounds by the light of the moon, with my son Stuart, a youth of nineteen years.

Owing to his absence from me at school, a couple of years before I left America, and my absence abroad for several years, and his recent illness, so prostrating him as to preclude a searching conversation, though the son of my youth, my first-born, whom I had carried on my heart to the mercy-seat every day of his life, he was almost a stranger to me. I knew he had joined our Church when a child, and at the age of eleven years professed to receive the regenerating grace of God, and that his teachers and his mother, had always given a good report of him, yet the details of his inner life had been a sealed book to me; but in our walk that night he unbosomed his heart, and gave me the history of his life. It was an event in my own life never to be forgotten. He had suffered great religious depression, had encountered great trials, but had held his ground all through from the time of his conversion. In the exhilaration of his returning health, he had said and done many boyish things, which led some to misjudge and misrepresent him, and cause anxious solicitude on the part of his parents; but his afflictions had been sanctified to his good, and he was now cleaving to the Lord, and happy in the love of Jesus. As I listened to the narration of his experience, I shed grateful tears, and praised God on his behalf. During my long Providential separation from my family, labouring for the salvation of strangers, and their children, I had maintained an unwavering faith that God certainly would not allow my children to perish, but would, through the agency of their dear mother, and other available instruments, fully supply the lack of service occasioned by my absence. Now I received a practical support to my faith, which greatly cheered me in my work.

Kamastone mission was commenced by Mr. Shepstone in 1847. The mission-house is plain, but spacious and commodious. Coming out on the front verandah, we see below us a large orchard of well-grown apple, pear, and other varieties of fruit-trees. To the right, distant perhaps a hundred yards, is the shop which furnishes supplies for the neighbourhood, kept by a good brother, who sold me a Kaffir pony, a superior "tripler," for £13, which carried my son Stuart seven hundred miles through Kaffraria and Natal. On each side, and in the rear of the mission-house, we see the huts and cabins of the natives, their gardens and cultivated fields, with their herds of horses, cattle, sheep, goats, dogs, and naked children. On the opposite side of the mission-house from the shop, and about the same distance from it, is the chapel, a cruciform, plain and substantial building, with sittings for about six hundred persons.

On Sabbath, the 14th of July, at ten A.M., we commenced our work there. Every square foot of space in the chapel is crowded. The space right and left, from the pulpit and altar, back to the side walls, is filled with the white colonial farmers from a radius of twenty miles. Next to them, on the right, and front from the pulpit, are nearly one hundred bastard Hottentots. Opposite to them, on the left, and through the whole body of the chapel, back to the door, and round the doors and windows outside, were all the varieties of Fingoes and Kaffirs. Christians, in European dress, and heathens in their native costumes and trinkets, packed together almost as snugly as herrings in a barrel. The preliminary service is conducted by the venerable superintendent; then he is seated in the altar, while I and Brother Pamla take the pulpit. While we explain to them God's provision of salvation, the personality and abiding presence of the Holy Spirit, and His methods of saving sinners through human agency, you feel and see the indications of a rising swelling tide of the Spirit's power, and you wonder that, under the pressure of such pent-up mental and emotional action, there is not a single audible response. All faces upturned, smiles, tears, distorted features, trembling limbs, but not a murmur. Lo! there's a man back near the door, who cannot longer restrain his feelings, but with one burst of half-smothered emotions, see him try to rush for the door, to take himself away, and not disturb the *umfundisi* or his hearers. In his attempt he falls down, but keeps moving on hands and knees through the packed masses who are standing and sitting in the aisle, out at the door he rushes, and away where he can roar till his over-charged soul is relieved. All this we see from the pulpit; but nobody is disturbed, all the rest remain quiet, and catch every sentence of Gospel truth we utter, and drink in the Spirit's influence as the thirsty land drinks in the rain. We close the service with singing and prayer, by Brother Pamla.

At two P. M., we again stand before a packed audience in the same order as in the morning. In the morning the preaching was to the believers, now we open a Gospel battery upon the ungodly, and the shafts of truth directed by the Spirits unerring aim pierced the hearts of hundreds. At the close of the sermon we proceed with a prayer-meeting. We invite the white seekers to kneel at the altar-rail, and the Kaffirs to commence with the front forms, and kneel at every alternate form back to the door, thus leaving space for their instructors to pass through them, and get access to every seeker. Soon the altar is crowded with whites, and about two hundred natives are down as seekers of pardon. Now their pent-up feelings get vent, and mid floods of tears, sighs, and groans, they are all audibly pleading with God in the name of Jesus Christ, for the pardon of their sins. No one voice is raised much above the rest, so that it seems to create no confusion.

Charles is a general in conducting a prayer-meeting, judiciously arranging everything, rightly employing every worker under his command, and setting all an example by working most effectively himself. A large number embrace Christ and find salvation at this service. Giving a little time for refreshment, we commenced another preaching service at seven, and continued the prayer-meeting till eleven P.M. It was a day never to be forgotten by any who witnesssed its scenes, and felt the power of the Spirit as manifested at the three services. On Monday, at eleven A.M., the chapel was packed as tightly as on the Sabbath. Brother Shepstone, as usual, conducted the opening service. As I always preached my sermon to my interpreter alone, and, as most of our time was occupied in public, we often took the time of the opening service for our preparation for the pulpit. At the Monday prayer-meeting, the crowd of seekers seemed almost as great as it was the day before, though several scores had been saved. Many whom we saw yesterday in their penitential struggle, apparently suffering the agony of death, weeping and piteously pleading for release from Satan, and the death-penalty of the law, are now with shining faces singing and witnessing for Jesus.

My son Stuart was greatly blessed, and for hours we see him labouring with a party of young men, several of whom he won to Christ.

See the altar crowded with whites, one after another they receive Christ, and are filled with unspeakable joy! Fathers and mothers embrace their saved prodigal sons and daughters in their arms, kiss them, and weep tears of gratitude, and praise God.

There's a heathen doctor among the seekers, decorated with strings of beads, shells, and all sorts of trinkets and charms. He feels that these things are hindering his approach to Christ, and now he scatters them. Nothing has been said about these things in the preaching, or personally to the seekers, but they are not simply the ornaments of their half-naked bodies, which might justly claim a little covering, even of beads, in the absence of something better; these were the badges of their heathenism, their gods and charms, in which they trusted for health, good crops, good luck in hunting, deliverance from their enemies, and all those demands of human nature which God only can supply. Hence, in accepting Christ, they violently tear these idols off, and cast them away. We see women tearing open the brass-bands on their arms, and throwing them down. They were great treasures before, but now they hate them. Many of those who, an hour ago, were roaring in the disquietude of their souls, are now sitting quietly at the feet of Jesus, with tearful eyes and smiling faces. Many, however, exercise their first new life in witnessing for Christ.

See that Kaffir Boanerges, how he talks! I wish we could understand his language. "Charles, what is that man saying?"

"O, he says, 'I never knew that I was such a

sinner, till the Holy Ghost shined into me, then I saw that I was one of the worst sinners in the world. O, I cried to God, gave my wicked heart to Him, and received Christ. Glory to Jesus! He has pardoned all my sins!'"

We'll look after the white seekers. There's an old man who has had a hard struggle. He was at it all yesterday; but now he has accepted Christ, and rejoices in the love of God. There is a little boy who was forward yesterday, but his countenance is bright; we'll see what he has found. "My little brother, have you given your heart to God?" "Yes, I have." "Have you received Jesus as your Saviour?" "O, yes, and He has forgiven me all my sins." "How did you feel when you came forward?" "O, I felt nasty." "How do you feel now?" "O, I feel nice."

A few feet from this boy we see a large, fine-looking Kaffir-woman, well-dressed in English costume, wearing a large scarlet shawl. We saw her bow down calmly as a seeker, with flowing tears and subdued utterances she gave herself to God, and received Christ, and obtained salvation in less than fifteen minutes. Now her countenance is beaming with joy unspeakable. "Charles, ask that woman where she belongs?" With what marvellous grace and eloquence she talks. "What does she say, Charles?" "She says she walked from Heald Town, forty-six miles, to get to this meeting. She could not get to your meetings in Heald Town, but heard of the great work of God there, and has come here to get you to tell her how to come to Jesus. She says she believed what her friends, at Heald Town, told her about the great salvation; but now she has found it herself, and says the half had not been told her."

There's a grand pantomime. We don't know what that Kaffir man is saying, but really his action is most earnest and graceful. "Charles, what is he saying?" He says, "I was going on in my sins, and did not know that I was in any danger till to-day. But to-day the Holy Ghost shined upon my path. I saw hell open just close before me, and I was rushing into it; but I turned to God, and laid hold on Christ, and He has saved my soul from hell."

See that old Kaffir-woman supporting her withered frame on sticks as she moves up and down the aisle in a regular Kaffir dance, and talking so earnestly. A more comical-looking old creature I never saw.

"Brother Shepstone, what's the matter with that old woman?"

"I don't know, she looks like a crazy person. I'll go and hear what she's saying." Down the aisle, amid the struggling masses of the seekers and the saved, the old missionary goes to hear the talk of the old woman. Returning with a smile, he says,— "She's not crazy at all, but has just come to her right mind. She has obtained salvation, and is exhorting the people to go on and tell everybody about

Jesus. She is in a transport of joy. I know her now. I have seen her at a heathen kraal in the neighbourhood; but I never saw her in the chapel before." "Her age must date back a long way towards 'the flood.'" "I don't know how old she is," replied the old missionary; "but her son, whom I know, is seventy-five years old." I look again at the old creature, and laugh and weep. She seems to be a relation to the antediluvians; whether this seventy-five year old lad was her oldest or youngest son, I did not learn, and yet as but to-day, "born again," and has become a babe in Christ. These are mere bird's-eye glances into a scene that cannot be described. We had a grand service on Monday night. On Tuesday, at eleven A.M., we preached on "Christian Perfection," went into the philosophy of the subject, and of the Spirit's gracious adjustment to the instincts, appetites, and passions, and explained clearly, even to Kaffir minds, God's purpose as to their existence, proper discipline, and appropriate exercise. The whole thing was simplified, so that every believing Kaffir could see it. Brother Shepstone said he never supposed before that the Kaffir language could be used to convey so perfectly the whole Gospel, and had never conceived it possible for an interpreter to put such a variety of English words and ideas into Kaffir. He expressed his surprise repeatedly, that Charles not only put my ideas into Kaffir to their nicest shades of meaning, but did it with such masterly facility. The fact is, though I gave him every statement of truth and illustrative fact in a sermon, just as I would give them in preaching directly to an English audience, yet I had always gone through each subject of discourse beforehand with him alone. If there was a word he did not understand, I at once ignored it, and substituted one that was familiar to him; but he was so thirsty for knowledge himself, that, if possible, he always preferred to learn the meaning of my words, and to select new Kaffir words to fit them, and the exact meaning of a foreign illustration he would give through a corresponding figure familiar to the Kaffir mind. For example, "An ivy crawled out from between the roots of a beautiful sapling, and entwined itself around the trunk of the young tree. It gradually absorbed the strength of the soil and moisture that the tree needed for its life, and tightened its manyfolded girth, till it obstructed the sap-vessels of the tree. The tree had grown tall and mighty, but the deceitful ivy did its deadly work. The noble tree declined, lingered long, but finally died. When I stood by the grand old tree it was dead, and all the dews of heaven, and the fruitful supplies of the earth, and all the skill of all the gardeners could not cause that tree to bud. It was dead. Application—the deceitful ivy of sin in the souls of all sinners."

There is no ivy in South Africa, therefore the literal base of that figure would be utterly lost on a

Kaffir, but the milkwood of South Africa furnishes a figure quite as forcible. It entwines itself around a tree as gently as the ivy, its hundreds of delicate tendril feelers encircle the tree, mat together, and then unite in solid wood, until it completely envelopes the grand old tree. The foreign thing at first simply seemed to hang on as a loose, ornamental foliage, but in process of time the tree within its folds is choked to death, and its gradual decay supplies nourishing food for its destroyer for generations to come.

I have often seen these noble trees of different kinds in all stages of this deadly process, and could not restrain a thrill of sympathetic horror of being thus hugged to death and devoured piecemeal.

When I first introduced my ivy illustration to Charles, he said, "The Kaffirs don't know what you mean by ivy." "Very well," said I, "we'll not use it." "No," said he, "it is too good an illustration to lose; since you have explained it to me I understand it well, and if you will give it as the ivy, I will give it exactly by the milkwood, which every Kaffir knows."

We closed our special series of services at Kamastone at 3 P.M., on Tuesday, the 17th of July. Just before we closed Charles gave them an account of the great work of God at Annshaw, and told them how they had battled for years to put away all heathen customs from among them, especially the drinking of Kaffir beer, with all its attendant abominations, and that the work of God never prospered among them till they had put away all these things and come out fully on the Lord's side, and then the Holy Spirit came among them, and saved hundreds of their friends and of wild heathens. While Charles was speaking, Brother Shepstone became so interested in his narrative that, he got up from his seat and stood before the pulpit, looking up at my man, and finally, seeming to forget himself, he shouted out, "Hear! hear! hear!"

During our series of two days and a half, in which we preached six sermons and held five prayer-meetings, Brother Shepstone took the names of two hundred natives and twenty whites, who professed, at those services, to find the pardon of their sins through an acceptance of Christ. In a letter I received from Rev. Mr. Shepstone, dated November 13th, four months after our departure, he says, "Since your arrival on this station up to the present we have added about two hundred and fifty to our society at Kamastone. On the 28th ult. I baptized from among the heathen one hundred and sixty individuals. About twenty of these were infants, the others have embraced Christianity, and almost all of these profess to have found peace with God through our Lord Jesus Christ. When I met the society last quarter for the renewal of tickets, there was such a union of love and Christian feeling among the members as gave me great pleasure. I was rejoiced to find that they had risen up into a higher region of Christian experience."

An eye witness to the baptismal service, admitting one hundred and forty adult heathens to the Church, as above stated, writing to a local journal in Queen's Town, and quoted by the *Wesleyan Missionary Notices*, says, "Many of the candidates for baptism were grey-headed men and women. In one instance we saw an aged man and his wife, tottering on the verge of the grave, who, a few months ago, were walking in the paths of sin, but now clothed, and in their right mind. Women, who, a short time ago, were found at the dance, besmeared with red clay, and indulging all the licentiousness of those abominable scenes, now were clothed in decent European apparel, not only being baptized themselves, but bringing their infants also. The large church was crowded with attentive observers, and no one could view the scene unmoved or without feelings of deep gratitude to the Great Head of the Church. In several instances these converts have suffered considerable persecution from their heathen relations, some have been driven from their homes, some have been severely beaten, others have been tied fast to the pole of the house and watched, that they might not go out and pray to the Great Spirit. Yet in almost every case persecution has only produced the same effects it did in days of old, to make the objects of it more determined than ever to serve God rather than man."

The following extract from a letter from Brother Shepstone, published in the *Wesleyan Missionary Notices* for December, will illustrate the further progress of this work of God, and "how the old missionary hero is renewing his youth:"—

In this district we have had a share, but the full results have not reached me yet. The Queen's Town Circuit will have had about one hundred Europeans added besides coloured men. Here at Kamastone we have added three hundred and forty, and, thank God, the work is still going on at both places. Besides this, it has spread to Hankey, a Station of the London Missionary Society, about twenty miles from this, where I am informed that one hundred and fifty have become earnest seekers for salvation; and to Kat River, where three hundred are said to have been added. Some of these people from Hankey were at Kamastone, and found peace. I desired them to go back to their own minister, and tell him what God had done for them, and I hear that they have been in no way ashamed to do this. It does seem that the seed of former days is being harrowed in by our American brother; and that God's Spirit is working in such a way as none have previously seen. We are all bowed down by a sense of God's condescending mercy, while we are lifted up with a thankfulness we cannot express. Some of us would grow younger at once (but nature will not alter her laws), that we might enjoy the progress of the Gospel in this long-benighted continent for another generation.

In St. Paul's great work of God in Antioch, in Pisidia, some of his hearers, to whom he made an offer of Christ as their Saviour, "opposed themselves, and blasphemed," and in Corinth they judged themselves "unworthy of everlasting life," so among these poor heathens many "opposed themselves," and rejected Christ, as may be illustrated by the following facts given by Mr. Shepstone, in a letter.

It has not been uncommon to see some rush out of the house of God during Divine Service, afterwards confessing that they felt if they remained longer they should have been obliged to give up their heathenism and their sins, which they were determined not to do. "Where are you going?" said a heathen woman lately to her husband, as he was putting on his European clothes. "To the service," was the reply (he was coming to chapel).
"Put them off! put them off! Do you not know that all who go there are caught?" He did put them off, and he is a heathen still, though I have some hopes he may yet be "caught," as hundreds have been caught, and we are still catching.
This heathen woman, you see, used the very same terms, and applies the same meaning as our Lord used to Simon. "From henceforth thou shalt catch men." (Luke v. 10).

Though our sojourn in Kamastone was so short, we were all so imbued with the unction of the Holy Spirit, and united together so closely in the bonds of Christian sympathy and love, that we found the parting to be a solemn affair indeed. Having to preach that night at Lesseyton, twenty miles distant, we had to take a hasty dinner, and then we bade adieu to the old missionary patriarch and his wife, and a hundred Kaffirs, most of them new-born souls in Christ, who were waiting to say "farewell." I gave them a talk for their instruction and edification, shook hands with each one and left, to see them no more till we meet before the judgment seat of Christ.

The interest of our farewell exercise was increased by a touching episode. Sister Turvey, the blind lady, before mentioned in connection with the work in Queen's Town, hearing that her son George, who had followed us with a heart of grief and sin to Kamastone, had found salvation, had come twenty miles to rejoice with him. As soon as George saw his mother led into the mission-house, he ran into her arms, exclaiming, "O, mother, my dear mother, I have found Jesus!" Though we were in haste to be off, we could but stop and wait, and wonder at and adore the mysterious providence and amazing mercy of God.

Here's a daughter of sorrow, who has walked in darkness, and has literally had no light for many years. She has struggled through the dark vale of her affliction to rear and educate her children. George had been a great comfort to her, but none of her children had embraced Christ. The mother had long been praying for them, and hoping that they would be brought to God, and go with her to meet their father in heaven. Now her prayers were answered. After her joyous meeting with George, she pressed my hand, exclaiming, "Oh, Mr. Taylor, I thank God that He sent you to Africa. You have been the means of saving four of my children." The tears streamed from her darkened eyeballs as she held my hand, and praised God for His abounding mercies to her own soul and to her children. Farewell Kamastone, we are off on our mission of peace, Brother and Sister Trollip and myself in the carriage, Charles and Stuart to follow on horseback. Away, out on a high-ridge, we take our last view of our recent battle-ground, and the beautiful surroundings of the Kamastone Mission Station, and then push on to Lesseyton, the scene of my former failure, which I feared I should not be able to visit again, but now glad of a chance to retrieve my lost victory there, and do successful battle for God.

CHAPTER XVI.

LESSEYTON.

CHARLES and Stuart were not quite ready when Brother Trollip and I left Kamastone, and our hope that they would soon overtake us was not realized.

When the darkness of a moonless night settled down upon us, we had about six miles yet to drive to reach Lesseyton. In working our way through the Mimosa Scrub we could not from the carriage see the road, and had to get out and walk. When we arrived, the chapel was crowded, but Charles had not come, and there was not a man there who could interpret for me. I thought, dear me! shall we suffer another defeat here? I knew Charles would certainly come if he could find his way, but as he was a stranger in those parts, that seemed very improbable. We waited anxiously for him for about an hour, when I heard the rattle of horsehoofs in a neighbouring scrub, and hailed, and got a response, from his familiar voice. Some one had recommended him to come by a more direct path, in taking which he lost his way. We commenced preaching about half-past eight, and continued the prayer-meeting till eleven P. M.

The Spirit of the Lord was present, and wrought "wondrously." About 150 seekers of pardon came forward, and about twenty of them professed to obtain it that night, but the mass of them were slow to accept Christ. Brother Bambana, the Tembookie, head man of the station, at the close of the service, conducted us to his house. Brother Trollip, being a merchant, and having always been greatly prejudiced against the blacks, would not have consented, a week before, on any account, to lodge at the house of a coloured man, but now he and his wife had the humility and simplicity of "little children." They had entered into the kingdom of heaven, and were "fellow-citizens with the saints and the household of God," to which fraternity, our sable host had belonged for many years, and it was their privilege to enjoy his simple genuine hospitality. He gave us good food, good beds, and good cheer. Mrs. Bambana would command respect among any class of sensible discriminating people, as a person of good common-sense, and great kindness of heart. She is a Class-leader, I was told, of rare excellence. They had two adult sons, who had received a fair education, and could speak English sufficiently to enable us to converse with them a little. They were both seekers of pardon that night. Brother Bambana was greatly interested in the account I gave him through my interpreter, of the 4,000,000 of Africans whom God had delivered from slavery in America, and of the efforts being made by their friends for their education and salvation.

The next day, Wednesday, the 18th of July, at ten A. M., we are again in the chapel, with a crowded audience. Besides Brother and Sister Trollip, and one white man, who followed us from Kamastone, there were no other whites present except a Dutch family, and they could not understand anything that was said, but the truth went home to the conscience of the Kaffirs, and nearly 200 of them came forward as seekers.

There we see them down in every alternate seat back to the front door. The struggle is long and hard; now they begin to get into "the liberty of the sons of God." How the new converts do talk and exhort. They are unusually demonstrative. See them with uplifted hands and streaming eyes, telling the wonders of the Holy Spirit's work in their hearts. There is a Kaffir-woman, with painted face, covered with heathen ornaments, but oh, how she talks. "Charles, what is that woman saying?"

"She says she has been a very great sinner, but has got all her sins forgiven; she says Jesus has saved her soul, and she don't know what to tell Him, to let Him know how thankful she is for His kindness. She wants all her friends to come to God. They are heathens, not one of them knows Jesus, and she never knew Him till now. She says she knows her friends will persecute her, and try to make her give up Jesus, but she is going to cleave to Him till she dies. She is begging all her Christian brothers and sisters to pray for her, that she may not only stand firmly, but lead all her kindred to Christ." Many of the converts, as soon as they get pardon, come up the aisle, talking as they pass along to the altar to tell me and Charles, what God has done for them.

A young Kaffir-man who came up and told us that God had saved him, then fell down, and, swinging by the altar-rail, wept for an hour. "Charles, what's the matter with that poor fellow? He don't look as though he was saved." Charles questions him, and replies,—" He used to belong to the school here for two years, and was taught to read God's word; but he says he was a scabby goat, and was turned out of the flock, and became a heathen. He says he has received pardon for all his sins, but has been so wicked and ungrateful, he cannot forgive himself."

There are Bambana's two sons down, pleading for pardon. They were there last night. Now one of them enters into liberty, runs and kisses his mother, and the father and mother embrace him, and weep, and thank God. Now the other accepts Christ, and joins in the family-bundle of grateful embraces.

A fine-looking Kaffir-woman walks up to the front, and, in a most emphatic, yet most graceful, manner, is telling Brother Pamla some marvellous story.

"What is all that about, Charles?"

"She says she once knew the Lord, and was a Class-leader, but had wickedly fallen away." Says she, "I was so foolish and false to God, that I went away and left the oxen, wagon, and precious cargo standing in the road; but oh, how wonderful is the love of God, He has forgiven all my sins, and restored me to my place in His family." See an old man away at the lower end of the chapel. He has just found Jesus. He mounts a form and talks to the people. Now he comes up the aisle, weeping and talking. Brother Bambana has seated himself at the end of a form near the altar. The weeping old man suddenly seizes Bambana's foot, and, nearly jerking the old man off his seat, kisses the bottom of his boot. We have heard of washing the disciples' feet, and of kissing the Pope's toe; but to kiss the sole of a Kaffir's boot, is a new idea. On inquiry, we learn that this old man, just converted, is Bambana's shepherd, and because his master was so faithful and kind as often to talk to him about his soul, he was very angry with his master; but now that he has found salvation, he sees that his master was the best earthly friend he had, and he has taken that method of expressing his humiliation and gratitude. These are but glimpses of the indescribable scenes of that day. The trouble was, that having to preach at three P.M. to the natives in Queen's Town, eight miles distant, and conduct a fellowship-meeting for the whites at night, our time in Lesseyton was too short. During our two services there, however, the names of fifty-eight new converts had been recorded, and about one hundred seekers left. Many of the young converts were aged persons.

At the close of our last service an old man stood up and made, what seemed a most earnest, yet very dispassionate speech, which was, in effect, as Charles interpreted, "I cannot let you go away, sir, without acknowledging the great obligation we are under to God, and to you, His servant, for these services. In these remarks I know I but express the heartfelt gratitude of all the people on the station." He used many figures to illustrate his statements. One was that on my first visit, I had hung up the "milk-sack; but that the milk was sweet, and they got no nourishment, but now the milk is good, and you have given us a great feast." Milk hung up in a cowskin-sack till it becomes sour and thick is a staple article of food among the Kaffirs, and the milk-sack is such a sacred thing that no woman is allowed to touch it, and but one responsible man, for the household has charge of it;' but a Kaffir, who would drink sweet milk, would be considered not a man, but a babe. We bade adieu to our dear friends at Lesseyton, and hastened on to our appointment in Queen's Town.

That was my last night in Queen's Town. The next night I expected to preach at "Warner's," fifty miles distant on our route through Kaffraria.

We had completed our arrangements, and were ready for an early start next morning. Our party consisted of my friend, Mr. James Roberts, and myself in the cart, Charles Pamla, on a little bay-pony, which had carried him over one hundred miles from Annshaw, and my son Stuart on a sorrel "trippling" Kaffir-pony I bought for him at Kamastone.

It was hard to part with such dear friends as Brother and Sister Dugmore. Two of their daughters and a son had been saved at our series, and three other sons were among the seekers. Up to that time twenty-three sons and daughters of our missionaries, in different parts of the colony, had found peace at our meetings. At our final farewell, Brother Dugmore, a man who gives to God all the glory for His work, but a dear lover of the brethren, hung round my neck and wept, and said, "God bless you, my dear brother, you have brought salvation to my house."

This was Thursday, the 19th of July. The progress of the work in Queen's Town, and Lesseyton may be illustrated by a few extracts from letters I subsequently received from Brother Dugmore.

By date of 31st of July, he writes, "Brother Bertram has got home. On Sunday he preached to the division of his people, speaking the Dutch language, (you did not see that location). The work broke out gloriously among them. In the afternoon at the Kaffir service, such an outpouring of the Spirit took place, that they could not get away till eight o'clock at night. Brother Bertram wishes me to tell you that he does not think there are any men left on the station who have not been brought into the fold of Christ. The Gospel has triumphed over the greatest enemies it had amongst them. The most bitter opposer, on finding peace, exclaimed, 'Now, Sandili, may come, now Krilie may come (two of the most notoriously wicked warrior-chiefs in all that region), 'since I, the greatest of enemies to Christ, have come to Him, nobody need stay away!'"

By letter of the 19th of August, he writes, "I have been hoping to hear the result of your visit to our Kaffirland Stations. I have heard some tidings that have gladdened my heart, none more than the conversion of my dear Brother Warner's wandering son.

The 'leaven' *leavens on* amongst us. I hope to begin the next quarter with an increase of two hundred members. Our services are seasons 'rich in blessing.' Our regular congregations steadily increase. Our older members are thirsting for a full salvation. God has in mercy baptized my soul anew, and I am reaching forward. We trust to hear blessed news from Natal. Why should not Colenso himself be converted?"

By letter of October 27th, Brother Dugmore writes, "The results of the awakening which God vouchsafed to the three Circuits of Queen's Town division (Queen's Town, Kamastone, and Lesseyton), "while you were among us, we cannot even yet fully estimate, but I think that not less than six hundred have been received into the Societies. God has enabled me to lay hold again of the blessing in which I rejoiced in years past. I walk in the light,

I feel that my soul has returned to her rest, and that it is glorious to have an abiding sense of that 'presence' which makes the Christian's paradise. Glory be to God for "full salvation!'"

Again, in my last letter from Brother Dugmore, before leaving Africa, he says, "I do most heartily adore the goodness of God in blessing your labours in Natal, as He has done. If the work after your departure follows the rule elsewhere, the numbers of conversions will go on increasing. In several places those numbers have doubled, or more than doubled, since you left."

CHAPTER XVII.

WARNERS.

THE residence of J. C. Warner, Esq., known by the name of "Woodhouse Forests," is the head of a new mission, embracing a portion of Tembookie territory, and a part of Fingo-land, under the superintendence of a very active, promising young missionary, Rev. E. J. Barrett.

Brother and Sister Warner are earnest and useful missionaries; in fact, as they once were in name and official relationship. He was a useful missionary among the Kaffirs for a number of years, but partly through failure of health for a time and other reasons, satisfactory, I believe, to all parties, he resigned his official relation, but has continued true to the Wesleyan Church and her mission-work in a different relation. He is "British Resident for Kaffraria;" the representative of the English Government to all the tribes living between Cape Colony and Natal, and being a Wesleyan preacher he is in a position of great responsibility and usefulness. He has always been opposed to the establishment of mission stations on the principle of vesting in the missionary magisterial functions to be exercised over the people on the mission-station.

The unmodified heathenism of Kaffraria at the time the mission-stations were established was considered so corrupt and so corrupting, and the civil administration of the chiefs so arbitrary, capricious, and so antagonistic to Christianity, that it was felt to be necessary to organize the people of the stations into a separate civil community, acknowledging the sovereignty of the chiefs, but protected and governed by the missionary under a kind of treaty stipulation with the chiefs. The Heathen chiefs are not supposed to be competent to govern a Christian community, and, I presume, in a majority of cases, prefer to be relieved from such a responsibility, and hence, by mutual agreement, that, devolves on the missionary, extending not simply to his church-members, but to all the people resident on the mission-station.

The mission-station, as per agreement, is a "city of refuge" to which persons suspected of witchcraft or other undefinable offences, endangering their lives, may flee and be safe, while they remain under the shield of the missionary.

The missionary, therefore, occupies the position of a civil magistrate, having jurisdiction over the district embraced in the lines of his grants for mission purposes. He must hear complaints, try cases, inflict penalties in the form of fines, or expulsion from the station, subject to an appeal from his decisions to the paramount chief. On the other hand, he is answerable to his chief for the good conduct of his mission people. I don't give this as the theory, with which the men of God, who hazarded their lives among those heathen, in founding those focal centres of Gospel agency, set out at the commencement, but the theory defining the developed facts as we find them.

An extract from a letter I received from Rev. Wm. Shepstone, dated November 13th, 1866, touching this subject, will show the legal status of the missionary in Kaffraria:—

A Kaffir chief has *Amapakati* in the different parts of his country. These preside over certain districts or rivers. In all cases of litigation the case should first come before the *Amapakati* to be settled, or adjudged, but either is at liberty to appeal against the judgment of the *Amapakati* to the chief. Now this is the power which legally belongs to a missionary in Kaffirland. He is no chieftain; but is a subordinate magistrate under the chief magistrate, to whom an appeal can always be made against his decisions, if either party desires it. Whatever he gains beyond this must be moral power, even such a diabolical practice as the *Umpouhlo*, the missionary must oppose by moral suasion. When Mr. Shaw and I entered on the Kaffirland mission in 1823, now forty-three years ago this month, the practice of *Umpouhlo* was rampant, revolting to every sense of moral feeling, to a degree one does not like to look back at. We were without any authority, we were no chiefs; but Mr.

Shaw succeeded in that tribe in getting it put down by authority, not his authority, but the chiefs. It was moral power. For this successful use of his influence, the women of the tribe gave him the cognomen of "Likaka laba Fasi"—the shield of the women: nor did I ever hear of the practice being revived or attempted in that tribe afterwards, and I am inclined to think that from that time the practice declined among the other tribes on the frontier.

That missionaries and ministers everywhere should prudently exert their influence for the removal of national sins, however disguised in legal livery, is a fact, that but few persons will deny; but how far a minister of the Gospel should encumber himself with administrative responsibilities, is a question to be carefully considered, and yet one which must be determined, in many cases, by the peculiar circumstances of any given case, which should come under the head of exceptions, as the rule certainly is that he should be a man of one work.

In regard to this mission-station question, a great deal may be said on both sides.

1st. It is a good thing for the missionary, as far as possible, to be able to make and execute all his arrangements for the salvation, the education, and the civilization of the heathen, without authoritative heathenish interference.

2nd. It is a good thing in those regions of heathenish darkness, where there is so much "smelling out," and murder, on a suspicion of witchcraft, to have a sanctuary to which the poor persecuted wretches may flee, and escape torture and death. Many lives have thus been saved at the mission-stations.

3rd. It is thought to be a very good thing for the converts from heathenism, to have the opportunity of "coming out from among them," literally, to live on the mission-station, where they may escape the daily taunts of their wicked neighbours, and the danger of contact with their abominable practices. Hence the rule has been for the converts, with but very few exceptions, to move at once, and become citizens of the mission community. There are, to be sure, some "out-stations," but they are under the same administration as that of the head station. I met with some good missionaries in South Africa, who consider it next to an impossibility for a converted Kaffir to live among his heathen neighbours, and remain a Christian.

But, on the other hand, it is said,—

1st. The missionary, having the responsibility of administrating this complex government of "Church and State," will so have his time and energies consumed with perplexing cares, as greatly to interfere with his ministerial effectiveness on his station, and leave him but little time or strength for proclaiming the Gospel beyond.

2nd. The station becoming the sanctuary and home for all sorts of refugees, attracts a great many worthless characters, who are often pointed at and quoted, by the colonists, as well as by the heathen, as fair specimens of the mission people, and however unjust the charge, the stations thus suffer great disgrace. The fact too, that so many supposed witches find a refuge on the mission-stations, a large proportion of the Kaffirs regard them as the home and haunt of the wizards, and therefore places to be dreaded and shunned.

3rd. That by collecting all the converts into one body together, the Gospel leaven is separated from the lump it should leaven, and a hot-bed, feeble type of Christian character is developed in the station, instead of a heroic martyr type, which alone can successfully grapple with heathenism defensively, and aggressively. Without going into the details of the subject here, I believe I have fairly stated the strong points on both sides, and I shall have occasion from personal observation, to furnish facts illustrating both sides of the question. It is by no means a mere abstract question, but a subject of vital practical importance to successful missionary enterprise in Africa, and in every other mission field in heathenism. When I entered Kaffraria, I knew nothing about this subject; I had never heard it discussed, and hence went into the field of observation, an unprejudiced learner, and came out with my facts and conclusions, which shall be forthcoming in due time.

That was a moonless night. From Queen's Town, we had travelled that day over a hilly rough road forty-six miles, and had yet four miles of our day's journey to make in the dark.

Rev. E. J. Barrett came to meet us and to be our

guide. We had in a pair of horses, that had been sent on thirty miles the day before, and they were fresh and fiery, and not so manageable as they became a couple of hundred miles further along. Descending what appeared to be a smooth bit of road, at the rate of about "eight knots," a sudden jolt sent us both over the "larboard," head foremost down the hill. We thought the thing had upset, but, relieved of our weight, it righted up; and when we got our "bearings," we heard the rattle of the horses' hoofs and the cart wheels away in the distance.

Brother Barrett, who was a few roads ahead of us, came rushing back, crying out—"Are ye killed?"

"Not dead yet, pursue the horses as fast as you can."

Away he galloped in pursuit.

We gathered ourselves up, and found that, though our clothing was torn, and we were scratched and bruised considerably, there were no bones broken, so we picked up a load of rugs and coats cast out of the cart, and worked our way in the dark to Mr. Warner's. About an hour later, Mr. Barrett arrived, telling how many miles he had travelled in different directions, but could get no tidings of the runaway horses and cart. A company of Kaffirs were then sent out in all directions. Different parties up to midnight reported no success. We had comfortable lodgings in Mr. Barrett's Kaffir hut, built by himself. It is eighteen feet in diameter, seven feet walls, with an elevation at the apex of about fifteen feet. The "British Resident," and family, live in a larger but more rustic Kaffir hut near by. He is building a good dwelling, which was nearly ready for the roof when we were there. At the dawn of next morning, Brothers Warner, Roberts, and Barrett, went to the place of disaster, and saw where the upper cart wheel had struck a large ant-hill causing our ejectment, hence tracing the "spore," they found that the horses had run down the hill, a distance of a quarter of a mile, and turned at a right angle away from the road. Further along, the cart "spore" was within three inches of a precipice, over-hanging a little lake, deep enough to have drowned the horses, had the cart gone over and drawn them in. About a mile from the road in the "veldt," they found the horses standing still, attached to the cart as when we were driving them, everything right, even the whip stood erect in its place. I was thankful, though not surprised, for I had said the night before that, as we were doing work for God, and could not replace our conveyance nearer than Queen's Town, and as our engagements demanded haste, I did not doubt that He who takes care even of the sparrows cared much more for the souls we might be instrumental in saving in Kaffraria, and would see to it that our animals and conveyance would be preserved from harm, and that we should pursue our journey in safety.

Rev. E. J. Barrett is a young man of great industry and useful missionary talents. He has been but three years in the work of the ministry, but has so far learned the Kaffir language as to preach through it fluently without an interpreter. He has no family, and while his head-quarters are at Brother Warner's, he is almost continually travelling and preaching among the Kaffirs, and lodging with them in their huts. His circuit, though on the borders of Fingo-land, lies mainly among the "Tambookie" tribe of Kaffirs.

He is preparing to build a chapel at "Woodhouse Forest," and another near a beautiful grove of timber, five miles distant.

On Friday morning, the 20th of July, I selected a suitable place for our preaching and prayer-meeting in a beautiful grassy vale, about four hundred yards from our hut. I took some healthy muscular exercise in rolling a large boulder to a suitable spot for a pulpit or platform from which to preach.

The population of this region is rather sparse, and the notice of our coming was very short, so that we did not see the crowds we had been accustomed to see in older communities. At eleven A.M. our service commences. As I stand on my rock pulpit, with my tall interpreter on my left, there is spread out before us a scene of great beauty. Just back of us is a little brook and reed marsh, obliging all our hearers to remain in front of us. From this brook, in our rear, rises a high, rocky, grassy, wooded hill, an angular branch of the main mountain to our right which is adorned with fine forest trees. In front of us rises a high, smooth ridge, covered with tall grass. To our left we see the huts of Brothers Warner and Barrett, the walls of the new residence of Mr. Warner, the native village, and an extensive open undulating country, with its lovely grassy slopes, enlivened by the herds of the Kaffirs, and their mealy patches. Circling in front of us, seated on the grass, are first the women and children, and next the men; on the outer edge of the circle, to our left, are a lot of painted heathens, with their red blankets thrown loosely round their naked bodies. The whole congregation numbers about two hundred persons. Our first sermon is to the believers, unfolding to them God's provisions and plans for the salvation of the world, administered by the personal Holy Ghost, who employs believers as His visible agents. We close by singing and prayer, and advise them to think much, and pray much alone, take some refreshment, and come again at three P.M. At the close of the afternoon sermon we invite the seekers of pardon to kneel down on the grass. About one hundred and forty bow before the Lord, and enter into a penitential struggle, with a general wailing of lamentation and tears, which cease not for three hours, only as they enter into liberty. We see among them several of the red heathens.

"Do you see that tall, well-dressed Kaffir down on his knees as a seeker?" "Yes." "That is Matanzima, a Tambookie Chief, a brother of Ngangelizwe, the paramount chief of the Tambookie nation." We see Charles bending over the chief for half an hour, trying to lead him to Jesus. Poor fellow, he seems to be an earnest seeker. Near the close of the meeting Charles brings the chief to me, and I explain to him the way of salvation by faith, and beg him to surrender himself to God, and accept Christ as his Saviour now. He seems very teachable and anxious to know God. Among a number of questions I put to him, that I may ascertain the obstructions in his way, and help him to consent to their removal, I said, "Matanzima, how many wives have you got?"

"Two," said he.

"How many children have you by them?"

"Two children by one wife, and one by the other."

"The laws of Jesus Christ will allow you to have but one wife. Are you willing to retain your first, as your lawful wife, and give the other one up?"

"Yes," he replied, promptly; "but what shall I do with her?"

"You must explain to her that you do not put her away in anger, but because you have consented to obey the laws of Christ, which allow a man but one wife; you must not send her away in poverty, but give her whatever she needs for herself and the support of her child, and let her go home to her own people."

"Well," said he, "I'll bring her to Mr. Warner, and let him settle it."

"Yes," I answered, "that will be the best way. Now having settled that matter in your mind, and consenting to give up all your sins, you need not delay your coming to Jesus Christ, but embrace Him as your Saviour now." But instead of a present surrender, and a present acceptance of Christ, I saw from his face that he was reconsidering the wife question, and wavering in his purpose to give up the sin of polygamy, and soon began to put on his gloves, for he was a fine-looking, well-dressed man, and said, "Now, I must go home." He did not tell me that he could not consent to Gospel terms, yet I felt but little doubt that, like the rich young man who came to Jesus, and hearing what he should "do to inherit eternal life," he declined and "went away sorrowful" in his sins. I was very sorry to believe, and to say to the brethren, that the chief wavered, and would not remain a seeker long.

I mention this case to illustrate one of the most serious difficulties to be encountered in bringing the Kaffirs to God—their ancient system of polygamy.

Meantime, about sixty persons of all ages professed to obtain the pardon of their sins. As fast as they got the witness of forgiveness they were conducted to a place to our left hand to be examined by the missionary.

"Now, Brother Barrett," said I, "you will please to hear the experience of these new converts, and get their names and addresses, so that you may know where to find them, and get them into class, and under good pastoral training for God. If any are not clear in their testimony to the fact of conscious pardon through the Holy Spirit's witness with theirs, kindly advise them to go back among the seekers and seek till they get it." Brother Barrett is an earnest and most industrious missionary, but seemed a little embarrassed in the midst of such a sudden break-down of so many Kaffirs, and rather incredulous as to the conversion of so many in one day, but I begged him to examine them closely and satisfy his own mind fully, and send back all who were not clear. He spent so much time with each one that he did not have time to converse with more than half of them. It was too cold to preach out that night, so we had a fellowship-meeting in Brother Warner's stable specially for the young converts. Over thirty of them arose voluntarily and promptly, one after another, and in great simplicity told what God had done for their souls. The experience of every one was clear except one man, who told about some great light that he had seen some months before and heard a voice telling him that he would be saved. Brother Barrett challenged his experience, and asked him several close questions. Charles also questioned him to draw out of him a testimony to a genuine experience of salvation, if he was in possession of it; but his tale was ignored, and the people warned against seeking to see sights and to hear audible voices, "for the Spirit itself beareth witness with our spirits," not to our eyes or ears but to our "*spirits*, that we are the children of God." It was a very profitable service for mutual edification. We gave them suitable advice, and I was much pleased to find that Brother Barrett's faith in the genuineness of their conversion had been fully confirmed.

Brother Barrett, in a letter, dated July 24th, says,

I thank God for your visit to this place. I see more reason to hope for the salvation of Africa than ever I did before. God evidently can and is willing to do a quick and true work among these people. Of those who were here some were from other circuits. Ten from Mr. Wakeford's circuit professed to find peace. Some of the Fingoes were blessed. I conversed more or less with them before they left, but have not yet had time to follow them to Fingo-land. Among the Tambookies of my own circuit I have had a better opportunity of understanding the work. I think all our members who professed any spiritual life are quickened. One man, formerly a dead member, who had never known anything of spiritual life, is clearly brought to God. He is now earnest and happy. Several backsliders have returned, among them is Klass, the head man of the station. The devil tried hard to keep Klass away from Christ. He had left a goat in charge of a Hottentot at the Tsoma river. The devil ordered his Hottentot servant to make off with the goat to Krielie's country. Klass heard of it just in time to take him away from your morning service. The Hottentot, however, got drunk, and was prevented from starting till Klass arrived and got his goat. We thought Klass had run away for fear he should get converted, but finding his goat he returned in time for the afternoon preaching, and the Lord brought him in.

Most of the former seekers have found peace, and a few, who were not seekers, have been brought in.

In a subsequent letter, Brother Barrett confirmed my fears in regard to the chief :—

I am sorry to say that Matanzima, the Tambookie chief of "the right hand house," has not retained the religious impressions produced on his mind by your preaching, and has not even permitted me to hold service at his place. (Herod heard John gladly, and "did many things," but did not give up his stolen wife, and soon after cut the preacher's head off.) How can he be a Christian when his powerful counsellors are heathens. I think the chiefs will have to be moved by the nation and not the nation by the chiefs. A Kaffir chief possesses power only for evil, to fight, to "eat up," and destroy, but not to improve the condition of his people.

I felt very sorry to leave "Woodhouse Forests" so soon. We had seen a good work indeed during our one day's services, but if we could have spent a week among them a great work might have been wrought, but my limited time and pre-announced appointments beyond obliged us to proceed on our journey. Saturday morning, the 21st of July, we bade adieu to this new and interesting mission-station, and commenced a journey of fifty miles that day to Butterworth. It is marvellous to look back and remember that the thrilling scenes and grand victories at Kamastone, Lesseyton, the native work and fellowship-meeting in Queen's Town, for the whites, and the campaign of yesterday at Woodhouse Forests, have all transpired within the past week, from Sabbath the 15th to Friday the 20th of July. Blessed God, the kingdom is Thine, the power is Thine, and hence the glory is Thine, all Thine, only Thine!

Brother Warner furnished us a pair of horses to take our conveyance twenty miles, to the "Tsoma river," and accompanied us on horseback several miles. At the Tsoma we overtook our horsemen who had gone on early with the horses, so as to give them a little rest, while Brother Warner's pair were doing the work for us. There is an old military station at the Tsoma, and at that time a small detachment of British soldiers, under Col. Barker. All the soldiers have since been withdrawn, and the station given to the Wesleyans for mission purposes, and the Fingoes left to themselves to keep the peace with their old Kaffir masters, or defend themselves till help can be afforded them from the colony. Col. Barker received us into his hut, with a cordial greeting, and entertained us with a good lunch, with genuine English hospitality. Rev. John Logden, the missionary at Butterworth, had been there a few days before, and prepared the way for us, and provided a relay of fresh horses at the Tsoma, which however we did not need, and respectfully declined the use of them.

The Tsoma, which is a fine African river, is deep, rocky, and dangerous for travellers, but the water being low in the winter season, we crossed without difficulty. On we go, over high hills, and across deep valleys, through a country abounding with grass, from one to two feet high, ripened and dried into a rich orange colour. This wavy ocean of grass, which stretches out in every direction into the immeasurable distance, is interspersed with occasional groves of timber, and island-looking rocky hill peaks and cliffs. About fifteen miles from the Tsoma, we met a Kaffir boy, who said " Mr. Longden has sent a pair of horses to Capt. Cobb's for you," pointing across the hills towards the Captain's house, nearly a mile off the main road. So we " out-spanned " our horses, and walked over. The Captain, who is a dashing, but generous pioneer Englishman, gave us a cordial welcome. He is a magistrate, under Mr. Warner, over a portion of Her Majesty's Fingo subjects. There we met the native teacher from Butterworth, who had come to act as our guide, and four or five English friends, who had been waiting at Butterworth for us two days, having come sixty miles from near King William's Town, to attend our meeting, and seek the Lord.

Captain Cobb gave us all a good dinner, and showed us his new house, orchard, and garden. It was really surprising to see such improvements, such beautiful beds of flowers, and flourishing fruit-trees, where, but eighteen months ago, the wild deer roamed without disturbance. The last eight miles of our long day's journey were made after the day had departed. The road was rough and dangerous, but our trusty guide rode before, and shouted, "To the right," and "To the left," alternately, turning us away from rocks and gullies which might have cost us an upset, at the peril of our necks.

By the mercy of our Master, we safely reached Butterworth about eight P.M., and were heartily welcomed and most kindly entertained by Rev. John Longden and his excellent missionary wife.

CHAPTER XVIII.

BUTTERWORTH (IGEUWA).

THIS mission-station was established under the general superintendence of Rev. W. Shaw, by the Rev. Mr. Shrewsbury, assisted by Rev. W. Shepstone, in 1827. The great Chief Hintza, of the Amagcaleka tribe, had not given his consent for the establishment of the mission in his country, but had not refused, so Mr. Shrewsbury proceeded in the work by faith. "But a few months after," says Mr. Shaw, "with great Kaffir ceremony, he sent to the station one of his brothers, and a company of his counsellors, mostly old men (counsellors of Kauta, his father) with the following remarkable message—'Hintza sends to you these men, that you may know them; they are now your friends, for to-day Hintza adopts you into the same family, and makes the mission the head of that house. If any one does you wrong apply to them for redress. If in anything you need help, ask them for assistance;' and as a confirmation of the whole, pointing to a fat ox they had brought, 'There is a cake of bread from the house of Kauta.'"

The mission, thus placed under the protection of law by the blessing of God, and the fostering care of several successive missionaries, grew and prospered for six years, when its harmonious relations were disturbed by the Kaffir war of 1833-4. Hintza joined in the war against the colonists, "behaved treacherously toward certain European traders, who were at the time in his country, and it was believed also, that he contemplated the murder of his missionary," Rev. John Ayliff, and the destruction of the station.

Rev. W. J. Davis gave me an account of how Brother Ayliff escaped, and, as it will illustrate a phase of missionary life in this place, now sacred in my own memory, I will give the substance of his narrative. "Hintza's purpose to kill Mr. Ayliff was revealed to him by Hintza's 'great wife,' Nomsa. All the trails and roads were guarded by spies, so that there was no possibility of his escape, but he managed to get a letter conveyed about fifty miles, to Brother Davis at Clarkebury. Mr. Davis sent to Morley Mission Station, thirty-five miles distant, and got the missionary there, Rev. Mr. Palmer, to join him in a trip to Butterworth, to try and rescue their brother missionary from the murderous designs of Hintza. On their arrival at Butterworth, after consultation with Brother Ayliff, they resolved that they would go and see the chief himself, and thus take the 'bull by the horns' at once. They immediately sent out runners, and collected a party of men as guides and guards, and set off to Hintza's 'Great Place,' about sixty miles distant. They rode boldly into the chief's kraal, and found him seated in council, surrounded by his ' Amapakati.'

"Having gone through all the ceremony common in approaching such a dignitary, Brother Davis, addressing the chief, said—" Hintza, we have come to talk to you about your missionary. We have heard that you have given orders to kill Ayliff, and now he has come, and we have come with him to see what you have against him. We know that you are at war with the English, but we are missionaries, we have nothing to do with the war. If Ayliff has done anything worthy of death, he don't refuse to die. You can try him and put him to death in an honourable way, but it don't become a great chief like you, to waylay him like an assassin and kill him behind a bush. He is your missionary. He came into your country with your consent, and put himself under your protection, and you should deal honourably with him. If he has done wrong then tell him so to his face; if guilty of anything worthy of death, convict him, and kill him. Or, if you want to get rid of him, give him a pass out of your country, and he will at once go away and leave you, but it would be a great injustice, and a disgrace to you as a great chief, to kill your missionary behind a bush.' Hintza seemed greatly agitated while Davis was talking, and was silent for some time. Then he ordered food for the missionaries, and told them to sit down for the night, and he would meet them in council the next day.

"That night, after the missionary party had sung and prayed in their hut, Nomsa, the chief's 'great wife,' came in and said, 'Sing again.'

"'Why should we sing again? We have just had singing and prayer.'

"'I have a word to say to you, and I don't want anybody but you to hear it. If you sing, they will think that after the singing you will be praying, and they won't come near,' so they sang again.

"Then said she, 'You have done well to come to the chief. It will be all right to-morrow, Ayliff will be allowed to remain, and get promise of protection. But if he remains he might tramp on a snake in the grass, and he had better not remain.'

"The next day they met the chief in council, and Hintza said, 'You have done well to come to me. Some miscreant might have done Ayliff harm, but it will be all right now. Ayliff may go back to Butterworth, and sit down in peace, and it will be all right.'

"They returned, and soon ascertained that there were no more conspirators in the way, seeking Ayliff's life, and as the way was now open, the missionaries unanimously agreed that it was better, in view of the war troubles, and all the circumstances in the case, that Brother Ayliff should take Nomsa's advice; so he made arrangements as early as convenient, and, with his mission people, left Hintza's country.

The chief complained afterwards of Ayliff's want of confidence in him, but his own subsequent record proved the wisdom of Ayliff's departure. Soon after the mission premises and village were plundered and destroyed, and, before the war was over, Hintza himself was killed.

The mission was re-established after the war, but was destroyed again in the war of 1846-7.

"Rili," or Krielie, as it is usually spelled to give the sound in English nearest to the Kaffir guttural R, the son and successor of Hintza, was anxious for the rebuilding of the mission-house and chapel, and gave for the purpose as many cattle as when sold, were necessary to cover most of the expense of erecting the mission-buildings, and compensate for the personal losses of the missionary.

At one time, when Rev. W. J. Davis was stationed there, the country was dried up, the cattle were dying, and there was a general apprehension of famine. The Chief Rili assembled a large body of "rain makers" near to the mission premises, and with a great gathering of the people, they went on with their incantations and "vain repetitions" daily for a week. Brother Davis kept himself advised, through his agents, of all their proceedings. Finally, the rain-makers said they could not get any rain, and had found out the reason why, and the cause of the drought. When the attention of the people was

T

fully arrested by such an announcement, they told their anxious auditors that the missionaries were the cause of the drought, and that there would be no rain while we were allowed to remain in the country. That brought matters to a very serious crisis, for the "rain-makers" are generally very influential, usually being doctors or priests as well. When the chief wants rain he sends some cattle to the rain-makers to offer in sacrifice to "Imishologu," the spirits of their dead, who are presumed to have great power with "Tixo" or God, who will send rain. If they do not succeed, the rain-maker returns answer that the cattle were not of the right colour, that cattle of certain peculiar spots were necessary. The details of these spots and shades of colour are so numerous that the rain-maker can not only drive a good trade in the beef line, but stave off the issue till, in the natural order, a copious rain descends, for which he claims the credit, and it is known all over the country as such a "rain-maker's" rain. Thus they maintain their influence, and when a number of such men combine against a missionary, it becomes a very serious matter. So when Brother Davis heard of the grave charge brought against the missionaries, and specially against himself and family, as they were the only missionaries there, he saw that he must act in self-defence at once. So the next morning, which was Thursday, he rode into their camp, while they were in the midst of their ceremonies, and demanded a hearing. They stopped their noise and confusion to hear what he had to say, and he proceeded as follows:—"I shall give you a very short talk. Your rain-makers say that the missionaries are the cause of the drought. I say that the rain-makers and the sins of the people are the cause of the drought. The missionaries are as anxious for rain as you are, and our God would give us rain, but for your wickedness and rebellion against Him. Now I propose that we test the matter between your rain-makers and the missionaries. They have been trying here for one whole week to bring rain, and have not brought one drop. Look at the heavens, there is not even the sign of a cloud. Now stop all this nonsense, and come to chapel next Sabbath, and we will pray to God, who made the heavens and the earth, to give us rain, and we will see who is the true God, and who are His true servants, and your best friends." Then Nomsa, the great wife of Hintza, who had interposed to save the life of Brother Ayliff a few years before, and the great chief Rili, her son, and their amapakati, held a consultation, and decided to dismiss the rain-makers at once, and accept the issue proposed by Brother Davis. The next day was observed by this missionary Elijah, and his Christian natives, as a day of fasting and prayer. On Sabbath morning the sun, as for many months past, poured his burning rays upon the crisped Kaffrarian hills and valleys, with their famishing flocks, without the shadow of an intervening cloud.

At the hour for service the usual congregation

assembled, and besides them the great chief and his mother, and many of the heathen people from their "great-place." There was a motley crowd of half-clad mission natives, a lot of naked heathens, the great chief in his royal robe, consisting of, a huge tiger-skin, his queen mother, with beaded skirt of dressed cow-skin, and ornamental brass wristlets, armlets, and head trinkets, and there, at their feet, the missionary and his family—a grand representation of Church and State, all sweltering with heat, all uneasy, all anxious to see a little cloud arise, but not one, even of the size of a man's hand, appeared when the service commenced. After some preliminaries, Brother Davis asked the people to kneel down, and unite with him in prayer to the Lord God of Elijah, to send them rain from heaven. The man of God pleaded his own cause, and that of the people at the mercy-seat, and importuned. No man was sent to look toward the sea; but while they remained on their knees in solemn awe, in the presence of God, they heard the big rain drops begin to patter on the zinc roof of the chapel, and lo, a copious rain, which continued all that afternoon and all night. The whole region was so saturated with water that the river near by became so swollen that the chief and his mother could not cross it that night, and hence had to remain at the mission-station till the next day. That seemed to produce a great impression on the minds of the chief, his mother, and the heathen party in favour of God and His missionaries, and Brother Davis got the name of a great rain-maker;

but signs, wonders, and even miracles, will not change the hearts of sinners, for Nomsa lived and died a heathen, and her royal son remains an increasing dark and wicked heathen to this day.

The Butterworth Mission Station was destroyed the third time during the Kaffir war of 1851-2, and lay waste about ten years.

About the year 1855, Krielie resorted to a daring and desperate plan for forcing his people into an exterminating war against the colonists, which destroyed thousands of his people, and deprived him of about half of his country, including the site of Butterworth Station. His plan was to strip his people of all their wealth, which consisted of "the cattle upon a thousand hills," and thus combine with their patriotism, and love of booty, a dire necessity, which would precipitate his whole people into the colony, "drive the whites into the sea," and seize the spoils.

So taking advantage of their superstitious gullibility, a prophet of renown among them commanded that all their cattle should be killed, and when all were gone, there would be a resurrection of all their cattle, and the cattle of their ancestors, greatly improved in size and quality, and countless in numbers, and all who would believe the prophet, and kill their cattle, should feast on beef all the days of their lives, but the disobedient would be turned into *moths*.

Tens of thousands of cattle were slain. Krielie's whole country was desolated and denuded of its fine supply of food. The colonists were in great alarm, and Sir George Grey was sent as governor, specially to meet the pending war emergency. By the time he was ready for war, he found Krielie's Kaffirs starving by the thousand, and instead of pouring into the colony as fierce warriors they came as beggars. Sir George wisely sent them supplies, and was soon able to dictate terms of peace to the haughty warrior chief, without firing a shot. In that treaty he got from Krielie all that fine country, lying between the "great Kei river," and the river "Gnabakka," which has since been given to the Fingoes, as a reward for their unwavering loyalty since their deliverance and adoption by the government in 1835. It is now known as Fingo-land. Butterworth is near the eastern boundary of it, and but fifteen miles from Krielie's "great place." The old chief, I was told, pleaded hard to be allowed to retain his mission-station, but it was thought, as his motives in respect to the station were purely selfish, and as it might more readily lead to complications with the Government, it was best for the colony, and for the mission, to keep it out of Krielie's hands altogether. Krielie's people do not now exceed thirty thousand. They have no missionary, and the old chief, owing to a petty difficulty which he last year fomented, at the Butterworth Station, about a pig, was forbidden by Captain Cobb to set his foot on the west side of the Gnabakka.

The Butterworth Mission has been established the

fourth time, and now promises to be more flourishing than ever before, under Rev. John Longden, who commenced operations there about four years ago.

We were comfortably quartered in the mission-house, and Brother and Sister Longden, with good fare and good cheer, rendered our sojourn with them very pleasant. On Sabbath morning, the 22nd of July, I walked round about their little Zion to find the most suitable place for open-air preaching, as we anticipated that the chapel accommodation for about four hundred would be inadequate. We selected a beautiful spot, a quarter of a mile distant, on the bank of the river, richly carpeted with grass.

At ten A.M., Charles and I stand before a motley crowd of about five hundred natives and a dozen whites. To our left is the river, in the rear a little cliff or point of rocks, jutting down to the water's edge; to our right a high rocky hill, at our feet the tongue or wedge-point of a valley, which rapidly widens, and opens the prospect to the mission-buildings on a high hill beyond; just in the rear of us are our European friends, who had come over forty miles for this occasion, and the mission-family; just in front are the native women and children, next to them, in a circling mass, the native men ; to our right and front, perched on the side of the hill, are about one hundred wild heathens, painted with red ochre, and greased till they glisten in the sunlight. Their clothing consists simply of a blanket painted red with the same native dye which covers their bodies. I greatly feel the embarrassment of the situation. I must preach to these believers to adjust them to the Holy Spirit's methods, so as to "work together with God" effectively in the salvation of sinners, and yet I must arrest the attention of the heathen and interest them in our work, or they will go away and we shall not get another shot at them, and there is scarcely time in one service to secure well these two ends, but we go on and combine the two objects as well as we can. All quiet and attentive, and a great interest manifestly awakened among the mission people.

"Now we invite all who fully understand the subject, who feel the burden of their sins, and have made up their minds to give themselves to God, and receive Jesus as their Saviour, to stand up. Let each one think well and act for him or herself. Let no one stand simply because another does. Let no one be afraid to stand up because of the presence of another. As we shall answer to God for ourselves, so let us say, 'Let others do as they will, but as for me, I will serve God.'" In about a minute we see about one hundred on their feet, including half a dozen whites. We now invite them to kneel, surrender to God, and receive Jesus Christ, whom He hath sent into the world to save sinners. An earnest struggle ensues, and a few enter into liberty, and witness to the fact in the story of their salvation to the missionary, who examines each one personally. After a service of three hours we dismiss them, and invite them to meet us there again at three P.M. "Charles," say I by the way, "the campaign of last week at Kamastone, Lesseyton, Queen's Town, and Warners, has nearly used us up. We are not up to our mark to-day. I don't feel the Spirit's unction as I usually do in going into the battle." "No," replies Charles, "your Father sees that your body can't bear it. He means to give you an opportunity to get back your usual strength of body. He does not want to work you to death."

I said in my heart, "Good for my Zulu, many a European or American enthusiast might learn lessons of wisdom from you."

At three P.M. we had about the same audience as in the morning. The preaching goes home to their hearts with increasing power. Many of the people are immigrant Fingoes, from Cape Colony, where they have been accustomed to hear the Gospel for years, and the station people have long been under the instruction of Brother Longden. These heathen know nothing about it, or, what is worse, they have heard more against the Gospel by the carnal opposition its glimmer of light upon their minds has provoked than they have learned of its power. After the sermon we call for seekers, and over a hundred go down on their knees, and an earnest struggle against the powers of darkness ensues. The heathen look very serious, but the most of them refuse to yield, a few of them are down among the seekers. A much larger number are saved at this service than at the first. Among the converts who report themselves, we see two old heathen men. "Charles, what has that old red blanket to say for himself?"

"He says he has been a very great sinner, but that he has found Jesus, and Jesus has saved him."

"What has that other heathen to say about it?"

"'I have been the greatest scoundrel in the world, but the *umfundisi* says that Jesus came to save the very worst sinners, and I have taken Him, and He has pardoned my sins, and I feel Him now in my heart.'"

Many of our hearers had come twenty miles to attend our services. They are not a people to carry food with them on so short a journey. They had now been with us all day, and were hungry, so we began to inquire if there were any "loaves and fishes" that we could set before them? After consultation, we announced to the congregation that all who had come from a distance, and were hungry, then, or at any time during our series of services, should go to the missionary, who would give each one a quart of "mealies," Indian corn, daily. Brother Roberts and I proposed to bear two-thirds of the expense amounting to a few pounds each, for the mealies thus consumed; but at the close, when we came to settle, Brother Longden would not allow us the privilege of helping him.

My labours with the heathen that day caused me to feel keenly my inability to penetrate their heathenish darkness, and grapple successfully with their prejudices and superstitions, from my want of an acquaintance with Kaffir life and customs, so I determined, by the help of the Lord, with the best sources available, though I should not have time during my brief sojourn to master the Kaffir language, I would master the Kaffir mind. I at once enlisted Charles in the work of studying native Kaffirism. At suitable times he got the oldest men together and questioned them about the customs and faith of their heathen fathers, and wrote down their statements; by this means, and by what we could learn from the missionaries and from *Kaffir Laws and Customs*, a book, compiled from the experience and testimony of several of the oldest missionaries, specially for the benefit of the government, we made progress in the acquisition of useful knowledge, which could not be obtained in any college in Europe, and knowledge that we both turned to good account by the help of the Holy Spirit.

We had preaching that night in the chapel, and a glorious harvest of souls. On Monday, Tuesday, and Wednesday, we preached in the forenoon by the river, and at night in the chapel. On Thursday and Thursday night there was a great marriage feast in the neighbourhood, which had been postponed several days on account of our meetings, so we took that day and night as a season of greatly needed rest. We resumed again on Friday, and closed our special series Friday night, and Saturday, the 28th, travelled nearly fifty miles to Clarkebury Mission Station. During our series at Butterworth, the missionary examined and recorded the names of one hundred and forty-seven converts.

While at Butterworth a fact transpired illustrating the magisterial authority of the missionary, and also the apparent necessity for such authority. A man on the station had a daughter, who had been in the mission-school, for years. It appeared that the father had a tempting offer of cattle for his daughter by some heathen man a few miles distant, who wanted to buy her, according to heathen Kaffir custom, for his wife and slave, whether first or fifth wife, we did not learn. The father knowing that the laws of the mission-station did not allow him to sell his daughter, nor give her in marriage, to a polygamist heathen, gave consent to the parties that his daughter might go to them to plough, and assist in putting in the crop of mealies, and several red fellows came accordingly for the girl. Brother Longden, however, having learned that such a negotiation was pending, promptly met the men, and told them to go away and attend to their own business, for he would not, on any account, let them have the girl. The fellows were greatly disappointed, and hung round some time before they would leave. Brother Longden told the father that if he meant to sell his daughter to the heathen, he must at once leave the station, for he would not allow such a man to live on the premises.

We shook hands with a distinguished old heathen at Butterworth. His fame was based on two adventures of his life. One was, according to the account in Kaffraria, that on one occasion when Rev. Wm. Shaw was trying to cross a swollen river, the current was too strong, and carried him down the stream, greatly imperiling his life. This heathen man plunged in, and assisted the "umfundisi" in getting safely to land. The other was, that in his early life he killed a "boa constrictor." That will give undying fame to any heathen Kaffir, as one of the greatest men in the nation, indeed, so great that his skull is, above all others, selected as the medicine-pot of the great chief. If such a distinguished individual, however, is allowed to die a natural death, the charm is lost, and his skull unfitted for such distinguished royal purposes. But the great snake killer, on the other hand, must not be surprised and murdered. He must yield himself a willing sacrifice, and abide in quietness for ten preparatory days, and then be murdered decently, according to royal decree. Many, I was told, had thus given themselves up to die, and be canonized among the most honourable "Imishologu." This old fellow, however, was not as yet sufficiently patriotic, nor ambitious of glory for that, but chose rather to retain his skull for his own personal use, and let old Krielie, his master, get on in his medical arrangements as best he could, and hence takes good care to keep himself beyond Krielie's dominions.

We were introduced to a much more remarkable character, at Butterworth, than the killer of the "boa constrictor."

Brother Longden gave us in substance the following history of "Umaduna." He said that some months before in visiting some heathen "kraals," he inquired at each one if there were any Christians among them. Coming to a kraal containing about three hundred souls, he put his question to many in different parts of the kraal, and received from all the reply, "Yes, there is one Christian in this kraal. He's a little one, but he is a wonderful man. He has been persecuted, many times beaten, and threatened with death, if he did not quit praying to Christ; but he prays and sings all the more."

Mr. Longden was greatly surprised, and pleased to learn that such a martyr spirit was shining so brightly in a region so dark, and sought diligently till he found the wonderful man of whom he had heard such things, and to his astonishment, the great man turned out to be a naked boy, about twelve years old. Upon an acquaintance with him, and the further testimony of his heathen neighbours, he found that all he had heard about him, and much more, was true. Hearing these things, we sought an interview with "Umaduna," for that is his name. He had attended our meetings from the first, and I had often seen him among the naked Kaffir children in my audiences but did not know that I was preaching to such a heroic soldier of Jesus, till the last day of our series. That day we sent for the lad to come into the mission-house, that we might see and learn of him how to suffer for Christ. He hesitated, but after some persuasion consented, and came. He was small for a boy of twelve years, and had no clothing, except an old sheep-skin over his shoulders. Quite black, a serious, but pleasant face; very unassuming, not disposed to talk, but he gave, in modest, but firm tones of voice, prompt, intelligent answers to all our questions. The following is the substance of what we elicited from him, simply corroborating the facts narrated before by the missionary:—

I said to him, through my interpreter,

"Umaduna, how long have you been acquainted with Jesus?"

"About three years."

"How did you learn about Him, and know how to come to Him?"

"I went to preaching at Heald Town, and learned about Jesus, and that he wanted the little children to come to Him. Then I took Jesus for my Saviour, and got all my sins forgiven, and my heart filled with the love of God."

He was not long at Heald Town, but returned to his people, and had since emigrated with them to Fingo-land.

"Was your father willing that you should be a servant of Jesus Christ?"

"Nay, he told me that I should not pray to God any more, and that I must give Jesus up, or he would beat me."

"What did you say to your father about it?"

"I didn't say much, I wouldn't give up Jesus. I kept praying to God more and more."

"What did your father do then?"

"He beat me a great many times."

"Well, when he found he could not beat Jesus out of you, what did he do next?"

"He got a great many boys to come and dance round me, and laugh at me, and try to get me to dance."

"And wouldn't you dance?"

"No, I just sat down, and would not say anything."

"What did your father do then?"

"He fastened me up in the hut, and said I must give up Jesus or he would kill me. He left me in the hut all day."

"And what did you do in there?"

"I kept praying, and sticking to Jesus."

"Did you think your father would kill you?"

"Yes, if God would let him. He fastened me in the hut many times, and said he would kill me."

"Umaduna, are you sure you would be willing to die for Jesus?"

"Oh, yes, if He wants me to."

"Are you not afraid to die?"

"No, I would be glad to die for Jesus, if He wants me to."

Brother Roberts gave him a copy of the New Testament in Kaffir, for his use after he shall have learned to read, and said he had intended to speak some words of encouragement to the boy, but on hearing him talk, he found the rustic little Christian so far in advance of himself, who had been but a few months in the way, that he could not say anything to him.

The subsequent progress of the work in Butterworth is indicated by an extract from a letter from the missionary, dated August 2nd.

I start this letter on your track, as I know it will interest you to hear that the revival of God's work, so delightfully begun on the occasion of your recent visit to Butterworth, is still going on. The evening of the day you left we had nearly twenty penitents; about the same number at mid-day prayer-meeting on Sunday, and twenty at the prayer-meeting following the afternoon preaching. We have had the same number, or more, at every public service since. Conversions have taken place, more or less, at every service.

The larger children of our schools, who remained apparently indifferent for awhile, have at last begun to seek the Lord, and literally roar in the disquietude of their souls. Those backsliders of whom I spoke to you, who seemed determined not to yield, have at last given way; and last night made the chapel ring with the backsliders' cry for mercy.

Six or eight fresh ones set out from the City of Destruction last evening, and so on, we trust, the good work will spread, until

   All shall catch the flame,
   All partake the glorious bliss.

Most of the new members have been got into classes, both here, and in what I may call the country societies.

On looking over my list, I find that a large number of our members have been converted, or re-converted, and the whole society has been much stirred up. We rejoiced greatly on hearing of your success at Clarkebury, and thought it would be so.

On Saturday the 28th of July we travelled nearly fifty miles from Butterworth to Clarkebury, our next field of labour.

CHAPTER XIX.

CLARKEBURY (UMGWALI).

"THE fifth mission-station established by our society in Kaffraria," says the old pioneer, Rev. W. Shaw, "was in the country of the Abatembu, under the great chief Vossanie.

"My first visit to this chief was during the journey of observation, which I performed in April, 1825.

"We reached the chief's kraal on the 9th of that month, and on the next day we had an interview with him, when, after we had submitted to the usual cross-examination, and afforded a full explanation of the objects contemplated in the establishment of a mission, Vossanie, in the presence of his counsellors and chieftains, promised that if a missionary came to them, they would receive him kindly, and give him land on which he might form a station. It was not till April, 1830, that we were enabled to commence this mission.

"The chief faithfully kept his word, and received Rev. Mr. Haddy," our first missionary there, "with evident satisfaction, giving him leave to search the country to find a suitable site for the proposed station." This mission-station was called Clarkebury, in honour of Dr. Adam Clarke.

The only Europeans killed by natives in connection with our Kaffrarian missions lost their lives in connection with this station. The first was Mr. Rawlins, an assistant, who was killed by a horde of marauders, not far from the station. The other was the Rev. J. S. Thomas, a thorough Kaffir scholar, an energetic brave missionary. In 1856, he had just removed from Clarkebury to a more suitable place, where he designed to establish the headquarters of that mission. Their cattle kraal was attacked at night by a band of marauders, which brought on a general conflict between them and the mission people. The missionary sprang out of his bed, and rushing into the midst of the fight to try to command order, was pierced with an "assagay," from the hands of one of the attacking party. On the death of this noble missionary, the removal of the mission site was abandoned. It should be said to the credit of the Abatembu nation, that they, as a people, had nothing to do with the assassination of those good men, but deeply regretted their fall, which was by the murderous hands of a band of robbers. The missionaries, however, have suffered endless petty annoyances from the heathen chiefs and people. The following story told me by Rev. W. J. Davis may serve as an illustration of this:

"When I was stationed at Clarkebury, in 1832,

the Tambookie* Chief, 'Vadana,' coveted a pot we daily used in our cooking. He came and begged me every day for that pot for a long time. I gave him many presents, but could not spare the pot, and positively refused to give it up.

"Finally, the chief said, 'Davis, I'll have that pot!' The next day Vadana came with thirty of his warriors, all armed with assagays—a kind of javelin, their principal war weapon.

"They stood in defiant array before me, and the chief said, 'Davis, we have come for that pot.'

"'We need the pot,' I replied, 'for cooking our food, and as I told you before, I won't give it to you.'

"'You must give it to us, or we'll take it.'

"'With thirty armed warriors, against one unarmed missionary, you have the power to take it, but if that is the way you are going to treat your missionary, just give me a safe passage out of your country, and I'll leave you.'

"'Davis, are you not afraid of us?' demanded the chief, sharply.

"'No, I'm not afraid of you. I know you can kill me, but if I had been afraid to die I never would have come among such a set of savages as you are.'

"'Davis,' repeated the chief sternly, 'are you not afraid to die?'

"'No! If you kill me I have a home in heaven,

* Rev. Wm. Shaw calls this tribe Amatembu, or Tembookies but they are now generally called "Tambookies."

where the wicked cease from troubling, and the weary are at rest.'

"Then, turning to his men, the chief said, 'Well, this is a strange thing. Here's a man who is not afraid to die, and we will have to let him keep his pot.'

"When the chief was turning to go away, he said, 'Davis, I love you less now than I did before, but I fear you more.'"

The chief never gave his missionary any further trouble about his pot, but showed greater respect to him than ever before.

On our journey from Butterworth to Clarkebury, one of our cart-horses got sick, and was scarcely able to travel, causing us much delay, so that we did not arrive at Clarkebury till nine o'clock at night, and having no moon we had to travel a couple of hours more by faith than by sight.

Rev. Edwin Gedye met us a little way from the station, and piloted us through the dark to the mission-house, where we were welcomed and kindly entertained by the missionary Rev. Peter Hargraves, and his truly missionary wife, who is a native of Kaffraria, daughter of a pioneer missionary, Rev. W. J. Davis. Rev. Brother Gedye was the missionary from Shawbury mission station, but had with his family recently fled to Clarkebury on account of fearfully complicated war-troubles at Shawbury.

They have capacious and comfortable mission buildings, and a beautiful garden containing fine oranges, and other varieties of fruit-trees, at Clarkebury, and a chapel to seat about five hundred persons.

My purpose was to remain there only till Wednesday morning, but Brother Hargraves said, that he had sent a messenger to Ngangelizwe, the great chief of the Tambookie nation, inviting him and his counsellors to attend our services, and that the chief had returned answer that they could not be with us at the commencement, but would come on Wednesday. So we consented to stay at any-rate till after Wednesday. On Sabbath morning, the 29th of July, we had the chapel crowded, Brother Hargraves read Mr. Wesley's abridgment of the Episcopal service, and his Kaffir audience repeated their parts of the service very distinctly.

We preached to the believers in the morning, and, without a prayer-meeting, requested them to retire, and spend as much time as possible in self-examination and prayer, and come together again at three P.M. A prayer-meeting followed the afternoon preaching, and also the preaching in the evening, and on each occasion, beside a gracious work amongst believers, we had probably one hundred and fifty penitents.

On Monday we had preaching and prayer-meeting both mid-day and evening. The same on Tuesday, and many souls were saved at each service. Among the converts were seven Europeans—Mr. Crouch, an old colonist who had come into Kaffraria with my friend Mr. Joseph Walker, a merchant of King

William's Town, on commercial business, Mr. Henry B. Warner, his wife, and four others. Henry B. is the son of the British resident for Kaffraria, J. C. Warner, Esq. Clarkebury was the place of Henry's birth, while his father was stationed there as a missionary, and having been brought up in the Kaffir mission-field, he is as perfectly familiar with the Kaffir language as a native Kaffir. He holds the office of magistrate in Fingo-land, and is the acting chief of a thousand natives. Now at the place of his birth he was "born again," and at once entered actively into the work, labouring personally, and exhorting publicly in the Kaffir language. He has gone rapidly forward in a career of increasing usefulness ever since, and is now preaching the Gospel. In a letter from Rev. E. J. Barrett, dated October 16th, he says, "Mr. H. B. Warner, a week or two ago, preached at Woodhouse Forest, and the Lord was working in the hearts of the people. If any one can move the Kaffir mind, I think he will."

Brother Hargraves, getting a hint that the great chief did not wish to come to our meetings at all, felt very anxious about it, and sent a messenger inviting him again, and proposing that if he preferred it, we would go to his "Great Place" and preach there. That led to a great council of the chief and his amapakati, who debated the question two days, and finally returned answer that the chief and his counsellors would go to Clarkebury on Thursday. The chief's position is peculiarly unfavourable to the success of the Gospel with him, or any of his councillors and chiefs. He had been to school a year and a-half at the mission-station, under Brother Hargraves, and became greatly concerned about his soul, and was "almost persuaded to be a Christian;" but when the time came for him to take the supreme chieftainship of his nation, the counsellors and chiefs, who had exhibited great jealousy and fear all the time he lived at the station lest the young chief should embrace Christ, demanded his formal renunciation of Christianity, or they would repudiate him, and support his younger brother. If he had been a Christian, he would have stated, and maintained his position on the Lord's side, and accepted the ultimate decisions of Providence, but he was not fully decided for God. He hesitated some time before he gave his final answer. I was told by Mr. J. C. Warner, and by the missionary, that the young chief went alone and wept, and it was hoped he would apply to God and get strength to stand up for Christ at all hazards; but, in a fit of weeping disappointment, he angrily clenched his fists, and said, "They are determined to have a heathen chief to rule over them, and I'll let them feel the power of a heathen- chief." It is believed that he will, if he lives long, take vengeance on the leading conspirators against Christ, who forced such terms upon him. He threw an assagay through the arm of one of them just before our visit.

Another case had just occurred still more peculiar and remarkable, illustrating the spirit of this chief:

Some of his leading counsellors brought a man who owned a vast herd of cattle before the chief, under a charge of trying to take the chief's life by witchcraft. The man had been duly "smelled out," and convicted by the priest or doctor. According to all precedent of Kaffir law and usage, the accused would have been tortured and killed, and all his cattle confiscated and driven into the chief's kraal. But in the face of hoary-headed usage, and the superstitious fear and cupidity which are so potent in such cases, Ngangelizwe turned to the accused, who stood in expectation of a horrible death, and said to him, "Go home, and sit down in peace, and take all your cattle, I don't want them." Then turning to his counsellor-plaintiffs in the case, he said, sharply, "Go home, and attend to your own business."

There is, therefore, a possibility that the counsellors and chiefs may be so filled with their ways, "sowing to the wind, and reaping the whirlwind," that the sad results of their wickedness may operate as a warning, and be employed by an overruling Providence to lead the nation nearer to God; but be that as it may, the present attitude of the chief, and the counsellors and chiefs who are engaged with him in this combination, is a serious bar to the progress of the Gospel among them, for every party requiring the chief to renounce Christ, he thus committed himself in a political compact against Christ. We had ample proofs of that fact, as my narrative will show.

On Thursday morning, the day appointed for the chief to come with his counsellors to our services, a messenger arrived, according to Kaffir custom, to announce the important fact that, "Ngangelizwe is in the path."

He had but fifteen miles to travel from the " Great Place" to Clarkebury, and we thought he might arrive by mid-day, but the three missionaries, Revs. Hargraves, Gedye, and Raynor, from Morley, thought, according to the ordinary ceremony and delay by the way, they might require the whole day for the journey.

About three P. M. his vanguard appeared on the high hill, half-a-mile east of the station, and took their stand. Half-an-hour later, another party came in sight and halted in like manner. It was then nearly an hour more before the great chief, with the main body of the royal cortege, appeared. The cavalry of the train, consisting of about forty counsellors, fell into line, single file, the chief being about the middle; and all came down the hill at a full gallop. Arriving, they at once dismounted, but all remained outside the mission-yard with the horses, except the chief and his brother Usiqukati, who came directly in. Brother Hargraves met, and shook hands with them at the gate, and introduced them to me and my party. All the ceremony required on our part, I learned, was simply to pronounce the name of the chief, and shake hands, and so with his brother. Having previously trained our tongues to a little familiarity with their names, we had no difficulty in meeting the requirements of the occasion. A sufficient number of huts had been vacated for the accommodation of the chief and his party, as long as they might desire to stay.

The chief's minor name was "Qeya," but accordin to custom, graduating to manhood and to his chieftainship, he got a new characteristic name, and being considered, even by disinterested parties, one of the greatest chiefs in Kaffraria, and by themselves the greatest among men, they gave him the name of "Ngangelizwe," which means, "Big as the world."

His brother's name is "Usiqukati," which means "strength." Though not so tall as the paramount chief, he has a breadth and depth of chest and development of muscle, indicating great strength of body, and a physiognomy bespeaking a strength of character and will greatly superior to that of his "big" brother. I said to the missionaries, that I believed as a Christian "Usiqukati" would be firm to martyrdom, but as a heathen chief he was capable of becoming as Hazael of Syria, or as Chaka, the Zulu. They replied that I had just expressed their own previous opinion in regard to him.

Ngangelizwe has a very extensive, rich, grassy, well-watered, undulating, beautiful country. His tribe numbers about one hundred thousand souls, of whom fifteen or twenty thousand are warriors. The chief is nearly six feet in height, straight, well-proportioned, of the copper Kaffir complexion, instead of black, a smooth, pleasant countenance, a sweet, charming voice, which I at once remembered was exactly like that of his brother "Matanzima," before mentioned, as being almost persuaded to be a Christian at "Woodhouse Forest." The two chiefs took tea with us in the mission-house, while the "Amapakati" and their attendants went to the huts provided for them.

The chiefs were well-dressed in English costume, but their men had each simply a "kaross" of dressed skin or a red blanket.

Soon we are all in the chapel for the evening service, Charles and I stand side by side in the altar; to our right and left sit the missionaries, Hargraves, Gedye, and Raynor; in the front seats before the altar-railings sit the great chief and his brother, and on the same seats in front about a dozen Europeans, including several British soldiers from Fingo-land. Then we see next the body of the chapel half way down, filled with these heathen counsellors and attendants, and a lot of red heathen from Fingo-land, making, perhaps, one hundred and fifty of this class; then, in the rear, and at all the doors and windows outside, are the regular worshippers to whom we have been preaching twice per day for four days.

Text: the third and fourth verses of the eighth chapter of Romans. We have learned to apply the moral law to Kaffir lives and Kaffir hearts, and to proclaim to heathen minds the Gospel tidings, proffering in Christ a perfect, present, available supply for every demand of their souls, and the personal Holy Spirit ever waiting to make the saving application to the hearts of all who will consent "to walk after the Spirit and not after the flesh." We observe profound attention and great apparent concern among our heathen hearers. They have been debating the cause for several days whether or not they would give us a hearing, have refused to allow us to go to "the Great Place" to preach, and have come here with the avowed determination not to submit to Gospel requirements, but the Holy Spirit is evidently laying the law to their hearts, and revealing to their dark minds the light that leads to life, if they will but "walk in the light while they have it." A mighty contest between the powers of heaven and hell is pending. This heathen king, his counsellors, and men, every one of them, consent to the laws of God that they are good, and that God's Gospel terms are reasonable and right, but there is that other "law in their members," the gravitating law of their carnal nature with its deep downward channels of sinful habit, and its accursed ramifications of heathenish superstitions and customs, all combining to strengthen their avowed political league against Christ, and all these complications of iniquity employed as leverage against their perishing souls worked by the "principalities and powers" of hell. Is it possible to storm these strongholds of Satan and rescue these heathen captives at a single service? Will they even tarry for the prayer-meeting?

We close the preaching service and dismiss the congregation, to give an opportunity for all to leave who do not prefer to remain for the after-service. Not one stirs to get out. We call for the seekers to kneel before God, surrender to Him, and accept Christ. Many of our former hearers "fall down on their faces and worship God," and soon "report" from a blessed experience of pardon that "God is in them of a truth."

The chief and his people sit, and gaze, and wonder. During the prayer-meeting Brother Henry B. Warner stands up near the window to my right, and by his commanding appearance, good voice, and eloquent euphonious ring of the Kaffir language, at once arrests the attention of the whole assembly, and, addressing the chief and his counsellors, tells them the story of his own conversion to God—they all knew him well from of old, and knew what a sinner he had been, and now learned the details of God's saving mercy to him, demonstrating the truth of the Gospel news they had heard that night—followed by an earnest exhortation to them to seek God without a moment's delay. Then we all kneel down in solemn silent prayer. Nothing is heard now but the suppressed sighs and sobs of wounded souls in the different parts of the house, pierced with the Spirit's "two-edged sword."

The presence of God the Holy Spirit, moving perceptively among the prostrate mass of men before us, becomes awfully sublime beyond description. The salvation of these heathens now hangs in the scales of a poised beam; many of us feel that the Spirit hath clearly offered to them the gift of eternal life in Christ. They are almost persuaded. They have reached a crisis. Let any one of these old counsellors avowedly take a decided stand for God, and the whole of them will follow his example. Unable to get beyond that point, we close the service at eleven P.M., and all silently retire from the field to come up to the work again in the morning.

Early the next day Brother Warner had a long talk with Ngangelizwe's counsellors. They admitted to him that what they had heard at the service the night before was true, and that they were conscious of an extraordinary influence on their minds, and that they believed their chief wanted to accept Christ; but said they, "Ngangelizwe cannot act alone, for he is bound by solemn promise not to be a Christian, and none of us can act alone, because we exacted that promise from him, and we are bound in honour to stand to our own position. We cannot go and do ourselves what we have bound the chief not to do." One of them proposed, and nearly all the rest concurred, that they should call a great council of all the chiefs and leading men of the nation, and debate the cause, and see if they will consent to abandon their old customs, and adopt the religion of Christ as the religion of their nation. Brother Warner came at once to me with their proposition to inquire whether I thought we had better entertain it.

I replied, "It may be a trick of Satan to keep some of them from a personal acceptance of Christ to-day; if not a device of the evil one, but, as I hope, a sincere expression of new desire kindled in their hearts by the awakening Spirit, it is a proposition that we cannot turn to account, as we will be leaving to-morrow, and, unless a much larger number of the counsellors and chiefs of the nation were brought under the awakening power of the Spirit than we have here, it would be hazardous to submit such a question to a national council, as they would be sure, by majority, to decide against Christianity, and thus lengthen and strengthen the wicked alliance already formed against it. Such a proposition, however, originating with the 'Amapakati' should be kindly entertained, and the spirit prompting it encouraged, but action in that direction now would be premature. We must urge them to accept Christ to-day, each one for himself, and take the consequences." That day we had the chiefs and councillors in chapel in the same order as the night before. We preached from St. Luke's abstract of St. Paul's preaching to a heathen audience on "Mar's Hill," on the "Unknown God." We traced the parallel between the moral condition and superstitious worship of the literary heathen of Athens, and the illiterate heathen Tambookies. We have clear indications in Kaffir traditions, sacrifices, and devotions, of the struggle of their moral nature to feel after the "Unknown God," and to find a supply for the conscious woes and wants of their souls. Having dug down effectually into the regions of their beliefs and conscious experiences, and having brought out their admitted facts demonstrating the truth of Bible delineations of human corruption, guilt, and bondage, and their vain efforts, by their sacrifices and sufferings, to atone for their sins, or give "rest for their souls," we declared to them the "Unknown God," and His glorious provision of mercy for them in Christ. We then pressed home the fact, that God "now commandeth all men everywhere to repent." Illustrating the work of repentance, wrought by the Holy Spirit in the hearts of sinners, resulting in their acceptance of Christ, I gave, among other examples, the cases of Thackenbau, King of Fiji, and of George the Third, King of the Friendly Islands. I showed that their complications in the sin of polygamy, and all forms of heathenism, were quite as bad as anything in Kaffirland, but that yielding to the Spirit they had triumphed, and had become Christians. I gave them the story about King George, as given me by the Apostle Peter—that old apostle to the Friendly and Navigators' Islands, Rev. Peter Turner. When their first chapel was opened, and the king came in and saw the preacher in the pulpit—a man higher up than himself—he was displeased. But instead of making any trouble about it, he had a pulpit built for himself the next week in the opposite end of the chapel, a few inches higher than the minister's pulpit. When the king saw the missionary ascend to his pulpit, he quietly went up, and seated himself in his pulpit.

After awhile the missionary and his leading men united together daily to read God's book of instructions to see how they were to proceed in their work, and prayed daily for the Holy Ghost to come down and "abide with them," and through their agency do His mighty work of saving the king and his people. After continuing thus to wait "with one accord" for many days, the Holy Ghost came in mighty power.

The news ran all over the island, that the Holy Ghost had come, and was waiting to lead them to Jesus, and save their souls. The people flocked together from every direction, and while they listened to the words of God from His Book, "they were pricked in their hearts," and many cried out in the agony of their souls, and were so affected by the awakening power of the Spirit, that to the number of from two to three hundred at one time they lay apparently dead for hours, but always came up rejoicing, and praising God for His great salvation.

The king himself was awakened, and came down from his high pulpit, and sat in the dust. His proud heart yielded to the Spirit's power. Still it did not give way all at once. He told the missionary he wanted to give up his sins, and seek God, but did not want to bow down with his common people, and asked the missionary to allow him to pray behind the altar-screen, which was a net-work of young bamboo rods, and would conceal him from the eyes of his people.

Brother Turner said, "Yes, King George, you may kneel down wherever you like, and give your heart to God." The king went behind the screen and fell down on his face and cried to God to have mercy on his poor soul. He is a man six feet four inches high, and rolling in an agony of soul he kicked down the screen and lay full length before his people, and cared for nothing but how he might save his soul.

His pride was broken, and he fully felt the burden of his sins, but got no relief till after he went home that night. About midnight, he gave his wicked heart to God, and received Jesus, and got all his sins forgiven, and received a new heart. He wrote a letter to Brother Turner that night, telling him that he had found Jesus, and that his soul was happy. Some days after, he had a great many of his people together, and told them that he had embraced Christ, and was happy, and said to them, "Do you see that post?" pointing to a post of the chapel building, "now, just as certain as you know that you see that post, just so certainly I know that God, for Christ's sake, has pardoned my sins, and made me his child."

"Many wicked people said," I continued, "as such will say about Ngangelizwe, that if King George embraced Christ, he would lose his kingdom, just as though the great God of heaven and earth, to whom all power belongs, could not, or would not, maintain the rightful authority of a ruler, because such ruler became loyal to God, his Divine Sovereign. Did King George lose his kingdom by becoming a Christian? Nay, many who were not his people have come under his authority because he was a Christian, and he became a greater king than ever before; he also became a preacher, and is employed every Sabbath in preaching Jesus to his people. A man forfeits no rights by accepting Christ as his Saviour, but he cannot accept Christ until he consents to give up all his sins, and submit that Christ shall take from him, or return to him, anything and everything he holds dear. A man who would not, if necessary, give up a kingdom to receive Christ, will, for the sake of a little bit of authority, which he can hold but a few years at most, reject Christ, and perish!"

We explain, in simplicity, the duty of repentance, and an intelligent acceptance of Christ by faith in God's own record concerning Him, and the Spirit's witness and renewing work, demonstrating the truth of the Gospel, and the saving power of Jesus. At the close of the sermon, we proceed as usual with the prayer-meeting. A large number of seekers come forward, and a similar struggle to that of last night, between the powers of light and darkness, ensues. Ngangelizwe shows great concern; his brother is evidently in an agony of awakening; some counsellors seem in great distress; others of them, by their looks, and a scoffing display of their great teeth, are using their influence against the work. One fellow, with a large cow-skin "kaross" over his shoulders, is "a child of the devil," an "enemy of all righteousness," as full of all subtilty and mischief as Elymas the sorcerer.

In the midst of the prayer-meeting, Charles rises from his knees, and stands within arm's length of the chief and his brother, and exhorts them personally for half an hour. You see at once that my Zulu is master of the difficult situation. The natural gracefulness and perfection of his action, and the power of his logic, told manifestly on the trembling Felix before him. The missionaries, and others who understood the Kaffir, said afterwards that they never heard such a display of Kaffir oratory in all their lives. He explained to Ngangelizwe that "the powers that be are of God," and hence it was for God, and not a lot of wicked counsellors, to put down one ruler and set up another, and that a man who will reject the counsel of God and follow the counsel of wicked men, shall as certainly come to grief as that the righteous God rules in the heavens.

"Kobi and Pato," continued Charles, "were great thiefs. Kama, their brother, was a boy, and had no people. These three chiefs had the offer of Christ, Kama was the only one that accepted Him; Kobi and Pato rejected Christ, and called Kama a fool, and said he would be a scabby goat, and never have any people. Their wicked counsellors told them, if they received Christ they would lose all their people, all their cattle, and have nothing, like poor Kama; but what was the result? God gave them up to follow their wicked counsellors, who advised them to go to war with the English. Kobi died a miserable refugee, and got the burial of a dog. Pato has spent many miserable years a prisoner on Robin Island. Kama remained true to God, and kept out of the war against the English, and now all the people of the Amaxosa nation, once ruled by Kobi, and Pato belong to Kama, who is going down to his grave in honourable old age, in the midst of peace and plenty, full of a glorious hope of a blessed home in heaven. More than one thousand of his people have accepted Christ, and all of them abide in the peaceable possession of their homes, under the protection of the British Government." This but indicates the range of Charles's inimitable discourse to Ngangelizwe, and he appealed most solemnly to Usiqukati to submit to God and receive Christ, whatever the chief and his counsellors might do.

The ground of Charles' special appeal to Ngangelizwe's brother was that, next to Ngangelizwe, he was the royal heir to the supreme chieftainship of the nation, and the rival that the people intended to promote, instead of his older brother, if Ngangelizwe had refused to remain a heathen. The illustrative points of his speech to Usiqukati were as follows, having previously expended on him the power of the highest moral motives, he now mixed them with political arguments with two edges, to cut both chiefs at the same time :—

"Now Usiqukati," said Charles, "if Ngangelizwe rejects Christ, and remains in his sins, you take my advice, just surrender yourself to God, as you know His Holy Spirit is now telling you to do in your heart, and receive Jesus Christ as your Saviour, and you will not only be saved from your sins, but you will take away the crown from Ngangelizwe while he is asleep. If you become a child of God, you are sure to become the greater chief. God is supreme, above all kings, and if you become a child of God, and Ngangelizwe remains a child of the devil, God will be sure to give you his state, as the great chief of the Tambookies.

"Be wise now, like old Kama, who first took the word of the great God, and after that became the chief of the Amaxosa nation, while his ruling brothers were cast down to destruction. Be wise, like King David, who took the Word of God first, when Saul, his father-in-law, was the great king of Israel; but Saul, like Ngangelizwe, refused God, while David remained true to God, and became the great chief of that mighty nation, and Saul came to a miserable end. Be wise, young man, like King Solomon, who was the wisest man in the world, and who took the Lord God of his father David for his God, and became the greatest king of Israel after his father's death. Be wise, Usiqukati, like the white men, who love God, and who, in spite of the bad men among them, have become the greatest people in the world, and the head of us all." Then turning to Ngangelizwe, he said, " I see that your younger brother is ready to take your State if you refuse; if you accept Christ, you will retain it; but if you reject, and he accepts Christ, he will be sure of your crown."

Our time for such a work was too short. I felt sure that they could not stand many such shocks of awakening truth, applied by the Spirit's power, as it was on the two occasions we had them before us. Ngangelizwe afterwards shook hands with Charles, and they had a friendly private interview. The political league seemed to be the principal barrier.

Ngangelizwe said he would stay and hear us again that evening; but about sunset a man came dashing down the hill at full speed, his horse in a foam of perspiration and panting for breath, and announced that one of Ngangelizwe's children was dying, and that the chief must return to the "Great Place" at once.

The chief said he was very sorry to leave, but that he was obliged to go. We had a private talk to him on his peculiar embarrassments and duties, and on our plan of enlarging the range of mission-work in his nation, having the station simply as the head, but regular preaching in all the principal centres of population, and to have his people who accept Christ not to leave their former homes and come to the mission-station to live, but to remain and let their light shine in the kraals to which they belong. I learned, some weeks afterwards, that Ngangelizwe invited one of the Local Preachers to preach at his Great Place, and after he had preached, told him to come every Sunday and preach to him, for he wanted "to have preaching at his place whatever the Amapakati might say." The missionaries believed that all that ado about the dying child was got up by some of those wicked counsellors to hurry Ngangelizwe away for fear he would that night become a Christian. The extraordinary unction of the Holy Spirit attending His truth on those two occasions leads me to believe that much greater results than were manifested at the time will "be seen after many days." Having thus lost the heathen portion of our audience, instead of preaching that night as we intended, we had a fellowship-meeting. Up to that period of our series of services, 185 persons, on a personal examination, had professed to have obtained the pardon of their sins. About seventy, principally the young converts, spoke at our fellowship-meeting that night. I sat beside Brother William Davis, who interpreted their talk to me. It was marvellously interesting; I can give but a few specimens, and they are as weak as water compared with their native Kaffir originals, accompanied by graceful action, and tears, and the peculiar idiomatic force of their language. A woman said, "I have for a long time been a member of the Church according to the flesh, but now I am a member of the Church according to the Spirit. Last Sunday in this chapel the light of God shone into my heart, and showed me my sins. I was stricken down by the power of His Spirit, but I cried to God, and received Jesus Christ, and He lifted me up, and made me His child." Another said, "My father was a doctor, and while he lived I thought there was no danger of my dying, so I gave no attention to my soul. But my father died, and then I felt that death was very near to me, and that I was not ready to die, so I tried to get ready to die, but I never saw what a wretched sinner I was till last Sunday; then I cried to God, and took Jesus as my Saviour! My soul is happy, and I am not afraid to die now! My poor father is dead, but Jesus is my doctor now, and He will never die!" Another said, "My father was a good man, and died happy in the Lord. When he was dying he called his children round him, and said, 'I have done all I could, my children, to take care of you, and bring you up to walk in the right way. Now I am going to leave you, and your mother has gone before me. Now, my dear children, my last words to you are, that you give your hearts to God, and take Him as your Father, for He will never die.' We all told our father that we would, and ever since that I have been praying to God, but never found Jesus as my Saviour, till last Monday night, in this chapel. Now I know that Jesus is my Saviour, and that God, who will never die, is my Father." A man stood up and said, "I always hated the mission-stations, and I hated all the people who went to them. Often when I have seen them going to chapel, I got so angry, I wanted to kill them. But I heard that Isikunisivutayo was coming and I came to see what was to be done. I stood outside the chapel last Sunday, and laughed and mocked. On Monday night I came in, and Isikunisivutayo set me on fire, and I felt that I was sinking into hell, I left as quick as I could, and started home, but my sins were such a load on me I could not run, but fell down, and thought I was going to die. The next morning I felt very glad that I was not in hell. I came to the meeting that day and received Jesus, and now my soul is full of glory."

"Isikunisivutayo" means a burning fire-stick or torch, used by the Kaffirs for burning the dry grass. In the fall, the whole country is covered with a thick growth of brown grass, from one to two feet in height. As spring approaches, to get the full benefit of the new crop for their cattle, they take their burning fire-sticks and soon set a thousand hills in a blaze, spreading and sweeping in every direction to prepare the way for the new harvest of grass. It is common with the Kaffirs to give every distinguished stranger some characteristic name, by which, instead of his real name, he is known among them.

I was told beforehand that I would get a new name, and there were not a few European conjectures as to what it should be. Some thought it would be "Longbeard," which bears no comparison to the appreciative, poetic, descriptive name which the Kaffirs gave me, "The Burning Fire-Stick," which the Lord was using to set the whole country in a blaze, burn up all their old dead works, and prepare the way for spiritual life, verdure, and plenty. Among the converted heathen at that fellowship-meeting, one old man arose, threw his kaross gracefully across his breast, and over his left shoulder, and told a marvellous story about his heathenish prejudices against the mission-stations and the missionaries. "My heart," said he, "was as tough as the hide of a rhinoceros, but last night the Spirit's sword cut right through it, and let in the light of God. I received Jesus Christ, and He gave me a tender heart filled with His love."

These are mere specimen illustrations of the experience of over sixty persons who spoke, and nearly all they said was repeated to me in English, sentence by sentence, by Brother William Davis; but the examples given may suffice. Brother Davis is a native of Kaffraria, and a fine Kaffir scholar. He is the translator of the "Pilgrim's Progress" into Kaffir. He is engaged in commercial pursuits, but received a fresh baptism of the Spirit during our series, and has since commenced preaching to the Kaffirs as a Local Preacher, and I should not be surprised if the Lord of the harvest should call him to devote his whole time to the work of gathering in precious souls. I got him to translate "The Eden Above" into Kaffir. It was composed by Rev. Wm. Hunter, D.D., Professor of Hebrew in Alleghany College, Pa., U.S. I introduced it into Australia, Tasmania, and New Zealand. Rev. W. Moor took it from Sydney to Fiji, and Rev. Brother Calvert inserted it into the new Fijian Hymn-book, so that it is being sung all through those portions of the southern world, and now the mountains and vales of Kaffraria echo its measures, as sung by the pilgrim bands of the sable hosts as they march along to the Eden above. I will first insert the hymn as we have it from the author, and then in the Kaffir, accompanied by a literal rendering of the Kaffir into English, which will illustrate the idiomatic difficulty of translating an English hymn into Kaffir. As I before stated, while we have many good Kaffir hymns, mostly composed by Rev. Brother Dugmore, we have but one of Wesley's incomparable hymns in the Kaffir. Yet it will be seen that Brother Davis not only put the poetic thought of "The Eden Above" in the Kaffir, but in some cases strengthened it, especially to a Kaffir mind.

"THE EDEN ABOVE."

We're bound for the land of the pure and the holy,
  The home of the happy, the kingdom of love,
Ye wanderers from God in the broad road of folly,
  Oh say, will you go to the Eden above?
    Will you go? will you go? will you go? will you go?
    O say, will you go to the Eden above?

In that blessed land—neither sighing nor anguish,
  Can breathe in the fields where the glorified rove,
Ye heart-burdened ones who in misery languish,
  O say, will you go to the Eden above?
    Will you go? &c.

No poverty there—no! the saints are all wealthy,
  The heirs of His glory, whose nature is love,
No sickness can reach them, that country is healthy,
  O say, will you go to the Eden above?
    Will you go? &c.

March on, happy pilgrims, that land is before you,
  And soon its ten thousand delights we shall prove,
Yes, soon we shall walk o'er the hills of bright glory,
  And drink the pure joys of the Eden above.
    Will you go? &c.

And yet, guilty sinner, we do not forsake thee,
  We halt yet a moment while onward we move,
O, come to thy Lord, in His arms He will take thee,
  And bear thee along to the Eden above.
    Will you go? &c.

Methinks thou art now in thy wretchedness saying,
  O, who can this guilt from my conscience remove?
No other but Jesus! then come to Him praying,
  Prepare me, O Lord, for the Eden above.
    I will go! I will go! I will go! I will go!
    O, yes, I will go to the Eden above.

ICULA ELITETA NGELIZWE ELI PEZULU.
A HYMN WHICH TELLS ABOUT THE LAND WHICH IS ABOVE.

Sikuyo indhlela yelizwe lobomi,
We are in the path to the land of life,
Ikaya labantu bahleli ngenyweba.
The home of the people who dwell in happiness.
Bahlukani no Tixo, endhleleni yokona,
Rebels from God, in the way of wrong-doing.
Nitinina? Noyana, noyana, pezulu?
What do you say? Will you go, will you go above?
Noyana, noyana, noyana, noyana,
Nitinina? Noyana, noyana, pezulu?

Usizi, usizi alunakubaku,
Sorrow or anguish cannot exist there,
Kwelozwe kuhamb' abangcwele.
In that country travel the holy.
Bankliziyo zinzima, nigqitywa bububi.
The ones heart burdened, ye who languish in misery.
Nitinina? &c.
What do you say, &c.

Kwelozwe akuko buhlwempu, nakanye;
In that country there is no poverty, not a bit of it;
Zindyebo ngendyebo, izinto izikoyo;
It is riches upon riches, the things that are there;
Isifo asiko, asingebiko.
Sickness is not there, it cannot be there.
Nitinina, &c.

Hambani bakonzi, elozwe, leletu.
Go on, pilgrims, that country, it is ours.
Sonqina, sinqina inyameko zalo;
We will prove, and prove again, the delights all;
Eweke, sohamba ngapezu kwentaba
Yes, we will travel upon the hills
Sisele amanzi ovuyo pezulu.
And drink the water of joy above.
Noyana, noyana, noyana, noyana,
Nitinina? Noyana, noyana, pezulu?

Kanti ke, moni, asikulahlile,
Yet therefore, sinner, we do not throw thee away,
Simil' umzuzwana, simele kwa wena;
We stand a little time, standing for even you;
Yizake ku Tixo, akusingate,
Come then to God, He will take you in His arms,
Akuse kwangoku, ekusa pezulu.
And take you even now, taking you above.
Noyana? &c.

"THE EDEN ABOVE."

Ndicinga ngokuti, usabunzimeni,
I think this wise, thou art in heaviness,
Usiti, ngobani ongalisusayo
You saying, who can take away
Ityala lingaka lisenkliziyweni?
Guilt so great which is in the heart?
Ngu Yesu kupela; Tandazake. Uye,
It is Jesus alone; Pray therefore. Going,
Ndohamba, ndohamba, ndohamba, ndohamba,
I will go, I will go, I will go, I will go,
Eweke, ndohamba, ndisiya pezula.
I will go, I going above.

CHAPTER XX.

MORLEY—INCANASEUE.

Morley mission-station was established by Rev. William Shepstone in 1829, and named in honour of Rev. George Morley, then one of the missionary secretaries in London.

Those were the days of wars and rumours of wars, under the reign of the Zulu chief Chaka. Qeta, one of Chaka's chiefs, taking the cue of his bloody master, revolted, and carried a desolating war into Pondo-land on his own account. His legions swept through a great part of the Amapondo nation like a tornado, leaving nothing but smouldering villages and the carcases of their victims behind them. Brother Shepstone and his family were right in their path. The missionary heard the crash of the coming storm, but remained at his post till he saw a neighbouring kraal in flames and the guerilla band advancing toward the mission premises. There seemed then no way of escape, but providentially, while the mission family was preparing for a hasty flight, they knew not whither, a dense fog from the river settled down upon all the adjacent vales and hills, under cover of which the mission family and their people escaped. "The pillar of cloud stood behind them;" "it was a cloud and darkness to them (their pursuers), "but it gave light" to the heaven-guarded strangers in the wilderness. I received the narrative of this marvellous escape from the lips of Brother Shepstone himself.

The invaders were soon after that overpowered by Faku, the great chief of the Amapondo, assisted by the Amabaca, and the Amapondumsi Damasi, chief of the Western Division of the Pondo nation, is said to have been a leading warrior chief in the final engagement, which utterly crushed the Zulu invader and closed the war.

The next year Mr. Shepstone rebuilt the Morley Station on a new site, some miles distant from the former site, in a more healthy location. After a few years of hard labour and fair success, the pioneer was removed to another new field, and was succeeded by Rev. Mr. Palmer. After Mr. Palmer's death in 1847, the mission declined, and lay waste for several years. The labour of those men of God, to be sure, was not lost, but their flock being left without a shepherd wandered off into other folds, and a few remained and preserved a name, which was revived by the appointment of the Rev. William B. Rayner as their missionary four years ago. Brother Rayner is a man of very small stature. On his arrival some of Ngangelizwe's counsellors scanned him closely without saying a word, till one of them, with an interrogative exclamation, said, "Have all the Englishmen run out?" But Mr. Rayner has, by his extraordinary zeal and effectiveness in his work, demonstrated the truth of Dr. Watts' saying, "the mind is the measure of the man." Brother Rayner has rebuilt Morley Station fourteen miles west of its former site, in the midst of a rich and beautiful country of hills, and valleys, and rivers of water at all seasons, belonging to the "Big" Chief, Ngangelizwe, who, though politically sworn to reject Christ, has three Wesleyan mission-stations and one Anglican within the lines of his domains.

Brother Rayner, with his own hands, assisted by his natives, has built a large comfortable missionhouse and a pretty chapel which will seat about four hundred persons, and has built also a small chapel in a village, five miles west of Morley. That part of Kaffraria is a famous place for "smelling out" and the conviction of men by their witch-doctors, for the crime of having cattle enough to excite the covetousness of a chief, or political influence enough to render him an object of fear, or from any cause laying him under suspicion.

Their mode of trial and conviction is thus described by J. C. Warner, Esq., in "Kaffir Laws and Customs."

"Kaffirs are firm believers in sorcery, or witchcraft, and they consider that all the sickness and other afflictions of life are occasioned thereby, and that were it not for the evil influence of the 'amaggwira,' none would die but in good old age.

"This universal belief in witchcraft has led to the almost entire neglect of the art of healing by medicines, and to cause them to trust wholly to the power of charms, incantations, 'amadini,' or sacrifices, &c.

"Hence their priests have little or no knowledge of the virtues of medicinal plants, and they trust entirely to such remedies as may be revealed by the 'Imishologu' (the spirits of their ancestors), and if, as is sometimes the case, they do make use of herbs, &c., they are always used in conjunction with charms and sacrifices, to the efficacy of which their virtues are attributed.

"They have, however, a few very valuable medical plants among them; but the knowledge of these is as frequently found among other classes as among the priests. When all ordinary charms and other means have failed to remedy sickness, &c., an application is made to the chief for permission to try the 'Umhlahlo' (smelling out for witchcraft), for no person can have the 'Umhlahlo' performed without the express sanction of the chief. When this has been obtained, the people of the kraal in question, together with their neighbours of the surrounding kraals, proceed in a body to the kraal of the priest whom they intend to employ.

"The people belonging to the priest's kraal, with those of the surrounding kraals, then assemble. Two semi-circles are formed; one of the party of the kraal seeking assistance, and the other, of the adherents of the priest.

"These semi-circles are so ranged as nearly to meet at their points, thus forming an almost perfect circle, leaving only just sufficient space between them to admit the priest and his assistants.

"The ceremony of 'Ukwombela' (the first process for detecting the witch) is now commenced, the hide drums are violently beaten, the bundles of assegais are struck together, accompanied by the well known humming and clapping of hands by the women. By-and-by, the priest rushes out of his hut, springs into the midst of the circle of human beings assembled, and commences jumping about in the most frantic manner, and performing all sorts of extraordinary gesticulations. This is called 'ukuxentsa.'

"The men now beat their drums, and strike their bundles of assegais together more violently than ever, and the women hum their exciting tunes, and clap their hands, in an increasingly agitated manner; vociferating all the while for help, and demanding who has bewitched them?

"This is continued until the priest is wrought up to the proper pitch of inspiration; when he suddenly ceases, and retires to that part of the circle formed by his own adherents. He then names the persons who have bewitched the afflicted party or parties.

"On their names being pronounced, that part of the circle where they are sitting rises simultaneously, falls back, and leaves the devoted victims sitting alone.

"This is the exciting moment, and all eyes are fixed upon them, while the priest describes their sorceries, and the enchantments used by them for their diabolical purposes.

"A rush is then made upon them, and every article—their kaross, ornaments, &c.—is torn off their bodies.

"They are then given in charge to certain parties appointed for that purpose, and led away to their respective kraals, there to be tortured in the most barbarous manner, in order to make them 'mbulula,' or reveal the materials by which they performed their enchantments.

"In the bush country, where the tree-ants are plentiful, their nests are sought for; the poor wretch is laid down, water thrown over his body, and the nests beaten to pieces on him.

"This irritates the ants, and causes them to bite furiously; they also creep into the nostrils, ears, eyes, mouth, &c., producing the most excruciating pain by their bites.

"Sometimes a large fire is made, and the poor wretch is tied up to a pole, so close to it, as literally to roast him alive.

"Large flat stones are also heated red hot, and placed on the groins, and applied to the soles of the feet, and other parts of the body. Another mode of torture resorted to is the binding of a string so tight around the thumbs as to cause the most acute agony, and unless the poor creature does confess something, and produce some kind of 'ubuti,' or bewitching matter, he must eventually sink under the torture.

"When the person altogether refuses to confess, which is sometimes the case, if the people are anxious to save his life, the priest is sent for, who produces the 'ubuti' for him, or assists him to find it, by refreshing his memory, as to its whereabouts; otherwise he is generally dispatched without ceremony for his obstinacy. But when an unfortunate victim has sufficiently satisfied his tormentors by his confessions, he is generally set at liberty.

"At this stage of the proceedings, the chief's 'imisila,' or sheriffs, make their appearance and demand the 'isizi,' or fine, and which is the same number of cattle as for any other kind of homicide.

"The 'isizi' is always paid by the person charged with witchcraft, even should the person supposed to have been bewitched recover.

"Very frequently, however, the chief acts in a despotic manner, and seizes the whole of his cattle (this is always the case when he is a political victim), but this is not according to law; but a mere arbitrary act of power.

"If the person charged with witchcraft dies under the torture, or is wilfully killed, without the sanction of the chief, the 'isizi' must be paid for his life also; at least, according to law, the chief has the power to demand it, though he often foregoes his claim."

"Persons charged with witchcraft are often put to

death by the express command of the chief; in which case he takes possession of the whole of his property, and frequently 'eats up' the whole kraal to which he belongs. This is always the case when the 'umhlahlo' is made use of as a political engine, to get rid of some influential but troublesome individual; for when once a person has been legally charged with this crime, it matters not how popular or respected he may have been before, he is at once avoided as the most noxious of human beings.

"The chiefs, therefore, find this a very convenient and powerful state engine to support their power, and enable them to remove individuals whom they would otherwise find great difficulty in getting rid of.

"After a person charged with witchcraft has satisfied all legal demands, and is set at liberty, he has the right of applying to a priest, who offers a sacrifice for him, and performs some other rites; after which he is pronounced clean, and again becomes as honourable a member of society as though he had never been punished for witchcraft. There is not the slightest doubt that the Kaffirs do frequently attempt to bewitch each other, and for which purpose they practice a great number of villanous tricks.

"They have also the knowledge of several vegetable poisons, and of which they make a very free use in getting rid of those they dislike; and, as poisoning is included by them under the head of witchcraft, there is no wonder at their superstitious fears having invented some kind of scheme to detect and punish individuals whom they believe to be guilty of these crimes."

As many as eight cases of smelling out and murder had occurred during the space of a year just preceding the time of our visit, the details of which, too numerous for my space, were given me by the missionary. A horrible case occurred near the station in 1864. The "lung-sickness" happened among the cattle of a native near Morley, who immediately employed a doctor to "smell out" the man who had bewitched them. The usual ceremony of "smelling out" resulted in the conviction of the man's own nephew. He was at once seized and tied to a post near his own hut, when a large fire was made in front of him, by which he was slowly roasted. After enduring these excruciating tortures for twenty-four hours, he was induced to confess his guilt. He told them if they would take him to the brook he would show them the poison by which he had bewitched the cattle. The poor fellow was made to go to the water. When dragged to the place he pointed out the "ubuti," a little root in the edge of the water, which caused the death of the cattle. Then the doctor jumped round and shouted glory to himself. The power to "smell out the witches," and the righteousness of his decision, were demonstrated before all the people. Then his poor victim was dragged back and tied to the same post, and the fires were rekindled, and while he for twelve hours more yelled in agony, his friends and relations were smoking their pipes, and taking their pleasure. The tortures of that poor fellow commenced at noon, and terminated in death at the middle of the second night. No doubt the relations of such victims manifest their indifference, and often their zeal in the execution, to avoid suspicion of complicity with the witch. The father of the poor man fled to the mission-station for refuge, and Brother Rayner asked him if he really believed that his son had bewitched his brother's cattle? "O, yes," he replied, "I believe he was guilty, because the doctor said so."

A heathen man's wife, near the station, was suspected of witchcraft. After being duly "smelled out," the penalty doomed her to be eaten alive by the ants. Her own brothers took her out, according to the judgment of the doctor, and driving down four stakes, stretched her out by an ant-hill, and lashed her wrists and ankles to the stakes to be devoured by the voracious insects.

The ants preyed upon the poor woman all that day, but her "sucking child," cried so for its mother that, I suppose as a matter of economy, they went out and untied the mother, who came home and took care of her child for the night. In the morning she was staked down among the ants as before, and at night was released again.

Such torture will ordinarily terminate life in a couple of days, but the respite of each alternate night prolonged this woman's agony, and after enduring this for six days, her tormentors said, "We can't kill such a witch. She won't die," so they loosed her, and "threw her away," which, with the Kaffirs, means such an "*anathema maranatha,*" that their faces must never be seen by any of their people again. In that dreadful condition she came to the "station." Brother Rayner told us that such a sight he never saw before. The surface of her whole body was lacerated and swollen; but her wrists and ankles were eaten down between the tendons, in some places to the bone. Her struggles caused the straps, by which she was bound, to chafe her wrists and ankles, and render them specially attractive to the little tormentors that were feasting on her. By very special care, Brother Rayner and his kind-hearted wife succeeded, by the mercy of God, in restoring her.

That very woman was converted to God during our series of services at Morley, and still lives at the station, a free woman in Christ.

Brother Rayner was at Clarkebury from Monday to Friday of our services there, and did us good service. On Saturday he conducted us to his house at Morley. Rev. Brother Hargraves and Brother William Davis accompanied us a few miles, and saw us safely over a dangerous "drift" of the Bashee, and bade farewell. After a rough journey of thirty-six miles, we reached the station a little after dark. We "out-spanned" by the way at a trader's station, and were kindly provided with refreshment by a widow, whose husband had died but a few weeks before. Brother Rayner visited him a short time before his death, and learned from him that he attended my series of services at King William's Town, and was greatly awakened by the Spirit; and though he did not go forward avowedly as a seeker, he did seek the Lord, and Brother Rayner had hope in his death. The widow was settling up his business, and preparing to leave such horrible associations.

On Sabbath morning, the 5th of August, I took a survey of the land to find a suitable place for out-door preaching. To the west of the house we found a beautiful grassy spot, but it was not sufficiently protected from an easterly breeze, which was prevailing, and, moreover, it was on the edge of a precipice which overhung the river, which curved round its base nearly 200 feet below, and we feared that, in a great crowd, some careless one might tumble over before they were ready. We finally selected a small level plot of ground, by a little stream, at the foot of the high hill east of the chapel. In turning up a large flat stone for my pulpit, I tore my coat. I got a few heathen Kaffirs then to help me, and prepared a good stone pulpit each for Charles and myself. I then slipped down the deep ravine, and prepared for the public service by doing a small job of tailoring, which closed the rent in my coat, which I thought might be damaging to my usefulness, and hence made a necessity of it. When I got my coat mended I buckled on the "armour of God," and returned to the field of action. Brother Roberts, Stuart, and Brother and Sister Rayner, were the only white hearers we had. There were probably three hundred persons of all ages in some way connected with the station there, and the village out-station, five miles distant, whose people, with their faithful head man, and Local Preacher, came in force; besides these we had nearly one hundred wild heathens. We stood on the precipitous bank of the stream, and cried "The Spirit and the bride say, Come. And let him that heareth say, Come. And let him that is athirst come. And whosoever will, let him take the water of life freely." We stated the first principles of the doctrine of Christ, and illustrated them by the realities of Kaffir life, in a thorough, but simple way, adapted to the capacity of heathen minds. The preaching occupied about an hour and a-half. There was marked attention, and evidently a mighty moving of the Spirit of awakening during the preaching; but, as usual, all were quiet. Having shown them that they were famishing in the dry desert of heathenism, and that God's provision of salvation for them was like a river flowing freely for all, we invited them to "come and take freely" by accepting Christ. About one hundred and fifty stood up to indicate their determination to "come" at once. They then "fell down on their faces, and worshipped God," and many of them that day drank freely, and were saved. That night we preached in the chapel, and had a glorious work of the Spirit. On Monday Charles preached in the chapel. He preached once at Butterworth, and once at Clarkebury, to the great astonishment of the missionaries.

On Monday night we preached again, and a great work was done. On Tuesday we preached again by the brook. On that occasion we had the chief of that part of Ngangelizwe's dominions, Ndunyela, twenty-four wives and women of his court, and about one hundred and twenty of his warriors. In each place we had visited comparatively few heathen came to our services, and the few who came did not put in an appearance—as in the case of Ngangelizwe's party—till near the time of our departure, when our limited time did not allow us to pursue and take them in the name of the Lord, so this influential band of heathen did not come, though specially invited by the missionary, till the last day. Ndunyela is a broad, thick-set man, of about forty years, fine open face, not black, but a reddish bronze. Some of his copper-coloured ladies had a fine Jewish physiognomy, and all were well attired in native costume. His warriors were naked, except a blanket or kaross thrown loosely round their shoulders. Brother Rayner made them a present of "a cake of bread," viz., a bullock, which they slaughtered and devoured in the afternoon. They are very expert in butchering a beef with their assegais, and in cutting out all the fleshy parts into strips, these they broil on the fire till about half done, and the smoking strips of rare roast are passed among the long circle. One fellow seizes it, and clenches one end of it with his teeth, and with his assegai cuts it off an inch or two from his mouth, just as much as he can get between his teeth, and passes it to the next, who follows his example. So on it goes round, strip after strip, a mouthful at a time, till nothing is left but the skin and bones of the beast. Every man has a right to a seat at such a feast. Whenever any Kaffir kills a beef, all the men within several miles round will assemble as promptly as birds of prey, and any one of them will eat as much as the owner. If a man should refuse to make it a free thing, he would be branded as a man too stingy and mean to live among them, and would be in danger of being "smelled out" as a witch. It is not easy for such people to appreciate English economy. To see a missionary kill a beef, and carefully cut it up and carry it into his house, and keep it to be eaten by himself and his own family, along at different times as may suit his convenience, why, to a lot of hungry Kaffirs it is the most shocking piece of business imaginable! Hence, if they want to berate a mean fellow, after exhausting their old stock of opprobrious epithets, they cap the whole by adding, "Why you are as stingy as a missionary." Brother Rayner gave the chief Ndunyela his choice, to take his people home in the afternoon, after they had eaten their "cake of bread," or to stay for the evening service. We were anxious for them to stay, but wished them to act with entire freedom of will. He sent his women home, but he and all his men remained. They occupied the front seats in the chapel, we gave them the Gospel message in all plainness, and they seemed deeply impressed but did not yield.

During the prayer-meeting Charles had a close talk with the chief. He admitted that what he had heard during that day and evening had convinced him that he was a poor sinner, that Jesus Christ was the only Saviour of sinners, and that he and his people ought to "receive" Him, and when Charles urged him to surrender to God and accept Christ, he replied, "I made Ngangelizwe promise that he would not be a Christian, and I am in honour bound to stand by our old customs, having compelled him to do so." After the prayer-meeting we had a fellowship-meeting, and those heathen heard the distinct testimony of more than thirty witnesses to the saving power of Jesus in their own hearts. On Wednesday morning we set out for Buntingville. The following extract from a letter written by Rev. Mr. Rayner, and published in the December number of the *Wesleyan Missionary Notices*, will furnish illustrative facts of the work of God in Morley.

That Sabbath was a lovely day; the sun shone with the genial warmth of approaching spring; and the chapel being too small to hold the congregation, we found a sheltered place by the river-side, and assembled the people there for the morning's service. I had long been conscious of a deepening work of God in the hearts of the people, and felt fully certain that Mr. Taylor would find them prepared to receive the word in all sincerity. Towards the end of the service the Holy Ghost descended with overwhelming power upon the congregation; and when the preacher called upon all those to stand up who were willing to come to Christ, nearly the whole congregation rose in a mass, and then with a "great cry" prostrated themselves before the Lord. It was a scene for angels to rejoice over. My feeling was one of inexpressible thankfulness; for I saw the fruits of nearly four years' sowing gathered at a stroke. Mr. Taylor stayed three days, and then passed on to Buntingville.

Soon after his departure I called a meeting of all the believers in the Circuit to form them into Classes, etc.; and upon counting them I found to my great surprise, that we had no less than two hundred and fifty present; and as the number of members before was a little below one hundred, there must have been, during those three days, one hundred and fifty conversions. There and then these were formed into sixteen classes When this was done, which was rather a tedious performance, I told each leader to meet his Class, as they sat in the different parts of the chapel, and inquire particularly into the state of each soul. They all commenced immediately, and after the hum of voices had died away, the leaders simultaneously rose, and announced the glorious fact, that with only two exceptions, the whole of the two hundred and fifty had a sense of sins forgiven, and enjoyed the witness of the Spirit that they were the children of God. You can understand the joy with which that announcement was received.

Six weeks have passed since then, and all these are walking consistently, and most of them are growing in grace.

We now present the unwonted spectacle of two native villages in the very heart of heathendom, where *more than half of the entire population*—I speak this advisedly—are converted to God, and living holy lives. Perhaps you would scarcely find a parallel even in England.

Of course all our efforts for the evangelization of the heathen will be prosecuted with renewed vigour. And, no doubt, amongst the young converts will appear some upon whom the Lord has laid His hand, for the future conversion of those who are still sitting in darkness.

We feel the increased responsibility laid upon us; but we are "workers together with God," and are resolved by His gracious aid to endeavour to lead these people on to holiness of heart and life, to build them up in the most holy faith until we can present every man perfect in Christ Jesus.

But while we had a good report of the great work of God, the work of Satan among the heathen continued as before, for owing to the wicked league of the nation and chief against Christ, but very few of the Tambookie heathen have been saved.

A horrible case of "smelling out" occurred at Morley, a short time after we left, which is described by Rev. Brother Rayner, in a letter, as follows:—

A few days after your departure, a man came running to me, saying that a woman had just fallen over the cliffs, and was lying at the bottom beside the river, dead. Thinking that perhaps she was only dead in a Kaffir sense, I gathered some men together and went down, hoping to be able to save her life. On arriving under the rocks by the river, I found that three heathen women from one of those kraals, which you saw on the other side, had gone down to gather firewood, one of them was standing between two large stones chopping a small tree, when the vibrations of the ground caused the upper stone, several tons in weight, to lose its balance and topple over. This caught the poor woman against the rock in front, and literally cut her in two, just across the loins. It was a horrible sight. The men of the kraal said she had buried herself, and had just sent the other women to pile a few stones over the body as it lay. The people said to me, " You will see that this is a case for the witch doctors." About a month after, a man came and told me that a woman was being tortured for this down by the river. I immediately sent down some Leaders to see what they were doing. They found that the doctor had said, " a certain woman of the same kraal of the deceased woman had brought a star from heaven, which caused the great rock to roll over and kill the woman. They had taken this woman, after she had been " smelled out " by the doctor, and, after a variety of tortures, they had driven four stakes into the ground, and throwing the poor victim on her back, had drawn her arms and legs to their utmost tension, and tied them to the stakes. One man stood by with a great nest of black ants, and another with a bucket of water. Occasionally one would throw some water on her body to cause the ants to take hold readily, and the other would shake on a lot of ants. The woman was wailing in agony, and the men were dancing round her. My men tried every means to set her at liberty until they were driven away at the point of their assegais.

On retiring that night I looked out at the bed-room windows and saw a great fire on that kraal, and the next morning we were told that it was the burning of the poor woman's hut, and that the woman had been sent home to her friends, but I think it more likely that she and her house perished together. This horrible deed appeared all the blacker from the flood of light which had just been poured into the minds of the people. We had often preached the Gospel to these very people, and most likely some of those very men who did that horrid deed heard you preach that morning when we gathered the outside people to hear you.

CHAPTER XXI.

BUNTINGVILLE—ICUME.

This mission, named in honour of that renowned patron of missions, Rev. Dr. Bunting, was established in the year 1830, by Rev. Wm. B. Boyce, so well known as a missionary in Africa, general superintendent in Australia, and now as secretary of the Wesleyan Missionary Society in London.

The Buntingville Mission was the first introduction of the Gospel to the Amapondo nation. The time to commence such a work was providentially opportune, for the whole nation were sitting in the ashes of their former wealth, greatly humbled. The Amazulu had just swept over their country, burnt their villages, destroyed their cattle, and had even eaten up nearly all their dogs. It is not likely that the invading savages preferred dog-meat to good beef, but the priest who, according to their custom, prepared them for war, no doubt commanded them to eat the dogs of the Pondos, and hence, when asked why they did so, replied, "We eat the dogs to make us more fierce and powerful in battle."

It was here that Rev. Mr. Boyce devoted himself so assiduously and so successfully to the philosophy of the Kaffir language, and discovered an essential key to it, which he called the "euphonic concord" of the language. He had the assistance of Theophilus, son of the old missionary, Rev. Wm. Shepstone, in this important work which furnished the basis of the subsequent grammars of the Kaffir language which have been produced.

The first site of this station was so dry and unsuitable for the cultivation of gardens, that after a few years it was removed to a more eligible spot. Faku, the great chief of the Amapondo nation, afterwards admitted that he selected the first site on very dry ground, so that the missionary would be obliged to pray for rain for his own garden, and thus the whole district would be watered.

It has been recently removed to a site twelve miles westward, on the banks of the Umtata River, and belongs to Damasi's division of the Amapondo nation, comprising about one-third of the whole population; the other two-thirds are under the rule of old Faku, his father.

This mission has been under the fostering care, first of Rev. Wm. B. Boyce, Mr. Fainton, a catechist, Rev. Mr. Satchell, Rev. James Cameron, now chairman of Natal District, then Mr. Boyce again, followed by Rev. Thomas Jenkins, who became the permanent missionary of that nation.

The Buntingville Station, though the mother of several other important stations, has been suffering a decline, so that it is now the feeblest mission in Kaffraria. It is now, however, under the care of Rev. Wm. Hunter, giving indications of new life and promise of great effectiveness in the future.

On Wednesday morning, the 8th of August, we left Morley for Buntingville Station, distant thirty-six miles. Rev. Wm. Hunter had been assisting us at Morley a couple of days, and was now ready to pilot us to his station. The bridle-path was five or six miles shorter than the wagon-road, and there was nothing to prevent us from driving our cart the short route, but an impassable drift at the Umtata River. However, a native man of some importance in that country, living near the said drift, who professed to have received good at our services, informed us that he had made a road out from the drift, and had also opened a road across the near way for wagons, so we were induced to take Dahveed's "new road," and accept his kind offer to pilot us through. Brother Hunter, Charles, and Stuart, took a still more direct path, and Brother Roberts, myself, and our guide, took the "new road," which we found was no road at all, and it was a marvellous thing that we got through. When we were descending the last mountain towards the Umtata drift, brother Roberts was almost out of patience, affirming that we had been humbugged, at the peril of limb and life, in taking that route, instead of the main road; but our guide was so kind and hopeful, that I begged Roberts not to hint his disappointment to Dahveed, but let him enjoy the satisfaction of doing us a great favour, as he evidently designed. As we were getting over the most dangerous part, near the river, Dahveed said, with an indescribable air of self-satisfaction, "This is my road." A field-officer, after a great victory, could not have manifested greater self-congratulation than did this native in getting us over his own road. Every reference to that trip afterwards threw Roberts into a spell of laughing, with a repetition of Dahveed's saying, "This is my road." When we drove into the "drift," one of the horses, in drinking, drew a buckle of the check-rain through a ring on the harness saddle, which we did not observe at the moment, but when Brother Roberts attempted to drive on, one line being fast, the other drew in the right wheel-horse, and the left being unrestrained, ran round the other, which turned their heads directly down the stream. Just before them was a ledge of rocks and deep water. Dahveed had dismounted to get a drink, and not knowing that we had no command of the team, was shouting at the top of his voice, "Pezulu! pezulu! pezulu!" He did not think of rushing to the rescue, but simply of giving the word of command to go above, so I stepped down into the river and released the lines, and we got through all right, and without much difficulty got up the steep bank, on Dahveed's new-cut road. He had done some digging there, let it be said to his credit, which rendered the ascent from the river possible. We reached Buntingville a little after dark, and found comfortable quarters in the new mission-house, but recently built by Brother Hunter, who, with his young and interesting wife, did everything necessary to make our brief sojourn agreeable. This new site for Buntingville Station is well selected on an elevation near the beautiful Umtata.

This mission, as has been intimated, belongs to Damasi, son of the great Chief Faku, who, though legally the king of the whole Amapondo nation, has for many years allowed Damasi the sovereign rule of all the Pondos west of the Umzimvubu river, and the two Governments are so distinct, that each can make war or peace with other tribes without involving each other. For example, when we were there, Damasi was at war with Umhlonhlo, chief of the Amapondumsi, but Faku's people were not; at the same time Faku was at war with the Amabaca tribe, but Damasi was not; so that Damasi, though not strictly in law, is in fact, a great paramount chief. It is difficult to get anything like a reliable census in Kaffraria. We were told, on what seemed good authority, that Damasi had 50,000 warriors under his command; but we learned from Rev. Mr. Jenkins, who has been among the Amapondo for over thirty years, that the entire population under Damasi is about 50,000, and that under Faku about 100,000. Damasi has furnished most of the funds, by the sale

AMAPONDO.

of cattle, for the erection of the new mission-house at Buntingville, and will pay a large proportion of the funds necessary for the erection of the new chapel they are preparing to build. There are but few families of natives resident on this new station as yet. There is still a society at old Buntingville, but at this new field they had only about twenty members, and Brother Hunter thought the most of them lacked the converting grace of God. He, however, had two or three really spiritual, and working members. Brother Hunter had hoped that we would spend a week with him, commencing our series on the Sabbath. I felt great sympathy with him in his isolated, difficult work, and great sorrow that my time was so limited, that we could remain there but two days. He sent out word among the heathen that Isikunisivutayo had come, and invited them to attend our services; but unfortunately "Vava," the nephew of Damasi, and chief of that district, had made a great marriage-feast for one of his relatives to come off on Thursday, the first day of our series, and therefore "they could not come," and prayed to be "excused." However, we got together a congregation of about one hundred, to whom we preached twice in the open-air, and nine of them professed to find peace with God.

On Friday the Chief Vava, his son, and about sixty of his counsellors and warriors, many of them with shields and assegais in hand, came, which added bulk and interest to our audience. Just from a marriage-feast, at which they had devoured a bullock or two, and swallowed streams of Kaffir beer, and now suffering a recovery, they were not in the best state of mind to receive the Gospel, but we remembered the saying of God, "Is not my word like as a fire; and like a hammer that breaketh the rock in pieces?"

By earnest, united prayer, we kept the Divine fire burning, and dealt heavy strokes with the hammer of truth upon the flint rock of their heathenish hearts. At first every stroke seemed to rebound without effect, except on our hearers of the previous day; but during the second service, by the action of the fire under the awakening Spirit, and the sledge-hammer of the Gospel, we made a break among the heathen; the chief, Vava, his son, and seven of his counsellors and warriors, went down on their knees as seekers, and most of them professed to have accepted Christ, and received the pardon of their sins. Vava seemed thoroughly in earnest, but though he professed to have found the Lord, we did not number him among the converts, till we should see the proof of it in putting away his plurality of wives. I am sorry not to be able to give definite information as to his subsequent life. Brother Hunter gave Vava a cake of bread (a bullock), according to custom, for their evening repast, and while the chief was in a hut, talking about the great salvation, his warriors devoured the beef, and poor Vava did not get enough to stay his royal appetite.

Vava asked Stuart if we were not going to the

"Great Place" to see Damasi? When he learned that we designed to go next day to Shawbury to spend the Sabbath, he said Damasi would be very angry if we did not go to see him; so he made an earnest appeal to us to go next day to Damasi's Great Place, distant nearly thirty miles, Brother Hunter supported it, and thought we might have a thousand heathen there to preach to. In consideration of this, together with the fact that Shawbury, the next station on our plan, belonged to Umhlonhlo, with whom Damasi was then at war, and the fear that if we should appear to slight Damasi, and give attention to his enemy, we might increase the already very terrible war-complications of the Shawbury Station, which we wished not to injure, but to benefit, we changed our plan, and consented to spend the Sabbath, August 12th, at Damasi's Great Place. On Saturday morning we bade adieu to Buntingville. Brother Hunter, Charles, Stuart, and Dahveed, went a nearer way on horseback; Vava, and a few of his men went on foot, while Brother Roberts and I, guided by a Mr. Morrison, a trader on the Umtata, who with his wife professed to find peace with God at our meeting the day before, took what was called "the road."

Much of the country through which we passed was very beautiful, with tall grass, and dense groves of timber on the eastern lee of the mountains and in deep gorges, where they were protected from the westerly winds. We saw a number of fine herds of rhei-bucks that day, and where we "out-spanned," while Mr. Morrison was preparing our lunch, I tried in vain to get near enough to some of them for a successful shot. They are hunted a great deal by the natives with their dogs, and are hence very wild.

We reached the Great Place about four P.M. Our horsemen had been there sometime before us, and had a hut arranged for our accommodation. Brother Hunter introduced me to Damasi, as Isikunisivutayo, a new *Umfundisi* from the other side of the great waters. The chief is over six feet in height, large, and corpulent, of a copper complexion, a generous open countenance, and altogether a fine specimen of a heathen chief. He took us into his palace, which is a round hut about thirty feet in diameter, the wall about six feet high made of clay, with a round roof of thatch, about twelve feet high at the apex. He introduced us to his "great wife," and some of his daughters, and showed his fine store of firewood, neatly piled up to the left as we enter, and his great earthen jars, cooking utensils, milk-sack, his royal robes, or tiger-skins, and his tiger-tails. If any Kaffir kills a tiger, he must at once inform the chief, to whom all the tigers are supposed to belong, who has the skin taken off with great ceremony, and dressed for himself. None but a royal Kaffir is allowed to own or wear a tiger's-skin. A tiger's-tail stretched over the top of a stick, about five feet in length, is a formidable sight before the hut of any Kaffir. When the chief wishes to call a man to answer for any offence, especially when a fine is to be imposed, or his property confiscated, he sends one of his "Imisila," or sheriffs, to set up a tiger's-tail in front of the offender's hut. When the poor fellow comes out in the morning, and sees the dreadful summons, for it is usually served when the man is asleep, he is filled with consternation, and must go at once and reckon with his master, who has the power to take his property or his life.

All the documentary details and process necessary to arrest and arraign a civilized man, are here accomplished at once by the magic spell of the tiger's-tail.

The chief pointed to a high perpendicular cliff, half-a-mile from his hut, and informed us that he threw his bad fellows over that precipice and dashed them to pieces. Many a poor wretch, no doubt, has found a quick passage out of the world from that cliff, and yet Damasi's appearance is not that of a tyrant, but of a kind-hearted generous man, and he is free from that mean spirit which most chiefs evince, of begging a blanket of every stranger who may visit them. When we subsequently sent word to the Great Chief Faku that we expected to visit him he replied to the messenger, "Is Isikunisivutayo travelling with blankets?" His more noble son Damasi supplied us with new clean blankets for our use, and everything we needed for our comfort during our sojourn with him, and scorned even a hint at pay in return. I was told of a clergyman who visited a neighbouring chief, who at once asked the "Umfundisi" if he had brought him any blankets?

"No," said he, "but I have brought you something better. I have come to tell you the good news about the Great God, who made the heavens above us, and who made the earth, who made us, who gave you all your lands, your mealies, Kaffir-corn, and pumpkins; and who gave you your cattle, goats, and sheep. He is our Father, and—"

The chief interrupting him, said, "Is He your Father?"

"Yes," replied the missionary; "he is my Father, and has sent me to tell you good news."

"Well," said the chief, with a grin, "if your Father is so kind as to give us all these good things for nothing, and if you are a true son of His, can't you give me one blanket?"

After Damasi had shown us the things in his house, his bloody cliff, and his great cattle kraal, said to be a thousand yards in circumference, and the largest one in Kaffraria, he said, "I am glad to see you, but the most of my people are gone. I will call all who are near to come to-morrow, but we are only a few now," and then went on to tell us, that, owing to the drought the preceding year, their stores of food were nearly used up, and that a large number of his people had gone to the "Umzimvubu," to get supplies of food; and that last night," "Umhlonhlo's" people had attacked his son's kraal and driven away a large number of cattle and horses, and that the war-cry had called a large number of his warriors away in pursuit.

The fact is, Damasi's policy is not to have a great number of his people settled near him, but to have them well distributed on the frontiers of his large and beautiful country, extending from the "Umtata" on the west, to the "Umzimvubu," on the east, and from the "Tsitsa," on the north down to the ocean.

Damasi, also, claims Umhlonhlo's country, lying north of the "Tsitsa River." When Kaffraria was being desolated by "Qeta," the revolted chief of Chaka, the Amabaca tribe to which the "Osborn" Wesleyan mission-station belongs, and the Amapondumsi, of whom Umhlonhlo is chief, to which Shawbury mission-station belongs, made common cause with the Amapondo, under Faku, who, with his allies, crushed the invader. These two tribes, however, were comparatively small, and were greatly scattered during the war. Soon after this, the representatives of the Colonial Government, wishing to have some powerful ally among the Kaffrarian tribes, with whom they could treat for the purchase of land, or for mutual defence, selected Faku as the most powerful chief, and asked old Faku to define his boundaries; and the old squatter laid down his lines from the Umtata. From the Umtata river to Natal, and from the great Drakensberg range to the ocean, comprising a block of land about 150 miles square. This grand survey,

A A

took in the countries of the two named tribes, and "Nomansland," which the colonial agents, I afterwards learnt, bought from Faku, and gave to Adam Kok's Hottentots. They have bought Alfredia also, which has been annexed to the colony of Natal.

The motives of these colonial agents were, no doubt, all right, but accepting Faku's geographical boundaries as valid, and forming a treaty with him on that broad basis of his pretended claims, Faku seems to take it for granted that his treaty with the English confirms his title to all these vast possessions, and hence he has for years been at war with the Amabaca to drive them off the land which they inherited from their fathers; and Damasi his son is on the same grounds fighting the Amapondumsi. These facts, which I received from Rev. Mr. White, and others on the spot, explain the ostensible ground of those marauding wars, so damaging to the Amapondo mission-stations, but more especially to "Shawbury" and "Osborn." I say "ostensible grounds," for their real motive is a love of plunder, which would be the same if the English had never seen their country. Rev. Mr. Gedye and his family had fled from Shawbury under Damasi's invasions but a few weeks before, and were then at Clarkebury; Rev. Brother White, at Osborn, remained at the peril of his life, under Faku's invasion of the Amabaca country.

The wars described by Rev. W. B. Rayner, in a letter published in the *Missionary Notices* for October last, occurred but a few weeks before our tour over their battle-fields, to proclaim the Gospel of peace. Mr. Rayner's letter, dated July the 20th, the week we were labouring at Butterworth, fifteen days before we visited him at Morley, describes the kind of field on which we had entered when at Damasi's Great Place, as follows :—

The present state of this country is not very favourable for missionary success. Hostilities have been going on between the Amapondumsi and the Amapondo for some time, and as the Tsitsa, on which Shawbury station is built, happens to be the boundary river between the two contending tribes, the marauding parties of either side must pass somewhere near the station; and thus either false or real alarms of war keep the station in a constant fever of excitement, until Mr. Gedye has at length been obliged to remove to Clarkebury.

A grimly amusing episode has just happened. Umhlonhlo, the Chief of the Amapondumsi, sent to Damasi, Chief of the Amapondo, saying that he was preparing to marry his *great* wife, and therefore he wanted the war to "sit still a little while." Damasi actually agreed, with the understanding that Umhlonhlo should let him know when he was ready to fight again!

It was during this lull in the storm, for Umhlonhlo's marriage to his seventh wife, that we came into Damasi's country, but now hostilities had been renewed, and the whole region was in a war-panic. Rev. Mr. Hunter had told us, that at Damasi's Great Place, I should have a congregation of at least one thousand heathens, and we had made up our minds to tarry there some days, if the Lord should open for us a door of access to them. This sudden turn of events was saddening to our hopes, but we arranged to spend the Sabbath, and do the best we could under the circumstances.

While we stood talking to Damasi, we saw a lot of young Kaffirs in pursuit of a bullock. Down the hill they came at full speed, and fetched up in front of us.

"There," said the chief, pointing to the panting bullock, "is a cake of bread for you." It was driven to the back of our hut, "assegaied," skinned and quartered with great despatch. The whole of the beef was hung up by quarters in our hut, and the skin laid in a roll underneath. According to custom, the whole belonged to the strange Umfundisi, who is expected to make a present of the hide to the chief, and also to send a fore-quarter to the chief's "great wife," and take the chief as his guest during his sojourn, all of which we performed with due ceremony. We had brought with us a supply of bread, coffee, and sugar, so with the beef broiled on the end of a stick, we entertained his royal highness in good style. We sent rations also to our friend Vava and his party, Mr. Morrison, Mr. Straghan, son, and son-in-law—three English traders—who came to attend our meeting, feasted at our common board. Charles, myself, Stuart, and our white visitors slept on the ground-floor of the hut, having each a Kaffir mat— about three by six feet made of reeds—and our rugs and coats, with a couple pair of extra blankets sent us by the chief, our saddles and other traps answered for pillows. On Sabbath morning, the 12th of August, our congregation assembled behind a hut near the chief's mansion, consisting of Damasi, his eight wives, and thirty or forty children (Damasi said he did not know how many children he had), and about one hundred warriors, armed with their assegais and shields, ready for war emergencies. Damasi came out in state. Instead of the red blanket he had worn the day before, he had a large tiger-skin over his shoulders, which constituted his entire dress, except a pair of rustic slippers on his feet. They all listened with great attention, but no decisive result was reached. In preaching to heathen on various occasions, beginning with first principles, and leading them on to a living Saviour in a single discourse, it required at least an hour and a half to deliver such a sermon through an interpreter, but we seldom failed to secure the end, the salvation of souls, on every such occasion. However, some of our friends thought we preached too long, so on this occasion we agreed to try a new plan, which was to preach half-an-hour, and then have a little talk with them personally, and draw them out, and after a brief recess resume the thread of discourse, and go on for another half-hour, and so on.

We got into the subject very satisfactorily. They appeared to understand it, and nearly all seemed to agree that our words were true, but we had not reached the vital point of convincing them of their lost condition, and of offering a present Saviour, when the time came for recess. We then asked them to talk, and ask any questions they wished on the subject of discourse. Some questions were asked and answered, when one of the counsellors said he "did not believe in a future state, or in Imishologu; that we all die like a pig, and there is no more of us." The chief replied to him, saying, "The man certainly could not be such a fool as that, for all our fathers believed in Imishologu, and so do we, and our people." The Kaffir infidel then got up and went away, and seeing that they all were getting restless, we thought it best to dismiss them, and have them assemble for another service in the afternoon. We felt that service to be very unsatisfactory. Charles seemed really discouraged, the first and only time I found him so. I assured him that "the result was what we might have expected, having opened our Gospel battery against such a stronghold of wild heathenism, we should have fired away, till they should at least feel the weight of our heaviest metal, but, instead of that, we called a parley just as we were getting well into range; we have not preached Christ yet at all, and we can't complain that they did not accept Him."

Charles cheered up, and we agreed that in preaching to the heathen, no matter what others thought or said, we would, regardless of the time required, never stop short of giving them the whole plan of salvation necessary to an intelligible offer of Christ.

In the interval, Damasi's counsellors gathered round him in a circle, and discussed the exciting topics of the day, especially the war with Umhlonhlo, and when we assembled for a second service, a number of the warriors who were with us in the morning found it convenient to be absent. The chief said their duties called them home. We did the best we could to make up for our failure in the forenoon, and at night we had a prayer-meeting in our hut. We had as seekers that night, the three white traders, Mr. Straghan, son, and son-in-law, two Kaffir men, one of Damasi's eight wives, and two of his daughters. Mr. Straghan, his son-in-law, and a Kaffir man professed to obtain peace with God. Next morning, before breakfast, we had a fellowship-meeting, during which Damasi came into the hut, Chief Vava, and two or three of his party, and the white men gave their testimony to the saving grace of God. Then old Damasi said, "I and my people are all Christians. We have all been Christians ever since Mr. Wakeford came among us." A hard old Christian, we thought, with eight wives, but he had received the missionaries, had helped liberally to build a mission-house, and was engaged in building a chapel, and when Brother Hunter's congregations fall off, he has only to inform his great chief to get a large audience of heathen, and why should he not have as much right to claim to be a Christian, as the mass of formalists, in Christian countries, who have superior advantages, and do less for the cause of Christ?

We felt very grateful for the old chief's kindness, and very sorry that he did not so feel his need of Christ as to accept of Him as a Saviour from his sins. On Monday, about ten, A.M., we bade adieu to Brother Hunter and his party, and to Damasi, and received his "kuhle hamba," and under the conduct of our former guide, Brother Morrison, pushed on in our journey toward Shawbury, distant about thirty-six miles.

The following extract of a letter from Brother Hunter, published in the *Missionary Notices,* will convey an idea of his estimate of the work of God, and its embarrassments in this field of labour.

It is with pleasure I write you a few lines to-day. My joy would know no bounds, and my whole nature would praise God if I could say that all the hindrances to our work here have been removed. This I cannot say, for alas! it is far from being true. Nevertheless I rejoice, because the Lord in mercy has visited and blessed us. Some of the worst of the station-people have been aroused to seek God, and some of them profess to have found the peace which passeth all understanding, and are joyful in the God of their salvation. All the old members have been quickened, and some twenty-three new ones have been received, so that we have now just doubled the number of members immediately resident on this station, which we had a little while ago. This work is of God, and our hope is that it will spread, and the world's Redeemer be glorified in the salvation of many of the perishing ones, by whom we are surrounded in this dark land.

CHAPTER XXII.

SHAWBURY—ELUNCUTA.

SHAWBURY was named in honour of the old pioneer-general, who planned, and superintended the founding of the whole line of old Kaffrarian Missions, the Rev. Wm. Shaw. For picturesque scenery—hills, dales, mimosa groves, cataracts, deep gorges, and precipitous cliffs, overhanging the Tsitsa river, a bold and beautiful stream—the site of Shawbury surpasses all the rest. It was established amid great hazards and difficulties by Rev. Wm. H. Garner, who was sent out by the Wesleyan Missionary Society in 1837; his widow now lives at Alice, near Fort Beaufort.

This became the most populous, and was hence thought to be the most promising of any of the Kaffrarian Stations; but while it reached a population of three thousand souls, its actual membership of professing Christians never much exceeded one hundred. At the time of our visit, the number was about ninety-five, and the whole station involved in war complications jeopardizing its existence.

It is located within the lines of the Amapondumsi Tribe, but the Tsitsa near by is the boundary between that tribe and Damasi's Pondos, with whom they are at war; yet the most of the mission-station people are Fingoes, and don't really belong to either of those tribes, and should not have been involved in the war at all, and would not, if they had improved their opportunities and become Christians. As they did not belong really to either party, they were under no legal obligation to fight, for both belligerent parties were bound by promise to the missionaries not to interfere with them; but those three thousand natives had their beautiful lines of huts on the mission-station, their fields of corn, and cattle, enjoying the ministerial and magisterial care of the missionary, released from the iron rule of Kaffir law, and the terror of the witch-doctor, and yet the mass of them refusing to submit to Christ, they waxed fat and kicked, and God gave them a little leeway to themselves, and they soon got themselves into an awful complication of war troubles. It was while I was labouring in Graham's Town, that I first heard of their sad state, by a letter from their missionary, Rev. Mr. Gedye, to Rev. W. J. Davis, in which Brother Gedye stated that he had received notice from Damasi to leave the station, as he would not be responsible for his life, or that of his family, for he meant to destroy Umhlonhlo, and take his country, and the mission-station was right in his war-path. But Umhlonhlo, on the other hand, had forbidden him to leave the place, so he and his family were in jeopardy of life. Our sympathy was greatly enlisted for him and his family, and also for his native teacher, whom he was protecting in a locked room in the mission-house against the threatened vengeance of Umhlonhlo, and earnest mention was made of them in our private and public prayers.

Some time after that, Rev. Mr. Solomon, on his way to Nomansland, spent a night near Shawbury, and hearing of the position of Mr. Gedye, sent for Umhlonhlo to visit his camp next day, and thus obtaining an interview with the chief, persuaded him to release his missionary and let him go away. Soon after Mr. Gedye took his family and went to Clarkebury, where I met him, his native teacher escaped also and went to Natal. Brother Hargraves from Clarkebury, and Brother Rayner from Morley, had gone to Shawbury, and had a council with Umhlonhlo and his leading men, to try to settle the difficulties between the chief and his missionary, and prevent the total wreck of the station, which was hard aground in a place where two seas met; but I believe they considered their mission a failure, and brought away the impression that the mission-people were so demoralized, that there was but little hope for them politically or spiritually, for after their missionary left they had a Kaffir beer-feast, got into a great fight among themselves, battering and cutting each other, and had actually killed one man. This briefly, leaving out many details, was the state of the case, so far as we had learned it before our visit to Shawbury; but we learned much more before we got through, as my narrative will show. As we have seen, the armistice secured for Umhlonhlo's marriage and honeymoon with his seventh wife, was now at an end, and hostilities had been resumed. On the last Friday preceding our visit, Umhlonhlo's marauders had invaded Damasi's country, and driven off a lot of horses and cattle, and on the Saturday night preceding, the Shawbury Mission-people had rescued a lot of cattle, which a band of Damasi's warriors were driving away from Umhlonhlo's dominions, so they were now in the midst of wars, and rumours of wars, almost daily. There was but little danger to white travellers in the day-time, but at night it was not expected that warriors should readily distinguish the colour of a man's skin, and Umhlonhlo had issued an order that no one should travel within his lines after dark.

We left Damasi's Great Place on Monday, the 13th of August, and it being but thirty-six miles to Shawbury, we hoped to reach before night, not only on account of the chief's orders, and the danger of travelling after dark, but also because of the very rough travelling near Shawbury, and the dangerous drift at the Tsitsa; but, unhappily, we got a late start, and were unnecessarily detained at the "Nokloka drift," where we "out-spanned," so that five miles of fearfully steep, rough roads, and the rocky diagonal ford of the river of about a hundred and fifty yards, had to be made in the darkness of a moonless night, through the lines of Umhlonhlo's armed sentinels. We worked our way slowly along, and told all the warriors we met about the great preaching services to commence next day at the station, and to be sure to come and bring their friends. When we got to the drift, it was so dark, we could not see the line of the ford, or where we should land on the other side; but we got a native guide, who piloted us through, and on to the station. Our guide had not to take off his clothes to wade across the river, for he had none on him, and had probably never been burdened with an article of clothing in his life. Neither he nor any of his compatriots have any laundry bills to pay. To our agreeable surprise we found Rev. Charles White, the missionary from Osborn Station, thirty-five miles beyond, had come to meet us, and was waiting to receive us at the mission-house. There was a white trader still remaining on the station, a good man, with a pious wife, who did what they could to supply all that we needed for ourselves and our horses. A kind native Christian woman did the honours of the kitchen for us, and with Brother White for our priest, we were all right, unless we should be surprised by a night attack from the Pondos, which we felt assured would not be ordered by our friend Damasi while we were there.

On Tuesday, at eleven A.M., we had the chapel crowded with five or six hundred hearers. From our stand-point we preached to them plainly, but kindly, illustrating from Jewish history the parallels of their own, and showed them that when the Jews were true to God, they enjoyed the peace of God in their hearts, and His protection against their enemies; but when they despised and abused their mercies, they brought guilt and remorse upon their own souls, and God, in such cases, after bearing long with them, and doing everything possible to bring them to repentance, delivered them over to their enemies, and all the horrors of the most desolating wars, and their only remedy was a return to God. They sat "in darkness and in the shadow of death, bound in affliction and iron"—chained in dungeons, approaching death casting its dark shadow upon them, and why? "Because they rebelled against the words of God, and contemned the council of the Most High: therefore, He brought down their heart with labour; they fell down, and there was none to help." Poor sinners, what did they do? "Then they cried unto the Lord in their trouble, and He saved them out of their distresses. He brought them out of darkness and the shadow of death, and broke their bands in sunder. Oh, that men would praise the Lord for His goodness, and for His wonderful works to the children of men." There was deliverance, and a shout of victory and praise to God for "His wonderful works."

"Now, see how this fits the facts at Shawbury. Here you have had the Gospel preached for thirty years. You have come to this beautiful spot from all parts, and have been living under the shade of God's missionaries. Besides a preached Gospel every week, you have had schools for the education of your children, and many of you have been taught to read God's Book; the blessing of God has been upon your fields, your cattle, your children, your homes, even your dogs have been exempt from the curse of the witch-doctors of the heathen! What have you done in return for all these mercies of God? Of three thousand souls on this station, not quite one hundred of you are connected with the society at all —one hundred and six a year ago, and now about ninety-five members on this whole station, and but a small proportion of them true disciples of Jesus—and "because ye have rebelled against the words of God, and contemned the council of the Most High," therefore, He is bringing down your hearts with labour, you are falling down, and there is no man to help you. We are not here to upbraid you, nor mock you in your misery, but to pity you, and beg you to consider your ways, and turn away from your sins, and cry unto the Lord in your trouble, who may save you out of your distresses." This is a mere illustration of the general drift of a discourse of an hour and half, which Charles sent home with the unmistakable ring of Kaffir periods which seldom missed their aim. We then called for penitents, and about fifty at once came out avowedly as seekers, and a small number were saved. We did not consider it safe to hold meetings at night as they had to stand by their assegais to guard their homes; but we announced for preaching again in the afternoon.

To our surprise at the next service our congregation did not exceed 150 persons, and they seemed more dead than alive. We had about thirty seekers, and they were in a gloomy unbelieving state, and but few of them accepted Christ. On Wednesday, we preached twice, but we only had out about 150, and it was a hard drag. An invitation had been sent to Umhlonhlo to attend the services, and on Wednesday he came to the trader's shop, but did not put in an appearance at the chapel, giving as a reason that Adam Kok with eight wagons, and many of his men, were passing through his country, and he had to go and meet them; so he went to meet Captain Kok, and took with him the head man of the station, whom we hoped to lead in a different direction.

On Thursday we left Charles to do the forenoon preaching, and Brother Roberts, Stuart, and I, set out for a visit to the Tsitsa Falls, five miles distant. As we were passing the line of huts eastward from the mission-house, we had an opportunity of seeing the Kaffir mode of storing away their corn. "Gideon" of old, "threshed wheat by the winepress to hide it from the Mideonites," so for a similar reason the Kaffirs hide all their corn. They dig holes in their cattle kraals, from eight to ten feet deep, and from six to eight feet wide, lined with waterproof cement. The shape is that of the old

Hebrew cisterns in Palestine, drawn in at the mouth to the diameter of about a foot, leaving space for a small Kaffir to descend to get out their hid stores as they are needed. Their women carry the corn in large baskets on their heads. Kaffir-corn grows like brown-corn, with a seed of double the size, and "mealies," a staple with them, is simply maize, or Indian-corn.

We saw them, on this occasion, pouring in, turn after turn, till the hole was nearly full of clean corn, in good order. Those holes are thus filled and covered with a broad flat stone, and then with the débris of the cattle kraal, and no stranger can tell from any outward indications whether there are any such deposits, or where hidden. During the wars, the colonial soldiers used to thump over the cattle kraals with their ram-rods, sounding for corn. If such a hole was partly empty it returned a hollow sound, but if full they were hard to find.

Stuart, in his journal, thus describes our trip to the Falls:—

We left our horses near the Falls in care of a Kaffir, while we took another Kaffir as a guide, and descended to the river below the cataract. The walk around was very long, and the descent very steep, but we were well repaid for our toil by the beautiful view we had below. Having gazed with admiration for some time from a good standpoint on the westerly side, we took off our boots and waded across the stream, in some of the deepest parts jumping from rock to rock, and then we clambered over a series of rugged ledges near the base of the mountain, and great boulders near the edge of the river, till we got up as close as the spray would allow us, to the falling water; and there we witnessed a phenomenon, to us new, and intensely beautiful. It was a rainbow formed by the reflection and refraction of the sun's rays upon the spray, so as to make a complete, though somewhat oval-shaped, circle. We stood in the lower rim of the great rainbow circle, and felt that for once we had indeed caught up with the rainbow, and stood in the midst of its glory more glittering than gold, yet "the bag of gold we found not." The Tsitsa Falls are 375 feet high, 200 feet higher than Niagara, and must be grand in summer when the river is in flood, but now the river is low, and is divided here into three principal streams which are about seventy feet apart, where they bound over the precipice to the depths below. Having made our observations, we proposed to ascend the cliffs from where we were—the opposite side of the river from our route of descent. Our guide who lives near the head of the Falls, said that no white man had ever gone up there. We determined, however, to go up as far as we could, and after hard climbing, and no small risk of falling and breaking our necks, we succeeded in reaching the heights, and having collected some pretty specimens of agates, rolled a few stones over the falls to measure the depth by the sound, had a good swimming bathe in the river, we saddled our horses, and turned their heads for the station. Passing the kraal, where we got our herdsman and guide, we stopped and sang in Kaffir, for the poor heathen men, women, and children, the hymn called *The Eden above*, to which they listened attentively, and seemed very much pleased.

On our return, we said, "Charles, how did you get on in the chapel to-day?"

TSITSA FALLS.

"We had out about the same number as yesterday, and I preached to them as well as I could."

"Did you have a prayer-meeting?"

"No, I thought we had better wait till you should get back."

Charles did not ordinarily wait for anybody where the Spirit led the way, but he felt the terrible repulsion which we all felt, but which as yet we could not understand. That afternoon we preached again, and had a few conversions, and among them Mr. White's servant-man, from Osborn. We had a fellowship-meeting, and he spoke like the Lord's freeman, as he was. About a dozen others spoke, professing to have obtained peace, but it was with trembling, and several who had professed did not speak at all, so that in everything there seemed to be the presence of some diabolical spell. That day I wrote to the Rev. William Shepstone, the chairman, explaining matters as I saw them, and begged him to do what he could to afford relief by his influence with the chiefs, which is great, and by sending some one to try to look after the scattered sheep. Brother Gedye is a fine Kaffir scholar, and a brother of zeal, but having had trouble there with Umhlonhlo, it was better to have a change. Next morning, when we were preparing to leave with Brother White for his station, we learned that the official members of the society wanted to meet us in council, to which we readily consented, without having the least hint of what was to be the subject of debate.

They soon gathered round us in the dining-room, squatting down on all sides and in every corner, a sombre-looking set of natives as I had seen at any time. I saw by their long pause that something solemn was pending, and soon perceived, by the direction of their eyes, who had been appointed to open the case, and who was to plead their cause. After a little time an old man, whom they called Elijah, arose, and with the gravity of a Roman senator, said, "We want to know why the district-meeting have thrown us away? What great crime have we been guilty of that we should be driven off like scabby goats, to be devoured by the wild beasts? It is not common to punish men till they have been tried and found guilty; even among the heathen a man is 'smelled out' before he is 'eaten up,' but here, in the midst of our dreadful punishment, we have come to ask you what is our crime?" I at once woke up to the subject, for I found that we were put upon our trial under a very grave charge, involving the issues of life and death. A lawyer, by the name of Job, was sitting beside Elijah, biding his time, and from his flashing eyes and swelling jugulars, I knew it was no child's play that we had to do. So by a few questions in an undertone to Brother White, I got an outline of the facts, and by this time Elijah was seated and Job was on his feet, and passing his blanket round his otherwise naked body, and throwing it gracefully over his left shoulder, proceeded in a subdued but masterly style of eloquence to say in effect:—" What my brother has just said is true. The district-meeting have thrown us away, and we are being destroyed. We have always had confidence in our missionaries and in the district-meeting, but our confidence has been betrayed and forfeited, and now we are ruined. The most of these people on the station are Fingoes. They have been brought up under the rule of the missionaries, and they came here into Umhlonhlo's country not to serve Umhlonhlo, but to live under the missionary. The missionary was our father, and we looked to him for a father's care. These people have no right to fight for Umhlonhlo any more than for Damasi, nor to be eaten up by him. I am not a Fingoe, I belong to Umhlonhlo, but the most of these people do not, yet the district-meeting has thrown them away, delivered them to Umhlonhlo, who says they must all fight for him against Damasi. Umhlonhlo himself has eaten many of them up, and they are all in jeopardy of their lives every day, and he is forcing old heathen customs upon them that they never were subject to in their lives." At the "Tina," an out-station, about twelve miles distant, " he has revived the horrible old custom of 'upundhlo,' requiring even Christian men to send their daughters to lodge for the night in the huts of the chief and his amapakati, and we know not what day the same brutal custom may be imposed on the people of this station. All this has come upon the people here because the district-meeting abandoned us to the rule of a heathen chief. We would gladly leave everything and go away, but the chief won't allow us to leave, so here we are, and we want to know our crime, and why the district-meeting has dealt with us so cruelly?"

Then it came to my turn to answer, and I arose and said, "Your case is very deplorable, and we are sorry for you indeed, but now we must find out the real facts in the case.

"Let us then look *first* at the action of the district-meeting, which you say is the cause of all your calamities. Whatever they did was done in the fear of God, as your friends and pastors, and they did not anticipate any of the evils which have befallen you, and but few of the things you are suffering have come from their action, as I will show you presently. It is not according to the Word of God that ministers of His Gospel should be ruling magistrates over a great community, of all sorts of sinners, such as are in this station. In establishing the Gospel first among the heathen in Kaffraria, the good men of God, in mercy to the people on their stations, whom they gathered in from among the heathen to live with the missionary, because they were Christian people, or earnestly seeking after God, and wanted for themselves and their children a Christian education, exercised all the authority, which they considered consistent with their own spiritual mission and the supreme authority of their paramount chiefs, for the protection and proper training of their people in everything necessary to qualify them to be good Christians, industrious workers, and good subjects of their chiefs, and also to furnish to the chiefs themselves a model of Christian government. Their one great work was to preach the Gospel and bring souls to Christ, and the magisterial office they consented to bear for a time, was an incidental thing, to be given up in due time entirely to civil rulers, whom God hath ordained separately for that work, just as ministers are called separately for their work. If the rulers are unwise or wicked because of the general wickedness of their subjects, then if God's people cannot correct the bad government, nor readily escape from the injustice they suffer, they must commit themselves to God, and endure patiently what God may permit for the trial of their faith, who will, if they endure hardness as good soldiers, make all things work together for their good. St. Paul did not gather a lot of his converts, and form a station like this, and rule over 2,900 rebels against God, for every 100 believers in his fold. No such thing. He preached the glad tidings to poor sinners, and when he got them to accept Christ, they would have been glad enough to have gone and lived with their Umfundisi, but what did Paul say to them? 'Let every man abide in the same calling wherein he was called. Art thou called, being a servant? care not for it; but if thou mayest be free, use it rather. Brethren, let every man wherein he is called, therein abide with God.' God will be with His people wherever they are, and if

God be with them, and they remain true to Him, He will either deliver them from their tribulations, or sustain them under them. That is God's way of spreading the Gospel in heathen countries, and in that way we will not grow sickly, dwarfish Christians, that can't stand a blast of wind, but healthy, strong men, ready always to do or to die for God. In that way we will not carry all the leaven and put it into a pot by itself, but will have it distributed through the lump till the great mass of heathenism is leavened. This you see is God's way. The most of the missionaries who have established the mission-stations and nourished the people at them so long, are now anxious fully to adopt God's way. Here, at Shawbury, the missionary being responsible to his chief for the conduct of 3,000 people, and having to settle all your disputes, what time had he left to give to his one great work of leading the people to Christ?

"He felt it, and the district-meeting felt it, and they in love to your souls thought it best to release him from that work, that he might devote his whole time to the work of teaching you and your children the way to heaven.

"There was no war then, and they could not anticipate any of the horrible things which have since come upon you.

"Now let us, in the *second place,* look at the real cause of your troubles. In the first place, the most of your people, under the name of being Christians, and enjoying all the privileges of a mission-station, are notorious rebels against God, and have no right to expect special favours from God or His people. In the second place you have not kept your treaty engagements with Damasi. At the beginning of this war, Damasi, by a special messenger, asked you three questions—1st. Are you Umhlonhlo's people, or are you not? 2nd. Do you intend to join Umhlonhlo in fighting against me or not? 3rd. If you do not intend to fight me, give me a description of your boundaries, so that I may not pass over them with my armies. Was not that so?" "Yes," replied the learned counsel on the other side, "that is true." "Well now, in reply, you said, '1st. We are not Umhlonhlo's people. We are mission-people, but we live in Umhlonhlo's country, and are bound not to break his laws. 2nd. We will not fight against you, unless you cross our mission-station lines. 3rd. Our lines are so and so,' and you gave him your boundaries." "Is not that true?" "That is all true," said Job. So far the thing was all honourable and fair on both sides. Now, if you had dealt honourably with Damasi, he never would have interfered with one of you, and your missionary would not have been disturbed, and you would have had his influence all this time to shield you from the wicked excesses of your chief. But what did you do? You got up a great sham fight for a lark, and though your missionary begged you not to go over the hill toward the river, in sight of Damasi's soldiers, you went in spite of him, and Damasi's soldiers of course thought you were going out to fight them, and put themselves in battle array. Then Umhlonhlo to help the devil to ensnare you, came along and ordered you to charge on Damasi's men, and when you refused, you got his ill-will, and then he advanced and shot some of Damasi's men himself, and you got the credit of all that on Damasi's books. Though you did not design it, you thus did so break faith with Damasi as to put it beyond explanation to him, and then having gotten yourselves into that mess, you gave up to Umhlonhlo, and have since been regularly joined to him in array against Damasi, and have not only thus brought all this evil upon yourselves, but jeopardized the lives of your missionary, and his wife and little children, and imposed upon him the greatest grief of his life, the necessity of leaving his work, and fleeing away to a place of safety."

Then Elijah arose and said, "The words of the Umfundisi are true words; but if the district-meeting felt it their duty to make a change of such importance, why did they not consult us first? We are official members of the Church, and we are a party directly interested in such a change. Moreover, as the most of us have been all our lives on the mission stations, and never felt the rule of a heathen chief, we should have been notified in time to prepare our minds for such a great change, so as to be able to bear it as good Christians."

Then Brother White replied, saying, "On my way home from the district-meeting, sometime before the matter was brought before Umhlonhlo, I told a number of your leading men what the district-meeting had done, so that you might prepare your minds for it." Meantime, I saw, from the flash of Job's eyes, that he considered us his game after all. Up he sprang, excited, almost beyond self-control; but he poised himself very quickly, and with true Kaffir self-possession and dignity, yet with great spirit, retorted, "Yes, you told us what you had done at the district-meeting as you went home. It was too late then for us to have any say in the matter. Why did you not tell us on your way to the meeting, so that we might decide what was best for us to do. If we had known that you were going to give us away to a heathen chief, we might have decided that it was better for us to pick up our assegais and blankets and go away to some other part; but after we have been sold for nothing, we are coolly told that the deed is done, and that we belong to a heathen master."

It then came to my turn to deliver the closing speech, and I said:—

"I see now how the case stands. We, the district-meeting, confess that we have made a great mistake in not giving you due notice of our intention, and in not consulting you, and fully preparing your minds for such a change, and

I think I speak the sincere feelings of every member of that meeting, when I say, we are very sorry, and all we have to plead is, what I have pleaded, our best intentions in doing a necessary thing to be done, but we should have given you notice of our good intentions. The reason, I believe, you were not notified and consulted is, that it was not till after the meeting had assembled, and the state of the work here made known, that it was felt necessary at that time to take such action. It was believed that the missionary was so burdened with magisterial duties in managing such a hard lot that the thing could not, in justice to your souls, be delayed, and there was then no opportunity of consulting any of you; but now we see that we made a great mistake in not waiting, to give ample time for consultation. But, while we confess to *one great mistake*, you will have to confess to *two great sins*, and then we must all humble ourselves before God, confess and forsake our sins, accept Christ as our Saviour, and ask God's gracious direction out of these dreadful tribulations. Your first great sin was to go, in spite of the wise counsel of your missionary, and break your solemn treaty with Damasi. Your second great sin is, that after bringing so many evils on yourselves, as we have shown, you have not only justified yourselves, and blamed it all on the district-meeting, but have gone on in greater excesses of sin, profaning this holy place with Kaffir-beer feasts, quarrelling, fighting among yourselves, and have even murdered a man, and have not confessed your sins, nor repented. Even while we have been here, who had nothing to do with any of your matters, but came purely to help you in your distress by leading you to Jesus, you have kept up a quarrel in your hearts against us, and have thus prevented a great work of God, which with your agency He would have done for you, by us His servants, just as He has done at other stations we have visited. Now you must have done with Kaffir-beer feasts, and with beer-drinking at home, surrender to God, accept Christ, and get right in your hearts and lives, and then we may hope that God, in some way, will give you relief, and spare your lives, that you may honour Him in the sight of the heathen. Meantime, I have written to Mr. Shepstone, the chairman, and hope that he may be able to do something for you; but his success depends on the mercy of God, and that depends on the course you take in regard to your sins."

Elijah said "These words are true," and pledged himself to do the best he could to promote a real reformation. Job said the same, and the rest assented. Then we knelt down and submitted the whole matter to God, and the Comforter was graciously present to quicken and to heal. Our horses were then waiting at the door, and we rose from our knees and bade our penitent friends adieu.

I said to Brother White, as we passed out, "Ah, if we had had that counsel on the first day of our series here, instead of the last, we would have had a glorious work of God." This was the terrible incubus which had strangled all our efforts, and added to it was a great disappointment growing out of a mistaken apprehension that I was coming as their missionary to live among them, and finding that I was only to be with them three days, many left in disgust; but if we had had the leading men with us, we should have overcome that, and had a grand victory. We had with us at our services at Shawbury, a native Local Preacher from Natal, who had come more than

200 miles to visit his brother there, and when we left off, he took up the work, and we learned that the following Sabbath he had the chapel crowded, and the Spirit of God was with him in power. Soon after, two of our missionaries went and gave them a helping hand, which Rev. Wm. Shepstone, the Chairman of the District, in a letter to me, describes as follows:—

My nephew found Shawbury so impressed on his mind, that he could not rest, so like the honest quakers of old, he yielded, and taking Hunter's station in his route, Hunter readily accompanied him. They spent four days at Shawbury, holding services, two or three times a day, and to use Rayner's words, "The Spirit of God came down upon the people," and they left about 100 souls who had, during their services, found peace with God, and joined the Classes. These, I believe, were all converts from amongst the heathen. Last week I received a letter from Brother Gedye, who had returned thither, and is labouring with all his might, and he tells me that since his return, about forty more have been brought in, and that "David Cobus," the man who was the devil's own agent, and the principal cause of all the Shawbury troubles, is now, like Saul of earlier days, preaching the faith which once he destroyed, or tried to. Gedye says he is helping mightily in the work of the Lord. That station is now in peace and quiet. The belligerents fight around it, but the people are not disturbed, and not a soul moves from the station towards the battle-ground. I had written a letter to Damasi, on the subject of the neutrality of mission-stations in war before your letter reached me, and obtained from him a promise that the missionary and all mission property should be respected.

Though Shawbury has been left without a missionary at a time it most needed one, God hath shown that, nevertheless, He can carry on his work in his own way. Umhlonhlo has not been to Shawbury since Gedye's return, but has sent a message that they must pray, but does not say for what. Gedye thinks he means for rain, which is the most likely thing he would wish to see.

A short extract from a letter from Brother Gedye, published in the *Missionary Notices*, dated November 30th, 1866, a few days after I sailed from Cape Town for London, may further illustrate the progress of this work. "On my return to the station, a fortnight after,"—the departure of Brothers Rayner and Hunter noticed above—" we entered upon a course of special services, which resulted in about fifty conversions during the week; and since then not a week has passed in which conversions have not taken place; so that we are enabled to report an addition of above two hundred persons meeting in Class. I have just returned from the Tina, where the Lord has given us twenty souls during the past ten days, and many others are under deep conviction."

CHAPTER XXIII.

OSBORN (TSHUMGWANA).

This mission-station, an offshoot from Shawbury, was established by Mr. Hulley, a Local Preacher devoted to the work of God, and for many years employed by the Missionary Society, under the title of a "Catechist." He is not in the employ of the Society now, but is nevertheless engaged in the mission work. He has settled his family on a farm near the west bank of the Umzimvubu River. His wife is a sister of Rev. H. H. Dugmore, and they have an interesting family of children. He has built a substantial hut-chapel, round, like a Kaffir-hut, about thirty feet in diameter, which will accommodate about 150 natives. He has organized there a society of natives, and preaches to a large number of heathen besides, and God is owning his labours. The Tshumgwana Station, established and sustained for a number of years under his administration, was called Osborn, in honour of Dr. Osborn, so long and so favourably known as one of the Secretaries of the Wesleyan Missionary Society.

Rev. Charles White, the present missionary at Osborn, brother to Mrs. Rev. Thomas Jenkins, and to Mr. Alfred White, who was the Lord's leading agent to induce me to go into those Kaffrarian adventures, is with Brothers Shepstone, Dugmore, Sargent, Bertram, and others, a Colonial-made minister, and none the worse for that, as the record of each one will show. The Osborn Station belongs to the Amabaca tribe, but like Shawbury, is situated near the borders of the great Amapondo nation, who are at war with the Amabaca, and it is therefore greatly exposed to the ravages of war. But a few weeks before our arrival, a large army of Faku's warriors came, variously estimated from 5,000 to 8,000 men, under the command of Faku's son, Umgikela. As this army penetrated the heart of the country, the Bacas fled before them, and the warriors were busily employed in gathering up all the live stock within their reach, till they got near to the Great Place of the ruling chief, Makaula. Tiba is nominally the paramount chief of the tribe, but his residence is in "Noman's-land," which was given, as before shown, to Adam Kok, the Griqua, who has laid Tiba under tribute, the mass of his tribe living beyond Kok's lines are free, and hence Tiba, though not deposed, has lost prestige, and Makaula is in fact the ruling chief, and being a young, brave spirited man, he succeeded in rallying his surprised and scattered people, and in person led them to the charge against the invaders, and after a severe hand-to-hand fight with their assegais, the Pondos began to give way, and soon in utter confusion and panic they retreated. They had to run ten miles to get to the Umzimvubu River, the boundary of their own country. The Bacas, flushed with victory, pursued, and strewed the route for ten miles with the dead bodies of their foes. The mission-station was in their path, and on the approach of the retreating army, the mission-people in the excitement fearing an attack on the station, turned out in a body, in spite of the remonstrance of their missionary, and poured a deadly volley in the front of the fleeing foe, which brought them for a little time to a stand, and the slaughter was fearful. A Brother Lee had a trading-station near, and the entrance to his house was blocked up with the bodies of the slain. One poor Pondo dashed himself through a window of the room, occupied by Mrs. Lee, with such violence as to cut an artery of his arm on the glass, and down he dropped beside the frightened lady, and without saying a word bled to death. A room of the mission-house, with an outer entrance, which happened to be open, was packed with Pondos, and Brother White stood at the door to shield them from the assegais of the Bacas. The pursuers came on in the rage of their human slaughter, and demanded access to the refugees in the room, but Mr. White said to them, "These men have placed their lives in my hands, and if you want them you will have to pass over my dead body." The Bacas seemed to think it hard that their own missionary should thus protect their enemies, but he taught them an example of forbearance and of justice to a fallen foe. That act, too, helped to mitigate the violation of the neutrality laws of the mission-stations, of which his people were guilty. He gave sanctuary to his prisoners that night, and sent them home in peace the next morning. The army of the Pondos were pursued to the Umzimvubu, and many were slain in the river, but the Bacas did not pass over into Pondo-land.

The Pondo army, to assist their flight, threw away nearly everything they had. Among the spoils were numerous shields and assegais, and seven hundred guns, of which it appears they had made but little use. Between four and five hundred Pondos were killed. Though they fled for life, when caught they died like stoics. For example, an old Pondo lay apparently dead, and a Baca exclaimed, "I killed him!" "No," said another Baca, "I killed him." With that the old Pondo opened his eyes, and said, "You are both liars; neither of you killed me!" Then the two merciless wretches took up stones and battered out his brains. Brother Lee, to clear his premises of dead Pondos, looped a "reim,"—a raw hide-rope—round their necks, and dragged them away, and as he was about to put the reim round the neck of one of the dead men, the corpse, as he supposed, opened his eyes and said, "Do please let me lie still and die."

The Kaffirs never bury their dead who are slain in battle; the dogs, pigs, wild beasts, and birds of prey did what they could to prevent effluvia and pestilence, by devouring their flesh, and the bones of their carcasses lay bleaching in the sun when we were there, a heart-sickening sight indeed. We had come as warriors too, had come to conquer, not to spoil and destroy, but to proclaim a life-giving Deliverer to the dead souls of the savage warriors still alive.

We left Shawbury on Friday the 17th of August. We out-spanned at Tina, the out-station at which Umhlonhlo committed the outrage before mentioned. We inquired of "Nicodemus," the head man, who had been a Class-leader there, but whose society had been broken up during the recent troubles, if the charge made against Umhlonhlo was so, and he affirmed that it was all true that we had heard.

Stuart thus briefly describes the rest of our journey that day:—

Soon after we crossed the Tina river, we came to a very steep and stony hill, where one of the horses became baulky, and seemed determined not to pull up the hill, and could not be persuaded, neither by coaxing nor the free use of the whip. After many unsuccessful attempts to get the beast up the hill at the great risk of breaking the cart, we put in another horse, which, going to the opposite extreme, dashed off, ran the upper wheel over a great stone, and upset the whole concern. By carrying our baggage up on our shoulders, we at length, after the delay of an hour, reached the summit; and passing through a beautiful, fertile, well watered country, reached the Osborn station just as the sun was setting.

Rev. Mr. White, the missionary, and his good wife kindly entertained us. They have no family, but have adopted a little prince, the son of Makaula. The little boy was very ill, the heathen doctors could do him no good, and when the chief thought he was dying, he brought him to the missionary and said, " Take my dying child. If he dies, bury him; if he lives, take care of him and teach him." He is now a fat little fellow over two years old. He is very fond of shaking hands, and is delighted with the ticking of a watch, and seems to understand such English as is addressed to him, for when we tell him to shut his eyes, and then to open them, or to laugh, he does so, and altogether he is a very comical little specimen of Kaffir humanity.

One embarrassment under which we had laboured in each place, in regard to the heathen, was that they seldom came to our services till near the close of the series, and we did not then have sufficient time to do a great work among them.

At Osborn we determined to try a new plan for getting them out to the preaching. So on Saturday morning, the 18th of August, Charles Roberts, Stuart, and myself, with " Petros," Brother White's schoolteacher, as a guide, set out on horseback, and visited all the heathen kraals within a few miles of the station.

We rode up to a kraal, and called to them, saying, " Bring out all your men, women, and children, and we will sing you a song about the country above." We then dismounted, and standing in a line, holding the reins of our horses behind us, we sang in Kaffir, " The Eden Above."

Then without adding a word we mounted and rode off, leaving Charles to tell them that a new Umfundisi from over the sea had just arrived, and had just been to pay them a visit, and sing to them, and would preach at the station that day at noon, and "he wants all of you to come and hear the good news he has to tell you." Then riding on to another kraal, the same was repeated, and so on till all within our reach were visited. In some places some of the men followed us to their neighbouring kraal, so that I could see at once that we were getting a hold on them. Sure enough, at noon we had the heathen to our meeting in force. The chapel would not hold the half of them; so we assembled them in the stable-yard, which, with various buildings of four sides, was a large open court. The first sermon, therefore, instead of being to the Church as usual, was to the heathen, from St. Paul's text about the "Unknown God." Having given a very brief history of St. Paul's work among the people in the great city of Athens, we came directly to our work.

We did not simply proclaim the truths of the Gospel to them, for the work of an ambassador for Christ embraces much more than that, but followed St. Paul's method. He never "begged the question." In preaching to the Jews, he based his arguments on the clearly defined prophetic Scriptures, which his hearers admitted. In preaching to heathens he went directly down into the regions of their own experience, and brought to light, from their admitted facts, a conscious demand in their souls which they were vainly trying to meet, but which the Gospel only could supply. If I could reproduce our discourses to the heathen there during our series of three days, my space would not admit them; but the substance of the first, and a specimen point or two of the others may serve to illustrate the method of preaching, which the Spirit of God was pleased to render very effective in the salvation of a large number of our heathen hearers.

At that first service, having introduced the subject of the "Unknown God," the following is an example of our method of preaching, which God used in bringing raw heathens to a saving acceptance of Christ, under a single discourse.

SERMON TO KAFFIR HEATHENS.

There is one Great God who made the world, the sun, moon, and stars, and every living thing; and who made man. That is a fact you all admit. Your old fathers who are dead believed that, and you believe it too. Your fathers called him "Dala," the Creator, or "the Great Hole," out of which all living things came; and they called him Tixo, God, the preserver of all things; and "Inkosi," the Lord, the Great Chief who rules all things. They did not know God, but they called Him by these names, and offered sacrifices of worship to him, and on many a hill in Africa, your "Isivivana" bear witness that they called upon His name (we saw by the path in a number of places on the hills a great pile of hand stones, about eight by sixteen feet, and six feet high. For generations, every heathen passing will add a stone, as an expression of thanks to "Inkosi" for helping him up the hill).

You then believe with us that there is one God, and that we are "His offspring." Come then and let us reason together about this Great God. If He made the sea, the earth, and the heavens above us, He must be a God of wonderful power. When His lightnings flash and He speaks to you from His "Great Place" above the heavens in tones of thunder, how you do tremble. Now, if we are the offspring of this Great God, which you all admit, let us examine His work, and see if He is not a God of love, as well as a God of power. Examine your heads, your eyes, your noses, your ears, your tongues, your teeth, your arms, hands, body, legs, and feet—what a wonderful piece of work! Everything about us witnesses, not only to the power and wisdom of God, but to His great love for us. If he had hated us, and had wanted to make us miserable, how easily he could have done it. Suppose he had made your ears of bone, they would have been knocked off long ago. Suppose he had put your eyes on the top of your heads, then you could not see the path; if He had put them on your forehead, long ago they would have been rubbed off, and you would be blind; but God, in love, has put them in the best place for seeing, arched them over with eyebrows to keep the sweat out of them, given us eye-lids to keep them moist, and guard them against dust, and walled them round with bones, so that a stroke on your face will not easily reach the eye; so with every other part of your bodies, everything is made just right, and all bear witness that the God who made us is a God of love. Well now, my dear friends, this wonderful body God has given us is simply the "hut" for the living Spirit which He has put into it. If the tent is such a wonderful thing, what must the tenant be? When you look upon a dead man, you see the whole body as complete as when he was alive; but it has no power to see, to eat, to smell, to think or to move. The fact is, the real man has gone away, it is his old "hut," that you are looking at, and soon it will crumble into dust.

You all know that you have a spirit, a mind, a living soul within your body, just as certainly as you know that you have a body. It is the spirit that thinks, reasons, plans, and executes our plans. You can at this moment, in your minds, see your kraals, all your huts, your cornfields, your cattle, your children and dogs. What is it that sees all these things? You don't see them with your eyes, for you are looking at me, and your kraals are away over the hills, quite out of your sight, but you have the picture of all these things in your minds. If you want to build a hut, the plan of the hut, its size and everything about it, is first the work of your spirit. If an Englishman wants to build a great ship, he first works out the whole plan of it in his mind, then marks it all down on paper. The ship-builders look at it, and go to work and make the ship, just as the man saw it all in his mind.

Now, my dear friends, the God who made us is the Great Spirit without a body, or hut, like ours, to live in, for all the heavens will not contain Him; but He has made us little spirits in His "own image," after His "own likeness," and has given us these huts of clay to live in till He calls our spirits to return to Him, and then they leave their huts, which are the dead men which you have seen, and go away into another world. Our spirits are suited to this world through the body; they employ themselves in planning and working for the body, and take pleasure in whatever is pleasing to the body; but our spirits don't belong to this world, and hence have wants that this world can't supply. You see a fish, it has fins, but no legs, and no wings, and you know at once that it don't belong to the earth, nor to the air, but its home is in the waters. There is a horse. You see that he has no fins, and no wings, but he has legs and feet, and you know at once that he don't belong to the air, nor to the sea, but to the earth. There flies a bird. You see it has no fins, but it has wings and legs, and you know without anybody telling you, that it belongs to the earth, and to the air above us. You see a man's body, it has legs and feet, and, therefore, belongs to the earth; but his spirit has no fins, no legs, no wings, and, therefore, don't belong to the waters, nor to the earth, nor to the air above us, but belongs to another world altogether. You know at once that this is all true, and hence when you bury a man, after you set him down in his grave, you say to his "umshologu"—his spirit—" don't say anything against us, but remember us kindly in that world you are going to." (The eyes of our heathen auditors sparkle under the light of a new association of admitted facts, and they look at each other, and nod assent, for like the Athenians they are always ready " to hear or tell some new thing.") Well, now, my friends, you see that our spirits belong to another world, and have wants that this world cannot supply. When we have taken all the pleasure we can get in this life, our spirits are still hungry, very hungry. They are always wanting to go somewhere, or to do something else to satisfy their great hunger and thirst, and to make themselves happy.

All animals have some kind of a spirit, but it is a low, earthy spirit, which seeks nothing more than to supply the wants of their bodies, and then their happiness is complete; but our spirits, as we have shown, belong to another world, and have powers suited to the world to which they belong, which we know, just as we know that the wings of a bird suit it for flying in the air. That pig has some sort of a low spirit, but you can't teach him your laws and customs. He has not the power to learn to read, or write, or to talk. Our spirits have the power to receive and to give instruction, to learn good laws, and to obey them, or to break them, and hence, also, we have a power in our own spirits which tells us that some things are right, and that we ought to do them, and that some things are wrong, and that we ought not to do them. If we do what we believe is right, that power in our spirits says to us, "You have done right," and we feel happy; but when we do wrong, it says to us, "You are wicked, you have broken the law;" then we feel guilty and miserable, an awful fear comes into our spirits that something dreadful will come upon us for our sins. So you see plain enough, my friends, that our spirits belong to another world; that they were made to be happy, and though they have some happiness in the pleasures of the body, they cannot find their real rest and full enjoyment in anything in this world. God alone has the real rest for our souls, and He alone can satisfy the hunger and thirst of our spirits. God is holy, and He made our spirits holy, so that they might live with God, and find their rest, and complete happiness in Him. Hence our spirits are adapted to receive and obey God's laws, which show us the right way to walk in, so that we may be ready to live with God when He calls our spirits away from our bodies. But you see, we may abuse this power of our spirits, and neglect, and break good laws, bring guilt and misery into our spirits, and thus get them so polluted with sin, that they are not fit to live with God at all. What, then, can God do with such wicked, polluted spirits? He has to "throw them away" (the Kaffirs' strongest term for hopeless abandonment), and they are dragged down into the dark hole where "Icanti" lives (an infernal umshologu, which assumes the shape of a huge snake; they often try to appease it by offering the sacrifice of beasts, throwing their offerings into deep holes in the rivers—a traditional idea of the devil, no doubt), the wicked spirit, the old serpent, called the devil—and Satan was once a happy spirit, and might have dwelt in happiness with God for ever; but he broke good laws, polluted himself by sin, and was driven away from God's fold like a "scabby goat" never to return. So all spirits, made to be holy, and to live in happiness with God, who follow Satan, break good laws, and pollute themselves with sin, are driven away also from God's fold to "the place prepared for the devil and his angels."

Well now, my friends, we have been looking at God's great work in our bodies and spirits. Let us next look into His great stores, and see what His wisdom and love have provided to make us happy. We will begin with the wants of the body. Our bodies can't live without water. See God's rills, and rivulets, and creeks, and rivers. See His clouds and dews, and showers of rain. How kind He is!

Our bodies need food. Hath God not given you a thousand grassy hills and valleys, and strong arms to cultivate them, and horses and oxen to help you? Hath He not given you Kaffir-corn, mealies, yams, pumpkins, and all manner of fruits? Hath He not given you cattle, sheep, goats, pigs, ducks, chickens, and geese? Where did you get all these things if God did not give them to you? All the men in the world could not even make one goose.

We need light for our eyes, and hath not God made the sun to give us light by day, and the moon and stars to give us light by night?

We need air for our lungs and blood, and hath not God supplied it abundantly? He hath poured it all round the world about fifty miles deep. Now if God provides such great treasures for our bodies in this life, which must return to dust, would He not provide as well for our spirits, which never die, but return to God who gave them? Would He not give us His good laws to mark out the path of holiness, that we may walk in obedience to Him, and thus be prepared to dwell with Him in happiness? Would He not? (Their eyes glance at each other, and they nod assent.) Well, now, God hath made us all of one blood. We have bodies just alike in all their parts, and our spirits are all of the same nature. God made one man, and called his name Adam, and then made one woman, and called her name Eve. He made their bodies of the dust of the ground, but their spirits He breathed into from Himself. Eve was the first mother of all the people in the world. God made Adam and Eve holy, and gave them a "great place" in the most beautiful garden that ever was made, called the Garden of Eden. It had in it every good thing that grows in the world, and God gave everything in it to the happy people He had made, except one fruit-tree He kept for Himself, and told them not to touch the fruit of His tree; and He gave them good laws for them, and all their children to keep, so as to get in this beautiful world the right kind of schooling to prepare them to dwell in happiness with God for ever.

His laws were all for their good, and allowed them everything they needed for their bodies, and for their spirits to make them happy in this life, and then, when they should be trained and prepared for a better home, to take them up to that glorious world where God abides. Was it not a fine arrangement for Adam and Eve, and for all their descendants? Oh, if they had walked in the path of God's laws, there never would have been any sickness in this world, nor pain, nor sorrow, nor crying, nor death. Then whenever they should have become holy enough to dwell with God, their bodies, instead of dying and returning to dust, would have been changed into such a glorious body, that instead of walking and running on the ground, they would have mounted up faster than the flight of an eagle to the bright world above. God was well known to our first parents, and came down and talked with them in their beautiful garden every day. Satan never was a human spirit, but a glorious angel spirit, but he became a rebel from God, and was "thrown away," a long time before Adam and Eve were made, and he was jealous of the happiness of our first parents, so he crawled into their beautiful garden, and had a talk with our mother, and persuaded her to disobey God, and she plucked off some of the fruit from God's tree, which He told her she must not eat, and she ate some, and gave some. to Adam, and he did eat. By listening to the dirty old "Icanti," they broke God's good laws, stole fruit from His tree, and thus sin entered into the world, and death by sin. Sin is such a dreadful thing, that through their disobedience all their children were made sinners, that is, sin so corrupted their spirits and their bodies, that all who were born of them were corrupt.

Then God drove them out of the garden, and they had to go and make a "kraal" among the briers and thorns. Still God was very sorry for them, and showed them great kindness in giving to them and their children all the good things in this world we have to enjoy, and He promised some day to raise up a great man from one of the daughters of Eve, who would crush the head of the old serpent, and deliver us from our sins. The children of Adam and Eve multiplied in the earth greatly, but broke God's laws more and more, and got so wicked that they did not like to retain God in their knowledge, and at last the old fathers who knew God died, and the foolish hearts of their children were so darkened by sin that they did not know God at all, but still they had the gnawing hunger and thirst in their spirits which God only can satisfy. They retained their powers of mind to receive instruction, to learn God's laws, and also a dreadful sense of guilt for sin: so when any great sickness came upon them, and their doctors could do them no good, they wanted to go to God for help, but they did not know Him. Then they built great houses, and altars of stone, where they offered bullocks in sacrifice to "Imishologu." In Athens they had one old Umshologu they called "Jupiter," and another they called "Minerva," and many others. When nothing ailed them they seemed to get on well enough with their Imishologu, but a dreadful sickness came upon all the people in their great city: then they offered bullocks to all their "Imishologu," but none was found to hear or save them. The cries of the orphan children, the shrieks of the desolate widows, the groans of dying men were heard in every street, and they found Imishologu had no power to help them, and then they built an altar for the "Unknown God," and offered bullocks upon it, and as soon as the smoke of that altar began to rise, the great God looked down upon them in pity, His heart of love yearned over them, and His hand, unseen, cured all their sickness, and health and prosperity returned to that city like the breaking of the morning. Then for six hundred years, though they kept up the worship of Imishologu, they also worshipped the "Unknown God."

Sin is the cause of this dreadful pollution of our spirits, and guilt, and fear, and sorrow, which the people of Athens felt, and which all of us have felt. That man who has sinned, even against his chief, how badly he feels. Before he did it he thought nobody would find it out, but now he thinks that everybody will know it, and every time he goes into a dark hollow, or passes a bush, he fears the chief's "Imisila" (sheriffs) will come upon him. Day and night he is in dread, and if he should wake up to-morrow morning, and find the tiger's-tail of his chief before his door, dear me, would he not be terrified? Perhaps his chief might not find him out, but you may be sure God will find out every sinner, for He is always looking at us. The pollution of our spirits, sin, guilt, and punishment, naturally follow each other. When the lightning strikes a kraal, and kills a beast or a man, you feel awful guilt and fear in your spirits, and know that "Inkosi" is angry with you for your sins, then you offer sacrifice to Him, but still you don't know "Inkosi." When you have great sickness among you, then you feel dreadful guilt and fear, and offer sacrifices to "Imishologu." You know that "Imishologu" can't save you, but you want them to plead with Tixo for you. You don't know Tixo, but as He took away the sickness in Athens, so He often takes away your sickness because He pities you, but still you know Him not, and you give all the praise due to Him for His great mercies to you to Imishologu, and to your priests. That is just the way they did in Athens, till Paul, God's great Umfundisi, went there, and made known to them the true God, whom they had ignorantly worshipped, and taught them how to worship Him aright. So you have been trying for more than six hundred years to worship the "Unknown God" here in Africa, and now God hath sent us to make Him known to you, and how you may come to Him.

We have told you how the early generations from Adam and Eve lost the knowledge of God, and His good laws; but in all ages there were a few men who would not follow Satan, but who earnestly sought after God; not in sickness only like you, and those miserable old sinners in Athens, but in youth and health, and God made Himself known to them, and told them His good laws for them to walk by, and to teach to the polluted families of men. One of those good men was called Abraham. He knew God very well, and God made His people a great nation. They lived in a country called Egypt, in the upper part of Africa, your own Africa; but the king of Egypt, who was called Pharaoh, subdued them, and made slaves of them for a great many years. There were many good men among them for a long time, and a certain boy was born whom they called Moses.

He grew up to be a very wise and good man, and got well acquainted with God; and God often talked to him, and told him a great many things to tell his people, and made Moses a great chief over all the nation that descended from Abraham. Moses was a holy chief; he had but one wife; he kept God's laws, and did justly to all men. When God had fully taught Moses to trust in Him, He told him to be up with all his people, and all their cattle, and everything they had, and He would lead them to a good country which He would give them for their own. So Moses and all the people went, and the wicked king who had oppressed them raised a very great army and pursued, and overtook them at a great river, or an arm of the sea. Moses and his people were dreadfully scared, and thought they would all be killed; but God commanded them to go right into that great river, and just as they began to wade in, God divided the waters and made a dry road for them, and they went clear across the great arm of the sea, without even getting their feet wet. When the wicked king saw that, he rushed right in with his great army, and chariots, and horses, and God brought the divided waters together and drowned the whole of them because they were so wicked. You see all that was easy enough for God, who made the sea and the dry land, to do.

Then his people travelled a long way through a desert, where there was no food for them or their cattle; but God sent them food daily direct from heaven, and that was just as easy for Him as to cause the food to grow out of the ground for us, but He thus taught His people His power and His loving care for them. One day God came down in a "thick cloud" to the top of a high mountain, mid "thunders and lightnings, and the voice of a trumpet exceeding loud, so that all the people that were in the camp trembled," and God called the man Moses to come up to Him, and there He told the great chief many things; but

He wrote down His principal laws on two smooth flat stones, which a man could carry. On one of the stones He wrote four commandments, to teach us our duty to God. On the other He wrote six commands, to teach us our duty to man.

God gave these laws to Moses for his people, the English, the Kaffirs, and everybody. They were written from the stones into books, and have been sent out among all nations, and we have them here in this book to read to you to-day. Now let us examine them, and see what good laws they are. "God spake all these words, saying, I am the Lord thy God, which have brought thee out of the land of Egypt, out of the house of bondage." God said to Moses, and He says to me, to you, to every man, woman, and child, "I am the Lord thy God." We see at once that the powers of our spirits, which came from God, made in the likeness of God, are so great, that God alone is worthy of our supreme confidence, loyalty, and love, and we see His great love to us in that He is not ashamed to say to every soul of man, so that all the world may hear it, "I am the Lord thy God." No living thing has dared to proclaim to any man, "I am the Lord thy God." Is it not a great shame that men should insult and reject this great and loving God, and put their trust in the ghosts of dead men, in their priests, and the poor trash they hang about their necks? Now hear what He says in the next command, "Thou shalt have no other gods before me." There is but one true God, but the thing to which we give the confidence, loyalty, and love of our spirits, which belong to God alone, whatever it may be, that takes the place of God, and such things are called gods, though they be such a bunch of bones, and beads, and birds-claws, as you have round your necks. God explains this, saying, "Thou shalt not make unto thee any graven image, or any likeness of anything that is in heaven above, or in the earth beneath, or that is in the water under the earth. Thou shalt not bow down thyself to them, nor serve them: for I the Lord thy God am a jealous God, visiting the iniquities of the fathers upon the children, unto the third and fourth generation of them that hate me; and shewing mercy unto thousands of them that love me, and keep my commandments." God is very kind, yet He is just. He could not consent to let us set Him aside, and put an idol in His place, no matter what it is, in heaven, or in earth, or in the sea. We see what a dreadful thing it is to reject God, and follow Satan and trust in men, and the things of this world. Such lose the knowledge of God, and their children for generations grope in darkness, and trust to charms, and to their priests or doctors, and to Imishologu. God does not want to visit the iniquity of the fathers upon the children, but the dreadful rebellion of the parents against God puts their children so far away from Him that they lose the knowledge of God, and go on in the wicked ways of their parents. But if the parents are true to God, and train their children to be true to God, then for thousands of generations they may walk in the ways of God, and enjoy His love for ever.

Now listen to God's third command : " Thou shalt not take the name of the Lord thy God in vain; for the Lord will not hold him guiltless that taketh His name in vain." Surely God could not allow us to mock, and insult Him, and scandalize His name.

Now for the *fourth* command, " Remember the Sabbath day, to keep it holy. Six days shalt thou labour, and do all thy work : but the seventh day is the Sabbath of the Lord thy God: in it thou shalt not do any work, thou, nor thy son, nor thy daughter, thy man-servant, nor thy maid-servant, nor thy cattle, nor thy stranger that is within thy gates. . . ." Now, see the kindness of God in all this arrangement. God knew that we needed food and clothing, and many things for ourselves and for our families, and He has given us the right to get and to hold property, lands, houses, cattle, money, and everything we need for our comfort, and He has given us the right to use six days out of every seven, and commands us during those six days to work and attend to all our business, and thus get property honestly, and have lack of nothing. But then the bodies of men, and women, and of beasts that labour for us, would break down if they did not get some rest-days, and God, who made us, knew just exactly how many were needed for man and beast, and set apart every seventh day for that purpose, and that while we were resting we might spend the seventh day specially with Him as a holy day, when all His people might meet together as children come to their father, and ask and receive his blessing. This is a law of God to man, and hence, if any man or beast is suffering in any way, and we can relieve them by work on the Sabbath, then the loving design of the law allows us to do such work, and it is pleasing to God. These four commands God wrote on one stone. They show us God's great kindness and justice. He is very anxious to have us keep His laws and be happy with Him for ever, but if we will not, then we bring pollution and death upon ourselves. The next stone had six commands written on it; the first is to our children. God loves our children, and says to each one, " Honour thy father and thy mother: that thy days may be long upon the land which the Lord thy God giveth thee." Our land is needed for our children's bodies when we are dead, and God is needed for their spirits. If they are not true to their parents they get into all sorts of trouble at home, and thus into wars, and finally lose their land and all their property; if they are not true to God they lose their portion in Him and go down to hell.

In the next command God speaks to every human being,

—"Thou shalt not kill." God has given us life, and kindly guards it by a command from that thundering mountain, "Thou shalt not kill." When a man breaks this command, and murders another, by God's laws his life is forfeited, and the judges may try him, and put him to death, for God says, " Whoso sheddeth man's blood by man shall his blood be shed." No man has a right to put even the murderer to death unless, after a fair trial, the Court has found him truly guilty, and commands him to be put to death. There are cases also in war, when men come into your country with the *intention* of murdering you and your families, and taking all your cattle, when the lives of many such persons are forfeited like that of the murderer. God gives you the right to defend yourselves, and your families, and homes, and He delivers over to your assegais such as He knows have forfeited their lives. We see, then, while God so kindly guards our rights to life, His justice sentences the wretch, who dares to commit murder, and break this law, to death. It is not because God has any pleasure in seeing the blood of the murderer shed, but He wants to make the law strong to guard our lives. Even in His justice He is very merciful to mankind. Now do you want to hear God's *seventh* command? Then listen, "Thou shalt not commit adultery."

In the beginning God made one man, and he was alone, and God said, " It is not good for man to be alone," and then he made one woman, and gave her to the man to be his wife. If God had designed man to have more than one wife, then He would have given the first man as many wives as He knew He ought to have, for Adam was not a poor man, for God had given him all the world and everything in it, and yet He gave him but one wife, for He knew that one wife was enough for any man. God thus gave to man the right and the command to form families, and the command, "be fruitful and multiply in the earth," and He thus showed clearly His law for forming families by the marriage union of one man to one woman. That was God's pattern for all people to follow, and He based a law upon it in these words, "In the beginning God created them male and female," and said, "for this cause shall a man leave father and mother, and shall cleave to his wife, and they twain shall be one flesh. Wherefore they are no more twain but one flesh. What, therefore, God hath joined together let not man put asunder."

Thus you see God's pattern and God's words together show His law for forming families as plain as daylight. Thus you see, if God had allowed a man to have more than one wife He would have given Adam just as many as He would allow any great chief to have, for Adam was the greatest chief and the richest man that ever was made, and then God's law from that pattern would have been "For this cause shall a man leave his father and mother, and take as many wives as he can buy or support," but you see that is not God's arrangement at all. You see, too, that God's law forbids multiplying in the earth except under His family arrangement, and also any waste or abuse of our powers for multiplying, which would in any way interfere with God's family law. The seventh command God wrote on the stone is to guard His arrangement for forming families and He says to every man and woman in the world, "Thou shalt not commit adultery." Are not all God's family arrangements wise, and kind, and good? The man or woman who breaks any part of God's good family plans and laws wickedly insults God, and sets Him at defiance.

Now let us examine the *eighth* command, and see what a good one it is. God has not only given every man the right to have one wife, and every woman one husband, to live together in union, and have children, and "Train them up in the way they should go," but He has given us the right to get and to own property for the comfortable support of ourselves and our families, and has given us the right to use six days in each week to work, and do business, and thus get property honestly, and He guards our rights to our property by a command to each man, woman, and child in the world, "Thou shalt not steal." How kind and thoughtful God has been for us, has He not? Now have you got any other thing dear to you that God could guard by His authority as our Great King in a command from the thundering mountain? What is the dearest thing a man or woman has that can be injured by another? It is your reputation, your good name. If a man tells lies of you, and gets your neighbours, the doctors, and the chiefs to believe that you are a witch or a thief, and gets them down on you, don't you see that you are ruined? God has given us a right to get and to have a good name, and guards that right by the command to every human soul who has a tongue: "Thou shalt not bear false witness against thy neighbour." Now there is nothing left that is dear to us that God could guard by another command, and yet there is another. What can it be for? Take it into your minds, and examine it well, and see what it is for. "Thou shalt not covet thy neighbour's house, thou shall not covet they neighbour's wife, nor his manservant, nor his maid-servant, nor his ox, nor his ass, nor any thing that is thy neighbour's." A desire in the heart for any of these things so strong as to lead us to be willing to break any of God's laws to get them, is to *covet* them.

A desire to get property is right, and, as you have seen, God provides for that fully, but if we allow that desire to get so strong that we are willing to get it by any dishonest means, that is *coveting* it, which is a dreadful heart-sin against God and man. A desire to leave father and mother and get married to one wife and have a family is right, and we have seen God's good pattern and law for all that, but to allow your desire to get too strong, and be your master, and lead you to be willing to use in any wrong way the powers God has given you to be used only in His wise family arrangement, that is covetousness, which is a great sin against God, because to gratify your wicked desire you will insult God and defy His authority. It is this dreadful heart-desire which wicked people indulge and allow to grow in their spirits till it masters them, and leads them to tell lies against their neighbours, steal their property, commit murders, and break all God's good laws. So you see, my dear friends, the first five commands of the second stone, each names the greatest outward sin against the best things God has given us to enjoy, but this last command strikes at the dreadful inward heart-sin of unlawful desire, which is the fountain from which all the rest flows. So you see all these commands of God reach from the highest outward sin to the lowest wrong desire of the heart. So the man who is guilty of murder in the sight of God is not only the man who assegais another to death from behind a bush, but the man also who allows the feeling of hate and murder to have any place in his heart. God says, "He that hateth his brother is a murderer." So also a man is not to commit adultery, nor is he allowed to look upon a woman for the purpose of indulging even a wrong heart-desire for her. What holy, just, and good laws these are! You see at once who made them, for no man could make laws so wise, so good, so broad, and so deep. If every one was obedient to these laws, then all the people in the world would love each other like brothers and sisters, then we would have no more wars, no killing, no stealing, no cheating, no telling lies, and injuring the good name of another; no more adulteries, nor any of the polluting wickedness of "ubukweta" or "intonjane." Then love to God, "peace on earth, goodwill to man," would fill the world with happiness and God would be well pleased.

Well now, my dear friends, don't you all say that God's laws are right and good, and that everybody ought to obey them? We all agree in that I see. Well, then, have you obeyed them? Why, says one, "How could we obey them, when we never knew them before?" Very well, you know them now. Are you willing to obey them? Are you willing to accept the Lord God as your God, the supreme Object of your trust, and heart-obedience, and love? Are you willing to give up all these wretched things you have been trusting in, instead of God? Are you willing never to speak His name but in reverence and love? Are you willing to work and attend to all your own business six days in the week, and remember the Sabbath, to use it only as God has appointed, as a day of rest, and the worship of God, our Great King? Now, to come to the laws of the second stone: Do these children consent to love and obey their parents, and so live at home, and away from home, as to bring honour to them? And do you, parents, consent so to teach your children, and to give them such a holy example of right-doing that they may, by obedience, bring honour upon you? When, in words or acts, you teach them wrong things, they will disgrace themselves, and dishonour you, even by obedience to you. Do you consent never to kill anybody, nor indulge angry desires in your hearts? Do you consent never to commit adultery, nor any uncleanness by the abuse of any of your powers which belong only to the family institution of God, and to submit to God's plan and law, of having but one wife? Do you consent never to steal, nor so desire the property of another as to get it by any unfair means? Do you consent never to tell any more lies, nor in any way injure the good name of your neighbour? I see some of you stick at one thing, and some at another, and at heart you are rebels against God. Though you have not known God, your ancient fathers knew Him, and these good laws of God; but they did not obey them, and their foolish hearts were darkened. Thus you have lost entirely the four laws of the first stone; but you have retained portions of five of the laws of the second stone. You have laws against disobedience to parents, against murder, against adultery, against stealing, and against lying; and you have fines and punishments for all these sins; but you have so corrupted and altered these laws of God that you confine them to a few outward things, and leave yourselves plenty of room for breaking the laws of God; and your laws don't go down into the heart like God's laws. So you see, my friends, you have closed your eyes against the light God has given you, and have refused to walk in the path of obedience to Him. Even now, when you see the plain, good path marked out for us all by His laws, you refuse to walk in it. Now, friends, let me tell you a great secret. You have seen that all the outward sins flow from a corrupt covetous source of sins in the heart, so all right obedience to God's laws must flow from holiness and love in the heart. You can't get salt water and fresh water out of the same spring. Now, if we have not that holiness in our hearts, shoving all the corrupt covetousness clear outside, then we cannot love God, nor keep His commandments. Alas! that is just the thing Adam and Eve lost when they first rebelled against God, and every child born since has come into the world in the sinful "likeness" and "image" of fallen Adam and Eve, with their corrupted nature in our spirits, and the love of God, and holiness to obey His laws are not there at all; and because our spirits are corrupt, we begin to go wrong when little children, and go on worse and worse. Now, that is the state of every one of you. Your spirits are corrupt as you feel and know. You refuse to keep God's laws, and can't keep them while your hearts are wicked. You are guilty, because you are sinners. You are under the sentence of death, because you have broken God's laws, for He says, " The soul that sinneth, it shall die." You are slaves of Satan, for having yielded yourselves servants to sin, and become rebels against God, He has delivered you over to Satan. What a dreadful state you are all in to be sure. Now, you know this is all true, and all your sacrifices to " Icanti " to " Inkosi " and " Imishologu," prove that you feel this dreadful guilt, and want to atone for it in that way. Now, what is to be done ? Every common crime against a chief must be atoned for by paying cattle; but some sins, such as murder and witchcraft, cannot be atoned for by the payment of cattle at all, the guilty man must die.

Now, sins of any kind against the Great God cannot be atoned for by cattle or anything in this world. All the gold and silver, and all the cattle in this world would not atone for the sins of one sinner. Now, as the whole world was guilty before God, and as there was no ransom for any of them, they were all going down into the infernal hole of Satan together, for they were so polluted and so guilty, they were not fit to live with God, and there was no other place for them. But though we were all such rebels against God, He loved us so much, and He was so sorry for us, He could not bear to see us all dragged by Satan down to hell, so He made a plan to give an atonement from heaven for the sins of all the sinners in the world, and send down a great Saviour to save all who would consent to obey God's laws, and receive the Saviour. There was " no man in heaven or on earth " who could find out how man could be redeemed from the death-sentence of these laws, or how our spirits could be washed from the pollution of sin, and made holy and fit to live with God, but God found out this great mystery, and made the whole plan Himself.

Now, my dear friends, we want to explain to you something about this great God. There is but one God, He hath told us that Himself, and He cannot lie, and we see the proofs of it in the plan of all His works, but in this one God there are three distinct personal spirits, exactly of the same nature, and the same power and love, which together constitute one God. They are called God the Father, the Son of God, and the Holy Ghost, "and these Three are One." This is a great mystery; you cannot understand it, and yet you know it is true. There is a mystery about everything you see that you can't understand, but when we have the proof that anything is true, we believe it, and don't trouble ourselves about the mystery at all. How do we know that in God there are three Persons? Because He hath told us so in His book, and in proof of it many holy men have got acquainted with God the Father, and with God the Son, and with God the Holy Ghost.

Well, the great plan that these Three in One agreed upon was, that God the Father should give His Son to come down into this wicked world, and be offered as a sacrifice for the sins of all the people, and the Son of God loved us so that He was glad to do that. But as He was all spirit, and had no body to offer as a sacrifice, it was agreed that He should lay aside all His glory, and all His great things in the glorious "Great Place" of His Father, and come down, and take a human body and a human spirit, be born a little child, and grow up to be a man, that He might be our Teacher, and die for the sins of the world.

This was the great Saviour God told Adam and Eve that He would send, who should be born of a woman, and bruise Satan's head; and God after that told many good men about Him, but He showed His great "purpose" more fully to Moses, for he was such a good man that he could understand it better. In the nation of Israel, of which Moses was a great chief, as we told you before, there arose many holy men who knew God, and God told them all about His "purpose" to save the world. He told them when His Son would come, and that He should be born of a virgin who had never known any man, and He should be born in a place called Bethlehem, and that though the second Spirit of God, called the Son of God, would be in Him, He would look just like any other man; that He would teach holy men all God's laws for mankind, which they had forgotten, and reveal to them the "unknown God;" that He would heal the sick, give sight to the blind, teach the poor people, and raise many dead men to life; that He would go about continually doing good. But God told them distinctly that because His Son was so good, and the world so bad, they would tell lies of Him, and beat Him, and scold Him, and that when He was ready to offer Himself up as a sacrifice for sins, He would just deliver Himself up to the wicked people and their rulers, who would nail Him to a tree, and put Him to death, and that God would accept His sacrifice for the sins of the whole world, and raise Him up from the dead the third day after, to be for ever our Great Priest and Saviour, that by Him all might have the power to come to God, and get forgiveness of all sins, and get their dirty spirits washed and made fit to dwell with God in eternal happiness. Well, all these words of God about His Son were written down in a book hundreds of years before the time set for Him to come, so that there should be no mistake in knowing Him when He should come. God's plan, too, was that through the promise of the Son of God to do all these things, all who would believe God's words about Him, and accept God's coming Son as their Saviour, should be saved, as certainly before as after His coming, and for fear that His words might not go deep enough into the minds of men, and that they might not trust in His only sacrifice for sins, to help their faith in His words, he told them to offer sacrifices of beasts to show their faith, not in the beast, but in the one great sacrifice of His Son. Many hundreds of years passed away, and many thousands of sinners believed God's words about His Son, and while they offered bullocks on God's altars, as pictures or patterns of the sacrifice God had promised, they accepted the Son of God as their Saviour, and they were saved, made holy, and went up to the holy place of God to be happy for ever. All who carefully read God's holy books about His Son knew when the time would come for His appearing among men, and they waited patiently, and at the time sure enough He came, and all the things that God had said, which had been written down by the holy men of God, were done. Everything about His birth, His life, His teachings, His mighty works, the persecutions He endured, His death and resurrection, everything came to pass just exactly as God said it would come to pass. The Son of God was called Jesus, which means Saviour, for He came to save the people from their sins. He was also called Christ, which means anointed, for God the Father set Him apart, and anointed Him to be the Saviour of the world.

Well, all these things that Jesus Christ did, and all that the people did to Him, which God had said would be done, were also written down in a book, so that all the world might read them, and learn about Him, believe God's words, and receive Jesus Christ as their Saviour.

He was " crucified, dead, and buried, but the third day

after He arose from the dead;" and then, in the same human body which had been put to death, He taught His learners and good men for forty days; and then from a mountain, called the Mount of Olives, they saw Him ascend up to heaven, out of their sight. I have seen all those places; where He was born, and lived, and taught, and died and rose again, and ascended to heaven. Now we have not time to-day to read to you all these words of God about Him. We have them all here in this book, but you know we would not tell you a lie about them. Here is the missionary, and plenty of these Kaffir people in the station, who have read them, and they will tell you the same things, and in proof of their truth, according to these words of God, we have received Jesus Christ as our Saviour, and He has saved us from our sins; and "we know God and Jesus Christ whom He hath sent," for He went back to His Father, not to leave us in our sins to perish, but to be our Great High Priest at the throne of the Great King of heaven, and He is as really the Saviour of sinners now as when He dwelt among men. It is from God's "Great Place," quite out of our sight, that he sends us rain, and supplies all the wants of our bodies, so from the same Great Place, Jesus Christ sends us salvation from sin and Satan, and makes us holy, so that we may keep God's commands. "But," says one, " Oh, He is a great way off; how shall I find Him?" Well now, we'll tell you another great secret. Before Jesus Christ left the world, He said to all His holy men, and they wrote it down, "If I go not away, the Comforter will not come unto you; but if I depart, I will send Him unto you." And again, " I will pray the Father, and He shall give you another Comforter." Jesus was then their Comforter, but was going away, but promised to send another to take His place, and abide with us; how long?—" that He may abide with you for ever." Who is this Comforter? " Even the Spirit of truth; whom the world cannot receive, because it seeth Him not, neither knoweth Him; but ye know Him; for He dwelleth with you, and shall be in you." "These things have I spoken unto you," said Jesus, "being yet present with you. But the Comforter, which is the Holy Ghost, whom the Father will send in my name, He shall teach you all things, and bring all things to your remembrance, whatsoever I have said unto you."

The Comforter he promised to send to live with us in this world for ever is the Holy Ghost, who is the third Great Spirit of the one Great God. He is an "Unknown God" to the poor slaves of Satan, because they don't see Him, but all the saved ones know Him, for He dwells with them, and teaches them, and comforts them every day; yet still they don't see Him, but they feel His power in their hearts. You can't see my spirit, yet it is my spirit that has been teaching you for an hour. You can't see Imishologu; yet you believe they live, and you have offered hundreds of sacrifices to them. You can't see the air you breathe, yet you could not live ten minutes without it. The air is the symbol God uses in His book to illustrate the presence and power of the Holy Ghost. The air is everywhere, so the Holy Ghost is in every part of this world. His first business is to shine into our dark spirits, and show us our pollution of spirit by sin, our deep guilt for breaking God's good laws, our exposure to the death-penalty of the law, our bondage to Satan, and to show us that we have no power to save ourselves. This light of the Holy Spirit shining into us stirs up all the bad in our hearts, wakes up the wicked spirits of Satan's fallen host, and then there is a great war in our hearts. The wickedness of our polluted spirits, called the "carnal mind," and Satan raises a great war against the Holy Ghost, to keep us from following the Holy Ghost, and accepting Jesus Christ as our Saviour.

But if we set our whole hearts to resist sin and Satan, and let God's Spirit lead us, He will make God's words about Jesus plain to our minds, and then if we consent to allow Him to take away all our sins, and cleanse our spirits through the blood of Christ's atonement, and receive Jesus Christ as our Saviour, God will at once give us the power to be His children. Do you hear these words? Are they not glad tidings to your ears? Yet you will not know God by hearing and believing that it is the truth that we are telling you, unless you submit to God's laws, and according to God's words receive Jesus Christ as your Saviour. Now remember, many of us have proved the truth of all this. We have both proved it (the two speakers) the missionary here has proved it, and many of his people here have proved it. We were poor sinners as dark as any of you. We remember well when the Holy Ghost shined into us and showed us our sins; we felt the burden of guilt heavy on our souls; we felt the mighty opposing power of Satan; we felt that there was no help in us; then we cried to God for help; We confessed our sins to Him, and submitted our wretched souls and bodies to His will, to do with us just as He pleased, but we believed His words about Jesus Christ, and received Him as our Saviour from sin, and the very moment we accepted God's Son as our Saviour, God pardoned all our sins. The Holy Ghost bore witness with our spirits that we were the children of God, and washed our spirits through the blood of Jesus, and filled them with His love. He did not bear witness to our eyes, or ears, but to our spirits; and we know that God's words are true for we have proved them, and we know that Jesus Christ is the Son of God and the Saviour of sinners, for He hath saved us; and we know that we are the children of God by His Spirit, which He hath given us, and by His purifying power in our hearts, and the love we feel for God and man.

E E

Now we accept the Great King as "the Lord our God," and gladly keep His commandments, for the fountain of our hearts has been purified, the bitter waters of covetousness have been cleared out, and the sweet waters of God's renewing love now flow out in willing obedience to all God's laws.

Now my dear friends, a great many of the things we have told you to-day *you* know to be true, from what you have felt and from what you now feel, and the rest *we* know to be true, for we have proved them, and we come to you as witnesses to the truth of God's words about Jesus. You know we would not tell you lies; even if the truth was not in us, we have nothing to gain by telling you lies. We are witnesses for Jesus that He came to save sinners, that He hath saved us, and that He is very desirous to save you to-day. Will you consent to let Him save you now? The Holy Spirit is now shining into the minds of many of you; you now begin to feel His mighty power, and the opposing power of sin and of Satan in your hearts.

You know the rising desire you feel in your heart to give up sin, and yield yourselves to God, is not from Satan, nor from your own bad hearts, and it is not from me, it is the awakening work of the Holy Ghost in your hearts. O, He wants to lead you to Jesus. He won't force you; but if you consent to be saved from all your sins, and walk after Him, He will lead you to Jesus. The Son of God don't wait for you to go up to heaven, to His Great Place, but whenever you are so sick of your sins as to give yourselves wholly to Him to save you, and receive Him by faith in God's words about Him, He comes down quick as thought, and delivers your soul from Satan, and washes it from its sins. Jesus loves you every one, and wants to save you now, and that is the reason He has sent His Spirit into your hearts to give you the desire you feel to come to Him

He is the only Friend you have, who loves you enough to die for you. He "hath tasted death for every man;" He hath poured out His heart's blood for you, each one, as the only sacrifice for sins. His love for poor sinners is the same to-day as the day He died for us, for He is not like a man to change; He is the Son of God, and hence the same in all the past time, the present, and for ever. He has a word for each one of you, "Come unto me, all ye that labour, and are heavy laden, and I will give you rest." You are heavy laden with sins, and sorrows, and guilt; you are weary with travelling in the dark way that leads to hell—you are the very persons whom Jesus invites, and He says, "Take my yoke upon you, and learn of me, for I am meek and lowly of heart, and ye shall find rest for your souls." Will you take His yoke, consent to be "in-spanned" and bear His yoke, and walk in obedience to all His laws; He won't lay too heavy a yoke upon you, for He says, to encourage you, "I am meek and lowly of heart," the most sympathizing, loving Friend in the world. If you take His yoke, submit to His will, and receive Him as your only Saviour, then ye "shall find rest for your souls." He will not deliver your bodies from the death penalty of the law. They will still suffer, and finally go down into the grave; but Jesus has promised to raise your bodies from the grave in the end, just as His human body was raised, and then our bodies will be so glorious and holy, as to be suitable for our pure spirits to live in at the "Great Place" of our King. Will you accept Jesus as your King, your Priest, and your Saviour, or not? Let every one think well, and decide for himself and herself to be the Lord's, and receive Jesus Christ, or not. Let no one try to come to Jesus, simply because another does. Let no one be ashamed to come to Jesus through fear of anybody. "God commands" each one of you to repent, and believe the Gospel,—to surrender to God, and on God's own offer, and invitation, and promises, to receive Jesus Christ. When He came to His people in olden time, many of them received Him not, and they perished in their sins; "but as many as received Him, to them gave he power to become the sons of God, even to as many as believed on His name." It is so now. Within the last two months we have seen about two thousand Kaffirs surrender to God, and receive Jesus Christ, and by the Holy Spirit every one of them received the power, renewing their hearts, and making them "the sons of God." If you fail to accept Christ, you will fail to receive this great salvation, and will die in your sins. Now God's great plan of salvation is before you, and you not only know that these things are true by what we have told you, but by the Spirit's light in your minds. Life and death are now before you; walk after the Spirit, receive Christ, and ye shall live; or, walk after your bad nature and Satan, and you will die in your sins.

Now all who have looked straight at God's words to-day, and who feel the Holy Spirit's light and power in their hearts, and who have decided to give up all their sins, and obey God; all who now consent to receive Jesus Christ, to be His, living or dying, to be true to Him, and have confidence in Him, and cleave to Him as your Saviour, as long as you live, let them stand up. Let none stand up but poor sinners, who now consent to be the Lord's, and receive Jesus Christ, but all such may stand up now.

About one hundred awakened persons stood up. A majority of them were persons on the mission, who had been long under Gospel teaching; but among them was a large number of raw heathen. Then we all kneeled down and prayed, and the power of the Holy Ghost seemed to shake the whole mass of believers and sinners in a remarkable manner, and many were saved at that service.

After the close of the day service the heathen returned to their kraals, not considering it safe, on account of their war troubles with the Pondos, to be away from their homes after dark. That night we preached in the chapel to the people living on the mission premises, amounting to about 400, including children. The next day, which was Sabbath, the 19th of August, we had the heathen out in still greater numbers than we had the day before, and after preaching to them in the same open court, from the third and fourth verses of the eighth chapter of Romans, we had a prayer-meeting, at which many were saved. At night we preached again in the chapel. On Monday we preached out-doors to the heathen again, from the Saviour's narrative of the prodigal son. After a suitable explanation of the subject, we used the prodigal's career to illustrate the spiritual condition of the apostate nations of Africa. I will merely state some of the leading points of the analogy, which we worked out in detail on that occasion.

1st. Every red Kaffir among you has been circumcised. Where did you get this ceremony of circumcision? About 4,000 years ago God made a covenant with Abraham, that great old chief we told you about the other day. The covenant bound him and all his seed to be true to God, and keep all His laws, and thus they would secure God's special blessings through all generations. And God said to Abraham, "This is my covenant which ye shall keep, between me and you, and thy seed after thee. Every man child among you shall be circumcised—and it shall be a token of the covenant betwixt me and you." The seed of Abraham from that time continued to circumcise their sons for about 2,000 years, till Jesus Christ came. Then God set the outward token of circumcision aside, and received all poor sinners of every nation alike into His church, who would repent of their sins, and accept Jesus Christ as their Saviour. Instead of circumcision He gave them all one outward sign for males and females alike—baptism by water, and the inward "washing of regeneration, and renewing of the Holy Ghost." You see that some of your ancient fathers knew God, and His covenant with men; but though you have kept to circumcision to this day, you have gone so far from home, that you have lost the knowledge of God and His covenant, and have therefore failed to learn His new Gospel covenant for all nations. Circumcision, till Christ came, was the ceremony of initiation into the Church of God, and the token of His Covenant; but you have made it the ceremony of initiation to the standing and privileges of manhood and citizenship, and the token for a system of corruption, most dishonouring to God and degrading to yourselves.

2nd. Where did you learn to offer sacrifices of bullocks as an atonement for sin? God appointed the offering of sacrifices thousands of years ago, as teaching types of the one great sacrifice of Jesus Christ.

When you kill a bullock as a sacrifice for a sick man, you split the beast in two, from the nose to the tail, right through the middle of the backbone. That is just the way Abraham did thousands of years ago. He "divided them in the midst, and laid each piece one against another."

When you prepare a bullock for sacrifice, you separate

all the fat, and offer that by itself. God said to Moses, thousands of years ago, the priest "shall take off from it all the fat of the bullock for the sin-offering, the fat that covereth the inwards, and all the fat that is upon the inwards, and the two kidneys, and the fat that is upon them; and the priest shall burn them upon the altar of the burnt-offering."

When you kill a bullock for a sick man, you catch the "blood in basins," and your priest sprinkles some of the blood upon the sick man, and on his bed, and the things in his hut. Then he digs a hole in the cattle kraal—(the most sacred place known to a heathen Kaffir, so much so, that women are precluded as from the inner court of the Jewish temple—and pours the remainder of the blood into the hole. God said to Moses, "The priest that is anointed shall take the bullock's blood, and bring it to the tabernacle, and shall dip his finger in the blood, and sprinkle of the blood seven times before the Lord. He shall put some of the blood upon the horns of the altar, and pour all the rest of the blood of the bullock at the bottom of the altar of the burnt-offering."

When you offer a sacrifice, you carry the bones of the bullock outside of the kraal, and burn them. God said to Moses, "The skin of the bullock, and all his flesh, with his head, and with his legs, and his inwards, and his dung, even the whole bullock, shall be carried forth without the camp into a clean place, where the ashes are poured out, and burn him on the wood with fire."

You see, my dear friends, from the many things you have, which are so much like the things that God commanded Abraham and Moses to do, that some of your old fathers knew God and his teachings to Moses; but one generation after another wandered away, like lost sheep, till you don't know the way to get back. You have kept one truth, that "without the shedding of blood there is no remission of sins;" but you have lost the knowledge of the only Sacrifice which can take away sins, the body of Jesus Christ. You have held on to the type or picture, but lost sight of the real substance.

That, my friends, is not the worst of it. You offer your sacrifices not to God, but to "Icanti,"—a great snake— and to Imishologu, who could not help you while they lived, and how can they help you now that they are gone?

When Abraham offered a sacrifice to God, he confessed his sins, and that for sins he deserved to be put to death, but his bullock was accepted, and slain instead of himself; but while he looked at his bleeding victim, he saw in it but a picture of the bleeding Jesus, whom God had promised to send into the world, as the only sacrifice which could take away sins.

When we come to God in praying, confessing our sins, and our exposure to the death-penalty of the law of God, we don't bring a bullock, for when the real sacrifice for the sins of the world came, then it was no longer necessary to use the picture or type of it, but to look directly to Christ. We have the plain words of God's Book to tell us the way, and we have the Holy Spirit of God to lead us to the living Jesus, and by His own precious blood He saves us from our sins.

The foregoing are some of the points brought out and illustrated on that occasion. Many prodigals came home to God that day and obtained a free pardon by accepting Christ. We preached again in the chapel that night, and God was with us.

On Tuesday we had a larger number of heathen than at any previous service, among whom was Makaula the Amabaca Chief. That day we preached from

"Choose ye this day whom ye will serve," and tried to influence them to a right decision by contrasting their system of heathenish superstition with the Gospel of Christ. The principal points were, First, Their dark traditions and God's plain Gospel teaching. Second: Their sacrifices to "Icanti" and to the ghosts of their old dead fathers, and the "body" God prepared and accepted as the only sacrifice which can atone for sins. Third: Their vain hope that Imishologu will be their mediator with Tixo (or God), and the certain fact that we have a Divine Advocate with the Father, and the only Mediator between God and man. Fourth: The broken reeds on which they lean, their priests, poor ignorant men like themselves, the charms which their priests bind about their necks, with the everlasting doubt which haunts them, and the utter failure of all these things to bring rest to their souls, and on our side the personal knowledge of God and Jesus Christ whom He hath sent, attained by all true believers, the security of dwelling "under the shadow of the Almighty," the sweet rest of soul which Jesus gives to all who come to Him, and the abiding presence of the Holy Comforter God hath sent to conduct us in peace to our home in heaven.

In showing them the folly of putting their trust in the charms or amulets they wear round their necks, instead of submitting themselves to Christ and putting their trust in the living God, I said, "Your country was invaded a few weeks ago by a large army of the Amapondo. They came to kill and destroy you and to take your cattle. Did not every one of those Pondo warriors go to a priest and get a protection which he thought would be proof against your assegais? Did not the priest hang a lot of roots, birds'-claws, tufts of hair, hoofs of beasts, and little horns, containing charmed stuff, round the neck of each one of them to make them courageous and strong, and to preserve them from death? Now, tell me, what good did all these things do them?"

I then drew out of my coat-pocket a double handful of charms, and holding them up to the astonished gaze of the sable audience (for if one of them should touch anything from the body of a man slain in battle they would be sure of being poisoned or bewitched by the touch) I said, "Look here! what a god in time of trouble? A poor Pondo got this lot of trash from a priest, and thought these would save him from death in the day of battle. What good did they do him? You slew him with all his charms on him, and this morning my boy here cut them off the neck of his carcase, and will you still reject the only true God, and put your trust in such filthy trash as this? The Pondos were invaders of your country to rob and to kill you, and God delivered the Pondos over to your assegais, because you were defending your homes, your cattle, your families, your own lives; and then, instead of giving God credit for His mercy to your nation, you had a great ceremony of thanks to Imishologu, and said that your priests and your charms made you strong and gave you the victory." The foregoing is a mere specimen illustration of many on that occasion adjusted to the capacity of their heathen minds. The Holy Spirit's application of truth and the effect upon the audience was quite indescribable. Many, with heads down, shed almost streams of tears, but I observed one old heathen woman who kept her wrinkled face up, in her hand she had a little instrument made of bone, in very general use among them. It is about six inches long, with a fork at one end, some with two, others with three, prongs about three inches long, which are used for picking their teeth, scratching their heads, and to stick into their hair as an ornament, the other end is cut into the shape of a salt-spoon, but not quite so large, which is used for dipping snuff, a favourite entertainment among the heathen as well as among the civilized people of Christian countries, but the old woman, having no handkerchief to wipe away her tears, used the little spoon for scraping them up, and tossing them away as they settled down in the furrows of her face.

That night, being our last, we had a fellowship-meeting. The chapel was packed somewhat after the style of packing herrings in a barrel. At the opening we told the old members that having so many new disciples present who had received Christ in their hearts, and were ready to make confession with their mouths, we specially desired the old ones to tell us a very short story.

Then an old man got up and said, that many years ago, as he was travelling from Shawbury to Tshumgwana, a lion jumped on him and broke his back and left him lying there, nearly dead. Several persons came along and looked at him, and passed by on the other side. Finally, a man took him to his hut, and after a long illness he got well, and God had been very kind to him, but he did not tell us whether or not he had been delivered from Satan, "who goeth about as a roaring lion, seeking whom he may devour." I then said, "Lion-stories are very interesting when we have time to listen to them, but we have no time now to hear anything but whether or not you have received Jesus Christ and got your sins forgiven?"

Then another old fellow got up and told a dream he had some years before in which a black man appeared to him. He thought it was the devil, and woke up in such a fright that he could not stay there any longer, and then he came to live at the mission-station, and had been trying ever since to serve God.

Then another arose, and said that many years ago he was baptized at Shawbury, by Mr. Garner, and drew out, what the sailors would call, "a long yarn," but with really nothing in it to the point. Then followed another, who, while living at Shawbury, was sick a long time, feared he should die, and was not prepared. In his distress he tried to pray, and one evening he looked toward the east, and saw Jesus sitting on a cloud, and heard a voice saying unto him, "Thou art a child of God." Said I, "Charles, this won't do. It gets worse and worse, not only unedifying, but misleading, for these young converts have not seen any sights, nor heard any supernatural sounds," and we had taught them not to expect such things, having a more sure word of prophecy through God's Word and the inward demonstration of the Holy Spirit, so I said, "Now we will all stand up and sing 'The Eden Above.'" After a grand concert of melody of thrilling effect to men, and probably to angels, I said, "Now we will give all the rest of the time of this meeting to the young converts." Then within the next fifty minutes one hundred and ten new witnesses came on with their simple, pointed, stirring facts. The whole time of the speaking was eighty minutes, but the old "fogies" at the beginning occupied about thirty.

The testimony of the new hands was clear, short, and to the point, with a great variety of expression and illustration, nothing commonplace or formal. Two or three illustrative specimens may suffice here: —A woman said, "When I came to these meetings I asked God for a great gift, and He showed me my sins! I then cried to Him to save me, and He gave me Jesus Christ, who saved me from all my sins, and filled my heart with His love."

A man said, "I was asleep. God opened my eyes to-day, and pardoned my sins for Christ's sake, and now I have light."

Another man said, "I have been trying to serve

God for seven years, but I had an old shield full of holes, it would not turn away the fiery darts of Satan, but last Sunday I saw that I was one of the very worst of sinners. I cried to God, and received Jesus Christ as my Saviour. Now I have peace, and God has given me a new shield."

That night, in spite of the perils of war, a large number of heathen came crowding round the chapel, unable to get in, so in pity to them we cut the fellowship-meeting short in the midst of a continuous press of witnesses for Jesus, and got all who were in the chapel to go out and let the outsiders come in. After an interval of about a quarter of an hour, we commenced a prayer-meeting for seekers, thirteen of whom entered into liberty. During the series of four days at Tshumgwana, Rev. Brother White examined and took the names of 167 persons, a good proportion of whom had come to the series as poor heathens, who gave to him satisfactory evidence of having been "justified by faith," a small number compared with that of some other places, but large in proportion to the population, and the limited time employed in the series.

CHAPTER XXIV.

EMFUNDISWENI.

OUR trip from Tshumgwana to Emfundisweni may be sufficiently illustrated by the following extract from Stuart's journal.

On Wednesday, the 22nd of August, 1866, at half past seven, A.M., we bade adieu to the battlefields of Tshumgwana. The Umzimvubu drift, a few miles distant, is very slippery, and hence considered very dangerous. We met a lot of Hottentots near the river, and Mr. Roberts got some of them to outspan and lead his horses over, and others to pull the cart. My father drew his boots and waded, but my surefooted "tripler" carried me over safely.

From the river we had to ascend a very steep hill, where we again had difficulty with the baulky horse, but finally mastered him. On a number of hills adjacent we saw lines of native hunters stationed. They stood about half-a-mile apart, with assegais in hand, and dogs by their side, to intercept the herds of deer as they fled towards the river from the driving hunters sent to the interior. We saw some bucks in their flight, but had not time to wait to see them surprised and taken. The distance from Tshumgwana to Emfundisweni is about sixty miles. The country is mountainous, and the way so rough that we only travelled about forty miles that day. Having the light of a full moon, we did not "out-span" for the night till about an hour after dark, then coming to a rill and a grove of mimosa-trees, we encamped in the 'veldt.' After a good tea by a cheerful log-fire, we had our evening prayers, and threw ourselves upon our beds of grass, and soon fell into the sweet embrace of Morpheus, and there, upon us all, 'tired nature's sweet restorer, balmy sleep,' shed repose until the morning bade us rise to the duties of another day. (Our camp was in sight of the copper lodes which are now attracting thousands of colonists into Kaffraria.) We had some difficulty in finding the horses, and feared some savage marauders had stolen them during the night, but finally found them, and resumed our journey mid wild mountain scenery and grassy valleys, with occasional herds of deer, and a few native kraals. We reached Emfundisweni about two P.M., and were most kindly received by a veteran old missionary and his heroine wife, Rev. Mr. and Mrs. Jenkins.

This is a new mission-station; the minister's house is a one-story cottage, substantially built of brick, nearly one hundred feet in length, with verandahs front and rear, and contains nine rooms. The second preacher's house occupies a pretty site across a hollow on a parallel ridge, occupied by the Rev. Daniel Eva, a zealous young missionary sent out recently from England. The out-buildings, beautiful garden, and orchard, are enclosed in a good palisade fence, all of which, with the ornamental avenue trees, the abundant supply of water conveyed from the base of a neighbouring mountain, and the pretty gothic chapel with a bell, display the energy and taste of the master-mind of the old missionary.

The present chapel, to seat about three hundred, is to be the school-house, when the large substantial church contemplated, shall have been built. Faku, the old Amapondo chief, who lives in a small, filthy hut, has contributed largely toward these fine mission improvements. This is the third mission-station established in Pondo-land, preceded by Buntingville and Palmerton.

The best illustration I can give of Christian adventures, patient toils, sufferings, and successes in Pondo-land, may be gathered from the following facts, which were told, and afterwards penned in a letter to me by the heroic old missionary himself. I give it verbatim, except to put in his name, instead of the pronoun representing it, and a very slight reconstruction of a few sentences :—

The Rev. Thomas Jenkins was appointed to labour in Amapondo-land, in the year 1838. He had been for some years in the Bechuana country, had seen much of what sin and the Prince of Darkness can do in debasing man, the noblest work of God, while labouring among Griquas, Bechuanas, Corannos, and Basutos ; but had really seen nothing compared with the low, dark, brutish heathenism of the Pondos. In a perfect state of nudity, their very appearance was most revolting. When a few of them first came round the missionary's wagon, Mrs. Jenkins almost fainted away. Wars and blood-shedding for generations had completely brutalized them. Wars were raging at that time, both among themselves and their neighbours, and the missionary and his wife had many a narrow escape with their lives. But a few weeks after their arrival in "Icume" (Buntingville), Mr. Jenkins went away one hundred and fifty miles distant to a district-meeting, and while there the report reached him that the "Ficani," the Zulu marauders, had devastated all the intermediate countries of the Tambookies lying between him and his family, from the Umtata to the Bashe rivers, and had burnt Morley Station, destroyed Icume, and that his catechist and family, and also Mrs. Jenkins were dead. The sun had set when these evil tidings reached him. In company with his native interpreter, he at once set out to know the worst. After riding fifty miles, he found sure enough that the "Ficani" had laid waste all the Tambookie country. The ashes of their villages were still smoking. During that night of terrors, as he was travelling along near the Bashe river, his life was in great jeopardy. A body of Tambookie warriors lay in ambush watching for the return of some of the invading hordes, and hearing the approach of Brother Jenkins and his interpreter, took it for granted that they were some of the straggling Zulus. They concealed themselves behind the bushes near the path, and suddenly rushed out upon the missionary with drawn assegais. Just in the act of their deadly aim they perceived that he was a white man, and a friend, and their assegais fell from their hands. About ten o'clock the next night they again rode into the jaws of death. They came suddenly upon a band of Pondo warriors, who, mistaking them for the enemy, rushed to their arms, and being close upon them, in another moment the missionary and his companion would have been killed, but for the instinctive sudden "face about" and flight of their horses, stimulated by the rush of the pursuing warriors. On and on they went for miles out of their course, and thus lost their bearings. The darkness and manifest dangers of the night were rendered more gloomy by torrents of rain. They came to a river flooded by the recent rains, till, to all human appearance, it was quite impassable."

There they were as desolate as old David on the hill Mizar on Mount Hermon, when he exclaimed, "Deep calleth unto deep at the noise of thy waterspouts; all Thy waves and Thy billows have gone over me." Behind the missionary and his faithful Kaffir was a band of infuriated warriors, in front of the raging river. "We plunged in," says Jenkins; "but how we got out, the Lord alone knoweth; but by His merciful Providence, we did get out on the opposite side. Then, after a long search, we found the footpath, thanked God, and took courage. We were nearly exhausted, but nearing our journey, the stimulus of hope and fear of the joyous or mournful scene in prospect, kept us up and on our weary way. At the dawn of the morning, we came in sight of our humble home in the wilderness, and to our inexpressible joy, embraced our dear ones in life and health. They had suffered great fear from the rumours of war around them, but had been preserved in safety."

Their daily hazards of life, however, from enemies at home, were almost as great as those occasioned by the invasion of foreign foes; as may be illustrated by the following incident which occurred but a few months after those terrible wars. Mr. Jenkins says:—

I was out some distance from the mission-station, where a number of my people were at work, when a party of marauding Pondos, who were returning from a nightly incursion upon some of their neighbours, passed by us. I spoke to them, and remonstrated against their thievish, murderous business. One of the party took offence, and said I had no right to interfere with their calling, and suddenly he got into such a rage, that he drew his assegai and made a drive at me, and would have thrust me through in an instant, but as he drew back to throw the fatal dart, a man behind seized his arm, and I was saved. One of our station men became so alarmed, that, without waiting to see the result, he ran home shouting, " The Umfundisi is killed! The Umfundisi is stabbed to death with an assegai!"

The men of the station, though few in number, seized their assegais, and rushed forth to avenge the death of their missionary; the women and children fled into the forests to hide themselves. Mrs. Jenkins in the general fright, took up her niece, a child of six years, and started off with the rest, but in a few moments recovered her equanimity, and exclaimed—"I will not fly! I am in the Lord's hands, if He delivers me over to the Pondos they shall kill me in my own house!" She at once returned to the house, but the native women ran on into the wild woods. During the first few years of missionary life among the Pondos, but few months passed without alarms, to the effect that the mission was to be burned and all the mission people killed. They could indeed say with the Psalmist, " the wicked plotteth against the just, and gnasheth upon him with his teeth. The wicked have drawn out the sword and have bent their bow, to cast down the poor and needy, and to slay such as be of upright conversation." Yet, " the steps of a good man are ordered by the Lord, and He delighteth in his way. Though he fall, he shall not be utterly cast down, for the Lord upholdeth him with His hand."

WITCHCRAFT.

In addition to the facts recorded in previous chapters, illustrating the horrors of witchcraft, or rather of the witch-doctors, I will give a few facts from the pen of Brother Jenkins, as follows:—

Under the pretext of witchcraft, it was common almost every week to see houses, and sometimes whole villages burnt; and the most horrible tortures inflicted upon their owners, often resulting in their death.

In no part of South Africa was this horrible thing carried on to the same extent as in Pondo-land. These things I have seen, when on my tours, preaching for weeks together from kraal to kraal. On one of those tours I came to a small valley, where five kraals had just been burnt to the ground, by order of Faku's brother, Umewenge. The witch-doctor, or priest, had sentenced the whole population of those kraals to death, by the most excruciating tortures that men and devils could invent. The exterminating decree was so terrible, that not even a dog should be allowed to escape; and thus every dog, man, woman, and child in that valley perished.

A case which occurred near Palmerton mission-station, not far from Brother Jenkins' house, may suffice to illustrate one of many methods employed by those diabolical doctors, and the slaves of their superstition, to render even the terrors of death a thousand-fold more terrible.

A poor woman was accused of bewitching somebody, and the doctor ordered that she should be tied to a post in front of her own hut, and by slow tortures roasted to death. A glance at the accompanying cut will give an idea of the tragic scene. It is too horrible to gaze upon! But if to look at a mere picture is so horrible, what must be the effect on the heart of the missionary living in the midst of such realities, what the horrible degradation of those who inflict such tortures, what the pains of the poor wretches who endure them? A sublime charity is the missionary enterprise, and what a work of mercy is the missionary's self-sacrificing life! "The dark places of the earth are full of the habitations of cruelty." After all the talk we are accustomed to hear about the virtues of the heathen, and the inherent goodness of human nature, the awful fact still stands out, that all is dense darkness where the Gospel is not preached; and although many who hear it do not accept Jesus Christ, still they are indebted to its elevating influence for all the blessings they enjoy above the common lot of the heathen. The day the poor woman was roasted to death, a young man came to Brother Jenkins so severely burnt, as scarcely to be recognized as a human being. It was a son of the woman who was being burned at the stake, as the best blood even of Christian England used to be treated in Smithfield. The young fellow yielded to his filial instincts, and tried to intercede for his dying mother. Her tormenters rushed at him, seized him, and threw him headlong into the flames, from which with great

WOMAN ROASTED BY ORDER OF WITCH-DOCTORS.

difficulty he managed to extricate himself, and fled to the missionary, under whose kind treatment he recovered, and is now living in Natal.

INFLUENCE OF THE GOSPEL ON WITCHCRAFT.

"It would occupy too much space," says Mr. Jenkins, "to tell of all the lives saved through the agency of the missionary. His very home is a sanctuary to which the suffering refugee may flee and be safe."

Just before my visit to Palmerton, a man who had escaped the death-sentence for a suspicion of being a wizard, by fleeing to the station, after remaining there in safety for some months, became emboldened, and though warned of danger, had crossed the station lines, and was at once arrested and tortured to death.

Every accident to a chief, or sickness of any kind, has always been attributed to witchcraft, and they believe that there can be no recovery till the wizard is "smelled out" and banished. Christianity is slowly sapping the foundations of this murderous old system, as may be illustrated by the following facts from Mr. Jenkins.

"Faku's mother, I think, was a true Christian. She died about twelve years ago, and left strict orders that there should be no 'smelling out' on her account, which orders were obeyed.

"Faku's great wife, we have cause to believe, died in the Lord, and she would allow no one to be put to death on her account. One of Faku's sons died a Christian. His good conduct so endeared him to the whole tribe, that his death was an occasion of mourning throughout the nation. The witch-doctors made it out that he *died through the Word of God*, and hence no one was put to death for him."

The son of this good young chief was converted to God during our series of services at Emfundisweni, and Brother Jenkins tells me by letter that he is growing in grace and usefulness.

The old chief Faku was very ill a few years ago, and the doctors would not allow any person to see him. As the case was of such vast moment, involving the life of the great chief, there must be a grand "smelling out," and a victim worthy of such an occasion. A chief, Faku's own brother, Cingo, was declared by the doctors to be the leading wizard who had bewitched the great chief, and he was accordingly sentenced to torture and death. Tidings of these proceedings reached the mission-station, and Brother Jenkins considered it unsafe to interfere, but Mrs. Jenkins, with tears and entreaties, persuaded him at the hazard of his life, to go and try to dissuade Faku from having his brother put to death. "I went," says Jenkins, "with fear and trémbling. It was a long time before the doctors would allow Faku to be told I had come. When he heard of my arrival, and expressed a wish to see me, the doctors would not allow me to see him in his royal hut in which he lay, so by his order he was carried into another hut, where I was allowed to see him. His condemned brother was present, and from his dejected appearance it was evident that he apprehended a speedy execution. After some preliminary remarks Faku said, 'Teacher, do you see how some of my own people hate me, in sending the wild cats to kill me?' His meaning was that they had bewitched him.

"I replied, 'Faku, to my certain knowledge there is not a man in the tribe who would do such a thing against his chief and father. They love you too well to think of doing such a thing.'

"'Do you think so?' he inquired, with evident surprise.

"'I am sure of it.' This led the way to a free range of conversation," says Jenkins, "by which I fairly won his confidence. I then said to him, 'Faku, Mrs. Jenkins, whom you know is your best friend, entreated me with cries and tears, and would give me no rest till I consented to come to you, and try to save your brother Cingo from death!' There sat the condemned Cingo, under the dark shadow of death, listening to all that was said on both sides. 'Faku, I plead for the life of your brother Cingo, because I know he is not guilty, and I know you are not the man to stain your hands with the innocent blood of your own brother!' Faku hesitated a few moments in deep thought, for it is a very serious business even for a great chief to ignore the judgment of the witch-doctors, then lifting up his eyes, he said emphatically, 'My Umfundisi, you have saved Cingo! He shall not be killed!' Oh, to have seen," exclaims Jenkins, "the effect of that announcement on Cingo! It was quite beyond any power of description, his eyes flashed with rapturous joy, and he hardly knew how to contain himself. He was saved that day from death, and is still alive, and very anxious to have religious services at his village as often as possible. One of his sons comes every fortnight, sixteen miles, to attend our Sabbath services, and is a promising young chief.

"Witchcraft is now altogether on the wane in Pondo-land, and I hope," says the good old veteran, "that it will soon be no more."

DEBASING EFFECTS OF HEATHENISM ON THE MIND.

The details of their legalized systematic customs of adultery and fornication are too polluting for the public eye, even in print. They had not only reached the lowest ebb in morals, but even the minds of the people seemed to be thoroughly darkened and debased, so that it was very difficult to get them to grasp any abstract truth. "Hence," says Jenkins, "a thousand questions from them such as these, 'If there is a God why can't we see Him?'

"'Why don't He show Himself that we may know Him?' 'Where does He live?' 'How many wives has He got?' 'If we have souls, what are they like?" 'How is it that we can't see them?' And, finally,

'If sinners are to be punished in another world, then, when we come to die, we will put our hands upon our mouths and stifle our souls, that they may perish with our bodies.'"

"I remember being at a hut one night," continued Jenkins, "and after closing a service by prayer, the hostess lighted a rush-candle, and diligently searched every nook and corner, and even the inside of her pots, and when asked 'What are you looking for?' she replied, 'I want to find God and see Him. The teacher has been telling us that He is here, but I can't see Him anywhere.'"

These are but specimen facts illustrating the state of those heathens thirty years ago. The great masses of the tribe are still heathens, but there has been a gradual improvement in their minds and morals. "Theft and robbery among each other in this tribe," says Jenkins, "seldom ever occurs, and though they keep up predatory wars with neighbouring tribes, neither the Government of Cape Colony nor of Natal has ever had a single case of complaint against Faku and his people. It was the only tribe that was not more or less led away by the mad infatuation, originating with an influential prophet in Krilie's tribe a few years ago, under which the people destroyed their cattle. The oracle announced that there would soon be a resurrection of their fathers, and of all their cattle, and all who believed it and would destroy their cattle should be sharers in this unending supply of new cattle, but the people who would not yield obedience and destroy their cattle, should not only forfeit the blessedness of this new creation, but should become *moths*. Express messengers were sent to Faku from this prophet, and the chiefs, who were in league with him, demanding that the Pondos should destroy all their cattle or become a nation of *moths*. Faku listened to their statements, and replied, 'In all great matters of this kind I have been accustomed to listen to my missionary. I will send for him and hear what he has to say, and be guided by his counsel.' The messengers tried to dissuade him from this, but seeing that he would not move in the matter without his missionary, they took their sudden departure out of his country."

POLYGAMY.

The practical workings of this ancient institution of iniquity are illustrated by the following facts from Mr. Jenkins:—"Polygamy is the most fruitful source of nearly every evil in this country. Unnumbered women as well as men used to be 'smelled out' and put to death in consequence of the jealousies and quarrels growing out of this system.

"I knew a case sometime ago of a man who had two wives. They were constantly quarrelling, and one day one of the women bit a piece out of the other's cheek, and in return, at another time, she bit the other woman's nose right off!

"To the people who have lived any length of time on the mission-station, polygamy becomes intolerable.

A man who lived for a time at our station and was married according to the Christian form, afterwards left, and went to live among the heathen. In course of time he took a second wife in spite of the earnest remonstrances of his first. Such quarrels ensued between the two women, that the man could have no peace. He then took a third wife, with the hope that as there would be two against one, he would surely get out of the scrape; but alas! he soon found that his case was more complicated and desperate than ever before. I met him sometime afterwards, and said he to me, 'my life is a dogging out of perfect misery! I wish I had no wife at all!'

"The result was, that his first wife left him and her children also, and went off 300 miles to Graham's Town. You may readily conceive, when the sons of these women grow up, the hatred to each other which will grow up with them, and give employment and emolument to the witch-doctors.

"To know the degradation, sin, and misery of heathenism a man must live among them. The half has never been told, and cannot be, and but for our faith in the Gospel of the Son of God and its adaptation to raise and transform every grade of human kind, we should utterly despair of its efficacy in this land, but we must obey the Gospel mandate, 'Go ye into all the world, and preach the Gospel to every creature,' and leave the result with Him who gave the command. The direct and indirect results of the Gospel among the Pondos may be summed up as follows:—We found them a blood-thirsty, warlike race. They are now comparatively a peace-loving people.

"They were so destitute of clothing that, in travelling among them for weeks, and sleeping in their kraals, I have not seen a particle of clothing, except occasionally a piece of a goat or sheep-skin a foot square, or a few rushes sown together; but now woollen or cotton blankets are to be found in every hut.

"Twenty-five years ago not a cow or even a goat could be purchased at any price in all Pondo-land. I knew a trader who came with a wagon-load of goods for trade, and after spending five or six months, he bought an inferior lot of calves to the value of £7 10s., which the missionary had previously secured for his own family use. Now thousands of cattle are bought and sent out of the country annually, and there are many successful traders established in the country.

"The wooden spade was formerly the only instrument used in tilling the ground; but now, within a very recent period, a single house in Natal sold 20,000 hoes and picks to the Pondos, besides many ploughs, and a few wagons. These facts are but an index to the general progress in every department of industry, and of household economy and comforts.

"As for direct spiritual results," continues the old missionary, "the light of eternity will reveal the extent of the Holy Spirit's saving work among the Pondos, yet we have seen many who testified in life and in death, that the Gospel to them was the power of God unto salvation; some of them were very triumphant in the hour of death, knowing that they were going to the better land. I have known and heard of not a few among them who heard the Gospel, embraced Christ, and died in the Lord. A young heathen man, a few years ago, attended our services regularly, in spite of the opposition of his friends, who accused him of wishing to become an Englishman, till he suddenly disappeared. I have every reason to believe that he was put to death, and preferred to die as a martyr than to give up Christ.

"An old heathen was brought to God years ago at Palmerton. When I left that station to remove to this, I advised him to remain, but he said, 'No, you brought me to God, and nothing but death shall separate us.' Soon after his arrival here he took ill and died. The evening before his death he said, 'The King has sent to call me! What am I that I should refuse to go?' In his last moments he said, 'I am going to the King above!' A moment after he was gone.

"A few years ago an old Pondo drank so deeply of the wormwood and the gall, that he had often to be carried home from the chapel. He found peace, and was made very happy in the love of God. He had a brother who tried by every means to get him back to heathenism. When his arguments failed, he resolved to murder him, and knowing where he went daily to pray alone in the bush, he took his assegai and followed him with the intention of stabbing him to death. The murderer came stealthily up to the sacred precincts of the good man's bower of prayer, where the prostrate Kaffir was doubtless defended by a body-guard of angels from heaven. He quite succeeded in his purpose of coming up close enough to drive his assegai through his brother's back without being discovered by him, but there he stood and looked at a man in audience with God, and heard him tell his great "Inkosi" all his griefs, and plead for his wicked brother. The assegai dropped from his hand, for the Holy Spirit's two-edged sword was piercing him, and he fell to the earth and cried for mercy. He soon after found peace with God, and became an Israelite indeed. Some time after the conversion of this persecutor, he, with others was called upon by the Governor of Cape Colony during the war of 1852, to go and fight the belligerent Kaffirs, Faku and his people being allies of the Colony.

When this converted heathen received the order to report himself for service in the colonial allied troops, he went to Mr. Jenkins and said, "*Umfundisi*, do you see this arm ? stretching out his right hand. With this arm I have killed many a man in war; but when God gave me a new heart, I vowed to Him that I never would kill another, not even to save my own life, and I cannot go!" To relieve his case,

Mr. Jenkins gave him letters to carry to Natal, and thus going on postal duty for the missionary, he was not pressed into military service. "He lived from the day of his conversion," says his missionary, "a faithful servant of God, and died in the triumphs of faith." The foregoing are but specimen examples of a great many cases, illustrating the saving work of God in those dark regions.

Our little party arrived at Emfundisweni Thursday afternoon, the 23rd of August, and preached that night, also on Friday mid-day and evening. At the three services Brother Jenkins reported over sixty souls saved. On Saturday, my friend, Mr. Alfred White, who first suggested my trip through Kaffraria, a brother of Mrs. Jenkins, drove me thirty miles westward to PALMERTON. Its native name is *Izala*. We left Charles Pamla to push on the work with Brother Jenkins; Brother Roberts and Stuart accompanied us on horseback, and went, on the following week, forty miles further, to the Umzimvubu mouth, and ascended the "eastern gate," an almost perpendicular height of 1,200 feet. My limited space precludes the details of their romantic adventures down this Hippopotami River, and of my labours at Palmerton. I may simply remark, we reached Palmerton in the rain which continued for four days, so that we did not get the heathen beyond the station lines to hear us. My interpreter there was the teacher of the native school, a fine young fellow from Verulam, Natal; but his knowledge of

G G

English was too limited for very effective preaching, and hence, though most kindly entertained by the missionary, Rev. John Allsop, and his good wife, it was a time of great trial to me. It is a beautiful station, but in a low spiritual state, and greatly needing help, and not to be able to lead them on to certain victory, because I could not talk to them, was too bad; but there was no help for it, and I patiently submitted. About thirty persons, however, were added to the church at Palmerton, during our crippled series.

We returned to Emfundisweni on Friday the 31st, and were greatly cheered by the accounts of the hard fighting and glorious victories, achieved under the leadership of Brother Jenkins and Charles. The heavy rains we encountered thirty miles nearer the sea had not extended to them in sufficient quantity to interfere with their services. I then saw clearly that God had hid me away at Palmerton that He might show to the old missionary and the Pondo nation, in the person of Charles Pamla, what kind of agents He designs to employ in the evangelization of the tribes of Africa, a thing that none of them believed before, or could doubt afterwards. I was glad to step aside, and yield the palm to my sable brother.

I had taken great pleasure in teaching Charles leading principles in psychology, logic, and the mysteries of salvation simplified, so as to make him "a workman that needeth not to be ashamed."

He has a philosophic cast of mind, can grasp the most abstruse principles readily, forgets nothing worth remembering, and after interpreting my sermons twice per day for nearly two months, it became a work of supererogation for me to preach through him, for he could do it as well, or better, without me. I had prayed that God would allow me to remain, at least a few years, to lead a victorious host of native evangelists into the interior of Africa; but I now saw that God would answer my prayer indirectly, by giving my mantle to my Elisha, and take me away, if not to heaven, to some other part of His vast dominions, where He may have greater use for me.

Brother Jenkins and Charles had carried on the services in the chapel, over the Sabbath and Monday night.

On Tuesday, they removed their "base" to a chief's kraal, some fifteen miles distant, and opened a direct fire upon the heathen, and stirring times they had indeed. Each service was commenced with direct familiar conversation with the heathen, by which their superstitions were brought to light, and defended by their own champions, and refuted by my Zulu, backed by the heroic old missionary, to whom Charles often appealed to clinch the nails he had driven in sure places. They thus not only swept away the rubbish, but cleared a basis of admitted truth in the minds of all who wished to come to the light, on which to build a Gospel structure of saving doctrines. The scoffers became very bitter in their opposition, and daily tried to divert the attention of the people from the preaching, by shouts and taunts, and by setting the grass on fire, and raising an alarm, obliging the people on two occasions to disperse in haste to save their huts from the flames. One of the worst opposers, and the man charged with firing the grass each day, was an ingrate by the name of Banbana, whom Mrs. Jenkins had a few years before saved from torture and death. He was under sentence for witchcraft, and with a *reim* round his neck was kept in a hut awaiting his execution. He asked to be allowed to go outside of the hut in the dark, to which his keepers consented, but they would hold on by the end of the *reim* (a raw hide rope) so that he should not escape. The wizard thus getting out managed to slip the *reim* from his neck, and tied it to a bush. The jailor inside feeling the steady pulling at the rope, had no doubt that his convict was fast at the other end, but at length became suspicious, and going out found a bush tied. Banbana fled to the river, and, through some friend, Mrs. Jenkins found him next morning hid at the water's edge among the reeds and bushes, and gave him a sanctuary at the mission-house, and finally succeeded in restoring him to the good-will of his people. Now she was almost ready to think that she had made a mistake in her merciful interference with the due course of Kaffir law, to save such a wretch.

But, in spite of the devil and his heathen host, a grand victory for God was achieved. Among the saved ones were some such as " Dionysius, Damaris, and others with them."

The whole number of the converts at that time, including those who were saved before I left for Palmerton, amounted to above 163 persons, among whom were a doctor and five young chiefs.

On our return from Palmerton, we arranged that while Roberts, Stuart, and myself, would go on and spend the Sabbath with Captain Kok's Griquas, at their request, and on Monday proceed on our way toward Natal, Charles should spend the Sabbath with Brother Jenkins, and help on the glorious work among the Pondos, and on Monday night meet us at "Ulbrichts."

That arrangement gave us over forty miles of travel on Saturday, out of our course, for Natal; and about thirty-five miles on our course for Monday, and gave Charles a journey on Monday of about fifty miles, to meet us at "Ulbrichts," where we might together enjoy the hospitality of a generous Christian Griqua family. So on Saturday, September 1st, we bade adieu to Emfundisweni, and set out for Kok's camp. That was a day to be remembered, for by the time we got off the main beaten Natal track into the dreary hills and mountains of "Nomansland," a cold drizzling rain set in, with a dense fog, which limited our field of vision to a radius of about fifty yards. Several times through the day we lost the trail, and much time was consumed in finding the "spoor."

About four P.M., we heard the barking of dogs, the squealing of pigs, the bleating of sheep, and the lowing of cattle, and hoped we were nearing the "Camp." Coming to a pioneer's hut and stock-yard, Mr. Roberts fought his way up through a pack of fierce dogs to the door, to inquire where we were. He found nothing there but dogs and a few children whose parents were out; Stuart and his father, and our weary horses, stood shivering in the storm till Roberts came and told us that the Dutch-speaking children said that it was fifteen miles to Kok's camp, and that we had a high mountain to cross.

On and on we struggled over the mountain, and down to a little river. It was now getting dark, and we knew not which way to go. We hoped we were near the Griqua camp, but we could see no lights, and hear nothing but the hollow moaning of the wind in the mountains, and the pattering rain upon us. When we got into places of great danger, Brother Roberts, finding that I was a good driver, and not wishing to be responsible for my life, found it convenient to get out and walk. So when we crossed the river, he gave me the reins, and went circling round to try to find the path. I drove up a hollow, and away on to high ground, hoping to see Kok's city set on a hill, called the "Bergliftig," but not a beacon glimmer shone out to cheer us. It was a moonless night, and with the clouds above us, the fog all round us, that was a darkness which we all felt. I waked the echoes of the mountains by shouts which I hoped might arouse the natives, but got no response.

I said, "Roberts, we have got into *Nomansland*, sure. I have not seen a tree for many miles back, but I saw a few bushes on the cliffs near the river. If we can back there over these dangerous gullies, perhaps we can get wood enough to make a fire, otherwise the severity of the cold and our wet clothes will finish the business for us!" Back we went to the river and "out-spanned." I felt my way among the cliffs to a bush about four inches through, which I cut down. It was green and wet, but by cutting kindling wood off the seat of our carriage, we at last succeeded in getting a fire. Thankful for a good cup of coffee and a supper savoury enough for princes, we endeavoured to devise some plan for the preservation of life through the night. We spent hours trying to dry our clothes, but while we were drying one side the other was getting wet with the fast falling rain. Stuart and I at last took a seat in the cart, which had a "bonnet," which gave us some protection from the rain, and wrapping up as well as we could in our wet rugs, we dozed, and dreamed, and shivered till morning. Roberts, meantime, dug a hole in the ground to get a dry place, and there, half buried, wrapped up in his tiger-skin rug, he "waited for the morning." The Lord graciously preserved us even from taking a cold, and in the morning, while Stuart was hunting the horses, and while Roberts was exploring the country to find somebody to tell us which way to go, I kindled a fire and prepared a good breakfast. Roberts found an English citizen of Captain Kok's kingdom, living not a mile distant from our camp, from whom we learned that we were quite out of our way, and that it was twelve miles distant to Kok's camp. He sent a young Hottentot to guide us. Mid rain, sleet, and snow we reached the town, where I had hoped to spend a quiet and profitable Sabbath, about noon. Captain Kok, who passed us in Umhlonhlo's country on his way to Cape Town, had not returned. His town has a population of about 1,000, built up of huts, with some pretty fair log and brick houses, and a fort with mud walls, about eight feet high, with piles of cannon-balls and a few big guns, with which to frighten the Kaffirs. In the midst of the fort is a good pioneer chapel, which will seat about 400 persons. A plain house was given us in which to sojourn. We met a young English trader, the son of Rev. Mr. Scott, of Natal, who, as a Christian, is trying to do good to the rising community. He and another young English trader furnished us grain for our horses, and other needful attentions; a kind Griqua family cooked for us, and we got on well considering the state of the camp and the weather. At three P.M. we had the chapel crowded, and I preached the Gospel to them through a Dutch interpreter, a pious intelligent man, the school-master for the town, and yet totally blind.

At night I preached in English to about thirty persons in a private house. We had reason to hope that good was done, and yet no decisive results were manifest. On Monday the sun shone out, and though the roads were thought to be so slippery that we should not be able to cross the "Zuurberg"—*the sour mountain*—we could not afford to lose time, and so pushed on our journey. We passed a number of new, fertile, well-watered farms of the Griquas, and after crossing the Zuurberg came through a Griqua village, where they also have a chapel, and regular worship among themselves. This village is near the lines of "Alfredia," the newly annexed territory of Natal. Just across the line a mean white man has opened a shop for enticing the poor Griquas to destruction by the sale of brandy. Our route of travel left Alfredia to our right, and continued in Captain Kok's country some forty miles further to the "Umzimvubu" river, which is the old west boundary of Natal.

We reached Ulbrichts before night, took tea, and drove on three miles further to Mr. "Bloms," where we spent the night. We waited on Tuesday for Charles till eleven A.M., and went on without him. In the afternoon of that day we reached Mr. Hulley's place, and preached in his large Kaffir-hut chapel, which will seat 150. Brother Hulley supports himself and his large family on a new farm in Kok's territory, on the west bank of the Umzimvubu, but is nevertheless a successful preacher among the Kaffirs, and has formed a society, and preaches to the heathen regularly in his own round native chapel. I was very sorry we could not command time to stay with him long enough for a grand advance among his people. We were very kindly entertained for the night, and next morning forded the river, which can be crossed only in a ferry-boat, except in winter; and spent an hour with Mr. Hancock and family, who are Graham's Town Wesleyans, and very enterprising, useful people. That day we travelled over forty miles through a picturesque country of hill, dale, and mountain, but few settlers, and much wild game. We saw more deer in greater variety that day, than any other day of the whole journey, though we saw many beautiful herds of "rhei bucks" in Pondo-land. We hoped to cross the Umkomas River before dark; but, though we sighted it from the mountain an hour before sunset, it was quite dark before we reached the ford, which we were told was deep, rough, and dangerous, yet our only stopping-place was a public-house on the other side. Near the river we met a native man, whom we found was from Indaleni, a mission-station about twenty miles beyond. He had been out among the Kaffirs with two wagons, selling Indian corn, and buying cattle in exchange. He was just the man of all others we most needed, to tell us about

AMAZULU.

the ford, to supply us with corn, and to help us over a high mountain, next day, tying our cart to one of his wagons, and driving our horses along with his stock cattle. As it was so dark and dangerous, Brother Roberts allowed me to drive across the river alone. He thought he could wade it, but failing in that, we sent a Kaffir with a horse to fetch him. We all got safely to the public-house. The proprietor was absent, but had left his Kaffir servant to attend to the wants of the travelling public. His beds were passable, but he had nothing to eat, except a few small potatoes and some bacon, but as we still had a supply of coffee, sugar, dried peaches, and bread, we fared well; and our "man of providence" brought us a bag of corn for our horses.

As we were getting ready to go to bed, our Kaffir landlord came running in to tell us "your horses have fallen into the ditch." Stuart describes the situation as follows:—

I knee-haltered my pony, so that when he was done with his corn he might go and graze, but three of the cart-horses were tied together. Near by was a trench, five feet deep, enclosing a paddock. The three horses, closely tied to each other, going too near to the trench, one tumbled in and rolled over, and drew the second on to him. The back of the first horse was wedged into the bottom of the trench, with his feet sticking up; the second lay on his side directly on the first; the third was standing with his fore legs set forward, to avoid being dragged in, and pulling back with all his might, was nearly strangled by the tightening of the *reim* round his neck. We soon released two of them, but the bottom one was wedged in so tightly, and was so exhausted with his struggles, that he seemed to have resigned himself to die.

We, however, went to work with pick and shovel and dug down the sides of the trench, till we got room enough to allow him to get his feet to the ground, then my father and the Kaffir seized him by the tail, while Mr. Roberts and I took hold of the *reim*, which was round his neck, and we pulled away. For a time the case looked very doubtful, and I felt some concern for the safety of his "fly-brush," but a final pull altogether brought him to his feet, and we were glad to find that none of them had received any permanent injury.

The next day we travelled to Indaleni, and were kindly entertained by the missionary, Rev. W. H. Milward, and his good lady. I arranged with him to have Charles spend the Sabbath with him, if he should come on all right. We had not heard from him since we left him at Emfundisweni. On the next day, Friday the 7th of September, we journeyed on twenty-five miles to Pietermaritzburg, the capital of Natal. From the time we left Queen's Town, I had travelled 613 miles, while Roberts and Stuart had travelled 700 miles. Stuart's Kaffir "tripler" carried him through without "giving in."

When Charles reported in Maritzburg the following Monday, we found that he was only about half a day behind us all the way from Ulbrichts to Indaleni. He left Emfundisweni on Monday according to agreement, but the roads were bad and the journey was too long. Finding that he could not reach Ulbrichts that day, he put up at a heathen kraal, near a chief's place. He got all the people together and preached to them that night, and again the next morning, and seventeen of them professed to renounce heathenism, and accept Jesus Christ. He wrote back to Brother Jenkins, giving him their names and whereabouts. He also preached to the natives at Mr. Hancock's place, but had not time to follow up the effort.

He preached Friday night, Saturday, and Sabbath, at Indaleni. An extract from a letter to me from Rev. W. H. Milwood will tell the story of that adventure :—

"Under Charles Pamla's preaching here, Friday, Saturday, and yesterday, many have been aroused to a sense of their danger through sin, and led to seek forgiveness and holiness through the blood of Jesus. About seventy, young and old, profess to have gained the pearl of great price, and a few others are yet earnestly seeking.

"This is a matter of great joy to me, and will be to you, I am sure."

From this stand-point we will look back and see how the work of God goes on at Emfundisweni. Many more were saved during the last Sabbath Charles was there, and in a letter from Brother Jenkins, dated September 18th, a few weeks later, he says :—

I am thankful to tell you that everything here is going on as steadily as could be expected. We have no great excitement; but we perceive a deep seriousness and devotion on every countenance, and as yet no falling off. For the present I meet all the new converts, both old and young, myself, to ground them well in Christian doctrine and experience. I look upon the young with special interest. We are endeavouring to take care of the young chiefs who were brought to God.

You will remember the young chief Umhlangazi. He, with a few others, went last week to see Chief Faku, his grandfather, and said, " We have come to lay before you a matter of very great importance. My mother, my two sisters, myself, and these, my friends, and many others of our kraals, have become Christians, and have fully made up our minds to follow the word of God, and cannot, therefore, any longer follow the customs of heathenism, and we thought it our duty, to our chief and father, to let you know the great change which we have experienced, and our purpose to cleave to Jesus Christ who has saved us from our sins."

Faku listened to all that was said, and remained silent for some time. He then expressed great surprise! After another pause he said, " My children, you have done right! Go and sit down in peace! We want to remove to that part and be converted also as you have been!" For this I am humbly thankful to God. The young converts, of course, have much to bear from the jeers and taunts of the heathen, but they stand firmly.

I hope the old chief may be awakened to the necessity of a personal preparation for heaven. A man one day asked Faku if he had any hope of getting to heaven, and the old chief inquired,—

" Is Jenkins going to heaven?"

"Undoubtedly, he is," replied the other.

"I'll go wherever Jenkins goes," said the old eathen, emphatically. "When Jenkins gets to heaven he won't stay there without me! I'm sure he'll come out and take me in with him!"

I said to Brother Jenkins, when this story was related at his own table, "I think when the Master calls you from labour to reward you, you'll treat poor old Faku somewhat as Rev. Valentine Cook did his wife. Cook was a celebrated pioneer preacher in the Western States of America. In 1832, when a shower of meteors came down all over the country, flying through the heavens almost as thickly as snow-flakes in a storm, there was great alarm throughout he land. 'The midnight cry' was raised, and borne along through many a hamlet and city. 'The world is at an end! the stars are falling! the Judge will soon appear!' Cook was suddenly aroused out of sleep by the cry and general wailing in the streets, and seeing through his window the flashing meteors, he took it for granted that it was all true, and as he made a dash for the door, his wife cried after him,—

"'Oh, Mr. Cook, wait for me! Do wait for me!'

"'No, my dear wife,' answered Cook, as he suddenly passed out of sight, 'if my blessed Jesus is coming, I can't wait for anybody!'"

Mr. Jenkins made an earnest request by letter to have us send Charles home through Pondo-land, that he might lead another campaign against the heathen, and, in the hope that he would come, sent an order on Mr. Cameron, the chairman, for the funds to bear his expenses back, and to strengthen his appeal, he adds, "Strange to say, some of the heathen chiefs have expressed a *strong desire* for Charles to visit them. This I take as from the Lord."

CHAPTER XXV.

NATAL.

IT was my purpose, out of a copious supply of materials, to fill four chapters with facts and incidents illustrative of this very interesting young colony, and the progress of the Gospel among its aboriginal and colonial populations, but my printer informs me that I have already greatly exceeded the limits of my book, so I must confine myself to a brief exhibit of leading facts and life scenes.

The colony of Natal lies principally between the parallels of 29° and 30° south, and longitude 29° to 31° west.

The climate is genial and healthy, the mean temperature for eight years past was 64° Fahrenheit, the highest, 97°, the lowest, 33°. The jungle and forest scenery, especially seaward, have quite a tropical appearance. The soil and climate are pretty well adapted to cereal grains and grass, but specially to the production of arrowroot, sugar-cane, and coffee, it is said also that cotton does well. There are many fine coffee plantations, and of the

108 mills in the Colony, worked principally by steam power, nearly 100 of them are sugar-mills. There are 4,667 farmers of different kinds in the Colony, 194 manufactories, and 57 commercial establishments.

The population, according to the census of 1865, was as follows :—

White males	79,990
White females . . .	78,590
Total . .	158,580
Native males	67,667
Native females . . .	70,069
Total . .	137,736

Indian coolies, 7000; more than four-fifths of whom are males, who are employed principally in the sugar plantations. The aggregate of those several classes swells the total population to over 300,000 souls. There are about 7000 native Zulu Kaffirs employed in service by the Colonists. They are much more robust, and said to be much more trustworthy than the Coolies, but being more free and independent than the poor Indians, they walk away if not suited, and hence are not so available.

The total revenue of the Government for 1865 was £176,295 1s. 9d.

Total expenditure, £179,883 7s., besides a public

YOUNG GENTLEMEN OF THE AMAZULU.

debt for unfinished harbour improvements at D'Urban, amounting to £110,000.

The Government appropriation for ecclesiastical purposes during the year 1865, principally for the support of Anglican and Dutch Reformed Ministers, was £1,150. For police and jails, £3,212, for the Judicial Department, £12,505.

Besides the various religious establishments common in English colonies, there are in Natal thirteen mission-stations among the Zulus, under the *American Board of Foreign Missions*. The Government has made to each a liberal grant of land, and fully appreciating the faithful labours of the American missionaries, and the influence of their practical American ideas on education, and all manner of handicraft for the natives, grants a subsidy for their schools, and £24 a-year towards the support of a periodical they publish for the Zulus, called the *Ikwezi*, so the Kaffirs have one newspaper, while the whites have four.

The Government appropriation in 1865, for all the industrial schools, three of the largest of which are under the Wesleyans, was £1000; For common schools, £909. In these several schools 1744 Kaffirs received instruction during the year. In the Industrial Schools 120 boys were at work, learning a variety of useful trades, and 372 Kaffir women were taught to sew. I am indebted to the Colonial "Blue Book" for my statistics.

Pietermaritzburg, the capital, with a population of

about 8000, is well located for drainage, health, and beauty, on a high ridge rising up from the banks of a small river, a branch of the great "Umgani." In every direction grassy hills stand out to view, with high mountains to the north and west.

The whole breadth of country, about 200 miles in width, from the "Drakensberg" range to the ocean, embracing the eastern province of Cape Colony, Kaffraria, and Natal, a distance of more than 1000 miles, is all of the same general appearance, just like the waves of the ocean, a vast sea of irregular grassy hills and mountains, with island groves of timber, the Kaffrarian waves being much more abrupt and high than those within British lines.

Up the river, seven miles from the capital, is the native village and Wesleyan mission-station called *Edendale*. It was founded by Rev. Mr. Allison, then a Wesleyan missionary, now a devoted and useful minister to the natives in Pietermaritzburg, not directly with us, but in good repute with all classes, and in good fellowship with his Wesleyan brethren. In founding Edendale, he bought a large tract of land, of superior quality, for the natives, and secured to them freehold titles. Their beautiful dale—near the river, with a grand waterfall in sight above, a good mill for grinding the millions of bushels of maize they grow on their little farms, their neat village of 1000 population, with nearly all the space along the sides of the streets and front and rear of their little houses, covered with fruit-trees, principally the peach; and two new chapels of brick and stone, in fine style, to seat about 500 each, all built by native mechanics—is not without reason called "Edendale." They have a fine young missionary, Rev. C. Roberts.

Distant from the capital fifty-three miles, is Port Natal, and the commercial town of D'Urban, with a population of nearly 10,000. It is located near the bay, on a vast plain of sand, which once belonged to the domain of the ocean, but the high "Berean hills," to which the town extends, covered with forests and tropical jungle, furnish fine background to the scene, and splendid sites for suburban residences.

Easterly from D'Urban, across the Umgani, twenty miles distant, in a country abounding with coffee plantations, is the rural village of Verulam. The daily labours of our brief sojourn of five weeks, were devoted principally to Indaleni, Pietermaritzburg, Edendale, D'Urban, and Verulam.

The services were held in the Wesleyan chapels, which are neat, substantial, and spacious, but we had the hearty co-operation of nearly all classes of Christian ministers and people. The effects of the searing blight of semi-infidelity, so famous in Natal, were so felt by the infant churches of the Colony, that all lovers of the Bible and its Author were ready to join hands with any agency whom God might send to help them in their need. In Maritzburg, besides Brothers Mason, Hays, and Cameron, Wesleyan ministers, we had Rev. Mr. Allison, before mentioned, Revds. W. Campbell and Smith, Scotch

Presbyterians, Rev. P. Huet, Dutch Reformed, and two zealous French missionaries, unjustly exiled by the Dutch Boers from the Free State, where they with their fellow-missionaries, thirteen in number, had laboured successfully for many years among the "Basutus." In D'Urban, besides the Wesleyan, Rev. J. Cameron, the veteran chairman of the district, his colleague, C. Harman, J. Langley, missionaries to the natives, Rev. Ralph Stott, a wise and indefatigable old Indian missionary, labouring among the Natal coolies, we had Rev. Mr. Buchanan, and Rev. Mr. Patton, his colleague, Presbyterian, Rev. Mr. Mann, Independent, and a number of the American missionaries, among whom we had special helpers in the persons of Revs. D. Rood, M.A., H. B. Wilder, M.A., W. Mellon, and that grand old pioneer missionary, D. Lindley, D.D. Rev. Mr. Mann brought his people in force, and nearly half the new converts belonged to his congregation, whom he organized into classes, after the model of Methodism, and, with such a body of new recruits, is going on with increasing success.

As I was straitened for time, and as the Natalians seemed to have but little appreciation of native stuff for the ministry, nay, strong prejudice against even the hope of raising up native ministers, and as my Zulu had become a workman that needed not to be ashamed, I thought it best to appoint him the general of the black legion, while I should bring up the smaller wing of the whites, and thus storm the citadel of infidelity and sin from two sides at the same time. So I commended my sable brother to the missionaries, and bespoke for him "an open field and a fair fight."

Bishop Colenso had just been booming away at an impregnable fortress of truth, the supreme Divinity of Jesus Christ, and issued his orders forbidding any to ask directly any favours from Christ, and ignored the very songs of Zion which contained prayers to the Son of God. The Colonial papers had given the Bishop all the "aid and comfort" they could, for his sensationalism is very edifying to the press, financially; but at the time of our arrival that novelty had lost its power of charming, and some new strategic dash was needed to revive the flagging spirits of the Bishop's troops; so on the first Sabbath night we spent in Maritzburg, the Bishop preached on "The Idolatry of the Bible," by which it appeared from his discourse, as reported to us by some who heard it, he meant an idolatrous reverence for the Bible. One of his illustrations was in substance as follows:—A young man, a printer employed in setting the type of one of his (Colenso's) first books on the Pentateuch, became so affected by the doubts thus excited in his mind about the truth of the Bible, that he went mad and committed suicide. The bereaved father of the poor printer wrote to Colenso, giving the facts about the dreadful end of his son, and charged the Bishop with his death, to which the Bishop replied that the father himself was the cause of the tragedy, by teaching his son such an idolatrous love for the Bible that he could not bear to see the truth of its stories called in question, and hence his madness and self-destruction.

The two Sabbaths we were in the capital, Dr. Colenso and his "thorn in the flesh," Dean Green, were booming away, just across the street in a diagonal line from our chapel.

While in Maritzburg, I delivered a lecture on "Reminiscences of Palestine," and as I had occasion to join issue with one of Colenso's arguments, in which he tries to prove the physical impossibility of executing the command of Moses, as recorded in the twenty-seventh and twenty-eighth chapters of Deuteronomy, to proclaim the curses and blessings of the law from the two opposite mountains, Gerizim and Ebal, to the assembled hosts of Israel between, having myself personally, by measurement and vocal power, demonstrated the entire feasibility of the whole thing in the very place where Joshua, in the eighth chapter of his book, informs us that all that Moses commanded was done, I requested my committee to present the Bishop with my compliments, and send him a ticket to the lecture; but he did not put in an appearance. I afterwards learned that the Bishop had left for D'Urban about the time the lecture was to come off, on a tour of episcopal visitation in that part of his diocese.

So when I went to D'Urban the Bishop was at his

post there. As I entered the town I saw the bills up, announcing that the learned Bishop was to preach next day morning and evening in the Anglican Church.

At Verulam he preceded us a week. Rev. Mr. Elder there tried to blockade his pulpit against the Bishop, and hence one of those scenes so common in his diocese, a violent removal of barriers, and "running the blockade."

The Sabbath I was in Verulam, Colenso was back in D'Urban. The papers puffed him, and eulogised his preaching, and a merchant of Maritzburg came to tea at the house of my host, Mr. J. H. Grant, in D'Urban, so drunk, he could not walk erect, and spent an hour in berating Christians and Christian ministers, and was sure that the eloquent Bishop, the most learned and reliable preacher in the world, would yet convert the whole of us. I happened to say, "Dr. Colenso," and he took offence, that I should be so irreverent. "Bishop Colenso! *Bishop Colenso!*" he shouted, "the most learned and pious man in the world!"

There are some very respectable families, in a worldly sense, and of good outward moral deportment, who are identified with the Bishop; but the majority of his followers are affirmed to be, by those who know them well, such persons as have good reason to dread the threatened judgments of the Bible, and therefore hope the book is not from God. Colenso, too, gains influence with many by his genial gentlemanly manners, and Low Church liberality, in contrast with the stiff, Puseyitical, Ritualistic character of the Bishop of Cape Town. Old Rev. Mr. Lloyd, Episcopal minister in D'Urban, in a friendly visit to my room, after talking to me sometime about the Bishops of Jerusalem, and Sydney, whom I had the pleasure of meeting, spoke of Colenso, who had been in his pulpit the preceding Sabbath, and said, "Poor Colenso, I believe he is a well-meaning man, but has got wrong in his mind. I believe he will be in a lunatic asylum before many years." Mr. Lloyd is a most kind-hearted old man, and would be glad to draw that veil of charity over the learned prelate's theological and moral idiosyncrasies. One of the D'Urban papers stated, as a proof that all the people had not lost confidence in the Bishop, that in his recent episcopal tour, he had "baptized two children."

During those eventful five weeks, in which the Bishop made his episcopal tour, and caused such a lively stir among the newspaper reporters, correspondents, and sensationalists of the church breaking order, and doing wonders in his way, and *baptized two babies*, my Zulu and his black legion, and I, with my pale faces, had marched steadily on against the armies of the aliens. The souls awakened by the Spirit, who surrendered to God, accepted Christ, and personally tested the truth of the Bible, and who got the demonstration of the supreme Divinity of Jesus, by the "washing of regeneration, and renewing of the

Holy Ghost," publicly confessed that they had received "redemption through His blood, even the forgiveness of their sins." They were also personally examined by their ministers, who being satisfied with their testimony, wrote down their names and addresses, so as to get them under pastoral training. These new witnesses, whom God thus raised up in refutation of the scepticism and infidelity of the times, numbered over 320 whites, and over 700 natives, of all ages and stations in life, making an aggregate of more than 1,000 persons. I only preached five sermons to Kaffirs during those five weeks, so that most of the success of that division of the army was under the leadership of my Zulu. I was glad of that, for it did more than volumes of argument could have done, to break down a foolish "caste" and "colour" prejudice, and thus open the way for the employment of native agency, which God will mainly employ for the evangelization of Africa.

When Brother Pamla first went to D'Urban, Mr. Henry Cowey, a merchant, an excellent worker, and Local Preacher, said to me, "There is a great deal of prejudice here against allowing a coloured man to come into the house of a colonist, but I have consented to take Charles to stop with me."

"You may think yourself very highly honoured, Brother Cowey, to have the privilege of entertaining such a messenger of God."

Brother Cowey afterwards reminded me of my remark, and said it was true, for he and his family had been entertained and benefited by Charles' sojourn with them.

PROMISCUOUS EXAMPLES OF NATAL ADVENTURES.

Dr. Colenso's attempt to popularise the Gospel to the Kaffirs, by his apology for polygamy, did not take with the Kaffir polygamists at all, for they were sharp enough to see that if Christianity differed so little from Kaffir heathenism as that, it was quite unnecessary to be at the trouble of a conversion from one to the other.

TRYING TO ASTONISH THE NATIVES.

When the first Anglican Church dean went to Natal, he visited the Wesleyan Mission at Pietermaritzburg, and Rev. W. J. Davis, the missionary, invited him to preach to his Kaffirs. The Dean accepted the invitation, and came before the audience in his white " surplice," a style of dress the natives had never seen before. After the service Mr. Davis asked some of the men what they thought of the new *umfundisi's* preaching? " Well," replied one, " it was very good, just the same things we had heard before; but we were wondering all the time why the man did not put his shirt inside of his trousers?"

CHARMING A LION WITH MUSIC.

When Rev. W. J. Davis was living in Pietermaritzburg, his little son John, a lad of four years, went too near to a chained lion in a neighbour's yard.

JOHNNY DAVIS AND THE LION.

It was called a pet lion, but was indeed so wild and vicious, that no living thing was safe within the radius of his beat. The unsuspecting child stumbled within his reach, and the lion instantly felled him to the ground, and set his great paw on poor little Johnny's head. There was great consternation among the bystanders, but none were able to deliver the child. Miss Moreland, a young lady, with characteristic colonial presence of mind, seeing the peril of the child, ran up-stairs, and with her accordion in hand, came to a window looking out upon the tragic scene, and with a shout, to arrest attention, played a tune for the entertainment of the so-called "king of the woods," and he was so delighted with her kind attentions and musical talents, that he released his prey, and went the length of his chain toward his fair charmer, and stood in rapt attention. Johnny meantime got up, and carried his precious little self off to his mother. He never thought of crying till he entered the house, and saw how they were all excited about him, and then quite out of danger, he had a good cry on his own account. John has grown up the stature of a tall man, and has been delivered from him "who goeth about as a roaring lion, seeking whom he may devour."

COLENSO'S ARK TAKEN DOWN BY A KAFFIR.

On our way to Pietermaritzburg, having crossed into the lines of Natal, Mr. H., a very intelligent and influential man, gave Charles Pamla a solemn warning against coming into contact with Bishop Colenso, which led in substance to the following conversation :—

"He is a learned, shrewd, dangerous man," said Mr. H., "and might shake your faith."

"Shake my faith in what?" inquired Charles.

"He might shake your faith in the truth of the Bible, and in the Divinity of Jesus Christ."

"I can't see how he could that," replied Charles. "I proved the truth of the Bible and the Divinity of Jesus Christ in my heart thirteen years ago. I was convinced of sin by the Holy Ghost according to the teachings of the Bible; I then walked after the Spirit according to the instructions of the Word of God, and He led me to Jesus Christ. I gave my guilty soul to Him and received Him as my Saviour, and got the forgiveness of all my sins through Him. None but God can forgive sins. It was on the truth of God's Word that I accepted Him as my Saviour, and then, according to the true promises of God, He saved me from my sins, a thing I know He never could do if He is not God. He not only saved me thirteen years ago, but He has saved me every day since, and saves me now. These are the facts that I know, and I can't see how any man's infidel speculations can shake God's facts revealed in my heart, which prove to me the truth of His book."

"Ah! but the faith of many strong men has been shaken by Colenso," rejoined Mr. H., "and you should be careful not to put yourself in his way, he might do you serious injury."

"Well, now, Mr. H.," said Charles, "will you please to give me the strongest argument Colenso ever raised against the truth of the Bible?"

"No, I should be afraid, it might do you damage." But Charles insisted on knowing the strongest thing Mr. H. could recall from Colenso's writings against God's book, and finally Mr. H. said, "Dr. Colenso shows, by an arithmetical calculation, that the Bible story about the ark breaks down; that it was impossible, according to the measurements given for the ark, to contain a pair of all the animals and seven of the clean animals, as stated in the story."

"Indeed," said Charles, "and that's it! Is that the strongest point the great man can make against the Word of God?"

"He makes a strong case out of that, and I can't remember a stronger in his writings," replied Mr. H., and Charles showed his splendid rows of ivory in a broad spontaneous laugh, peculiar to himself, and then said, "Well, now, seriously, Mr. H., whatever may be our ignorance of ancient measurements, the fact is, if God should command me to build an ark, give me the pattern and dimensions, furnish plenty of timber of the right sort for such a ship, and plenty of ship-builders, and 120 years to fulfil my contract, I'll warrant you I would make it big enough, and I have no doubt that old Noah was as sharp as any Kaffir in Africa."

The fact is, taking the "cubit" at twenty-one inches, the measurements given in the narrative are adequate; but my Zulu took the Bishop on his own ground. The Jews had a measure called a "cubit," the Chaldeans had a very different measure called a "cubit," just as we have different measurements bearing the same name now; for example, a mile in Ireland is about one-third longer than a mile in England, and an acre in England, Ireland, and Scotland represents in each country quite a different measurement of land, so Charles at a glance grasped the fundamental points in the story, and furnishing the clearest presumption of its truthfulness.

THOMAS PALFREYMAN AND THE TIGER.

The South African Tiger is of the bright-spotted leopard species, not quite so large as the Asiatic tiger, I believe, but very fierce and formidable. When we were at Maritzburg a young man, near York, twenty miles distant from us, discovered a tiger near his residence, and shot at the beast two or three times, but without much effect, except to enrage the animal, which joined issue with him, teeth and claws against his powder and bullets, and the young fellow cried for quarter. His shouts brought his father to the spot. The young man escaped with his life, but his father was killed by the tiger almost instantaneously.

Thomas Palfreyman, a young Englishman, was away back of Pietermaritzburg, toward the great Drakensberg, when some frightened Kaffirs came running to him, crying, "a tiger! a tiger!" pointing to the woods and cliffs near by. Palfreyman ran with his gun into the "bush" and came in sight of the beast very soon.

The tiger stood his ground, the young man advanced close to him, took deliberate aim at his head, and fired, but produced no effect beyond the flash and report of the gun, and the slow retreat of the tiger. The young fellow then, upon reflection, was convinced that in his haste he had forgotten to put in a ball, and had, therefore, merely burnt a charge of powder in his first attempt to kill a tiger. He had only been a little over a year away from England and was not well up in that kind of Colonial work. He then put in a good charge of powder and ball and pursued. The Kaffirs kept out of the bush in the open ground where they would have plenty of lee-way all clear, so that if they should deem it expedient to do any running, they might do it to the best advantage for themselves, for the Kaffirs, brought up from childhood in terror of the tiger, their great "Inkosi" of the forest, have a mortal fear of them. Palfreyman was feeling his way along a narrow path on the side of a cliff, eight or ten feet above its base, looking ahead for another sight of the tiger. The great beast meantime, with sharper sight, was looking for him, and was now crouched on a ledge of the cliff just above him, ready to pounce down on his hunter as he was passing below. The young hunter was quite outgeneralled by the strategic movements of the enemy, and when he came within range, the tiger with one long leap came down upon him.

Hearing the spring of the tiger, he suddenly drew up his gun in the direction of the bounding beast and fired, but without effect, except, perhaps, to give him a wholesome admonition with the smell of burnt powder.

As the tiger struck him he set the nails of one of his paws deeply into one of Tom's shoulders and his teeth into the back of his head, and knocked him heels over head down the cliff, eight or ten feet into the jungle below. In their sudden tumble over the ledge of rocks the tiger lost his hold, and retreated into a jungle a little further on. Tom gathered himself up, and finding he had the use of his limbs, though badly wounded and bleeding profusely, he put into his gun a heavy charge of powder, and rolled in a handful of naked bullets, and was ready to renew the attack. His *English* pluck was up by this time, and he rushed into the bushy retreat of his foe, and there he was waiting for him, calculating, no doubt, and on very plausible grounds too, that the victory and the spoils would be his. The young Englishman advanced upon him till he could see the flashing glare of his eyes, and with good aim drove his full charge of bullets into his head, and dropped him dead in his tracks. Tom showed me the skin of the tiger, which measured nine feet from the nose to the end of the tail. He

TOM PALFREYMAN AND THE TIGER.

was preserving the skin, waiting an opportunity to send it to his parents in England.

Thomas drove me from his uncle Thomas Palfreyman's, house, eighteen miles, to my appointment at Richmond, where I preached two sermons and got my tiger-killer converted to God.

THE DUTCHMAN AND HIS HOLLAND BIBLE.

Two Kaffrarian missionaries, Rev. W. J. Davis, and Rev. John Ayliff, in one of their journeys, put up at the house of a Dutch farmer.

During their evening conversation, Mr. Ayliff introduced the subject of vital, personal godliness, and was urging upon his host the necessity of being "born again," as a mere form of religion would not secure him a passport to heaven, nor a fitness for it. The Dutchman listened so attentively for some time, that the missionary was quite encouraged with the hope of winning his man to Christ; but at last the Dutchman interrupted him, by saying, " Mr. Ayliff, what did Cain kill his brother with ?"

Mr. Ayliff replied, " The Bible does not inform us what kind of instrument he used, and hence, we do not know."

The Dutchman went and got his large Holland Dutch Bible, and laid it down on the table, and with his hand upon it, said, "See here, Mr. Ayliff, this is my religion. This is a duly authorized Holland Bible, that cost me one hundred dollars (Rix dollars—

£7 10s.). A Holland Bible, Mr. Ayliff, in black letters, duly authorised! That is my faith."

He then opened it, and turned over many pages with large illustrated black letters and pictures, till he came to the story of the first murder, and there was a picture representing the murderer with a great club in his hands, and, pointing and looking with an air of triumph, he said, "There Mr. Ayliff, do you see that? Don't you see it plain enough that Cain killed his brother with a club?"

"Ah, but my dear sir," replied Ayliff, "that picture was not a part of the inspired narrative. The artist might have put a sword into his hands instead of a stick, except that at that period they had clubs, but not swords. The murderous weapon was most likely a club or a stone, but the sacred writer has not told us which."

The Dutchman retorted in a spirit of indignation, "Now when a man, professing to be a teacher of religion, comes and tells me that my duly authorised Holland Bible, which cost me one hundred dollars, does not tell the truth about Cain, I want to have nothing more to do with him."

REV. MR. BUTLER AND THE ALLIGATOR.

Some of the rivers of Natal abound with alligators, and many a poor fellow has been dragged down and devoured by them. Rev. Mr. Butler, an American missionary, was crossing the Umkumas River on horseback, when a huge alligator seized his leg.

REV. MR. BUTLER AND THE ALLIGATOR.

He held on for life to his horse, and dragged the savage beast ashore, and happily for him a number of Kaffir women were near, who ran to his rescue and beat the horrible creature off him. The wound, after a long time, was healed, but the minister never fully recovered. He has since returned to America.

THE LAWYER AND HIS ADVOCATE.

Mr. Pincent, of D'Urban, in Mr. George Cato's judgment, though not an eloquent pleader, is the best law counsellor in South Africa. After he had been forward with our seekers several times feeling after God, his case, to his own mind, became desperate, and after giving me a relation of his rebellion against God, he inquired, "Now, do you think there is any chance for such a vile creature as I am to be saved?" (He was regarded as a moral, right-minded man, but now the Holy Spirit had revealed to him, what every sinner must see before he will consent to God's terms of salvation, "the exceeding sinfulness of sin.")

I assured him "that it is a faithful saying, and worthy of all acceptation, that Christ Jesus came into the world to save sinners"—even the very chief of sinners—and that if he would but surrender to God and accept Christ, he would prove the truth of that glorious announcement straightway. We then went into the details of the struggle, and he was so sick of sin, that I had but little difficulty in getting him to consent to a divorce from all sin, and to accept God's will as the rule of his heart and life, but he stuck sometime at the believing point. He wanted to pray on till God, for Christ's sake, would give him peace, and then he could believe. When I got him to see clearly that he must have confidence in a physician, and accept him before he could hope to be cured by him, he next stuck at the mystery involved in such a work. Realizing his antagonism to God's immutable laws, and that a judgment had been given and recorded against him in heaven's court, under the clearly revealed law, "the soul that sinneth, it shall die," "He that believeth not is condemned already," he could not see how it was possible for his legal relations to God's government to be adjusted so that he should be fully reconciled to God.

After fully explaining the Gospel plan of salvation by faith, I finally got him down to the saving act of faith, by the following illustration. Jesus Christ is our "Advocate with the Father."

"Now it is fair to presume that He understands His professional intricacies and difficulties. If He had not been perfectly qualified for that responsible position, He would not have been admitted to the bar of heaven's court at all. Now suppose, Mr. Pincent, that one of your clients should elbow you round the corners of the streets, and keep insinuating, 'I can't see how you are to conduct my suit to a successful issue. I can't understand the complications of the the case, it seems all dark to me, and I'm afraid you'll not succeed.' Then when the case comes on for trial in court, and your client insists on standing by you to tell you how to conduct the suit, and every few minutes gives you the benefit of his counsel, and dictates to you how you should attend to your own business. What would you do, sir? You would return him his brief straightway! Now that illustrates your treatment of 'our Advocate with the Father, Jesus Christ the righteous.' If a client understood the business, he would not employ an advocate, and when he employs one he thus admits that he does not understand it, but that his advocate does, and having faith in his advocate, allows him to conduct the suit in his own way, and is not concerned to know the intricacies involved, but the successful issue." This being the last point in the penitential struggle of my lawyer, he thus saw it clearly, and at once gave his case fully and unreservedly into the hands of his heavenly Advocate, and that very day he got his discharge from the death-sentence of the law, in the court Divine, certified in his heart by the Holy Spirit. The very moment God saw that, under the leading of the awakening Spirit, he fully surrendered himself to God, and accepted Christ, at the instance of his "Advocate," the Father "justified him freely"—changed his relation from a condemned criminal to an adopted child, and then being a son, "He sent forth the Spirit of His Son into his heart, crying Abba Father."

From that Brother Pincent became decidedly active as a witness and worker for God, and very useful in leading poor sinners to Christ.

But says a hypercritical soul, "Why make such a free use of a gentleman's name?" Suppose I ask why St. Luke gave the name of Sergius Paulus, the governor of Cyprus, who believed under Paul's preaching, and why tell us, that under his sermon on Mars Hill one of the judges of that august court, Dionysius, was one among others who believed? Such facts judiciously stated block the game of a class of depreciative croakers, common in all countries, who are always ready to insinuate that the believers in Christ are a sorry set of weak-minded souls, composed largely of superannuated old women and little children; and then, when such are forestalled by such examples as Governor Paulus and Judge Dionysius, they are greatly shocked that the names of such should come to light. I made an allusion to Mr. Pincent's conversion in Cape Town, and one of those hypercritics made a blow in the papers about it, no doubt expecting to turn even my lawyer against me for using his name; but I had the pleasure of stating at my next service, that it was by Mr. Pincent's own authority that I made use of his name, having said to me, "So much of my life has been wasted, that for the rest of it I wish my time, talents, and testimony, all used in any way that will promote the glory of God and the salvation of sinners, and you are entirely at liberty to make any use of my name you like for such purposes." In the colony of New South Wales, eight lawyers received Christ at our meetings, and one of them, a barrister and crown prosecutor, has been used by the Holy Spirit in the salvation of a number of prominent men in the colony.

THEORY OF THE "WISEACRES."

We have seen the theory of the heathen Kaffirs at "Annshaw" for solving the mysterious phenomenon of God's work there, on seeing hundreds of their fellow heathen subjugated to Christ, but now the enlightened sages of Natal try their hand. Seeing bankers, merchants, mechanics, and all classes from the highest to the lowest yielding to the invisible mysterious power of the Holy Spirit of God, they could not deny the presence and moving power of some wonderful agent, so their magical brains went into labour, and brought forth the much desired solution—for it was a very serious time with them, we had carried the strongholds of infidelity by storm, and the kingdom of their father in that colony was shaken to its centre. Well what was their grand solution? *Electro-biology and mesmerism.*

Their darling, however, had but a puny existence for a few days, and suddenly died. My friend, Mr. George Cato, drove me twenty miles to "Amanzimtote," one of the American mission-stations, for a couple of preaching services, through a pioneer interpreter, Mr. Joseph Kirkman, who was the speaking medium for Rev. Dr. Adams and Rev. A. Grant, American missionaries there from the year 1838, long before Natal became a colony, and the night I was absent the work in D'Urban was rather more successful than usual, and many souls were saved. The "mesmerizer" was gone, and yet the power remained, so that their confusion was doubly confounded.

GEORGE C. CATO, ESQ.,
Consul of Sweden, Norway, and Denmark, Consular Agent for the United States of America for Natal, merchant, sugar planter, free counsellor on all colonial matters, agent for the American missionaries, and liberal patron of good things, is an *institution* of the country worthy of a much larger space than my limits will allow, but the following extract of a letter from him will furnish illustrative glimpses into the character of the man, colonial pioneer life, and the recent work of God.

Natal, 13th January, 1867.
My dear and beloved Friend,

It was with unspeakable pleasure that I read your two notes you very kindly wrote me, the last one written near St. Helena. We prized the likeness of yourself and your good wife that you sent, and shall respect the giver while life shall last. It is not very likely we shall forget you. Some of us in this country reckon things and times by epochs, such as when the Zulus came down on the natives here, but finding them cooking human flesh so disgusted them, that they would not soil their assegais by killing the cannibals, and hence left the country; then the arrival of the Dutch Boers; then the Zulu war, which a good and wise Providence allowed to sweep off all the old English residents, who were living with and like the natives, and who, if they had remained alive, would have been the cause of much cold-blooded murder. Then the first occupation by British troops; then their leaving, and giving up the country to the Dutch; then their coming back again, and our fight, and my being made prisoner, and put in irons by day and stocks by night; then the first and second flood of the Umgeni River, and our starting at midnight with a boat to see if any of the residents of the lowlands were in danger, and saving the Smith family, who had got to a small hill, and was then standing in water breast high. Then the arrival of Bishop Colenso, one of the most extraordinary men I ever knew, and beyond my poor comprehension. Then the arrival and final departure of our good Governor, one of my best friends, Mr. Scott, with a few smaller advents, until the coming and going of not the least of my remarkable days—when you came and went. I don't wish you any harm, but I wish the chapter of accidents would just land you here again. I have come to the conclusion in my own mind, that human nature is human nature under all circumstances, and a predominant feature thereof is an insatiable greed, never satisfied—some crave one thing, and some another, consequently if you think there are not souls enough to be saved here to satisfy your craving, then we will annex the Zulu country, and the Dutch, inland. I think you would find enough here to make stars for your crown, and we should welcome you in all love and respect. I cannot conceive that you will find a country where your good would be more enduring than it appears to be here. As a matter of course, I know the fountain from which this good comes, and that strengthens my argument, you had the approval of your Master. Since you left I saw a letter from one of my friends to another, saying that he was at church the other night, and if I had been there I should have been delighted, as the Bishop said during his sermon that some men were specially gifted by God with powers to awaken their fellow-men; that these powers did not depend upon great learning, but were a special gift to convey His messages to mankind: that we may not scrutinize the messenger too narrowly, but must obey his message; among such men he named a Wesley, a Whitefield, a Spurgeon, and a Taylor.—Now after that I think you had better come back.

It may be worthy of remark, that near the close of our campaign, Bishop Colenso called at the house of my host, Mr. J. H. Grant, in D'Urban, to see me, saying, "I wanted to see you and shake hands with you before you leave. God has given you your work to do, and you are doing it, and He has called me to another work and I am doing my work. You don't suppose that all those who have been brought in at your meetings will stand, do you?" I replied, "I certainly do suppose that the most of them will stand to the death, but a few of them, owing to their very bad habits, bad associations, and the influence of bad examples, may relapse into sin." Our interview being short, but little passed between us beyond the facts given. I could readily see how by his kind gentlemanly manner he won the friendship of many persons, who say they receive him as a gentleman without any reference to his ecclesiastical character and relations.

FRANCIS HARVEY, SEN., OF VERULAM,

Is one of the natural *curiosities* of the Colony. The

following scrap from his journal may suffice to introduce him :—

"This happy morning, at five o'clock, the exact anniversary of my birth, seventy-four years since, I find myself by the special favour and goodness of Almighty God, in superior health and energy of body, and rich in the full enjoyment of every faculty and power of mind, intellectual, emotional, and spiritual, as much so as at any former anniversary of my entrance on life's pathway; and in all and everything of blissful possession and sublime hope, I cannot believe there exists in Africa, or in the wide world, one more blest, or more conscious of entire unworthiness of the least of all God's mercies."

Francis Harvey is a real progressive, a teetotal lecturer and Local Preacher, of more than ordinary cleverness, but luxuriates on his bright memories of the past. Among many other interesting things, I heard him relate the story about Mr. Charles Wesley and the king's "men-of-war's men" with so much graphic power, that I requested him to write me the story, and he gave me the following.

A century since, on a Sabbath afternoon, the Rev. Chas. Wesley was preaching at Portsmouth in the open air; a godless naval officer, heated by the demon spirit of wine, and heading a party of blustering, swearing men-of-war's men, came furiously towards the assembled hearers, purposely to disturb and drive them off. Mr. Wesley wisely called out to the people, "Open there, right and left, and let His Majesty's brave tars come near me." The effect was electric, they who were ready for any work of wicked violence became in a moment disabled and dismantled to the very clew-lines of their hearts; their leader, the half-drunk lieutenant, paralysed and truly taken aback, confused and utterly confounded, dared not look a man in the face; honest, weeping, broken-down veterans for the Devil, were helpless as maimed infants, and the old lion of hell himself had to skulk away, tail between his legs, as best he could. The sailors had come up singing a roystering bullying song, and when all was still and lulled to a peaceful calm, Mr. Wesley, who was pleased with the lively air, and smiling all over his radiant face, offered to give them a song of his own, to their tune; and he did so, and they sung heartily and lustily, as Jack in a storm can sing:—

> *'Listed* into the cause of sin,
>   Why should a good be evil?
> Music, alas! too long has been
>   *Pressed* to obey the devil
> Drunken, and light, and lewd the lay
>   Flowed to the soul's undoing,
> Widen'd and strewed with flowers the **way**
>   Down to eternal ruin.
>
> Who, on the part of God will rise,
>   Innocent sound *recover*,
> Fly on *the foe* and seize the *prize*,
>   *Plunder* the carnal lover,
> Rob him of every moving strain,
>   Every melting measure,
> Music in virtue's cause retain,
>   *Rescue* the holy pleasure.
>
> Who hath *a right* like *us* to sing?
>   Us whom the Spirit teaches?
> Merry our hearts, for Christ is King,
>   Cheerful are all our faces.

Heaven already is begun,
Open'd in each believer;
Only believe, and still sing on,
Heaven *is* ours for ever!

Written purposely for the Rev. Mr. Taylor, this happy 11th of October, 1866, by his loving friend, Francis Harvey, Verulam, Natal, in his seventy-fourth year, and without glasses.

At the first service held in D'Urban by Bishop Colenso, on his arrival in the colony, Father Harvey was present, and tells the following :—

"The Bishop entered the plain church, as it was then, walked to the pulpit, sat down, and made a scrutinizing survey of the rustic audience. I being the oldest man in the house, with a white beard, he no doubt thought I was a vestryman, and came down the aisle to me, and said, 'Are you an officer in the church, sir?'

"'Yes, sir, I am the superintendent of a Sabbath-school, and a Local Preacher in the Wesleyan *Establishment.*'

"'Ah, ah, indeed!' replied the bishop with an air of disappointment, and walked back to the pulpit.

"After a little he came to me again, and said, 'Have you been long in this country?'

"'Yes, sir, about ten years.'

"'What induced you, at your time of life, to come so far?'

'"I had some promising sons for whom I thought I could do better in a new country.'

"'From what part of England did you come?'

"'Cornwall, sir; where your father used to live before he removed to Devonshire. I used to go to school to your uncle, William, in Cornwall.'

"By this time all who were sitting near, hearing the conversation, became quite interested.

"'My uncle, William?' inquired the Bishop.

"'Yes, sir, your uncle, William Colenso, I went to school to him many a long day. He was a Wesleyan Local Preacher like myself.'

"Sensation among the listeners."

The bishop took it very kindly, and soon returned to the pulpit. He left the old officer in the Wesleyan Establishment.

Father. Harvey presented me with a little poem he composed for the daughter of a minister, a member of his class, who was then seeking the Lord, and afterwards became a very exemplary Christian:—

"*Saw ye him whom my soul loveth?*"—Canticles, iii. 3.

> Where the friends of Jesus meet,—
> Where they hold communion sweet,—
> Where the Lord himself is seen,—
> Where His presence oft has been,—
> Where the Holy Spirit rests,—
> Where He visits Sion's guests,—
> Where the Father's love is known,—
> Where He dwells amongst His own,—
> Where His children still are fed,—
> Where He breaks the living bread,—
> Where the Shepherd's Tents are seen,—
> Where the pasturage is green,—

Where the living waters flow,—
Where the trees of healing grow,—
Where the vale-birth'd lily grows,—
Where blooms Sharon's fragrant rose,—
Where the Flocks in peace lie down,—
Where the Shepherd guards his own,—
There, thou wilt thy Saviour meet,—
Haste thee,—worship at His feet.

F. H., sen.

One of Colenso's friends in Verulam was telling Father Harvey about the Bishop's eloquent sermon there the Sabbath preceding my visit, and said that nothing could come up to it. Harvey did not join issue with him on the literary merits of the sermon, but said, "As for the demonstration of the Holy Spirit applying the truth, and the saving power of God, I'll explain to you the difference between Colenso's operations last Sabbath and the work now progressing in the Wesleyan chapel.

"See a silversmith, with a beautiful tiny hammer, hammering the link of a delicate gold chain, and then look at one of Nasmyth's mighty hammers, twenty-five tons in weight, stroke after stroke, crashing down on red-hot iron. Imagine a moonbeam reposing on the crest of an iceberg, in contrast with Nebuchadnezzar's furnace 'heated seven times hotter than it was wont to be heated.'"

REVIVAL INCIDENTS AT VERULAM.

STIRRING incidents they were too, and enough to fill a volume, but my space will admit but a 'meagre skeleton of a few. I will insert one from Pamla's division, as given by Charles.

A heathen man at the Inanda, near Verulam, came to one of my meetings when I was there. After preaching, when I called for penitents, the heathen man came forward. I asked him, "Do you give up your sins?"

"What sins?" he asked.

I replied, "Man, don't you know what sins are?"

"I never did commit any sins."

"Man, did you never quarrel or fight with the people?" And then he got up immediately and looked in my face and was very angry. He said:

"What sort of a preacher are you? Do you think you are a better preacher than our preachers here? You are not. It is not a sin to hit another man. Why did David kill Goliath? Now if David was a good man and could do that, it is not a sin. I may fight too. Do you think that I would let another man come and kill me? No."

I told him that David was allowed by God to kill Goliath because Goliath was a great enemy. You are allowed to defend your country and to kill people in battle yourself, but not at home; God says, "Thou shalt not kill nor hate thy brother." The next time he came to my meeting he was sorrowful, and told me that he was a great sinner and kneeled down, gave up his sins, received Christ, and found peace.

The engravings of the "Zulu young gentlemen," and "Captain Ngoya," are specimens of the naked neathen daily seen in the streets of the towns, as well as throughout the country; but the saved heathen are "clothed and in their right minds," like the Gadarene.

CAPT. NGOYA IN NATIVE HEATHEN DRESS.

At my last service in Verulum, forty-two souls entered into liberty. A man said "Mr. Garland, go and talk to that poor fellow" (pointing to a man down on his knees among the penitents), "he is a Roman Catholic, and needs help." Garland went to him and said, "Are you willing to give up all your sins and surrender your soul to God?"

"I have done that, sir," replied the Catholic.

"Are you willing on the faith of God's record, concerning His Son, to accept Christ now as your Saviour?"

"I have accepted Him, sir."

"When did you accept Him?"

"To night, sir, since I knelt down here."

"Does He save you from your sins?"

"Yes, sir, He has saved me. I feel it! I know it, He's my blessed Jesus!"

A young colonist among the seekers, who received Christ and obtained the renewing of His Holy Spirit, at once went to work in his blunt simplicity to help his struggling friends to come to Jesus, and was made a blessing to some; he said to a young friend who was weeping and praying, "Believe, Jim! accept Christ now! Do it sharp as I did! He'll save you this moment if you'll only accept Him!" His friend came to the point, believed "sharp," and was saved. Miss Cubit, who was saved at D'Urban and was made very useful at our Verulam Meeting, said to me in the last hour of our last service, "Do come and speak again to Mr. Fynney, he seems to be sinking into utter despair."

As I approached him, he exclaimed, "O, Mr. Taylor I am lost! I feel the dreadful 'ivy of sin' around my soul, and I can't break it. I feel that there are at least 1,000 devils in me, they are all alive in me, and I can't get them out! Do you think there is any chance for me?"

"Your case is bad enough you see, and all the good men, and good angels in the Universe combined, could not eject a single devil from your heart, but Jesus Christ can save you this moment. He cast a legion of devils out of the Gadarene by a word, and He will save you if you will surrender yourself to God, and believing His testimony, receive Christ as your Saviour. You are under the sentence of death, your life is forfeited, and you can't do better than throw your whole being on the mercy of God, in unreserved submission to His will, to do with you as He likes. Do you surrender to Him?"

"O yes, I do by His help give myself to God to do with me as He wishes."

"Have you sufficient confidence in Jesus, from what you have read and heard about Him, to accept Him as your Saviour?"

"O yes, I am willing to accept Him, I have no hope in any other."

"Thank God for the willingness, that is the fruit of His awakening Spirit, but it must be developed into the fact of an actual acceptance of Him. Do you accept Him now?"

"O I can get no light!"

"No, and you never will get the light till you receive Christ."

"O, but I can't feel His love!"

"No, and you never will feel His love, till you believe on Him and take Him as your Saviour. You want to feel His pardoning love and then believe. That is expecting the cure before you accept the physician, which is quite out of the question."

"O I feel so utterly wretched! Is there no hope for me?"

"None whatever, while you look to yourself. The sailor said to his fellow, 'You may just as well look into the hold of the ship to find the north star, as to look to your self for salvation.' You must accept the Great Physician by faith, faith in His Gospel credentials, give your case into His hands, consent to His treatment, and leave Him to exercise His own wisdom and skill to cure you in His own way."

"But what if I get no relief? I can't feel any witness of the Spirit."

"You still want to get relief, and feel the Spirit's witness before you are pardoned, which is utterly impossible. The witness and renewing work of the Holy Spirit are as much a matter of provision as the atonement itself and as immutably reliable. That is not your part of the business. Your business is to "repent and believe the Gospel"—surrender to God, and accept Christ, and you may be sure the Holy Spirit will not fail to fulfil His engagement in the matter. Do you, my dear brother, now accept Christ?"

"I don't feel that I do."

"It is not by feeling, but by believing, not presumption, but the most intelligent faith in God's most intelligible testimony. If you believe what God says about Christ, is Christ not worthy of your confidence, and if so, why not entrust your case in His hands, and take Him now as your Saviour? If you have any mental reservations you are not accepting Him, but dictating terms to Him which He will spurn. You can accept Him only on His own terms as a Saviour *from sin*, with your hearts' *consent*."

"O I do give up everything! I'll die if I don't get relief!"

"Yes, and you will perish eternally if you do not receive the only Saviour of sinners. Now in full confidence in the blood shedding of Jesus for the sins of the whole world, His prayers, as your Great High Priest, His power to save the very chief of sinners, His invitations and promises, confidence in His willingness to save to the uttermost all that come unto God by Him,' accept Him as your Saviour. He is 'meek and lowly of heart,' your most sympathising Friend, the only friend you have who loves you enough to die for you, and His heart of love is just the same now as when He poured out His heart's blood on the cross, Jesus Christ, the same yesterday, to-day, and for ever, and you have not to ascend or descend to bring Him; He is nigh thee. Do you accept Him?"

"Yes, I do accept Him! I do accept Him! I do accept Him—Glory be to God, He saves me! He has pardoned all my sins and delivered my soul! Glory to God and the Lamb, I'm saved!" His mother, a good woman who had been telling me that day with tears that poor Fred was possessed, and she feared would never be saved, embraced her returned prodigal and shed floods of grateful tears, and could truthfully exclaim, " This my son was dead, but is alive again, he was lost but is found." The next morning, Frederic B. Fynney, for that is his name, said to me, " I know four African languages. I know the Kaffir better than I know the English, and I owe such a debt of gratitude to God for saving my soul, and I feel such sympathy and love for the Kaffirs, that I believe God has called me to devote my life in leading them to Jesus." He commenced preaching straightway; we'll hear of him again.

J. W. Stranack, a clever young man, who was said to have been the special correspondent who did the puffing of Colenso's recent sermons in Verulam for a D'Urban paper, surrendered himself to God and accepted Christ on the faith of God's record, on that memorable "last night" in Verulam.

The following extract of a letter to me from him will tell its own story :—

Verulam, Natal, May 10*th*, 1867.

My dear father in Christ, for such I must ever regard you, I have purposed ever since my uncle, Garland, heard from you, to write you some account of my own progress, and that of your Verulam converts, and also to tell you of the work we are each endeavouring to do for Christ. A sceptical view with which I had become accustomed to regard every thing connected with personal religion and a contempt for professors of religion, who were, as I considered, credulous enough to accept the dogmas of Christianity merely because they were told they were so, had become so settled, that I regarded my own conversion as certainly the most unlikely thing under the sun. You came; I attended the Wesleyan chapel as usual, new feelings, new desires were awakened. I saw truth as I never saw it before. The sermon on Wednesday morning, October 10th, on Christian perfection, fairly brought me to the point. I saw Christianity to be something worth having, grand, noble, and I resolved that I would count all things loss if I might gain Christ. I went to the altar of prayer the same evening, was enabled to " surrender and to accept Christ." The following Tuesday evening, at the prayer-meeting, I felt the witness of the Spirit clear, unmistakable, that I was accepted of God, and a settled peace filled my soul. Since that time I have had seasons of temptation, severe indeed, but am still able to maintain my facts, and am resolved, in every purpose and power of my being, to be fully the Lord's. I felt at once the necessity of doing something for God, both for the sake of my own maintenance of spiritual strength, and in order to save souls, and promote the cause of our common Saviour. A month after my conversion one of our Local Preachers took me with him to preach at one of the two services he had to conduct. I went out, also, during the four or five months following with three other of our local brethren, and on two occasions went alone as a supply. The brethren considered me qualified for the work, and have placed me on trial as a Local Preacher. I preached on Sabbath evening in D'Urban and had the glorious privilege of seeing one make a stand for God, and find peace through Christ.

CHAPTER XXVI.

THE MISSION WORK IN SOUTH AFRICA.

THE letter embodied in this chapter, published in the *Graham's Town Journal*, and republished in the *Watchman*, and in the *Wesleyan Missionary Notices*, in London, contains a brief outline of the Gospel theory for evangelizing the world, illustrated by numerous facts in these pages, and also practical suggestions bearing specially on the mission work in Africa, entitled, it would seem, to a permanent record in a bound book, and hence its insertion entire just as it was first written. I thought of putting it in as an appendix, but I don't fancy postscripts and appendices, and have decided to give it the place to which in the order of events it belongs—the close of our campaign in Natal. I was not able to gratify Rev. T. Jenkins by sending Charles back through Pondo-land, having already detained him a month longer than the time agreed upon with his superintendent, so I sent him by steam-ship to Port Elizabeth, nearly a week before I and the other two members of my party sailed. James Roberts fulfilled his part nobly, not only in bringing "me on my way," but in pointing penitent souls the way to Jesus. He was thoroughly enlightened by the Spirit, and not one believer in a thousand could explain the simple way of salvation by faith so clearly as could Brother Roberts. He accompanied me to Cape Town, and helped me in my meetings in different places in those memorable places, where Rev. Barnabas Shaw, the first Wesleyan Missionary to Africa, planted the Gospel standard over fifty years ago. Mr. Roberts provided an excellent nurse for Africanus, our seventh son, then but two months old, to serve us during our voyage to London. The blessing of our covenant-keeping God rest upon my dear brother James Roberts.

The following letter was written on our voyage of 1,000 miles from Natal to Cape Town.

As I am now returning to Capetown from my tour of special services in the Eastern Province, Kaffraria and Natal, and expect to proceed to England by the November mail, I wish, through your popular Journal, respectfully to submit a few thoughts on what I regard the best methods of evangelisation. The mission work, commenced through the ministry of the Rev. Barnabas Shaw in Cape Town about fifty years ago, and by the Rev. Wm. Shaw in the Eastern Province about forty-six years ago, has, through the prayers and liberality of good people in England, and the persevering efforts of faithful missionaries and their friends here, under the fostering care of the Great Shepherd, gone forward and prospered.

The Wesleyan Missions in Southern Africa, embracing white colonists, according to the returns of last year (1865) report : 138 chapels, 359 preaching places, 63 missionaries and assistants, 389 local preachers, 8,331 church members, 1,235 on trial, 54,790 attending public worship, 128 Sunday-schools, 10,163 Sunday-school scholars, 103 day-school teachers, 11,457 day-scholars. When we weigh these figures, and take into the account the widely extending influence of such a work beyond ; not to speak of the great work wrought here by other branches of the Christian Church, which my limited space will not allow, we may well exclaim, " What hath God wrought ! "

But glorious as is the work accomplished, I believe the mission-stations of Southern Africa, extending coastwise for nearly 1,500 miles, with a similar line on the West coast, constitute but a base line and depôt of supplies necessary to a more direct decisive movement into the interior of the continent.

The establishment of a mission-station in a purely heathen country appears to require something like the foundations of a " new state," civil and religious. A large grant of land is secured from the chief, with treaty stipulations that while the mission-station is his, the missionary being answerable to him for the good conduct of the people in this new community, the chief is not to interfere with the internal government of the mission people. It is, indeed, designed to be a model of Christian government, embodying Gospel teaching, schools for education, mechanical industries, in short, a miniature Christian nation, for the government of which a heathen chief has no qualifications. The mission station, too, is by consent of parties, a sanctuary to which all persecuted people under suspicion of witchcraft, or other undefinable offences, may flee and be safe, while they remain there. The missionary practically becomes the chief of this mission tribe. He is the minister, the magistrate, the superintendent of the schools, and often the teacher as well, the master mechanic, the patron in general of all the arts of civilization which the heathen should learn, and he soon gets work enough on his hands fully to employ, and often utterly consume, his energies and his life. The uninitiated, especially now that heathenism in these parts is awed by the presence of English Colonial Governments, can form no adequate idea of the complicated difficulties our missionary fathers had to encounter in planting the Gospel standard in this empire of darkness; and far be it from me to indulge a thought, or drop an insinuation reflecting on their wisdom or fidelity in establishing the missions just as they did. They have done their work nobly, and many of them have already received of the Master the "Well done, good and faithful servant, enter thou into the joy of thy Lord." While they enjoy the glory of God in heaven, let them be honoured by men on earth. But now that they have established a base of operations, the time will come, and I believe has come, when we should, from this base, develop a more simple, direct, economical, and a more thoroughly effective system of evangelization for the conquest of the entire continent. The necessity for such a movement may be seen from the following facts: According to published statistics, there are in the Cape Colony and Natal nearly half-a-million of African natives. It is believed by old Missionaries and others who have the best means of forming an approximately correct idea, in the absense of a census, that the different tribes of Kaffraria amount in the aggregate to at least 250,000 souls. (Rev. E. Solomon says 300,000.) Add to these the tens of thousands embraced in the lines of the Bechuana district, and in the Free State, and we shall have nearly a million natives within the bounds of our South African Missions. Among all this mass of heathen population, accessible to the Gospel, according to last year's report (1866), we have 8,247 Church members.

We have up to this day but one Christian ruling Kaffir chief, and his is the only Kaffir tribe that has to any great extent received Christ; the great majority of our stations being composed of Fingoes. This vast field, white for the harvest, to say nothing of the millions of souls in the interior, calls loudly for additional labourers, while the Missionary Society is calling out for retrenchment. Now what is to be done? I would not give up to the authority of heathen chiefs the mission-stations which have grown up under the civil administration of the missionary, as in the case of Shawbury. Let them remain as seats of education, and " cities of refuge," as long as such a protective arrangement may be necessary.

But unless a very clear Providential necessity should arise, let no more mission-stations be established on that plan. Education and all other appliances of civilization will follow in the wake of Gospel triumphs, and should be amply provided for, but if all these must precede the Gospel, or go abreast with it, as part of the missionary's work, they will so circumscribe and trammel his movements that he will have but little time and strength left, for carrying " the war into Africa," beyond the lines of the station.

I do not propose any fundamental changes in our itinerant system, but having our mission stations with all their resources, with the Bible in Kaffir, Zulu, and other African languages, I would respectfully submit what I believe to be the best method of greatly increasing the working effectiveness of our missions, without greatly increasing the cost to the Missionary Society of carrying them on. I don't propose any new plan, but the old plan so successfully worked by St. Paul and his fellow-missionaries. I will give an outline of what I regard the purely

EVANGELICAL PLATFORM.

The Gospel is adapted to humanity in all its forms, from

the most learned philosopher to the most degraded heathen. All the knowledge essential to the salvation of a poor heathen may be acquired in a very short time—his pollution of soul by sin, his guilt, his condemnation and exposure to penalty, his bondage to Satan, and that God hath provided and now offers to him, in Christ, a ransom, a cleansing fountain, an Almighty deliverer. Through the quickening power of the Holy Spirit he may learn all this under the preaching of a single Gospel sermon, or even under the prophetic witnessing of a few laymen. " If all prophesy, and there come in one that believeth not,"—a poor sceptic, who had heard, but did not believe these Gospel tidings— " or one unlearned,"—a poor heathen who knew nothing about them—" he is convinced of all, he is judged of all; and thus are the secrets of his heart made manifest, and so, falling down on his face, will worship God," and finding salvation in Christ, will be able, as a witness for Jesus, to "report that God is in you of a truth." The Gospel plan not only embraces " pastors and teachers " for the watch, care, and edification of the Church, but also " apostles, prophets, and evangelists," for the development and effective employment of the combined forces of the Church in bold aggressions into the kingdon of darkness. "*The Acts of the Apostles*," extending through a period of over thirty years, though full of thrilling history, was not written merely as history, but the Holy Spirit evidently designed thus to illustrate the practical application and effects of Gospel principles, doctrines, and methods necessary to the salvation of the world.

Every fact, therefore, is an authoritative teaching fact, and every character portrayed, a representative character. Nearly the whole record of facts from the travels and labours of Barnabas and Paul and their coadjutors, authoritatively teach and illustrate God's own methods of spreading the Gospel. Whether in Jerusalem, at the great Pentecost, or subsequently in Antioch, Athens, Corinth, or Ephesus, and all other illustrative examples given us by St. Luke, the plan was to consecrate their most effective forces "daily," and thus they added daily to the Church such as were saved.

This is not at all in conflict with the ordinary methods of " exhortation, edification, and comfort," of believers, and individual efforts to win souls to Christ. The aggressive methods should not be allowed, in any degree, to supersede the ordinary means. Like the various departments of military warfare, they are so many essential parts of one great plan. The recruiting, daily drill, reconnoitering, and skirmishing are not to supersede the forward march of the grand army; nor are the victorious charges of the grand army to do away with these preliminary departments of the service. Special revival efforts to be sure, involve hazards, as all great movements do. When the " Church maketh increase of herself" by ordinary means only, the increase is principally of those who have been under training in her Sunday Schools and stated ministry, persons whose general moral character and associations would be a guarantee for their good behaviour as church members, whether they were truly converted to God or not. Whereas a special revival effort is like dragging the "great net," bringing up all sorts of fish, rendering it necessary to select " the good and throw the bad away," as the Saviour illustrates. On the other hand, I believe that nearly one-third of the converts in a great revival, were nominal members of the church at the time of their conversion. After many years of patient drilling and preparation in Southern Africa, we have recently tried this Gospel method of a daily " concentration of effort " for a few days together in different places. In every place there has been a hearty co-operation of ministers and people. God hath in every instance owned their labours, and crowned them with success, so that in Cape Colony, Kaffraria, and Natal, during the space of five months and twenty days, the ministers, on a personal examination of each case, with record of name and address, reported over 4,000 souls converted to God. (That turned out to be but the first gathering of the harvest as we went along, but the full returns a few weeks later, swelled the aggregate to about double that number). Over one thousand of these are whites, a large majority of natives under training on the mission-stations, with a good sprinkling of heathen. Probably one-fourth, or more, of the whole were nominal members of the church. On at least two of our large mission-stations, the missionaries say all their people are now converted, and hence such another harvest on the same field cannot soon be gathered; but with good drilling, these communities can make new aggressions into the regions beyond. The unsaved millions of this continent belong to the heritage of Jesus, and should be brought home to His fold. Plenty of work for everybody. Let every believer be always trying to save somebody. How shall we best conserve and extend this great work of God? I can only plead for a fair trial of the

APOSTOLIC PLAN

What is the ordinary mode of aggression beyond our base —the mission-stations? I believe it is to send out local preachers as pioneers among the heathen kraals every Sunday, with an occasional tour and periodical services by the missionary, when his unceasing pressing duties on the station allow it. After the labour of years, a little society is formed, composed, it may be, of a few superannuated old heathen women, and an old pauper man or two. This society, under the title of an "out-station," is to the surrounding heathen an exponent of Christianity, a representation to their minds of the work of the great God we tell them about, and but excites their scorn and contempt. We, however, pity their ignorance, and go on fostering this little society, till in the progress of years it grows to a respectable church, and a really good work is wrought and many souls saved, but the mass of its contemporaneous heathen have meantime gone down to perdition.

Now, instead of this plan, or rather in addition to it, in humble reliance on the broad charter of the Gospel and the power of the Holy Ghost, I would select a few of the best native preachers in the country.

We would go then into the principal centres of population, and pitch our tents, and by all legitimate means arrest the attention of the people, and "dispute with them daily," till the God of battles would give us 1,000 or 3,000 souls according to the extent of the available population. We would immediately organize a church, and establish good discipline, under an effective pastorate. From such a centre, under the influence of such an exhibition of the saving power of Jesus, we would send forth into the neighbouring kraals, Local preachers, and all sorts of lay agency, and give them healthy exercise and good vantage ground for winning souls. So soon as we should thus get the work in a new field thoroughly organized, we would strike our tents, and be off to another great centre of population, and so "speak that a great multitude would believe." By-and-by, Barnabas and Mark could go to Cyprus, while Paul, Silas, Timothy, and Luke should press their way into new and more extensive fields.

In praying the God of the harvest to send forth labourers into our new fields, whether as evangelists, pastors or teachers, we would expect that most of them would be Native Africans, who would gladly submit to the general superintendency of the white missionaries so long as the Providential necessity for such agency might exist.

This will lead us to consider the

KAFFIR STANDARD OF MINISTERIAL EDUCATION.

Nearly every Kaffir you meet is an orator. Their power as law pleaders is proverbial, and every Kaffir child speaks its language correctly. Rev. Mr. Appleyard, who has given to the Kaffirs the whole Bible in their own language, told me that he never heard a Kaffir make a grammatical blunder in speaking the Kaffir language. To teach a Kaffir Latin and Greek, to prepare him to preach to Kaffirs, in a language without a literature, is not only a waste of time, but is likely to remove him, in his feelings, modes of thought, and habits of life, so far above his people, as greatly to weaken their mutual sympathy, and in many ways increase the difficulty of his access to them. Of course we would not object to the multiplication of such men as Rev. Tyo Soga, but shall the car of salvation stand still and millions of heathen perish while we are waiting for the schools to turn out such agents as he?

When the tribes of Africa become Christianized and civilized they may require a high literary standard of ministerial education, and would also have the facilities and the men to use them. For the present, our Kaffir ministers should be able to read and write well in their own language; and, as far as practicable, to read and write the English. They should be holy men of God, called by the Holy Ghost to preach the Gospel,—men thoroughly instructed in our doctrines and discipline; men who, individually feel that "Woe is me if I preach not the Gospel," and who have "gifts, grace, and fruit"; men who will cheerfully consent to go anywhere, this side the gates of perdition, to save sinners—ever ready to preach or to die for Jesus.

WHERE ARE WE TO GET THE MONEY FOR SUCH A WORK?

Whenever we shall succeed by the renewing power of

the Holy Spirit, in getting "a great multitude" converted to God, we should say to them, "God designs you to be men, and not a set of children to be hanging on the coat-tail of some foreign 'umfundisi.' We will together thank God for sending missionaries over the sea to give you the Gospel, and we will always reverence and love them; but now that you have embraced the Gospel, God requires you to support and extend it. He hath given you land, grain, and cattle in abundance; He hath given you heads, and hearts, and hands; and now, through faith in Jesus, you have received the 'gift of eternal life.' Now you need a chapel, a preacher's house, and school-house, and God expects every one of you to help in this great work." We would at once show them the plans, and systematically organize them for the work. A little sweep was seen in a snow-storm running down a street in New York city. "Hallo, Jack! which way are you going?" "I'm going to the missionary meeting; I've a share in the concern; I gave a shilling to it last Sunday." Thus we would give every saved heathen "a share in the concern." Drawing them out of the channels of their heathenish habits, we would give them plenty of new and useful employment, and allow them no time for backsliding. We would thus make our infant churches self-sustaining from the start. St. Paul's new churches, among the heathen, were not only self-supporting, but gave liberally for the support of their poor widows, and for the poor Jews in Judea besides. In some cases, to be sure, St. Paul refused to receive a support for himself, but it was no doubt because he was establishing for the church God's own system of finance, and he would not leave a peg on which his slanderers might hang a suspicion that his grand financial scheme was for his own personal advantage. According to this system every one of them was expected to lay by in store—the first day of every week, according as the Lord had prospered them,—at least a tenth of their net income, with "free-will offerings" besides, according to God's ancient law for mankind, and to which the Jews of those days yielded ready obedience.

While we "have the poor with us," and while the Gospel is preached by men, this law will be necessary, and hence obligatory.

Our native ministers would not require more than one-fourth of what is necessary to support a foreign missionary. It would not be best to raise them above the people too fast, but to advance as fast as they could raise their people with them. We would promise our men plenty of hard work, hard fare, and a martyr's crown if they could fairly win it; and they would have an opportunity, no doubt. This brings to view a glimpse of the MORAL EFFECT of such a movement upon the church. Mr. Geo. Cato said to me the other day, "Why is it that the Gospel has so little effect upon the Mohammedans?" "Mohammedanism," I replied, "is so bitter in its opposition to Christianity, and has such a tenacious hold upon its devotees, that the mild conservative type of modern Christianity is not adequate to grapple successfully with such an organization of superstition and sin; nor indeed to gain very fast on heathenism, or successfully to resist the inroads of infidelity, and worldliness, even in Christian countries." I felt it to be a humiliating confession to have to make, but does not the logic of facts prove its truth. But let us have a healthy development of the essential aggressive spirit of the Gospel, carrying the "glad tidings" from city to city, and from country to country, according to the Gospel precedents adduced—now a chief or king converted to God, now an evangelist martyred, now a city conquered,—the sympathy, prayers, and co-operation of every Christian in the world would be freely invested in such an enterprise. Everybody would be inquiring daily about the progress of the great work of God in its grand march to the conquest of the world. We would have a living thing worthy of God and humanity, and adequate to its ends. Such a work would wake the heroic elements of man's nature. How they are brought out by the tocsin of war! Within the last five years, nearly a million of men have laid down their lives on the altar of patriotism. A low type of Christianity that does not enlist and employ the whole man, sinks down to a formal secondary thing with him, and the active elements of his nature are carried off into other channels of enterprise. The heroic power of man's nature, enlisted and sanctified by the Holy Spirit, is essentially the old martyr spirit, which kept the Gospel chariot moving in the olden time. What had Garibaldi ever to offer to his soldiers? But did he ever call in vain for an army of heroes ready to "do or die?" He knows how to arouse the heroic element of men's hearts.

Every passion and power of the human mind and heart should be sanctified by the Holy Spirit to the purposes for which they were designed. There is no field of enterprise to which the heroic element of our nature is better adapted, or more needed, than the great battlefield for souls, enlisting all the powers of hell on the one side, and all the powers of heaven on the other. What an heroic record the Gospels give of the labours, sufferings, death, and resurrection of the "Captain of our Salvation," and the noble army of martyrs trained under his personal ministry.

Give these Gospel methods of aggression a fair trial in Southern Africa. Hundreds of natives who have recently been converted to God can read and write, and we also have many native whites who are as well acquainted with the Kaffir language as with the English. With such resources, under continued and improved facilities of education, and the fostering care of our faithful missionaries, now in the field, the God of the harvest would doubtless raise up all the labourers the increasing demands of the work might require. The native agency already employed by our missionaries at Fort Peddie, Annshaw, Morley, and elsewhere, has been worked very satisfactorily, and the four native brethren just admitted as candidates for the ministry, promise great usefulness to the church.

Such a movement as we have described would, under the leading of the Holy Spirit, bring out hundreds of Africa's sons who would gladly share the greatest hazards of missionary life. They would not unnecessarily provoke persecution; would patiently endure it, or "flee from one city to another," if necessary, but if such should be manifestly the will of God, they would die for Jesus as cheerfully as the martyrs of the Apostolic age.

My convictions of the importance of this movement, and my desire to help my dear brethren in the full development of this plan in practical effect in Southern Africa, have so occupied my mind and heart, that for months past I have been praying to God, that if it were his will to adjust my family and Conference relations to this work, and call me to it, I would gladly spend and be spent in this great battle for African souls. I have, however, finally come to the conclusion that God designs the glorious work here to be carried on by others, and will employ me in the same work in some other part of the world.

If my fellow-labourer, Brother Charles Pamla, and a few others were set apart as were "Barnabas and Saul" for this work, and properly sustained in it, I believe the Holy Ghost would do a work through them that He could not so readily do through me.

Let this aggressive method, so fully illustrated in the Acts of the Apostles, be adopted and wisely worked throughout the world, and we would, under the Holy Ghost, develop a healthy heroic spirit of Christianity, which would throw off the incubus of unbelief and spiritual death against which it is struggling, and would enable her successfully to grapple with the insidious forms of worldliness and sin in Christian countries, with Mohammedanism and all forms of heathenism. Then the darkness would soon be past. The dismal cry, "Watchman, what of the night?" would be heard no more. Then we should see the mellow light of millennial glory reposing on the tops of the mountains. "The glory of the Lord would be revealed, and all flesh would see it together." The jubilant shout of the final victory of our all-conquering King would pass along the lines of the sacramental hosts, and be echoed back from every island, mountain, and continent, "Hallelujah! the Lord God omnipotent reigneth."

WM. TAYLOR.

Steam-ship *Mauritius*, off Cape of Good Hope, *October* 18*th*, 1866.

CHAPTER XXVII.

REVIEW OF THE WORK AND ITS PROGRESS TO THE PRESENT TIME.

"PAUL said unto Barnabas, Let us go again and visit our brethren in every city where we have preached the word of the Lord, and see how they do." Would that I could do the same in Africa! I will, however, take my dear reader to those places where I have "preached the word of the Lord," and we will learn from the brethren "how they do." From the most reliable sources I will respectfully submit statistics and facts, which will at least furnish an index to the manifest extent of the work of God in those fields during my sojourn in Africa, and up to the time of my departure; and although my limited space will not allow a review in consecutive order, I will select from a large amount of interesting matter in hand, a few miscellaneous facts, illustrative of the progress of the work to the present time.

Rev. Thomas Guard, in a letter dated November 14th, 1866, says :—

I have been to Somerset, to Queen's Town, and to Fort

Beaufort since your visit to those towns, so that I am able to give you the latest information respecting the progress of the work.

Last Tuesday was a thanksgiving day of our Church in this city (Graham's Town). Thanks for rain; thanks for payment of debt on our Chapel—£3,000; thanks for the grace of God in connection with your, ever to be remembered, visit—showers of rain, of gold, of grace, but the greatest of these is grace; and I am glad to assure you the grace abides. Classes, prayer-meetings, Sunday and weekday preaching services, all continue to evince the power and mercy of the God of Hosts. In Queen's Town nothing could be more delightful than the state of our Society, "in fellowship, breaking of bread, and prayers." I could see the change more clearly than you, as I had been there but a short time before your visit. Dugmore is in a most heavenly state of mind, and preaches with unwonted might and unction. In Beaufort Brother Wilson rejoices over the most prosperous and growing state of spiritual life. In Somerset, especially in the country, whither many who were converted in town carried back the flame, the good work triumphs, and finds in Brother Edwards an indefatigable overseer.

Cradock is remarkably advancing, every service adds souls to Christ; the town is all a-fire with zeal and love. Those brought to God in this city, with very few exceptions, stand fast in the faith. One or two young people, of whom we had some doubts, have gone aside; but we trust to see them reclaimed, or really converted. * * *

Annshaw heads the list as to the numbers saved during the season of refreshing.

Rev. Brother Lamplough, by letter, November 7th, 1866, says:—

Charles arrived at home all right, and very glad I was to see him again, though I am thankful to say I have got a first-rate interpreter, indeed, I think he surpasses Charles in that line, and is also a very powerful preacher, though in the latter work we have no one here to come up to Charles. I am very pleased that Charles went with you to Natal, and that you had such a glorious journey. It is truly wonderful to hear of all the wonders wrought by the Lord among the heathen in so short a time. * * You will be pleased to hear that the work still continues to progress in this circuit. I have lost count almost of numbers; but at least 1,200 profess to have found peace with God on this circuit, and there seems every reason to believe that we shall have a fresh ingathering on a large scale, soon. The best of it is, our men are beginning to work so beautifully, and if they only keep up to the mark, as they are at present, I see no reason why the work should not continue to go on. The clear experience of those who, until just lately, were heathen, and the wonderful way in which the little children speak about the things of God is most astonishing. The last quarterly visitation for tickets, was one of the most delightful seasons I have ever experienced.

For purposes of mutual edification and Christian fellowship, all the members of the Wesleyan societies are divided into classes, to be met weekly by a leader, who is a sub-pastor, and quarterly by the minister.

Brother Lamplough, in a more recent letter, speaking of the effect of the revival on the "Native Helpers," says:—

A young Kaffir, a candidate for the ministry, has been greatly owned of God in the conversion of about 300 souls the past year. Another, an elderly man, who can do but little more than read a hymn, has also been very useful among the red heathen. His method is as follows: Having selected a particular village, he spends about a week in earnest importunate prayer for that village, sometimes rising in the middle of the night, and going into the chapel to wrestle for the souls of the heathen, until he has confidence that souls will be given him. He then sets forth, taking with him a few earnest men to help him to sing, pray, and exhort; and after continuing thus to labour for some days, employing the time between the services in visiting the heathen in their huts, he calls for those who are awakened by the Spirit, under the preaching, to come and bow down in prayer as seekers, and very soon he is surrounded by weeping penitents, who are soon changed into happy believers. The believers and penitents are then brought to the station, where special prayer-meetings are held until all are enabled to rejoice in God. One day I heard the sound of joyful singing, and looking up I saw a sort of triumphal procession coming over the hill. In front was one of our leaders, carrying on a long stick a number of heathen ornaments; behind him were about a dozen heathen who had torn off their ornaments, some were weeping bitterly, and others manifesting joy and gladness; behind them were other leaders and members, to the number of about twenty, who, as they came to the station, were singing a hymn of triumph. It seemed like a miniature representation of the last time, when "the mountain of the Lord's house shall be established in the tops of the mountains, and all nations shall flow into it." I must not dwell on this subject. I may just say that the greatest blessing in connection with your visit amongst us, was the wonderful effect it had on our *Native Helpers*. They became new men, and not only displayed remarkable zeal in working for souls, but much wisdom in winning them to Christ. Your coming seemed to be like a new life opening before our native labourers; they became, not only more willing to go forth to work for Christ, but were taught how to do it successfully. Even the new converts at once go to work for God, with success. A heathen man, in the midst of a large village of red people (wild heathen, painted with red ochre), after his conversion, stood up and declared that God's word was true, and told the people what he felt. He then proceeded to address them in a most wonderful way, and the power of the Holy Ghost was so remarkably manifested, that it seemed that the whole village was moved. I might tell you of many heathen men, who have given up their plurality of wives, and retained only their first; but these things we expect, and therefore they have not produced much impression on our minds."

The old veteran missionary, Rev. Mr. Shepstone, chairman of the Queen's Town district, writes under date, May 1st, 1867, saying :—

"You will be glad to learn that the work of God which you saw begun here on this station, as well as on the others, where we had the satisfaction of seeing such blessed results of your labours, did not die with your departure, nor diminish in your absence—we added more in number on this station after you left, than we had done while you were with us—some, after public service came forward and voluntarily confessed their sins before all. One woman after confessing various sins, said, 'it was I who stole the thatch that was to have thatched the school-house.' This woman was a thorough heathen, living about seven miles from the station. A man near the same place, was putting on his European clothes, when his wife, a heathen, saw him, and asked 'Where are you going?' 'To the chapel service,' was the reply. ' *Take them off! take them off!* don't you know they catch everybody? You will be caught. Take them off!' And he did, and he has not been caught yet! But many more have—many have been known to run out of the service, simply because, as they confessed, that had they remained, they must have yielded to the convictions that came upon them.

Some have been beaten, some have been tied fast to the posts of their houses by persecuting heathen husbands that they might not attend the means of grace, and in one instance, the poor woman has yielded for the present. Others have persecuted their children and succeeded in keeping them back; whilst others have been bold as champions for the truth, and though young, their Christian courage is delightful.

At one place, about seven miles from us, there were two young girls, of about the age of sixteen years, two cousins, daughters of a head man and his brother. These were converted while you were here, but having been found praying in the mountain together by the father's younger brother, the father told them he would have no praying in his family, none had ever prayed, and he would not allow it. If they would persist, they should leave the place, which they did and came to me. I sent for the head man to know the truth. He denied any knowledge of the girls having been driven from their homes, and promised to allow his daughter full liberty of action. He was as good as his word—she returned home with her father, and a few days afterwards, the old chief bought her proper clothing to attend God's house. The other being the daughter of the most insolent opposer, refused to return with her uncle until he had come down and seen me—I sent for him to ask him how it was his daughter was a wanderer. He of course denied the persecution. I had a fine opportunity of giving him a personal sermon, and inviting him to the mercy of God.

The old grey-headed polygamist, promised the same liberty, and both have ever since I believe been growing in grace—besides that they have been instruments in bringing nearly twenty other young people at the same river, to embrace the Gospel of salvation. But the old heathen parents, have by one stratagem or another, succeeded in keeping back the greater part, or sending them away to heathen friends at a distance. Still the word of God is not bound."

Another venerable old missionary, Rev. J. Cameron, Chairman of Natal district, writes as follows:

The Lord made you an instrument of much good to many souls in this country, and the memory of your visit, will be cherished with delight.

The work which began in D'Urban when you were here is still going on, though with less outward demonstration, than under your personal ministrations. The new converts, I am thankful to say, with but few exceptions, are progressing in divine life. All the means of grace are well attended, and characterized by much of the unction from the Holy One. The noon-day prayer-meeting, in the Chapel, is still kept up, though the attendance is not so large as formerly. Those who do attend, can generally say, "Master, it is good for us to be here." We have a fortnightly public band-meeting, which has proved a great blessing, especially to our young people, many of whom bear delightful testimony to the fact of their continued interest in Jesus. Some of the young men who speak the Kaffir language, manifest great zeal for the salvation of the Kaffirs. We have put some half-dozen on the plan, as Kaffir exhorters, and they are going on with their work. Bro. Langley has engaged to meet them once a week for the purpose of giving them special instruction as to the best modes of getting and communicating knowledge. Still, with all our precious means and appliances, we need much larger baptisms of the Holy Ghost, which we hope will be vouchsafed to us. Instead of twos and threes occasionally crying for salvation, we want to hear crowds doing so every time we meet. We have much agonising prayer for this, and much faith too, which I am persuaded cannot be in vain. In Kaffir land we mean to adopt more strenuous measures for the conversion of the heathen, and are only waiting for the sanction of our Home Missionary Committee to a plan for this purpose submitted for their consideration. The plan agrees with your views, so far as the agency we can command will allow, and if carried out successfully, will encourage us to do something on a larger scale, by-and-by.

Rev. Ralph Stott, the indefatigable old Indian missionary, who is now in charge of the 7,000 Coolies in Natal, says of the work in D'Urban, by letter in *Wesleyan Missionary Notices*, for February, 1867,

I have been in several revivals within the last 45 years, in connection with David Stoner, Thomas Walker, Joseph Wood, Messrs. Palmer, and in Batticaloa, and have often seen glorious results, but was never in a revival which pleased me so well.   *   *   *   *   *

Numbers who have been converted in this revival are now, under the influence of the love of God shed abroad in their hearts, working for God both amongst the English and Kaffirs, and thus new centres of light and influence, and power, are established in the land, which will in time tell on thousands beyond. Many young Englishmen have

Kaffir tongues, and renewed hearts, and they are using both for God. I wish some of them had Tamil and Hindustani tongues.

Rev. Richard Hayes, Jun. minister in Pietermaritzberg, writing for the *Missionary Notices* for January, 1867, says of the work there :—

At Pietermaritzberg the members of society have been strengthened and established in the faith, and not a few have been added unto the Lord. The good work has gradually advanced: none have fallen away, and a good many have been added since Mr. Taylor left us. The simple but clear and scriptural narrations of conversion, to which we have listened, and the evidences of fruit in the life, have produced the conviction that the work among those newly converted has been genuine.

Rev. H. S. Barton, superintendent of Verulam Circuit, writes for the March number of *Missionary Notices,* saying :—

As before, so since Mr. Taylor left, the work has been going on, so that at our last Quarterly Meeting, we were enabled to report a hundred and six English, and a hundred and ninety-five natives, on trial, being almost as many as our present members. We have taken one new English preaching-place on the plan, and five native places, with three English young men on trial as Local Preachers; and nine young men, English and native, to engage in native work. My heart does indeed rejoice in the Lord's work; and I feel I can heartily bless God for bringing men so devoted to His work for a time into our neighbourhood. The success is more marvellous when the spareness of the population is considered.

As the greater part of my work in Africa was in the Eastern Province of Cape Colony and Kaffraria, principally in the Graham's Town and Queen's Town Mission Districts, I will extract from the annual Report of the Wesleyan Missionary Society a tabular view of those two districts, which will furnish a statistical index to the late work of God, and also furnish an illustrative specimen of the working appliances of Wesleyan Missions.

TABULAR VIEW OF THE GRAHAM'S TOWN DISTRICT.

CENTRAL OR PRINCIPAL STATIONS OR CIRCUITS.	Number of Chapels	Number of other Preaching-Places	Missionaries and Assistant ditto	Catechists, &c.	Day-School Teachers	Sabbath-School Teachers	Local Preachers	Number of Full and Accredited Church Members	Increase	On Trial for Membership	Number of Sabbath Schools	Number of Sabbath Scholars of both Sexes	Number of Day-Schools	Number of Day-Scholars of both Sexes	No. of Attendants on Public Worship, including Teachers and Scholars
1. Graham's Town (1st)	6	7	4	—	1	58	11	461	158	6	5	355	1	49	2,500
2. Graham's Town (2nd)	3	8	1	3	1	30	11	298	110	119	2	385	1	184	800
3. Salem and Farmerfield	5	1	1	1	2	16	7	310	128	96	2	193	2	109	1,000
4. Bathurst	4	2	1	—	2	27	6	162	16	11	6	266	2	52	870
5. Fort-Beaufort	5	5	1	—	—	25	8	201	73	74	5	279	—	—	600
6. Heald Town	3	6	1	1	5	39	20	318	20	358	4	386	4	489	1,500
7. Port Elizabeth	2	4	1	—	4	56	8	209	42	99	4	543	3	186	850
8. Uitenhage	1	1	1	—	—	12	1	58	12	17	1	81	—	—	300
9. Cradock	3	12	2	—	—	36	5	335	126	130	3	280	—	—	1,500
10. Somerset, East	3	9	1	1	—	19	1	312	108	49	2	186	—	—	960
11. Peddie and Newton Dale Decrease 120	10	27	1	1	10	59	34	567		397	10	738	9	473	2,500
12. King William's Town	5	12	1	1	5	35	21	505	39	189	3	581	5	251	1,850
13. Mount Coke	2	3	1	—	4	19	14	142	2	138	4	245	3	199	800
14. Annshaw	8	46	2	4	6	40	44	810	196	736	13	666	6	218	3,300
Totals	60	143	19	12	40	471	191	4,488	1030 Minus 120	2,419	64	5,192	36	2,210	20,530

TABULAR VIEW OF THE QUEEN'S TOWN DISTRICT.

CENTRAL OR PRINCIPAL STATIONS OR CIRCUITS.	Number of Chapels	Number of other Preaching-Places	Missionaries and Assistant ditto	Catechists, &c.	Day-School Teachers	Sabbath School Teachers	Local Preachers	Number of Full and Accredited Church Members	Increase	On Trial for Membership	Number of Sabbath Schools	Number of Sabbath-Scholars of both sexes	Number of Day-Schools	Number of Day-Scholars of both Sexes	No. of Attendants on Public Worship, including Members and Scholars
1. Queen's Town	3	5	2	—	—	26	4	201	120	34	3	223	—	—	1,000
2. Kamastone	1	5	1	1	5	7	7	465	249	31	1	118	5	236	1,000
3. Lesseyton	—	5	—	—	1	7	} 5	343	171	88	} 4	100	1	82	2,300
4. Mount Arthur	—	—	1	—	—	—		139	—	2		—	—	—	—
5. Isokebeni	—	—	—	—	—	—	—	64	—	17	—	—	—	—	—
6. Isomo	1	28	1	3	1	—	21	71	139	59	4	184	1	146	2,000
7. Butterworth	1	19	1	2	1	12	18	251	122	246	2	116	1	87	2,500
8. Clarkebury	2	4	1	2	2	10	10	237	145	204	2	210	2	165	2,000
9. Morley	1	10	1	1	1	5	6	230	25	65	2	120	1	45	1,000
10. Buntingville	1	5	1	—	1	6	3	64	—	5	1	100	1	65	1,000
11. Shawbury	1	3	1	—	1	5	7	92	—	181	1	114	1	105	1,000
12. Osborn	—	—	—	—	—	—	—	97	7	205	—	—	—	—	1,000
Totals	11	84	10	9	13	78	81	2,244	978	1,137	20	1,285	13	931	13,500

An egotistic display of numbers, even of a work of God, is abhorrent to any person of common sense, but an occasional judicious representation of facts is due to the credit of God's work, and a means of stimulating the faith of His workers. We could have formed no appreciative idea of the Holy Spirit's great Pentecostal work in Jerusalem if St. Luke had not said, "Then they that gladly received his word were baptized: and the same day there were added unto them about three thousand souls." In regard to the further statistical exhibit I propose to make for the glory of God, I may remark, I never number the converts myself, but note the numbers if furnished to me by the ministers, who personally examine them and record their names and addresses; their examination by the pastors is to assure themselves that the persons professing to find peace with God can give satisfactory testimony to a real change of heart from the witness and renewing work of the Holy Spirit. If their testimony is clear, their names and addresses are recorded for the purpose, not of numbering simply, but of putting them definitely under pastoral care and training.

The six thousand and upwards, before mentioned, as having been examined and reported saved at my services in Australia, New Zealand and Tasmania, embraced simply those professing to find peace with God at my immediate services, but this African exhibit will embrace not only those saved immediately at my meetings, but those also saved in the districts in which I laboured simultaneously with my services during the period of seven months. The annual returns in Wesleyan Missions there are made in the month of September, so the returns would embrace the first fruits of our series, who, having fulfilled a three months' probation (six months with American Methodists), are returned as members under the head of "increase," but the majority were "on trial," not having had time to fulfil their period of probation; and the fruits of D'Urban and Verulam in Natal, and four weeks' subsequent labour in Cape Town District were after September, and, hence do not appear in the "annual report." It will be seen from the foregoing tables that the net increase in those two districts was 1,888 members, 3,556 remaining on trial, making an aggregate of 5,444. In Natal there were of natives who professed to obtain peace with God 735, whites, 320; of natives at Emfundisweni, over 150, making an aggregate of 1,205; to these may be added over 200 in Cape Town District, making a total of 6,849 souls duly examined and reported from without. Then in the societies, besides the great quickening of believers in many places fully one quarter of the regular seekers and converts were at the same time Church members. About 250 such were among the Annshaw converts, and about 200 Brother Sargent reported at Heald Town, and a similar proportion, so far as we could learn, in all other places; but if we put the proportionate number of converts among the previously enrolled members in the Graham's Town and Queen's Town districts at one-fifth instead of one-fourth, it will add 1,088 to the list of converts in those two districts. Besides these, Brother Edwards at Somerset says, many of our converts belonged to other organizations there, " and were lost to us, but not to God." Brother Shepstone writes that the fire spread into other denominations, and at Kat River, 300 were added to the Church ; at Hankey, 150 ; and so in many other places the work spread out from the centres in which our meetings were held; but not counting any of these—not being personally examined and reported by our regular missionaries, though all saved we hope—by adding the 1,088 aforesaid, we have a grand total brought to God within the space of seven months of 7,937 souls. Of these, about 1,200 were Colonists, and the remainder Kaffirs. Glory be to God! Amen!

Now for a few facts illustrating the genuineness and continued progress of the work, and the multiplication and increased effectiveness of the workers.

INDICATIONS OF PROGRESS IN KAFFRARIA.

Rev. Peter Hargraves writes concerning this work in Clarkebury under date of May 1867, ten months after my departure, as follows :

Here we have abundant cause to remember your visit and to feel grateful for the " showers of blessings " which accompanied and followed your faithful and zealous labours amongst us. We are not the same people, the Mission Station is not the same. Grace has wrought a great and blessed change in the moral and mental habits of the people around us.

The blessed revival of religion did not cease when you left us. It continued, and continues even to this day. When it commenced there were scarcely one hundred persons meeting in class, and but few of these could give a satisfactory testimony of their conversion to God. Most of them were formalists, and believed the class to be the means and end of salvation. Now, blessed be the name of God, there are more than four hundred and sixty persons in society with us.

Testimonies to the change wrought in the moral habits of the people have come from all quarters. Some time back a counsellor of Ngangelizwe was on the station for two or three days, and on leaving he told one of the traders that Clarkebury used to be like a large canteen, but during this visit he had not been able to get any beer or find any beer drinkers. The Chief visited and remained with us two days. When leaving, he took my hand and said, "I believe in this people now, they serve God in truth." Testimonies like the above might be multiplied to any number.

This blessed work has not been circumscribed by the boundaries of the station, but has affected and influenced many heathen families residing miles beyond the station. At one kraal, under a head man named "Pelshana," we have had between twenty and thirty conversions. At another kraal in the "Bololwa" we have been able to form a class of ten members. At the Cwecweni the number in society has risen from eight to twenty-eight. At Kubi's kraal we have a society of nearly forty members. At the present time we have societies in the different places beyond the limits of the station, composed of more than one hundred and twenty members.

"I enclose you a late plan of our preaching appointments, and though it does not show all our labours—it will prove that we are beginning to do something in the way of carrying the Gospel of Christ to the heathen around us. Our present plan has on it the names of twenty-seven Local Preachers, and twenty-one places where services are held every Sabbath, and occasionally on the week days.

I meet the Leaders and Local Preachers every Friday, when we read over the appointments for the coming Sabbath, and then each leader reports the state of his class.

I must say but little of our chief. We have services at his place every Sabbath. The attendance is good, but we see little or no effect. The chief himself has given us great trouble during the last few months. We have had great contentions. It is only within the last few days that the chiefs of the tribe have refused his unjust decisions and done us all the justice we claimed.

H. B. Warner, who was saved at our Clarkebury series of meetings, has gone forth, and continues preaching to the Kaffirs with great success. The Clarkebury Mission is now spread out among the heathen, embracing eighteen different preaching-places, filled by twenty-eight different preachers, belonging to the circuit. Rev. P. Hargraves, the missionary, at the head; W. S. Davis, who translated "The Eden above," second; H. B. Warner third; and then the native force of Local Preachers.

Brother Warner has recently written me a brief history of his rebellious life against God, his conversion, and subsequent experiences, which I would gladly insert if my space would permit. The first leading instrument of Satan, by which he was led into wicked association with the heathen, was the "pipe," and it was the last thing he surrendered in his penitential struggle before accepting Christ. He says it is a sign and leading means, to the most sinful vices of heathen Kaffirs, and while he would not judge any Christians uncharitably for using it, nevertheless, if Christian laymen and ministers in Africa could appreciate what he knows of the significance and diabolic use of the pipe among the heathen, they would abandon it at once and for ever. Rev. W. B. Rayner writes me that 100 heathens, under H. B. Warner, have been converted to God.

Rayner has been removed from Morley to the *Tsomo*, and lives at the old military station, where we dined with Colonel Barker. There was no society there then; but now Brother Rayner writes me he has a large circuit there, with 170 church members, and daily increasing.

Rev. T. Jenkins writes from Emfundisweni, in April, 1867, nine months after our departure, saying :—

We rejoice over the souls brought to God when you were here, as those who have found great spoil. Heathenism then received a great shock, and a few more would make the powers of darkness tremble to their foundation. A few days ago some of the converted women, residing about ten miles off, were here, and in conversation with Mrs. Jenkins, said, "Before the word of God came to our hearts we lived like beasts, we scarcely knew that we belonged to human kind; but now we know that we are the children of God." Nothing but the grace of God would induce such people, who never attended the house of worship, to come as they do now, ten, fifteen, and twenty miles to our Sabbath services. "It is the Lord's doing, and marvellous in our sight."

The work in Natal is progressing quietly, but steadily, aggressively, successfully, especially among the natives. The new workers, who know the Kaffir language, are owned of God in their work.

When I was in Palmerton, Rev. Mr. Allsopp, the missionary who came from Verulam, Natal, the preceding year, received a letter from a young native interpreter at Verulam, saying that the Quarterly Meeting proposed to employ him for twenty years as interpreter for the missionaries, and hesitating to make so long an engagement, he wanted to consult his old pastor. I said to Allsopp, "You will see that God will raise up so many native preachers, that long before twenty years shall pass, you will scarcely hear of such a thing as an interpreter in the country."

An extract from a letter, written by my host, Mr. Thomas Garland of Verulam, will illustrate the expansion of the work in that direction.

My nephew, John William Stranack, is one of the most complete *conversions* I ever witnessed, or anybody else *here* ever knew; he has been working in the Sabbath-school, going out to *country places* to hold *prayer-meetings*, and is on our plan on trial as a Local Preacher. Everywhere, so far, the people are more than pleased with his sermons; their literary worth is much beyond the ordinary productions of young men. You may look for his name amongst the itinerant lists in a year or two, so I believe, for he has talents, and they are all now dedicated to God and His cause on earth.

F. B. Fynney continues faithful, and has laid himself out to work for God, and is anxious to be a missionary. I am sure this young man is called to preach. The success that marks his labours everywhere are in proof of that, and to this I attribute the terrible mauling the devil sometimes gives him. He is naturally impetuous, and this with other difficulties has given him trouble, but he is braving the storm manfully.

Fynney, young Campbell, and Blainey, started off on a tour to Zulu country, intending to visit Ketchwayo, the ruling Prince of that land, and they got nearly to the place of his residence, but he had gone away to be absent for some weeks; but they held services every day with the Kaffirs, and everywhere good was done. They met with one young man, a Kaffir, who had left our station here and forsaken God. Fynney asked him how it was he left following Jesus. "Well," said he, "I was on your side of the river long while, and was very happy; but looking over to the side I am now on, I saw lots of *shining white stones*, and I wanted to be rich; so I said, that's the place, I leave *this side* and go there. I came and found ah, *alligators*, and I am now being *devoured*. What a fool I was." "But," said Fynney, "why not go back?" "Well, but I cannot." "Why not?" "The river is deep, and when I get over who will care for me." "Why, don't you see Jesus standing there waiting for you?" "Oh, no, He won't love me again." "But look, there He stands." "Well, I can't see Him, and I cannot get over the river; to make the attempt is to be lost; I must *die* where I am." "Well, if you had a boat, would you go?" "Well, yes; oh, yes." "Then see, here is a boat;" a promise of God's word was given. "Well, I cannot row, I want *oars*."—Some more truth was furnished from God's record. "No," said the man, "I don't believe it's any use; I don't believe Jesus is there; I must give it up." Fynney prayed with him that night, and they had a prayer-meeting. Next morning it was very cloudy and wet. About eleven o'clock Fynney met this same man. "Good-morning, Jonas," "Sacaboni umgane." "Well, where is the sun, Jonas?" "Oh, there, overhead." "Oh no, Jonas, sun is not up yet." "Not up?" said Jonas. Yes it is. I tell you 'tis up there." "Well, Jonas, you must be cheating me. I cannot see the sun, and yet you say it's there; must I believe it, Jonas?" "To be sure you must," said Jonas, "if you are not a fool you will." "Well, I do, Jonas, believe it.—Jonas, can you believe Jesus waits on the other side to receive you?" Jonas hung down his head, covered his face with his hand a moment, then said, "I see it; I see it; I will pull, I will cross. I believe everything; I'll go to Jesus, He will save me." And he did it, and was saved, and was "shouting happy."

At the same place Fynney was preaching, discussing the theory of *snake transmigration*, in which they believe. When he suggested that it would be well for all who really believed they should become snakes hereafter, just to practice it a little, and get ready to move amongst the snake fraternity, and asked all such believers just to have a trial of moving on their bellies, down this grassy hill near by; and this simple touch of the ludicrous did more than an hour's argument; they gave a unanimous vote that day, that they did not and would not believe in snakes.

At several places the natives crowded round this band, and implored them to stay and preach again, and repeated this request till Fynney was left alone, not getting home till eight or nine days after the others, and *everywhere* many of those poor dark, uneducated men received the Gospel, and were made happy. At the American Mission

Station, under the Rev. A. Grout, the people sent a request to their minister, that Mr. Fynney should preach to them as he passed, and though it was the middle of a working day, all left their work, and the chapel, holding 500 people, was comfortably filled; and then, outside for two hours, Fynney discussed the way of salvation, the people weeping, and begging him to stay longer. Mr. Grout thanked him heartily, and invited him to come at any time to preach. Fynney has spent much of his time at Verulam with Mr. Kirkby, and a great many of the natives have been brought in. We have now, in addition to those above named, Mr. Hill, Foss, and Daddy, living in Verulam, all, especially Hill, who has traded in Zulu-land for years, are well acquainted with the Zulu language. Hill is a reclaimed backslider; a very determined character, of good practical sense. These have engaged to preach to Kaffirs, and on our plan is a list of places to which they go regularly every Sabbath; so that we have, what we now call, our *Kaffir band*, numbering nine, in all, in our circuit, and it is to the Kaffir kraals they go; an agency is thus commenced for carrying salvation to this people, such as we have never seen before. Other young men are studying the native tongue, anxious to be of this *band* of evangelists. I have realized, in a degree I never did before, the purpose of God in bringing *us* to this land. Since these young men have set to work thus to spread the Gospel, I feel it is enough to compensate for being here, if nothing more was accomplished, thus to see the beginning of God's purpose developed in this manner.

At Umhlali we had three members when you came to Verulam. Eight or ten persons from there, came and heard you, were saved, went back and told what God had done for them, and the work of the Lord *began* to spread. We had the new chapel opened there just four weeks after you left, and a large party of us went; we had public meetings, anthems, and speeches. I was called to take the chair. Mr. Barton and Kirkby were there. I wanted it to be a salvation meeting, and spoke accordingly. Messrs. Barton, Kirby, and Tyler (American missionary), all threw their prepared speeches to the wind, and spoke to the point, the power of the Lord came down. An altar of prayer was formed, eight or ten persons came forward; amongst them, Mr. Tyler's son, a young man of seventeen years old. The whole community seemed moved with deep concern about their souls. Mr. Kirkby remained, and held a series of services every night, and now we have two classes, numbering altogether thirty-six members, and a chapel filled every Sabbath, large Sabbath-school, and week-day services, just the same as in Verulam.

One man there, an old Local Preacher from Bristol, was nearly ready to drop into hell through strong drink. I have often warned him, and the Holy Spirit has striven with him again and again; but he seemed bent on his own destruction for time and eternity. I wrote and urged him to come and hear you in Verulam, but he did not; but some of my words in that letter troubled him, and he was among those brought in with his wife and two sons at Umhlali—a clever man—but sin has nearly unfitted him for service in God's cause. He has, of course, also taken the pledge of teetotalism, and so the work goes on, and many are added to the church, such as are saved by faith in Jesus.

Rev. Charles Harmon, junior minister at D'Urban, Natal, writes for the *Missionary Notices* for October, 1867, saying:—

I rejoice to be able to inform you that the work of God

is still progressing in our midst. Those who prophesied speedy reaction, and foretold disgraceful declension of professed converts, have been disappointed. With very few exceptions, those who professed to find salvation are giving the best proof of its possession, a consistent godly life. The Kaffir-speaking young men who were brought to God at the revival of last year, and who at once went to work among the heathen, are still gladly and diligently doing the work of evangelists.

Rev. Thomas Kirkby, junior missionary in Verulam, writing for the *Missionary Notices*, for June, 1867, says : "In the native work generally, we are progressing. In the English Circuits the Lord has triumphed gloriously, and is still showing that He is above men, devils, and sin. He is converting men who have been down to the gates of hell."

Some of the converts have died in the Lord. Rev. T. Kirkby, in a letter published in the *Missionary Notices*, for September, 1867, gives the following interesting account of the death scene of a Christian Zulu girl, who was brought from heathendom to the mission-station to die :—

When she arrived on the station, there was only a faint hope held out to her of the possibility of her recovery, and when told about a week after this that she must die, "O," she said, "I am not afraid. I have been ready many days." It was about ten days afterwards that she departed. About midnight, when all but the sick girl were fast asleep, a sound stole across to the ears of the sleepers who were near her, a sound which came from the dying girl, as she talked with the Invisible. She was praying the last prayer, and these were some of the words that the waking listeners heard: "O Lord, come and meet me!" One of the women asked her if she needed anything. She told her to call her father, and then told him to pray for her; and when he had given expression to his desires for his child's safety, he asked her how she felt in prospect of death. "O," she said, "it is all right now! God is with me! I am safe!" and then came the last struggle. Lying on a mat in the low room, open to the roof, with her head upon her mother's breast, and her feet almost touching the blazing fire that was on the floor in the middle of the room, she said, "Put my feet nearer to the fire, I am so cold." Ah! poor child, the fire could not give her poor body warmth; already she was in the cold river of death, and the water was deep, but He was there. Feeling anxious to leave a clear testimony, as well as to do what good she could, she said, " Give me a little water, that I may speak a little more. God may help me to say that which may do good." The father then called to a neighbour, and said, " Come, and hear my child; she is going to God. He has come to meet her." The end was near; and so to her was the heaven side of Jordan. Fixing her eye on something she appeared to see approaching, she slowly breathed out, " The wagon is coming to—to —fetch me;" and with a last effort she said, " It is here!" These were her last words.

In the Queen's Town District we have very encouraging reports of progress. Brother Dugmore, however, says a few about Queen's Town have fallen away, but the mass of the converts stand firmly.

A few incidents and facts may suffice to illustrate the onward movement in Graham's Town District, and finish my task. W. A. Richards writes from Graham's Town in April 1867, ten months after my departure, "We are not having many conversions in our church just now, but the members are earnest in seeking higher spiritual blessing, some have grown colder, and one or two have backslidden. But why should we not make inroads on Satan's kingdom, now as well as when you were here? We have the ever-present Lord Jesus with us, and He it is who works. The fault must be in us, " Oh that the church would purge herself from dead works."

Rev. W. J. Davis writing me from Graham's Town, under date June 13th, 1867, a year after my services there, says:—

You will rejoice to hear of the prosperity of our work here. The Lord is still working among us, and many souls are being saved. We have had this month a series of special services in all the circuits in the district, which we intend to hold each succeeding year in commemoration of your visit here last year. It was so much blessed to us all as ministers, and resulted in so much good to our people. In the services just held, many hundreds have been converted, and our societies have been greatly blessed and revived. I have a letter from Brother Charles Pamla, who is in the Peddie Circuit, in which he tells me of more than two hundred being added to the church there during the special services. I have faith to believe that the whole of Kaffirland shall soon stretch out her hands unto God. It is the greatest happiness of my life to have been spared to see this work of God. Thirty-five years ago I began to "go forth weeping," bearing indeed " precious seed," but almost despairing of ever seeing that seed produce so glorious a harvest; but now I return rejoicing, bringing my sheaves with me. 'Tis worth living for this."

Rev. Robert Lamplough, who has been for six years at Annshaw, and who now is labouring at Heald Town writes under date July 10th, 1867, saying; "The work here is not very satisfactory at present; we have some conversions but we want the power of the Holy Ghost. Nearly 300 profess to have found peace since we came here, but the work is not what I should like to see it. I very much miss my efficient Native helpers at Annshaw. The people here have not been trained to work, though I hope they are getting into the way. Siko Radas went to Somerset the other week and had thirty-three souls brought to God, under his preaching." Siko has commenced preaching since he went with me as interpreter at Somerset and Cradock, and is preparing for the regular ministry. The Lord bless him, and give him wisdom to win souls to Christ. Brother Lamplough had only been in Heald Town five months, and had about 300 souls saved in that time, but was not satisfied. In his official report from Annshaw, for 1865, he says: "This Circuit has prospered spiritually during the year. Discipline has been beneficially exercised. Conversions have resulted in several instances. The officers of the Church have been much quickened. The three Evangelists referred to last year (1864) have been diligently employed in preaching at the heathen kraals during the greater part of the year. There is reason to believe that, partly through their efforts, one or two conversions have taken place amongst the heathen, and in other respects their labours have been attended with much good."

Last year he had 1,200 conversions in Annshaw Circuit, and now looking at the resources of the Gospel, available for the salvation of all Africa and the world, with his heart of love for precious souls attuned to the loving heart of Jesus, to spend five months in getting 300 souls saved is a disappointing business to my dear Brother Lamplough.

Charles Pamla was appointed Junior Minister at Fort Peddie Circuit, and lives at Newtondale. At his first service he had the two wives of a leading chief, converted to God, with a number of others. The following extract of a letter I recently received from him, gives a very brief notice of what an affair it lead to with the chief:—

I have no time to tell you all the facts, but must tell you about the conversion of the Chief Maxwayana. His two wives came to the meeting the first Sunday I preached at Newtondale, and were both converted, to the astonishment of both heathen and Christians. But God showed that His Gospel has all the power to save the worst of sinners. Some heathen thought they were mad. Their husband was not at home. When he came home he wanted to bring a case against me about his second wife, because now she was converted, she refused to live with him. But his elder wife and two friends persuaded him to come to the service himself, and he was converted, with many other heathen. Such is the power of the Word of God here at present.

Some of my friends think I shall spoil Charles Pamla, by telling the whole truth about him, but I know my man, and he is blessed with a sick wife, and plenty of jealous friends, and bitter enemies, all of whom the Holy Spirit will turn to good account, for the development of his patience, meekness, and humility.

Brother Lamplough, writes me again as late as August 7th, 1867, as follows:—

Heald Town,
7th August, 1867.

My dear Brother,

I enclose a letter from Charles Pamla, who has been spending some eight or nine days with us at Heald Town, conducting special services. We have had some very good seasons, and about sixty souls have professed to enter into the enjoyment of salvation. The results would have been much greater, had not the revival services been interfered with by missionary anniversaries here and at Fort Beaufort, which took up half the time of Charles's visit.

I was very much pleased with Charles; he is still as earnest and devoted as ever, and is, doubtless, a chosen instrument for accomplishing great good in South Africa. I believe some six or seven hundred have been brought to God since he went to Peddie last March, and the work is still going on.

The Church here has been much quickened and blessed through Brother Pamla's visit, and if we can only get our leaders and members into a better state, I have no doubt we shall soon see a glorious work at Heald Town. Kaffir beer is all but done away with, as well as other heathen customs, which is no little thing.

As a closing illustration of the progress of the work of God, and of His workers in South Africa, I will insert a letter from my Brother, Charles Pamla:—

Newtondale, July 18th, 1867.

* * * I will tell you the great objections the heathen have been making against the work of God and against me.

First objection:—This man is trying to get all our people converted so as to get lots of tickets and class-money, and also to increase his salary from the white men, and become the richest native in Africa. We will not go near him to be converted by him and increase his salary.

Second objection:—This man, Pamla, got some poison from that white who took him to Port Natal. He carries it in a black bag. He calls the foolish people to come to him and kneel down, so as to get at them and poison them, and then they become more foolish, and believe that they have been converted, when they are not. 'Tis not the work of God, for we never saw such a work before. If it is the work of God why did not the other ministers, who have been labouring amongst us before, do such things? We never saw so many people converted amongst us heathen before.

Third objection, based on a false report:—A stranger, from Annshaw Circuit, who is a heathen, told the heathen round here, "This is the very man who was removed from Annshaw by our white men because he was doing the same work there. The white men will soon find out that he is here cheating the people in this way, causing the people to give up their second wives and pleasures, and keeping services even during the week-days. He deceives you because you are black, but the white men will soon find him out and drive him away."

Fourth objection, also based on a false report which went round as an alarm:—" Tell all the heathen people not to come near that man, for a person has just brought the news that the people who were converted by this, man, in all places before he came here, are all dead, and it will be the same thing here soon." When the new converts here heard this, they said, " If that be true, we will go to heaven at once!" Their reply was a great disappointment to the enemies.

Fifth objection, based on a reform from the drinking of Kaffir beer;—Many of our mission-people have given up the custom of drinking Kaffir beer, and have openly broken their beer-pots. The enemies became very angry indeed, and said, " What! what, breaking pots!—breaking pots! We never heard of such foolishness before. Shortly something will happen." They were specially shocked that their Chief, Matomela, broke his beer-pots and gave up the beer-drinking, and the enemies said, " What a pity we are under the British Government, we would kill Charles Pamla, because he is a false prophet, and because he has persuaded our chief to give up our grandfather's best food, which is beer, and if we had the power we would put Matomela out of his state, as chief, for giving up the beer, and put another in his place who would drink beer."

But notwithstanding all this opposition, the work is growing stronger and stronger. We get fresh converts from the heathen every week—men, women and children. Some of their chiefs and two of the richest heathen men in the country—Giba and Cwati—have been converted to God. Besides the converted chiefs I have named before, I will add the name of Chief Mbilase. I will be able next time to tell you the number of converts gathered in since I was appointed to this circuit."

Brother Lamplough, at a later date, says that between 600 and 700 have been converted to God, under Pamla's ministry, during his five months labour in his new circuit. Pamla continues:—

I have been preaching almost every day, except a few Fridays and Saturdays, once a fortnight.

Now I will tell you how I have answered some of those objections of the heathen. I went to the Great Place of Chief Fundakube, and laid these things before the chief. I then asked him to gather together his counsellors and best men, and lay the subject before them, and select a heathen, whom you all can trust, who can read the Kaffir Bible, and I'll debate my cause with them. The chief and his people were very glad, and so a day was appointed for the public discussion of all these points. The day appointed was a Monday. Due notice was given, and at the time set there was a great gathering of our mission people and the heathen at the Great Place of Fundakube, but we found the chief and his party tipsy with Kaffir beer, so we appointed to come again on Thursday. When we came on Thursday we found them all right. They had selected a heathen man, by the name of Mawomba, who was a great enemy to religion, well respected by the heathen, one whom they could trust, and who could read the Kaffir Bible well. So we opened our service and took up the objections in their order. In regard to the first, I said, " I do not get any money from the white men for the new converts. If you like, I will give you an order to go and draw in my name all the money which you say I get for the new converts from the white men. As for the ticket and class-money, which amounts to a few shillings weekly, that goes to support the Gospel, and is almost nothing compared with what you pay the Kaffir doctors, in oxen, goats, money, and Kaffir beer, while we furnish medicine to our members free."

They answered "Yes."

In regard to the second objection, I said, "I have no poison from Mr. Taylor. This converting power was an old work before Mr. Taylor was born. I have the Bible to prove that this work did not begin with me here nor with Mr. Taylor. Now we will take up that part of your objection about calling sinners to come to Christ, and about them kneeling before the Lord their maker to pray to Him." Then I called upon Mawomba to read from the Gospel by St. Matthew, xi chapter, 28 verse, "Come unto me all ye that labour and are heavy laden, and I will give you rest."

Also Revelations, xxii. chapter, 17 verse, "The Spirit and the bride say, Come, and let him that heareth say, Come, and let him that is athirst come, and whosoever will, let him take of the water of life freely."

Mawomba read them distinctly, and I said, "These passages refer to the calling of sinners to come to Christ, now having been sent both by God and by His ministers, have I not a right to call sinners to repentance? In regard to penitents kneeling, I will ask Mawomba to read the 6th verse of the xcv. Psalm. Mawomba read, "Oh come, let us worship and bow down, let us kneel before the Lord our Maker." Then I said, "Are you satisfied?"

They answered, "*Yes.*"

"In regard to your objection about so many heathen converted in so short a time, and why the other ministers did not do the same work in the same manner, I answer, first in regard to the work done by the ministers who have been labouring amongst you. They did a great work. They did the same work for our fathers who received the Gospel preached to them by those men of God. They bowed down on their knees also, and were not too proud to worship their great God and Creator as you are now. But while many of our fathers were converted, you were against the ministers who laboured amongst you. I know what sort of feelings you had against the Word of God and against those ministers. You were not their friends at all.

"When you went to hear them preach you at once began to talk to each other, and said, 'What has he been saying?'

"Another answered, 'He was talking about some wind in the air which he called God.' Another says, 'He was talking about death and dead people.' Another replies, 'What have we to do with dead people, we are not dead?' Another adds, 'He says after we are all dead, then we will all go to hell.' Then they all laugh and say, 'We be all dead, who will go to hell?'" This is but an example of the bad feeling and prejudice of nearly all the heathen people against the word of God, then and now, and that is the reason why the gospel has not been more successful among them. I then told them how ungrateful it was for them to say anything against the old ministers, for it was through them, and especially Mr. Ayliff, that their fathers were led out of Kaffir bondage (for they were Fingo heathen) and that thousands of them had since been converted to God.

At this point they replied, "Our complaint is not that the people are being converted, but that so many are converted in so short a time."

I then asked Mawomba to read the 41st verse of the

2nd chapter of the Acts, and he read: "Then they that gladly received his word were baptized: and the same day there were added unto them about 3,000 souls." Also the 3rd and 4th verses of the 4th chapter, "And they laid hands on them, and put them in hold unto the next day; for it was now eventide. Howbeit many of them which heard the word believed; and the number of the men was about 5,000." Then I said, "What have you to say to that? about 3,000 souls converted in one day, and about 5,000 converted on another day." I then told them about the great work of God with Mr. Taylor among the English at Algoa Bay, Graham's Town, King William's Town, and the same work among the natives at Annshaw and all round, right up to Port Natal, where there was also a great work among the English. Then I said, "Now I will tell you what those people get who come and kneel down as penitents, whom you say I poison," and I called on Mawomba to read to them from Romans 5th chapter, 1-3 verses, "Therefore, being justified by faith, we have peace with God through our Lord Jesus Christ: By whom also we have access by faith into this grace wherein we stand, and rejoice in hope of the glory of God. And not only so, but we glory in tribulations also." I then explained to them the new birth which these new converts had experienced, and got Mawomba to read to them a part of the third chapter of John, "Verily, verily, I say unto you, except a man be born again, he cannot see the Kingdom of God." I told them, when the penitents are thus born of God, the new law of God is written by the Holy Ghost in their hearts, and I got Mawomba to read the 37th verse of the 22nd chapter of Matthew, "Jesus said unto them, Thou shalt love the Lord thy God with all thy heart, and with all thy soul, and with all thy mind, and thou shalt love thy neighbour as thyself." I explained it to them and shewed the proofs of it in the lives of the converts. After all this talk Mawomba stood up and read the 4th verse of the 150th Psalm, to try to support their Kaffir-beer—dancing feasts, " Praise Him with the timbrel and dance: praise Him with the stringed instruments and organs."

In my reply I said, " How do you explain that passage? Did David mean that dancing which the heathens and drunkards do in worshiping the devil? I ask you, father, did David mean that the people should worship the devil instead of the true God?"

Mawomba said, "I can't explain it. You will please explain it to me."

I said, "David feared God, and would not do anything which would displease God. He had a harp that he played in worshiping God, just as the English have an organ in their churches to assist them in singing praise to God. Again David praised God with all his things, all he had was devoted to God, even his pleasures were done unto God." I saw that the man's pride was gone and that his power failed him, and he stood up and said, "I never understood these things so clearly as I do to-day, both in regard to the work of revival, and my own questions." (A Kaffir is a noble antagonist, when fairly beaten in argument he will promptly and honestly own it.)

Then the great chief Fundakube said, "No man after these things which have been done to-day should ever complain against the great work of God. We are all satisfied. Our own man has read these things out of the Book of God."

Then I said, "Who can prevent me from calling sinners to-day to come and kneel down before God?"

The Chief replied, " No one can prevent you. Your way is clear, but we will go home to-day, and we will think over these things. We are all well pleased, and will hear you again." Our meeting then adjourned.

In the next service I held at the Great Place of Fundakube I called for penitents. The Chief came and talked to me privately, and said, "I will kneel down before God, but not before you."

I said, "Kneel down where you are, well and good. I don't want any sinner to kneel to me, and it don't matter about the place if there is a broken and a contrite heart submitted to God."

Four of them, the Chief's mother, and two of her children, and his brother's wife, found peace with God that day, and the Chief seems to try very hard to seek God. I will let you know next time how he gets on. I have not time to tell you more to-day. I may say, however, while there are many enemies, thank God there are many kind friends also, who love Jesus, and love me at the same time. I find Mr. Holford to be a kind friend and Superintendent. I have a native friend who goes with me to help me in the work, and he is very pious, and a great assistance to me."

In this work, in those barren wastes of Africa, we see the fulfilment of God's own words, "For as the rain cometh down and the snow from heaven, and returneth not thither, but watereth the earth and maketh it bring forth and bud, that it may give seed to the sower and bread to the eater, so shall My Word be that goeth forth out of My mouth; it shall not return unto Me void, but it shall accomplish that which I please, and prosper in the thing whereto I sent it." "In the wilderness shall waters break out and streams in the desert. And the parched ground shall become a pool, and the thirsty land springs of water: in the habitations of dragons where each lay, shall be grass, with reeds and rushes. And a highway shall be there, and a way, and it shall be called the way of holiness; the unclean shall not pass over it, but it shall be for those who are 'cleansed through the blood' of Jesus;" "the wayfaring men" who, like those saved sons of Africa, obey God, and walk after His Spirit in this holy way, "though fools, shall not err therein."

WORKS
BY THE REV. W. TAYLOR.

Reviews.

SEVEN YEARS' STREET PREACHING IN SAN FRANCISCO.

"It is a very entertaining volume, full of adventure, grave and gay, in the streets of a new city, and among a peculiar people."—*New York Observer.*

"And the book itself so thoroughly good, so deeply interesting, and so replete with wise counsels, and examples of what street preaching ought to be, that we cannot but wish for it a wide circulation. The writer tells his story with the simplicity and directness of a child, and the incidents related are of a most unusual and romantic kind. Too much cannot be said in praise of the nervous, plain, vigorous style of the author's preaching. For clearness, directness, and force, the specimens given in this book have never been surpassed."—*London Quarterly Review.*

This book had numerous commendations from the press, but the best proof of its worth is the fact that over 32,000 copies have been sold.

Works by the Rev. W. Taylor.

THE MODEL PREACHER.

"It is a book calculated to stir the soul to manly and bold achievements in the service of Christ, in the great work of preaching His gospel."—*Methodist Recorder.*

"The Saviour is Taylor's 'Model Preacher.' I wish to say, moreover, that although the book is addressed to a preacher, and on the subject of preaching, yet its treatment is such that almost any religious person will be deeply interested in perusing it. There is a charm about it, like the author's preaching, a freshness, a raciness, an abundance of apt illustration, that captivates the ordinary reader, and leads him from chapter to chapter, to the end of the book."—*Professor Wm. Hunter, D.D.*

Over 20,000 copies have been sold.

———◆———

CALIFORNIA LIFE ILLUSTRATED.

"Full of interesting and instructive information, abounding in striking incident, this is a book that everybody will be interested in reading."—*New York Observer.*

"Scenes of thrilling excitement, of touching tenderness, of noble heroism, and of dark crime—not concocted in the brain of the novelist, but enacted in real life—are here depicted."—*Ladies' Repository.*

"It is replete with such pictures as the British eye never sees. It is better worth hundreds of thousands of editions than the most brilliant novel that has yet seen the light."—*British Standard.*

This book has reached a circulation of 30,000.

Works by the Rev. W. Taylor.

RECONCILIATION; OR, HOW TO BE SAVED.

" The volume before us contains, in six chapters, the author's mode of teaching the great Christian doctrines of salvation, repentance, and faith, and some striking illustrations and anecdotes enrich its pages. We wonder not that a teacher so fearless and outspoken should have been honoured by God in the conversion of many from a life of indifference and vice, to one of faith and godliness."—*Christian Times.*

The third edition of this book has been issued within a few months.

INFANCY AND MANHOOD OF CHRISTIAN LIFE.

" What a glorious event in the history of any soul, to be born again, to become a babe in Christ, an event that we will celebrate in eternity; but to remain a babe is to become a dwarf, and fail to attain the end for which we were born."—*Extract from Book.*

" Mr. Taylor's style is direct, vigorous, and sometimes colloquial. Clear statement and forcible reasoning are relieved and made more effective by apt illustration. Christians of other denominations may here learn, without any undue mental exertion, the views held by Wesleyans on the doctrine discussed by our author, and, even when unconvinced, they can hardly fail to be interested and profited."—*Christian World,* May 3rd, 1867.

The volume is pervaded throughout with an earnest purpose, and the writer, in many a powerful passage, speaks straight to the conscience and to the heart."—*Methodist Recorder,* June 28.

www.ingramcontent.com/pod-product-compliance
Lightning Source LLC
Chambersburg PA
CBHW021227300426
44111CB00007B/448